WHERE BIGFOOT WALKS

Books by Robert Michael Pyle

Watching Washington Butterflies

Handbook for Butterfly Watchers

The Audubon Society Field Guide to North American Butterflies

The IUCN Invertebrate Red Data Book
(with S. M. Wells and N. M. Collins)

A Field Guide to Butterflies Coloring Book
(with Roger Tory Peterson and Sarah Anne Hughes)

A Field Guide to Insects Coloring Book
(with Kristin Kest)

Wintergreen: Listening to the Land's Heart

The Thunder Tree: Lessons from an Urban Wildland

Where Bigfoot Walks: Crossing the Dark Divide

WHERE BIGFOOT WALKS

CROSSING THE DARK DIVIDE

Robert Michael Pyle

A MARINER BOOK

HOUGHTON MIFFLIN COMPANY

BOSTON · NEW YORK

For information about permission to reproduce selections
from this book, write to Permissions, Houghton Mifflin Company,
215 Park Avenue South, New York, New York 10003.

Library of Congress Cataloging-in-Publication Data
Pyle, Robert Michael.
    Where Bigfoot walks : crossing the dark divide / Robert Michael Pyle.
        p.   cm.
    Includes bibliographical references (p.   ) and index.
    ISBN 0-395-44114-5   ISBN 0-395-85701-5 (pbk.)
    1. Sasquatch. I. Title
QL89.2.S2P95   1995
001.9′44 — dc20   95-2506
                            CIP

Printed in the United States of America

QUM 10 9 8 7 6

Book design by Melodie Wertelet

The following excerpts are reprinted by permission: from Margaret Atwood's
poem "Oratorio for Sasquatch, Man, and Two Androids," copyright © 1970 by
Margaret Atwood; from "Footsteps on the Wind" by Glenn and Dotty Dorsch,
copyright © 1989 by Willow Run Music Co.; from "Dyin' for a Metaphor" and
"The Roman Road" by Jack Gladstone, from *Buckskin Poet's Society,* copyright ©
1992 by Jack W. Gladstone/BMI; from "The Man in the Mirror" by J. W. Sparrow, from *Dances with Words,* copyright © 1995 by J. W. Sparrow; materials from
Weyerhaeuser Company Archives.

FOR THEA

For all the searchers and dreamers
For the Ones who walk in mystery

Contents

CONTENTS

A giant has swallowed the earth,
And when he sleeps now, oh when he sleeps,
How his eyelids murmur, how we envy his dream.

— Pattiann Rogers, *Firekeeper*

Introduction: Bukwus and

Dzonoqua at Play

This was D'Sonoqua, and she was a supernatural being, who belonged to these Indians . . . I said to myself, "I do not believe in supernatural beings. Still — who understands the mysteries behind the forest? What would one do if one did meet a supernatural being?" Half of me wished that I could meet her, and half of me hoped I would not.

— Emily Carr, *Klee Wyck*

SOMETHING IS DEFINITELY AFOOT in the forests of the Pacific Northwest. Either an officially undescribed species of hominoid primate dwells there, or an act of self- and group deception of astonishing proportions is taking place. In any case the phenomenon of Bigfoot exists. Whether the animals themselves are becoming scarcer or whether they even walk as corporeal creatures at all, their reputation and cult are only growing. More and more people, including credible and skeptical citizens and scientists, as well as the gullible, the wishful, and the wacko, believe that giant hairy monsters are present in our midst. What does this mean? Who is this beast described by the great ecologist G. Evelyn Hutchinson as "our shadowy, perplexing and perhaps non-existent cousin"?

Bigfoot, also commonly called Sasquatch (from the Salish *saskehavas*), is the North American counterpart of Yeti, or the abominable snowman, in the Himalaya. Cryptozoologists, who study undiscovered animals, now recognize at least four possible species (other than humans) of upright apes in Asia, of which Yeti is one. They tend to think that the North American animal represents a single, different species. Although reports, tracks, and putative sightings have come from almost every state in recent years, most of the lore centers on the Pacific Northwest, from northern California to central Alaska, and especially southwestern Washington.

Arriving on the continent, European settlers encountered a rich and varied array of native tales concerning giant, hairy, humanlike monsters. Native Americans, from the Hoopa of the redwood forests to the Athabascans of the Yukon River, have stories of hairy giants. And the Sasquatch stories did not arrive with trade beads; for centuries the Kwakiutl of the British Columbia coast have consorted with the wild men and wild women of the woods.

Mountain men, trapping far beyond the westward advance of their racial kin, brought tales of ape-men along with beaver pelts to the rendezvous at Jackson Hole. Teddy Roosevelt, in *The Wilderness Hunter,* recorded the story of one such trapper raked off by an unknown beast at his campfire while his partner checked the trapline; Roosevelt called it "the Snow Walker." Pioneer trainmen in the Fraser River country stopped to catch and cage a baby ape found near the rails; named Jacko, he was extolled in the press and exhibited for a while, then disappeared. A British Columbian fisherman, Albert Ostman, returned from a wild inlet to tell of being kidnapped by a family of Bigfeet and kept captive until he freed himself by sharing his snuff. The same year, 1924, the famous Ape Canyon incident took place, when miners in Washington's Skamania County reported shooting a Bigfoot and then being attacked by several others.

Reports continued to generate from Skamania County, and in 1969 an ordinance was passed protecting Bigfoot. Monster hunter Roger Patterson, encountering a female ape of great proportions on a northern California stream, returned with a shaky film shot on the run when he was bucked from his horse. Shown worldwide, the film set off an epidemic of hunters, who dispatched reports no more or less compelling than the hundreds of tracks and glimpses and fuzzy photos and hanks of hair turned up by ordinary folk with no monsters aforethought. Bigfoot societies were formed and expeditions mounted, as hundreds of huge humanoid tracks were discovered, from Maryland to Minnesota, from Pike's Peak to Mount Hood.

Most academics and forest managers remained firmly unconvinced, while the growing cadres of true believers argued over whether or not to kill the animal when it was found. Movie spoofs and tabloid dramas fanned the flickers of the faithful while degrading a once-powerful set of native traditions into a staple of kitsch journalism. Thus have we come from the early frontier fables of bogeymen, which accompany every advance into the wilderness, to a state of mass fascination mixed with general unbelief.

As assembled from some hundreds of eyewitness reports, traditional legends, tracks and other signs, a few vague photographs, and the famous filmstrip made by Patterson and Gimlin at Bluff Creek in 1967, a portrait of Bigfoot emerges fairly clearly. The animal is large or immense, from six to ten feet in height and weighing perhaps three hundred pounds to half a ton when mature. It stands upright, and though its powerful arms are long, they do not touch the ground, as those of the great apes do. Russet, beige, brown, or black fur covers the massive body except for the palms, soles, and most of the face. The neck is short, the sagittal crest pronounced, the brows heavy and beetling. Bigfoot may have red eyeshine in headlights. Males have small genitals and are half again as large as females, whose breasts can be pendulous, as Patterson's film shows. Almost all observers agree that the animal leaves behind a very strong, disagreeable odor and that the face is more humanlike than animal.

The most frequently described feature, and the most prominent, is the feet, which are, in a word, big. Tracks commonly measure fifteen to eighteen inches or more in length. They have five toes, a double muscle-ball, and a low arch. Grover Krantz, a professor of anthropology at Washington State University, has analyzed many tracks and has pronounced some of them genuine. He hypothesizes that Bigfoot represents a living population of the huge primate *Gigantopithecus,* known from Pliocene and Pleistocene fossils in Southeast Asia. Most cryptozoologists believe that if the big galoot exists, it is a relict hominoid ape that occurs in dispersed populations totaling several hundred or several thousand across the forested montane Northwest.

Many relict species — animals or plants extinct over most of their range but surviving in pockets — are known. The tailed frogs of the Northwest, whose only relatives occur in New Zealand, are a good example. The mountain gorilla is another. And some such species have remained hidden until recent times. The fact that *Gigantopithecus* did exist makes it impossible to dismiss giant hairy apes out of hand. The idea that a large bipedal ape might have evolved, died out overall, but survived in remnants strikes no biologist as outrageous. The problem is not whether Bigfoot *could* exist but whether, if it does, how it has remained so long unknown.

Obvious difficulties arise in any conversation about Sasquatch.

Why isn't it seen more often? Why haven't any bodies, or even any bones, ever been found? Why are all the pictures fuzzy? How could something so large be so hard to find? Wouldn't loggers, hunters, and others who spend their time in the woods be well acquainted with such a dramatic animal in their midst?

Believers reply that encounters occur often; that we seldom find bodies or bones of bears or pumas because scavengers eat them; that no one would believe in the authenticity of a clear picture of Bigfoot; and that if you were intelligent, hunted, and extremely adept in the bush, you too could stay hidden in the huge, rough territories in question. As for sightings by those who work and play in the woods, many of the reports do come from loggers and hunters. And, the believers add, how are the tracks to be explained? Hundreds of clear, consistent casts that pass podiatric and forensic examination in terms of weight, stress, indentation, and stride have been recovered from scores of disparate, remote locations. And so the dialogue continues, between nay-sayers and yea-sayers unable to either embrace or demolish each other's arguments.

In many ways the search for Bigfoot brings to mind the popular preoccupations with UFOs, aliens from outer space, and the Loch Ness monster. In fact it has something in common with each of these. Statistically the likelihood of alien travelers is not so very remote, as cosmologists such as Carl Sagan contend. Also the body of UFO sightings that are difficult to dismiss grows by the month. Likewise, reputable zoologists consider the possibility of relict plesiosaurs in Loch Ness and several other deep lakes to be considerably better than nil. Yet most of us feel that disturbed or disingenuous people have invented bogus incidents that have obscured the real issues. And the tabloid-type hysteria that accompanies serious inquiry makes it tough for sensible people to sort the possible from the preposterous and makes them fear that open-minded will appear oatmeal-minded. We feel justified in ignoring those who present the cases of aliens, UFOs, Nessie, and Bigfoot as if they were somehow related, part of the same weird parade, usually wrapped up with paranormal phenomena and interdimensional travel.

Any of these phenomena *might* be real — but how can we know? In each case the problem seems to be one of agreeing on acceptable evidence. As skeptics insist, extraordinary claims require extraordinary proof. That leaves us with an uncomfortable question: will it be necessary to bring in a body before any as-yet-unseen form of life is considered real? And if so, is the prize worth the price? Beyond the question of mere belief, this is the issue that sharply divides the several camps of eager Bigfoot hunters.

- - -

Each year hundreds of Sasquatch seekers take to the woods, and some lesser numbers gather in annual jamborees, such as the one known as Bigfoot Daze in Carson, Washington. To get a feel for their motives and modi operandi, I joined them at the Bigfoot Trailer Park one recent fall. There, following the beefy fumes of a barbecue serving Bigfoot Burgers, I found the assembled enthusiasts of the Western Bigfoot Society.

As the October light faded into vague mothglow, the Coleman lanterns came out. In the absence of a campfire, the members gathered around a Coleman to share Bigfoot tales old and new. Martin Witter, an older man with a silky white beard, recounted his wife's sighting of a seven-foot ape on their honeymoon forty years before, as Lusette nodded approvingly. A hunter told of finding eighteen-inch tracks all around his RV in an apple orchard near the coast.

Datus Perry, a white-bearded old-timer with wild eyes and a jack-o'-lantern grin, described the latest of his many sightings near his cabin in the hills outside of Carson. He demonstrated the sign you must make — crossing your arms over your chest and patting — to show apelike interlopers that your intentions are peaceful. Behind him stood a life-size Bigfoot model he had made, with the peculiar pointed head and deerskin shawl that he insists upon.

Peter Byrne, khaki-clad dean of the Northwest Bigfoot students and leader of the well-funded Bigfoot Research Project, listened with narrowed eyes and an analytical set to his handsome Irish jaw. Eventually he was persuaded to tell something of his days in Nepal in search of evidence of Yeti. The evening aged, tales dwindled, and most of us drifted off to our accommodations as winy accounts of UFOs took over.

Back at our cabin at Carson Hot Springs, Byrne and I exchanged news of our inquiries into the nature of the Sasquatch phenomenon and shared our frustration over the difficulty of sorting the chaff from the kernels, if any. I confessed that I was as intrigued by the people who share a common infatuation with the beast as with Bigfoot itself. Who are they? Why do they care so deeply about something that might not even exist? And what does the growing passion for monsters among us mean for our own self-image, our fears, our wild hopes? Peter said to let him know if I figured it out, and we retired. I fell asleep with gentle giants on my mind.

The next day the testimonies continued, as a teenaged girl in a monkey suit infiltrated the small crowd. I had known Ray Crowe, the founder of the Western Bigfoot Society, as a dedicated lepidopterist before Bigfoot captured his fancy. The hefty, mustachioed bookseller emceed in between selling Bigfoot books, newsletters, and plaster casts of footprints, Eventually the voices and stories ran together, and my head was spinning from the muddy mix of information and dreams. It occurred to me that this business was like one recipe for adobe bricks: a certain amount of solid earth blended with horseshit and bonded with hair — Bigfoot hair.

Heading for home, as I crossed the toe of the Cascades on small logging roads, I found myself watching for shadows behind every fir, imagining tracks around each muddy bend.

- - -

Certain social anthropologists like to consign Bigfoot to the category of archetypal myth: the contemporary expression of Beowulf's Grendel, the modern manifestation of the medieval Green Man — the wild counterpart to our domestic selves that all folk seem to need. Probably it works well for this purpose, for we do require bogeymen. But is there more to it than that? Looking at the traditions of Northwest Coast Indians, we see through the moss and the mist a furry figure who fits that deep myth of the monster-beyond-the-fire-circle, while clutching about itself a coarse-haired cloak of reality.

For the Kwakiutl, Bukwus is the Wild Man. On totems and masks he wears a wild face and a shock of black, unruly hair. Dzonoqua, when appearing as the Wild Woman, purses her lips to whistle. According to one tradition, when a young man, the Hamatsa, is to attain chiefdom, he goes into the forest for several weeks. Roaming the mossy damps, he might encounter the cannibal spirit Bokbokwollinooksiway, from whom Bukwus and Dzonoqua receive their power. The wanderer acquires some of that power through his ordeal and the winter ceremonial dances that greet his return. The rest of the year the Wild Man and the Wild Woman abide in the deep shadows, vaguely disturbing and malevolent presences capable of stealing children and souls. Other clan stories have interpreted these figures quite differently, but all recognize that giants walk among them.

All of this lore would be only colorful and strange, and we would show the same polite interest we use to patronize native traditions everywhere, if it weren't for the fact that Bukwus and Dzonoqua are still around. While modern Kwakiutls have left Tsitsiutl the sea serpent and Thunderbird behind in the realm of imaginative myth, those who still live on the northern fjords and in the forests accept the wild people the same way they accept frogs, ravens, and bears — as literal facts.

Throughout the reported range of Bigfoot, American Indians who go often into the woods still fear the Sasquatch, and from time to time some of them see it. I have heard stories that appear in no book concerning personal encounters with Bigfoot figures — not only venerable traditions but recent tales as well. For example, an Athabascan teacher I know told me that as recently as the spring of 1992, a fishing village in Alaska was abandoned because the Woods Man had appeared nearby. The teacher was reluctant to say more because her people have such a powerful spiritual regard for their Sasquatch figure, in whom they believe literally and passionately. Martha's story is dramatic but not unique.

The hairy-giant theme is hardly limited to Native Americans. Tales of the abominable snowman among the Tibetans and other peoples of the Himalaya are well known. In western China accounts of a large primate have become so prevalent that expeditions have been undertaken there recently, with the full blessing of Chinese scientific academies. In the villages of the Caucasus Mountains in southwest Russia, spring festivals include the arrival and slaying of Quidili, a shaggy giant. This has much in common with the winter ceremony of the Kwakiutl, except that instead of the monster appearing in person, the Hamatsa dancer brings forth its spirit. Clearly, forms of Bigfoot appear in widespread cultures.

Bukwus and Dzonoqua probably haven't stolen any children lately, but they still steal souls. I have known good men to give up their jobs, families, and reputations to go in search of the big-footed ones. Certainly the tabloid writers who degrade honorable native traditions into idiot-pulp have long ago abandoned their souls, and the "professional" Bigfoot hunters looking for the fortune its skin would bring have severely compromised theirs. Even those who insist that it will be necessary to kill one Bigfoot to save the rest have left a chunk of their souls on the barbed-wire fence of conscience.

If Sasquatch lives, the concerted efforts at searching for it must soon succeed. Or maybe not. Unlike Indian legends, modern experience and present-day folklore paint Bigfoot as generally harmless and reclusive. The coastal natives had no experience with primates besides humans, who were often warlike. A gigantic hairy "man" would naturally be seen as a threat. But Europeans, aware of gorillas, chimps, orangs, and monkeys, have been able to picture Bigfoot as part of that gentle lineage. Without the fear of a hostile tribe of giants, Bigfoot seekers such as Peter Byrne have been free to abandon the hostile approach.

Byrne characterizes this other ape as a harmless presence deserving a peaceful overture, whom we would be very wrong to kill. His former coworker, Dede Killeen, in an editorial aimed at scientists who want a specimen, prodded them to consider "the natural rights of Bigfeet." Yet many seekers of fact and fortune still advocate greeting at least one Bigfoot with high-caliber gunfire. I can well imagine that a sentient animal aware of armed pursuit could become that much more difficult to find.

- - -

Bigfoot might or might not exist in the sense that we and other known animals exist. Answering the question of its existence is not the purpose of this book. How our hearts are carried off by hairy monsters that may live only in our minds, how we behave when we suspect that stunning discovery and great reward might lie on our own overgrown doorsteps, and how much wildness will survive our rough handling of the land — these are some of the questions I explored in the territory of the Dark Divide.

Whether heavy on its feet or as light as a ghost that never was, Bigfoot walks the Northwest woods. As we attempt to walk alongside, Bukwus and Dzonoqua are having a hell of a time watching us.

1 - PAN'S BRIDGE

1

Not Looking for Bigfoot

Sometimes the things you believe in become more real to you
than all the things you can explain away or understand.
— Tommy Albright in Lerner and Lowe's *Brigadoon*

IT WAS HALLOWEEN NIGHT OF 1970. I was twenty-three years old, camping near Mount St. Helens. I couldn't sleep, and then the cries began.

A little less than half a century before and some five miles away, a pack of miners claimed they had shot at a giant, hairy ape and then been attacked by a group of them. The seven-foot-tall ape-men threw massive rocks onto the cabin roof, the miners said. The next day the men escaped downhill to Kelso and led a posse back in search of the "vicious monsters." None were seen, but witnesses returned with stories of huge stones on the cabin roof, tracks, a twisted rifle, and other signs of a struggle. The slain Sasquatch supposedly fell into an abyss, which ever since has been known as Ape Canyon. A nearby lava tube, the biggest in the world, became Ape Cave. Since then the region around Mount St. Helens has been the epicenter of Bigfoot lore.

Intrigued by the stories, I had decided to take a look for myself. My wife, JoAnne, and I set out for St. Helens in a red Volkswagen Beetle, driving south from Seattle a hundred miles on the freeway and U.S. 99, then up the Spirit Lake Road east from Toledo. A swarm of big autumn alderflies glittered in the afternoon sun as we drove up the Toutle River, which would become hot mud toddy when Mount St. Helens later erupted. Autumn regalia of yellows and reds draped the black cottonwoods, bigleaf maples, and dogwoods of the Cascade foothills. Vine maples burned candy-apple red, and the cascaras were hung with lemon drops.

When the day went cold, we stopped for coffee at Spirit Lake

Lodge, a three-story beauty of huge fir beams and basalt blocks built in 1940 by Gus Gustafson. Gus had lived by the lake since 1917, a neighbor of the Harry Truman who would become briefly and post-humously famous for his sit-down strike in the face of the 1980 erup-tion. Over a hot mug I asked Gus about Bigfoot. Gus claimed that his grandfather had helped to promulgate what he called the Sasquatch hoax. As he told it, a church group on a picnic was accosted by miners in bearskins, who wanted to scare people away from their unpatented mine. Grandpa Gustafson spread the tale of the "apes," thus (accord-ing to Gus) starting the local Sasquatch legends. Of course, I knew that the other miners' story had preceded this one and that numer-ous Indian traditions were earlier yet, but I just listened.

I found it strange that a man living near St. Helens for fifty-three years wouldn't have encountered so much as a track if something *was* there. But I'd heard that no one sees Bigfoot except by accident, and I knew that locals are often the least inquisitive about their back yards. At this point I was strongly inclined to believe in the possibility of Bigfoot, so I tucked away Gus's version of the creature as hoax without putting too much store by it.

JoAnne and I were tempted to check into the warm old lodge, but even seven dollars for a double was more than we could manage on our graduate students' ragged excuse for a budget. So as dusk came on we drove up the road to the Timberline viewpoint and beheld the youngest and least glaciated of the Cascade volcanoes. Its sides lay under deep, creamy snow, as did the trail we hoped to take the next day across the Plains of Abraham to Ape Canyon. On the broad, flat surface of that old ash flow might there not be tracks?

A purple sheen fell over the silky slopes. Loo Wit, as the Indians called the mountain, became a cold blue snow cone against the subtle pallor of the winter sunset. We couldn't go far in the gathering dark and the deep snow, so we merely stretched our legs before returning to Spirit Lake to set up camp. After a little wine and some wursts cooked over a reluctant fire of damp wood and old-man's-beard, we crawled into our down bags. I felt just a mote of unease in the quiet, closed campground.

It felt great to get away from the city into the solitude of the high country. But the solitude and silence vanished abruptly. This was deer season, and suddenly hunters appeared with headlights and racing engines. A jeep buzzed the campground again and again. Someone hauled a snowmobile up to Timberline and ran it over those snowy mantles for hours. After their ruckus subsided, my back, tight from the drive and from too much time spent hunched over my desk at the university, took on a spasm. In the cold it throbbed like a broken bone badly healed, preventing me from getting any kind of sleep.

And then the cries began. From the southwest, up toward the Plains of Abraham, they boiled out of the night like bats from a deep and silent cave, each one an invisible note on the staff of the black sky. At first the calls resembled shrill barks, but not canine in the least. Then they accelerated in tempo, grew in volume, and rose in pitch until they sounded more like whistles.

I'd been studying ornithology and mammalogy with Professor Frank Richardson, a great naturalist, and we had gone over the known vocabularies of Washington's birds and mammals. I'd heard many in the field and had listened to recordings of most of the others. I ran again through the species that might have produced that tortured concert: elk, coyote, red fox, bobcat, puma, the winter owls. The calls I was hearing were not in the repertory of any of these, as far as I knew.

My back was crawling as well as yowling itself, so I lay still and listened. The sound of the chorus changed again to suggest the crying of babies. The snowmobilers had long since left; there was no one up there. The cries persisted for many minutes, subsided, resumed, then played on into the predawn. They might have been a dream, they were so strange and unworldly — or, rather, deeply visceral, but different from anything I knew in the world. Yet this was no dream. Nor was it the wine, little and long gone.

JoAnne never woke up. Finally I dropped off to sleep, and when I awoke it was dawn and the world was silent. I listened, crawled deep into my down cocoon, and slept again.

The next thing I knew, weird cries were in my ear again, very close. A gray jay was perched on my shoulder, calling for breakfast. I rose, chilled and a little shaken. JoAnne was already up. Over our breakfast of instant oatmeal and coffee I chatted with the insistent camp robbers. Ill content with bits of wurst and flakes of oatmeal, they cocked their gray masks and asked for more. But the voices: JoAnne had heard nothing. Should I be content to consider them an anomaly of an odd night, maybe an artifact of the wind in concert with owls or virtuosic coyotes? No. They were still as real and fresh in my mind as if the eerie, whistle-cry chorus had just ended.

Spirit Lake was lustrous in the clear morning, and St. Helens an almost clichéd image of mountain glory, its glacial shadows outlined and emphasized by the oblique rays. Snowy ash fields rolled below the cone. Out on the snow an ancient language of runes had been inscribed by the small-track makers: juncos, jays, deer mice, varying hares. A great horned owl chasing a hare made a snow angel, but the hare got away. It was interesting to decipher the night's script with the aid of my Rosetta Stone, Olaus Murie's *Peterson Field Guide to Animal Tracks*. But the book didn't contain the tracks I was especially seeking.

Well, what did I expect? If it were that easy, everyone with an ounce of curiosity would be up here looking. We stomped over to the edge of the Plains of Abraham but couldn't get farther without snowshoes.

Later, heading back down the Toutle, we attuned ourselves to the very real wonders of the Cascade autumn. Bigfoot maple leaves floated down like great yellow bats in glide. A saffron tortoiseshell butterfly seeking a hibernaculum flashed above the stream. Below, the water ran deep magenta with the spawning of chum salmon. In the concrete reality of the salmon's flash, Sasquatch seemed somehow unnecessary.

At home in our small apartment on Brooklyn Avenue, we looked through the mail. In the October-November issue of *National Wildlife*, my eyes were drawn immediately to an article entitled "On the Trail of Bigfoot," by the magazine's managing editor, George H. Harrison. The National Wildlife Federation had cosponsored the American Yeti Expedition 1970, led by Robert W. Morgan, and Harrison had gone along. Just five months earlier the expedition had made camp very near where we had just spent the night. The crew had found several sets of sixteen-inch tracks, including fresh ones made in the night after Morgan set up a sound device he hoped would attract his quarry. So we might have found tracks there — unless the expedition was the target of a hoax.

But for me the most striking thing about the article was Harrison's description of "eerie and frightening sounds of the night" when he camped on the slope of the volcano. When I read his words, I might as well have been reading my own night notes.

- - -

Five years later field work took me back to the Northwest. JoAnne had gone on to another life in Alaska, and I had remarried. Sally and I were sharing an overstuffed Volkswagen Beetle with my brother, Bud, field assistant David Shaw, all our camping gear, and a summer's worth of provisions. We were traveling Washington's back roads in search of data on butterfly ranges for my dissertation. When we got to Mount St. Helens the subject of Sasquatch came up. David and Bud were enthusiastic; Sally, an English botanist, was tolerantly amused. We combed the mountain's forest fringes looking for intact butterfly habitats.

But the roads we used were there to serve the logging trucks; the land was largely clear-cut, and incessant rain kept the butterflies under cover. David observed that Bigfoot must like mud if it lived around there. Bud added that there seemed to be about as many butterflies as Bigfeet, and they were both proving boring. That night, near Harry Truman's lodge, we had a brief thrill as a large, dark figure lumbered down the road toward our headlights. This was how most of the sightings occurred, according to the Bigfoot books. But the figure turned out to be a substantial drunk. We stayed at the same campground where I had heard the calls, but we heard only a great horned owl. I slept well.

The next day we headed up the Columbia Gorge to find sun on the east side of the damp Cascades. We were joking about Bigfoot, its capacity for alcohol, and our imaginations, when we came to The Dalles, a town on the Oregon bank of the river. As we uncoiled ourselves from the confines of our old gray bug at a gas station, I noticed a prefab building across the street with a clear sign on the front: Bigfoot Information Center. Of course we went in, prepared to guffaw quietly at a roadside attraction of the Tom Robbins variety. But we didn't laugh. Far from tacky, the exhibits were impressive, the tone discreet, and the printed interpretation intelligent.

I introduced myself to the director of the center, an Irishman with a British colonial background named Peter Byrne. With the understated manner of an Oxford don disturbed in his rooms at Balliol or Magdalen, he explained the objectives of his project. His khaki dress and educated accent placed him somewhere between that don and a white hunter on safari. A Bigfoot expedition in northern California funded by Texan Tom Slick had brought him from Nepal. Later Byrne decided to take his mission into Washington and Oregon.

Although his search for the so-called abominable snowman had not been conclusive, Byrne felt the chances of finding Sasquatch were better. Toward that end he had begun gathering all of the reports he could find, interviewing the principals, then retaining in his database only those reports that satisfied the rigorous dictum "When in doubt, throw it out." He had rejected hundreds of bears, drunks in the night, shadows, hoaxes, hallucinations, and who-knows-what. That left him with a few dozen "encounters" that were extremely difficult to dismiss out of hand. I'd heard of some such: a doctor who watched a Bigfoot for twenty minutes at close range in clear light; five policemen and a parson who swore to the authenticity of an array of tracks found in the winter of 1953; a long string of perfect tracks in remote wilderness; and so on. While maintaining a degree of clear-headed skepticism toward the majority of the "sightings," Byrne and his partner Dede Killeen had become convinced that Bigfoot exists.

– – –

That autumn, back at Yale, I was appointed to the seminar committee of the School of Forestry and Environmental Studies. It occurred to me to invite Peter Byrne to speak. The venerated school did not routinely give audience to speculative subjects. Topics might include "New Methods of Increasing Pulp Production in Tropical Cut-over Stands" or "Biomass Studies in Relation to Biological Diversity in a Connecticut Woodland." They did not address monsters. Yet the novelty of the topic and my enthusiasm for Byrne finally won Dean François Mergen's approval, and Vice President Henry Chauncey, Jr., signed off on it — a formality deemed judicious in this case.

Byrne spoke at Yale with charm, confident yet self-effacing good humor, and gentle authority. He showed the famous 1967 Patterson-Gimlin filmstrip from Bluff Creek, recounted the most substantive reports from his files, shared photographs and casts of tracks, and adroitly fielded all the usual objections to the existence of such an animal. Afterward a barrelful of Yale's best biologists, primatologists, and anthropologists filed out of Sage Hall's gothic auditorium scratching their heads. They might have come to ridicule the subject and the speaker, but when they left, not one would tell the press that they thought the phenomenon certainly a hoax or a misguided obsession. Of course they had not become convinced, but many minds had been opened that afternoon. Mine had opened wider.

Over the years I had formed something of an emotional attachment to a creature that I did not necessarily believe in. I suspect that many people harbor similar feelings. Bigfoot represents many motives in our society, from blind faith to curiosity, from superstition to wild hope. As for me, the keen interest in this outlandish subject shown by people I respect has been a pleasant tickle. Something in the mix of myth and tradition tells me that this thing warrants my attention.

I think of Bigfoot as an emblem of the Pacific Northwest, standing for the residents' earnest and whimsical frontier curiosity, for their eagerness to grasp the essence of the land and its life. It reflects our fascination with the bizarre, the monstrous, and the mysterious — the more like us, the better. As a fuzzy sort of grail, Bigfoot positively shines with the hopes, both noble and pathetic, of the outsider, the searcher, the latter-day Linnaeus, the wannabe Darwin, or maybe Barnum. It mirrors our schizoid approach to the universe, now crying out to be gulled, now hard as bones against belief.

In her book *Stepping Westward,* Sallie Tisdale says she feels sorry for the "true disbelievers" in Sasquatch, who "have lost their own mammalian vigilance about the greater earth." I agree. Because most of all, Bigfoot shows what could have been and what still could be, if only we treated the land as if it were really there. For the very wildness from which the Bigfoot myth emanates is disappearing fast. The struggle for the leavings — the roadless zones, the old growth — is vigorous and current.

If we manage to hang on to a sizable hunk of Bigfoot habitat, we will at least have a fragment of the greatest green treasure the temperate world has ever known. If we do not, Bigfoot, real or imagined, will vanish; and with its shadow will flee the others who dwell in that world. Looking at that tangled land, one can just about accept that Sasquatch could coexist with towns and loggers and hunters and hikers, all in proportion. But when the topography is finally tamed outright, no one will anymore imagine that giants are abroad in the land.

- - -

I've been looking into Bigfoot but not looking for Bigfoot. Plenty of others are doing that — true believers, whose hearts, souls, and wallets are on the line. I am not one of these. Even so, I felt the need to take my research to the hills, to confront the concept of Sasquatch on its own ground. I wanted to get inside the head of Grendel, to watch the fleeing forest from within. Most of all, I wanted a perspective only the mountains would give.

The mountains I chose were Washington's southern Cascades, a region of intense Bigfoot activity, judging by the density of reports over the years. Specifically, I zeroed in on a range of black peaks running crosswise to the main north-south axis of the Cascade volcanoes. The name Dark Divide applies both to this chain of impressive basalt extrusions and to the roadless area that surrounds it. The divide, which separates the Cispus and Cowlitz river drainages on the north from the Lewis River on the south, lies roughly in the middle of a diamond formed by Mounts Rainier, Adams, St. Helens, and Hood.

My plan was to trek across the Dark Divide from top to bottom. I would enter the northern end of the roadless zone and hike south on trails and cross-country. After reprovisioning at two road-access points, I intended to cross in turn the Indian Heaven Wilderness Area and the forbidding Big Lava Bed and arrive on the shores of the Columbia River in early October. I gave myself a month for the journey. Early fall made sense because it was after my busy season of field work and teaching but before the autumn rains and mountain snows. I hoped that the mosquitoes would be finished, the huckleberries at their peak.

And so, like another man who courted large subjects a bit beyond his back yard, I went deliberately into the woods. Twenty years after the night of the wild cries, my wife, Thea, and I, not in a Volkswagen, pulled into Tower Rock Campground in Gifford Pinchot National Forest. And I went from there.

2

Juniper Ridge

It was there for the first time that she felt that special hallucination peculiar to country people alertly watching for the
apparition of some fantastic animal, the passing of the "Great
Beast" which nearly all of her companions had seen at least once.
— Emile Caro, *George Sand*

OUR TENT LEANED into the green shade of sword fern, hemlock, and corydalis foliage. The mosses, ferns, and vine maples,
backlit by the late evening sun, fashioned a chartreuse scrim around
the campsite. What looked like a big, flared cedar was a false front —
a snag, whole on one side, with a hemlock growing out, giving it a
crown. Oxalis sprinkled the floor like shamrocks. And intermingled
with the plants and creatures of the wild Cascades were cut logs,
asphalt pads, city weeds, and European garden slugs — field marks of
the standard U. S. Forest Service in-between land that American car-
campers come to know so well.

After supper we watched the stars recruit campfire sparks for a
while, then walked down to the Cispus River, spanned by an old
bridge closed to cars. It was paved with pellets that we took for deer
droppings but that turned out to be goat. We listened to the sounds of
the river trundling round stones along its bed, a kingfisher zipping
up the night, and the goats bedding down, then we did the same. As
we lay still in our sleeping bags, a pair of fighter jets tore past Tower
Rock at a few hundred feet, sounding like Armageddon. Then silence
took over until ravens and jays claimed the next day as their own.

Winter wrens attended our breakfast: carrot muffins and good
Gray's River water from home. Soon everything I drank would be
filtered or boiled. I wished I could travel as light as that minor fluff-
ball, the wren. Repacking and adjusting my backpack took much of

the morning. Pulling out everything I thought I could live without, I reduced its weight to seventy-five pounds. Too much! But I wasn't willing to omit anything else.

After loading the pack into the Subaru with difficulty, I visited the only small building in sight. I sat in the outhouse with the door open to ferns and fresh air, enjoying the last such perch I expected to have for a month. The day was clear with a light breeze, 70 degrees or so — ideal for setting out. I was ready to let the adventure begin.

Thea drove me up the steep logging road past Tongue Mountain. At noon we hit the trailhead for Trail No. 261 to Juniper Ridge: my way into the Dark Divide. Thea picked huckleberries as the engine cooled down, and a raven crawed our intrusion to all who would hear. Its relative, Clark's nutcracker, yelled back and made desultory swoops at the butterflies of late summer. The objects of its attention, California tortoiseshells and hydaspe fritillaries, coasted about the road crest and into the trees, flashing their personal shades of orange.

I hauled out my Kelty Sherpa pack and climbed into it like a moth mashing itself back into its earthbound pupa. It was damned heavy, and got more so as Thea tied my water bag to the back. With my tent and Therma-Rest sleeping pad strapped to the sides, my day pack with optics, maps, and trail food hanging from the rear, and gallons of water slung here and there, I looked about as sleek as an avalanche. I weighed as much as a small Bigfoot (close to 330 pounds, all told), but I was far less fit. Old-man's-beard hung from the firs and from my face, and I wondered if I reflected the lichen's pale green shade. But as I adjusted the weight and breathed the terpenes of the astringent mountain air, I felt fine.

The trail looked steep and beat up by bikers, and the sign had of course been stolen. I clumsily hugged Thea and headed out, taking her kiss with me. "Be careful," she called as I clumped up and around the first bend. "I love you!" She did not expect to see or hear from me until we made our first resupply rendezvous on the Lewis River in ten days' time. I was excited to be off, and a little appalled.

- - -

When I decided to walk across the Dark Divide, I should have thought about an earlier outing to a place coincidentally known as the Dark Peak.

The Dark Peak trek took place in March 1972. I was studying in England that year, and I wanted to see something of wilder Britain.

My friends Jim Conway and Barry Hayward, biologists with the British Antarctic Survey, suggested a hike on the long and rugged Pennine Way. We began at Edale, a remote outpost in the high Pennine Mountains of Derbyshire. Jim, an Aberdonian, wanted to walk all the way to the Scottish Borders. Shortly after we set out, Jim remembered that we'd forgotten matches. Instead of loafing on the steep hillside and schmoozing with the sheep while someone went back for them, we kept on the move: Jim ran back to the inn while Barry carried both their packs up the steep incline.

By the next day we were deep into the bogs and moors of the Pennines. Jim followed his compass one way, Barry another, and I took an averaged route in between. The third day found us cold, wet, and fogbound on a precipitous edge of the Dark Peak itself, besotted with the vapors and oozings of the black bog. We managed to skirt the cliffs without incident. Across a long, Baskervillian moor known as the Moss Castle, the shallow trench of the Pennine Way continued north, perhaps forever.

Eventually we came to a road, which we followed to a ponderous Victorian guest house. The landlady nearly shut the door on our peat-smeared and bearded visages, but Barry thought fast and said, "It's *Doctor* Hayward of the British Antarctic Survey," in his best Cantabrigian accent. That got us in. Before the fire, curled up with hot tea and a bull mastiff that would have given an unwary traveler on the moor a heart attack, we pondered our next move.

I chose to take the road to Glossop, then a bus for Birmingham and a train for Cambridge. Thence to my thatched cottage, where a coal fire, a hot cup of coffee, and chocolate digestive biscuits awaited. I was ashamed but comfortable. Barry and Jim proudly carried on, but only, as it turned out, for another day or so. The Dark Peak in March had chewed us up and spat us out. The Pennine Way would wait.

Two summers later, lulled by Denver's dry heat into forgetfulness of the aborted hike on the damp moors, I embarked on a walk along the High Line Canal, a century-old irrigation ditch running from the edge of the Rocky Mountains out onto the High Plains. I had held a lifelong fascination for the prairie watercourse and a desire to walk its entire ninety-mile length.

I set out from Waterton with my heavy pack full of roasted soybeans, maps, cameras, plant presses, and other nonessentials. The first ten miles were beautiful, through red hogback foothills, old farmsteads, and cottonwood glades draped with white clematis bunting. But soon I entered the urban fringe. There was nowhere to camp with any peace of mind. The temperature was in the nineties, the mosquitoes were terrific, I was out of water, and there was a nice little log tavern I knew on the Sedalia road . . . My friend Chuck Dudley met me there, and after a few beers I decided to head back into town with him. The next day I got a job in a doughnut shop to pay my way back east. Spring, I decided, or perhaps fall, would be a nice time to walk the canal. And I later did, but in sections, not all at once.

Although walking is one of my primary pleasures, I am not by nature a long-distance trekker. So I should have known better than to think of crossing the Dark Divide to become more intimately acquainted with Bigfoot country and lore. Not that my objectives were terribly impressive. The distance was roughly comparable to that of the Pennine Way or the High Line Canal — something under a hundred miles. Much of it would be on trails, although there were some cross-country legs, and the terrain was a good deal rougher than anything in the Pennines. But dozens of people walk the entire Pacific Crest Trail, some two thousand miles. I knew a singer-songwriter in Montana by the name of Walkin' Jim Stoltz who has hiked well over eighteen thousand miles in the wilderness, and the meter is still ticking. And I knew a Paiute Indian named Benjamin Bill who had walked more than forty thousand miles on sponsored walks for charities and who hoped to either raise a million dollars or walk a million miles before he quit. A month's backpack trip over the territory between Mount Rainier and the Columbia River is not that big a deal.

Still, the trek represented a substantial challenge for me as well as a chance to immerse myself in the putative habitat of Bigfoot. And perhaps a way into its mind, or at least into the part of my own mind where Bigfoot dwells. It really didn't matter how long the route was nor how the miles were covered. What mattered was the time I'd set aside to sort out the findings and ponderings of decades; the solitude; and the Dark Divide itself.

- - -

The day came hot. Mount Adams stood immanent to the southeast. Red-leaved berry bushes slathered the open slopes like coals pouring from an open forge, lending even more heat to the steamy scene. Cool breezes took over as I entered a forest of middle-aged firs with downed giants lying about. One of these had left a section of trunk five feet across, and a five-inch seedling was growing from it. King boletes and coral-root orchids, both blown, studded the needle mat: fat, frowzy yellow caps next to pale pink seed stalks. At a water bar, bug-chewed leaves of false hellebore dangled seed pods like the Jolly Green Giant's ears from the spent tassels where the corn lilies once bloomed.

My trail mix, specially formulated by Thea, seemed redundant when giant ripe huckleberries and ruby thimbleberries decorated the trailside in every sunny patch. After gorging, I plunged back into the shadowed forest, where scarlet fruits of false Solomon's seal and deep blue ones of queen cup lilies took over, perched on long stalks. These were not to be eaten, yet they nourished my eyes, already growing jaded with green. In the next sun spot I filled my free hand with the blue globes of huckleberries, then littered the ground as I popped them toward my moving mouth.

My plantigrade tracks beat a dull cadence. To divert my attention from the pain of being a beast of burden, I watched everything I could. Thin, many-browned *Zonatrichia* shelf mushrooms made somber sunsets on the floor. Some call them turkeytails, and so they look, except for the absence of the amazing iridescence that let us use all the brightest crayons when coloring tom turkeys for Thanksgiving windows in grade school.

The next switchback marked the county line — my first milestone, where I passed from Lewis County to Skamania, known far and wide in the right circles as Bigfoot Country, where a county ordinance actually protects Sasquatch. I hadn't even thought of Bigfoot until then. Maybe my walk was just a cunning plan to get back into the wilderness I'd too long neglected. Looking back over my right shoulder, I glimpsed a fabulous view of Mount Rainier through the thinning trees. Salmonberries appeared. Even ripe, the orange drupelets are the tartest of the Northwest *Rubus* berries, making a welcome change from the sweets of all the rest. Their color reminded me of citrus. As the path rose, the Cispus retreated farther and farther below.

One elk track marked the switchback's westerly elbow; any others that might have been there had been erased by motorcycle tracks. I felt myself sneer — here was a fine scapegoat for my discomfort. The previous morning Thea and I had pulled into the ranger station at Randle to pick up any new maps and register for backcountry hiking. "Oh, you don't have to do that," said the young clerk in the Forest Service uniform.

"I was under the impression that wilderness travel required a fire permit," I said. But this was not a formal wilderness area, so the formality was forgone.

"We don't worry about you up there," she said, dismissing me.

"How about trail conditions?" I asked, wanting something to show for my trip to the station. She hadn't a clue but said the bikers liked it fine. "Mountain bikers?" I asked.

"No, trail bikers — you know, motorcycles." That was the first I'd known that the Dark Divide was biker country. Earlier I'd heard of a petition to the U.S. Forest Service to make the area, if not wilderness, then a "national hiking area." Apparently the district ranger had seen fit to do the opposite.

The bike damage was not bad so far, on the better soils and reasonable grades. The bikers' dust was soft to walk in, but the tracks were an unpleasant presence, like tire marks on a beach. And as the grade increased, so did the damage. The gouging of the steep switchback showed the potential for knobby tires to lacerate the land. A crushed water bar and a shard of red taillight lens emphasized the point.

The trail grew steeper. Sweating hard and grunting, I made slow, steady progress. Keeping my eyes down in the steeper bits showed me a pine siskin's yellow fluff in the trail, along with the tracks of bobcat and deer, the scat of coyote, a puma-hued *Amanita pantherina*. Up in a great Douglas-fir snag, six feet in diameter, I beheld a masterwork by woodpeckers.

The wonderful yellows, browns, and off-greens of gracefully decaying leaves of corn lilies, currants, and trilliums massaged my mind but not my aching feet. I finally rested below Juniper Peak. Taking the pack off was a job, but not as bad as the reverse. I adjusted my boots and the infinitely adjustable Sherpa, hoping that I would notice the difference. I had lunch, then scrunched against a bank to get the pack back on.

Up through more steep forest, then poof! I came into a clear, sandy, subalpine draw, then to a mini-cirque below a mini-rockslide at the foot of Juniper Peak's pale point. Marmots and pipits briefly shared the rockslide with me and with a parnassian butterfly nectaring on a mauve aster. After I emerged from the deepwood for the last time, the scene changed. A dry slope of white cinders glanced off to Adams, its summit now wreathed in the lenticular cloud that so often wraps the afternoons of the Cascade volcanoes. Kinnikinnick and prostrate juniper made a kind of heath below Juniper Peak. I carried the sweet smell of fir needles crushed on my boots into the hot open.

Finally topping out, some 4,800 feet above Puget Sound, I gained the spine called Juniper Ridge. A big orange day moth wafted overhead, and a huge nymph of a short-horned grasshopper, about as fast and graceful as I, trundled up the trail. Given the choice, I would be the moth.

Soon I came close to flying like the moth. In the band of my gray felt hat I was wearing a small, mottled gray and beige feather. Perhaps it had once belonged to a solitaire. When I reached the ridgeline at last, feeling lightheaded at this little success and the grand views, I stood, legs apart, and gazed east. A plucking breeze licked up the slope from the Cispus far below, took my feather, and dropped it on a rock just over the edge. Thea had made me promise not to chase butterflies in my heavy pack; but this seemed safe, so I inched over, cleverly facing uphill so as to keep my purchase on the slope. I bent, reclaimed the feather, and stood up. Then, having risen to a lighter head than I remembered, I began to fall over backward.

Swinging at thin air with Marsha, my big butterfly net, I caught enough breeze to tug my higher-than-usual center of gravity back across the fall line and landed on my knees facing uphill. Crawling to the ridge I sat, shook, and looked down the route I'd almost bought. The long, steep slope offered no arrest for hundreds of yards. Rolling over the sharp and lumpy pumice, my joke of a load shoving my face into the cheese-grater slope, I could have been badly injured and stranded far below. I branded BE CAREFUL, DUMMY! on my frontal lobe, rose with difficulty, and went on.

- - -

Juniper Ridge stretched ahead forever, a bony jawline hung with a gingham bib of mountain ash, huckleberry, and bleached bunchgrass. Mount Rainier, otherwise known as Tahoma, loomed up behind me, and Mount Adams, or Pahto, lay ahead to the left: a pair of white incisors. The far, pearly canine of Mount Hood (Wyeast) stood framed by two black molars in the Dark Divide on the south, while from the massive abscess on the right side of St. Helens (Loo Wit) gasped wisps of steam.

Termites glittered amber in the dropping sun, and it was time to look for camp. I stopped at the base of a hillock trending easterly on the ridge beyond Juniper Peak. From there I could see three of the volcanoes clearly — almost four, but Hood's fang had ducked behind one of the black molars. There were juncos up here, and big lumbering deer flies, to whom I gave about a pound of flesh. Fortunately, I said, already talking to myself, they're slow, loud, and dumb. But so am I. Brothers of the peak. I didn't bite them back, but I damn well bapped them if they hung about too long. The sandy path was knitted with coyote tracks of varying sizes, and elk bones lay alongside the trail, paler than the volcanic sand.

There was scarcely room for the tent on the knife-edged arête. Eventually I was able to pitch it in a spot marginally wider than the rest. With the wind beginning to rise out of the west and my close call fresh in mind, I stapled the tent to the ridge with a dead tree to keep me from rolling or blowing into the abyss in the night.

I boiled some water over my blue Gaz stove and cooked some ramen noodles. I'd drunk about as much as I should have on the long hike up, and already the water I'd brought was much reduced in weight — and availability. I was careful with what I used, but not stinting. Coyotes barked and yipped somewhere down the ridge. And then the ghost moths came out.

3

Ghost Moths at Moonrise

The point of having a Sasquatch on our minds is that it makes us pry into the thickets and walk over the horizon, hoping always to see something take wing in the ghostly silver light.

— Peter Steinhart

THE SUN FELL BEHIND Loo Wit, dragging pink streamers all the way from Mount Rainier. A gray-green plume crept from the gaping crater of St. Helens, and the full moon rose right out of Mount Adams. My tent was a hammock suspended between the sun and the moon, guarded by three volcanoes. I watched the sunset's afterglow through a sheaf of tall bunchgrass that sprang from a carpet of red huckleberry and blue juniper. All the tones deepened.

The first ghost moths appeared a half-hour after moonrise; half an hour later they were gone. It was easy to imagine that they hadn't been there at all. But they had, and their shimmering spiral flights turned the mountain heath phantasmagorical for the few minutes they deigned to fly.

Ghost moths belong to the primitive but successful family Hepialidae, part of an ancient suborder of the Lepidoptera whose females' sexual equipment is uniquely arranged. Of some five hundred species of hepialids, about twenty fly in North America, most of them limited to the Pacific Northwest. While tropical ghost moths can be big and brilliant, ours tend to be small and subtle. An inch or so in wingspan, they range from beige to russet in color, often displaying metallic markings on their forewings. Their very short antennae and peculiar habits give them away.

Unlike the many moths that fly throughout the night, ghost moths appear only briefly, each species at a predictable time of day, dusk, or night. The larvae of most butterflies and moths eat the leaves of specific plants. Hepialid caterpillars, in contrast, bore into the roots of a wide variety of grasses, herbs, and shrubs, mining their underground or even underwater parts. And instead of laying her eggs directly on the host plant, the female hepialid broadcasts them by the thousands as she flies — but not until she has mated. Prior to coitus, females of some kinds are flightless . . . as if the "kiss" of the male releases them to the air. The females of other species fly up from the herbage in search of mates, reversing the usual roles of moth partners. In either case, with their antennae like a baby's eyelashes and their tiny, jeweled eyes, the ghost moths find their way through the mountain maze to the bower of their waiting mates.

The lekking flight of the male ghost moths is their most distinctive trait, giving rise to their common name. In leks, such as those of sage grouse, birds of paradise, and swarm flies, males forgather to display communally to the females. By flying together they superstimulate the females to be receptive. Leks account for some of nature's most spectacular displays of sexual energy and adornment. The brief twilight leks of ghost moths might seem subtler than the daylight displays of bright-colored birds, yet when the males swivel in place on the air as if hung from a skein of spider's strands, the sight is dramatic.

Cornell entomologist Robert Dirig described the sight of an eastern species thus: "Imagine three large tan moths about ten feet above the ground hovering and swaying back and forth in this strange rhythm, against the greenish-black backdrop of the alders and distant forest beneath a purpling sky . . . lending by their brief adult existence a touch of faerie and romance to the remote wetlands."

The twilight flights of the males spiral over the vegetation in shifting columns that seem to evoke glowing spirits hovering over the turf. The name Hepialidae, given to the family by the French entomologist Fabricius in 1775, comes from the Greek *hepiales,* deriving from *epialos* (nightmare) or *epiolos* (moth), or perhaps both. The moths' ghostly reputation grew from their luminous pallor and common occurrence over foggy moors and graveyards.

Try to approach them and they do seem to be phantasms: you see them, then you don't. Their rapid flight gave the group its alternative English name, the swifts. They seldom come to lights, and the adults do not feed, so flowers don't draw them, as they do sphinx moths and millers. Till that time I'd seen few ghost moths and caught fewer. But David Wagner, a University of Connecticut professor and hepialid specialist, had asked me to procure specimens for his ongoing studies of the Northwest species. So when I saw these wraiths rise from the heath on Juniper Ridge, I attempted to collect a small series for him.

I had already shed my boots to cool and rub my feet, sore from the rocky trail. Birkenstock-shod, I bumbled among the huckleberries in the full moon's light, lunging at the luminaries. I managed to catch only one of the many flitting around, always just beyond the reach of my net. Not only were they swift and spectral, but at times they seemed not to be there at all. Then, within moments, they disappeared for real.

Moonlight mothing, chasing ghosts. It brought to mind a charming essay on these creatures by Harriet Reinhard, a pioneer Northwest lepidopterist. She wrote:

> As children, we lived during vacation time at our family cottage at Ocean Park, Washington. Each year during the last week of August at sundown my sister and I set out for the spot where we had discovered the ghost moths, for only at that hour and season did they materialize.
>
> Pulses and footsteps quickened as we drew near. Almost invisible, they danced and darted from bush to bush as twilight deepened into dusk. We netted what we could until darkness prevailed, then trod light-footed homeward with our harvest. Scientists called ghost moths choice and rare.

That was in the early twenties. Sixty-two years later, Harriet met David Wagner, then a graduate student at Berkeley, quite by chance. Learning that she had collected the well-known series of Ocean Park ghost moths, David plumbed her memory, hoping to go there and find the moths himself. "I looked into the eager young face," Harriet wrote of the occasion, "and knew that the excitement I had felt in 1921 would blaze again, could he but see the ghost moths dancing in the dusk at end of summer."

I wonder if that's what my friend Jeanne Gammell saw. A present-day resident of Nahcotta, just a mile or two from where Harriet had chased the ghost moths more than seventy years ago, Jeanne told me of an experience she once had while camping in the wilderness of Washington's North Cascades. It was early October. After a storm she peeked out of her tent at two-thirty in the morning and saw what she thought were stars.

But the "stars" were moving within the tiny clearing in the deep woods. There were dozens of what Jeanne took to be small lights, nearly equidistant from each other, moving "in a gently undulating spatial dance, counterclockwise, never touching or crossing the path of another, as though directed by an unseen choreographer." Jeanne stood and reached up as one circled near her, then climbed up on a stump and stretched toward them. But she couldn't reach the "lights," which seemed to give off a "warm gold-white glow, pulsating as they moved." They were about the size of butterflies. Completely unsure of what she'd seen, Jeanne retired to her tent with her mind wide open.

Now, in the evening of this other October, a hundred miles south down the spine of the Cascades, I watched my own parade of dancing lights. To my eyes the ghost moths didn't seem to generate light, but in the pale moontorch and sunfade they could be said to glow. Their dance, if not quite as regular as what Jeanne saw, arced like a signal-man's swinging lantern. And they *were* almost impossible to touch, as I found with my net. Clearly they exploited the faint ultraviolet better than I was able to use the last visible light.

The ghost moths fell back into the heath as ineluctably as they'd risen. To spend the better part of a year enclosed — first as a senseless egg in the winter; then as a burrowing wormoid in some cold, tight root; next a dumb pupa within a silk-battened cavity — then finally to fly free in the alpine air for all of two hours! The life of a ghost moth suggests a Cinderella whose ball is not only brief but final.

As I retreated into my own cocoon of rip-stop nylon and fiberfill, I took with me the glimmer of the moths' soft wings on the soft night air. These fleeting lives leave powerful visions behind, beguiling a small number of lepidopterists while giving shivers to dusk-watchers and night-campers who haven't a clue what to make of these strange sights, "dancing . . . at end of summer."

- - -

I have little doubt that many UFOs, fairies, and specters could be handily explained in lepidopterological terms. Yet I suspect that such an explanation would hardly satisfy Jeanne Gammell. I have seen things in the night myself that have nothing to do with moths or anything else I know in the "natural" world . . . yet they were surely part of nature, which is all. Reluctantly yet inescapably, we admit to having seen certain night lights that are not readily explained as ghost moths or headlights or airplanes or weather balloons.

In the same way, after all the shadows and bears and monkey suits and plankwood footprints have been eliminated, a residue of Bigfoot remains. Tucked in my ridgetop camp, I turned my thoughts back to hairy giants. After all, my mission wasn't one of moths. I laid my buzzing head against my air pillow and thought about how we'd arrived at the present Sasquatch tradition.

Every culture has had its monsters and giants, its myths of the Green Man and the Wild Woman, but no culture has ever been so confused as ours as to what it really believes. Are we such wonderful observers of the natural world that we should expect to know everything that looms, walks, creeps, or grows outside our doors or beyond the city wall?

The orderly pace of taxonomy has been steadily eroding the biological unknown since before Aristotle, through Buffon, beyond Linnaeus, and right up to one Professor C. P. Alexander, who described more than ten thousand species of crane flies. Lately this leisurely enterprise has taken on an air of urgency as the rate of species extinction has come neck and neck with that of description, for only by knowing what's out there can we hope to conserve it.

With the accelerating effort to catalogue life before it disappears, our estimates of its overall proportions expand. New information from the rain-forest canopy has raised the projected tally of the world's insect species (and thus, most of life) from around a million to more than thirty million. Journals of systematics tumble over themselves to place new taxa on the docket. Still we know just the meager margins of the totality of natural diversity in any depth whatever.

David Wagner plans to name several new species of ghost moths. For the time being he has placed the dusk-flying swifts of the Cascades in the species *Hepialus roseicaput* — the red-headed ghost moth — for the reddish ruff of furry scales on its bulky thorax. Far from phantoms, these flesh-and-blood redheads are real enough to earn scientific names, the number of which might soon increase.

It may seem a matter of little moment just how many species of obscure moths actually occupy a remote wilderness. Yet knowing what they are and where and how they live might help us know better how to care for the high country — a landscape under pressure from acid rain, grazing stock, forestry, and recreation. Even if the naming yields no practical application, it somehow seems better to know the world in its secret detail than to take its diversity for granted.

Yet who knows the ghost moths? I had seen a total of perhaps a dozen over a decade — a few of Harriet Reinhard's ocean-beach species in my own domain, one broad-daylight type on the pre-eruptive slopes of Loo Wit, another on her sister Komo Kulshan (Mount Baker) to the north — prior to the night of the moonrise fliers on Juniper Ridge. That's a dozen more than most people have encountered. Yet because something hasn't been seen, does it therefore not exist? Who, upon hearing of its bizarre life history and eerie twilit transience, would not be forgiven for wondering whether such a thing as a ghost moth was *real?*

If something we see lies beyond our ordinary experience, do we shrug and say it is nothing at all? This is the central question surrounding Sasquatch. Possessed of soft evidence, most people react with either hopeful credulity or hostile indifference. Only a few ask the hard questions, keep an open mind, then stay tuned for answers that might never come. A few others resort to the supernatural to explain the unexplained, as they always will.

For myself, I feel that nature is good enough and rich enough that a "supernatural" is not required. Therefore I try to look at the imponderables as things to ponder, certainly not to be dismissed as fantasy, phantasmagoria, or spectral deceits. If it was difficult to imagine the dusky shimmer of the ghost moths prior to my own encounter with them, then it is just as hard to accept a hepialid whose wings span eight inches of emerald green — yet just such a beast is a common pasture pest in Australia. When the world proves larger than we expected, we need to let out the seams in our mindset, and there should be no limits.

It's a long step from even a very big moth to the smallest Sasquatch, and I hadn't expected to find a clue to Bigfoot in the ephemeral flight of a night-fly. The objections to a second North American hominid are many, and my scientific skepticism counsels caution. But the long litany of belief and tradition courts fair consideration, as do the numerous clear tracks found in disparate wilds and the many sightings by seemingly reliable folk. To dismiss the unknown out of hand is even more foolish than to accept it unquestioned, more foolhardy than to fear it.

- - -

The next night I camped several miles down the ridge. I cooked a curry and sat back to await the silver discus of the moon. Mindful of my poor mothing the night before, I resolved to try again. I knew the moths were there, at rest among the tussocks and clumps. Even so, when sunset came, I waited with some trepidation to see if they really would come out again . . .

They did. Just after moonrise I saw them darting above the dull blood dropcloth of the heath. Again they flew for just half an hour. Dave Wagner had written that net collecting could be rewarding, "if one is fleet-footed." That let me out. Even so, he said, "a dozen adults may be missed for every individual netted." I missed many more than that but finally caught six males for Dave, my only evidence that these living lanterns weren't simply a trick of the moonmist.

- - -

So far, Bigfoot is proving even harder to catch than ghost moths. Let us earnestly hope it stays that way. In the absence of specimens, no one can prove that Bigfoot is *not* out there. Meanwhile, perhaps we should not be too eager to consign a perfectly good myth to the litter bin of lies. In the end, when we come to plot the vague landscape of what's what and what's not, maybe a moth is as good as a monster.

4
Sunrise with Bears

And I with my long nails will dig thee pig-nuts,
Show thee a jay's nest, and instruct thee how
To snare the nimble marmoset. I'll bring thee
To clustering filberts, and sometimes I'll get thee
Young scamels from the rock. Wilt thou go with me?
— William Shakespeare, *The Tempest*

WHEN I AWOKE the second morning, the volcanoes suspended Juniper Ridge in a cat's cradle of sunrise beams. Dawn is not my common companion. I love the morning, but I have seldom come to it gladly except from the backside. Let me stay up all night and swallow morning like a sleeping draft before bed and I find it sweet. But the actual rising, the opening of the sandpit eyes and raising of the stoneset body, are tough for me. So when I awoke wide-eyed in my tent's mouth, gazing out at sunrise and ready to go, I was surprised. I didn't know if it was the altitude, the exercise, or the dawn, one of the most glorious of the few I'd beheld.

The moon was still high. Color began to mix in the east, beyond the pale lump of Mount Adams. Pink mares'-tails rode in above the Goat Rocks, and a red flush appeared where the sun soon would, almost exactly where the moon had risen the night before. Mauve smears intensified by the minute and became purple knives shooting up and through the mountain from the south. A parasitic wasp and a termite both climbed my safety rail, as if to get a good seat for the show but actually to reach the warmth. As it turned out, the night and I had been still, and I hadn't needed a crib. Now tufty grass heads wriggled in a light breeze, silhouetted against the lightening eastern sky. The purple knives turned scarlet, their deed done.

I dressed and climbed the nearby knoll to see Mount Rainier in the first flush of the chilly dawn. This greatest of the Cascade volcanoes shows itself only fitfully. Though I've known hundreds of days when "the mountain's out!" as Puget people say, my views have mostly been from lower elevations, where hundreds of feet of city dust or forest haze cloud its grand clarity. I had seldom seen it from such an altitude and nearness, and I found it stilling. Juncos, maybe jaded by the sight, crowded a clump of fir, cedar, and mountain hemlock with their waking busyness. Hummingbirds tore open the morning with their shrieking plummets above my blue tent, and a great horned owl called faintly a couple of times from the valley to the west. Violet-green swallows shone like chips of jade and amethyst in the same blaze that lit the mountains.

Shifting to another spot on the knoll, I could see Rainier, Adams, and St. Helens all at the same time. I seemed to be almost equidistant from the three, an illusion based on Tahoma's disproportionate eminence. The sun seemed to hasten while the moon lingered, both on very nearly the same track. Glittering like a snail's slime trail, an inch of the Cispus River shone far below. I'd awakened thirsty, and I began to wish its water were within easy reach.

After repacking, my Sherpa seemed a bit more compact. As I hoisted it off an ancient stump I realized that my shoulders were bruised; but I felt strong even as the sweat began to pour. Almost as soon as I started walking my thirst came on sharp. I had enough water for another day or so, and I wasn't sure how soon I would find more. But I was in sight of roads, in earshot of truck horns, and I wasn't going to die. Not that it would be a bad place to go if they left me here, as in Ed Abbey's last request, under "lots of rocks."

Butterflies hilltopped the ridge as I followed it south into the warming morning: anglewings, tortoiseshells, painted ladies, fritillaries, coppers, sulphurs, skippers, all seeking mates. These colorful bits of living confetti helped keep my mind off the hard work. The grade was easy, but deep dust in the narrow motorcycle furrows, cut down two feet below grade, made the trail tough going. Hot needles pierced the fourth toe on my left foot as I took a downgrade through loose, sharp rocks.

This I had not expected after having a pair of boots custom-built. My feet, wide of instep, narrow of heel, and with an arch so high it could be a croquet hoop, have never known a really good fit in their lives, besides air and Birkenstocks. Many hikes had been less than pleasurable because of a disagreement between my feet and their wear. So when the grant for this book became available, I went to see a bootmaker.

I had long planned to visit the Buffalo Shoe Company in Seattle, a venerable firm that had shod generations of loggers, but by the time I got to it they'd gone out of business. Asking around, I located a respected private bootmaker on the outskirts of Portland. Bill Crary, the son of the founder of the Danner Boot Company, grew up around fine bootmaking. He and an Armenian assistant craft footwear for all manner of workers, riders, dancers, and others who need something beyond the common-denominator shoe-store offerings.

The rich smells of leather and waxes permeated the small shop and my untanned nose. Boots stood everywhere, ranging from husky black "corks" (hobnail loggers' boots) to a pair of shiny black riding boots for a woman with eight-foot-long legs and calves as big around as my wrist. Out from under a heap of leathers emerged a stocky, balding man in an oxblood-stained apron. That is, oxblood polish; they don't actually make the leather on the premises, just the shoes.

Bill was brisk and professional but friendly. Quickly and carefully he determined what I wanted and what my feet required. He whistled at my arch. He took measurements for a last to be crafted from an ancient form made of tulip-tree wood. And from these he fashioned my boots: four pounds of Norwegian ox, kangaroo, bonded rubber, and sturdy foam. They were magnificent, if more like Frankenstein's clogs than the sleek, hardly-even-there, New Age pseudo-booties so popular now. I broke them in on the flat, and they felt like clouds on my mutant hind paws. Heavy clouds, waterlogged perhaps, but I didn't mind that — I like a substantial shoe. And that they were: but for their waffle-stomping soles, my tracks in the loose pumice would surely have excited fresh reports of Bigfoot among the next party of hikers or bikers.

Those wonderful boots cost $445, and I expected them to be good. So I was taken aback when my feet started hurting one day into the hike. The boots worked fine on the level and on good trail, but when I had to descend, especially in rocky places, or climb through the trenches left by bikers, one toe hurt like hell. It wasn't the fault of the bootmaker — he'd done his best — but of my weird feet. I was a victim of Morton's metatarsalgia, a common pressure affliction of hikers. Today I wore thinner socks, laced my boots less tightly, and moleskinned my toes. Still, that toe shrieked in the dirt-bike ditches.

After one particularly painful descent I stopped for a lunch of cheese, water, dried apricots, and Thea's wheat crackers in a cool hemlock grove. I'd been inhaling water, and the containers were low. Just around the bend from the grove lay a melt-water pond in a little grassy cirque at the base of Sunrise Peak, the first water I had seen. I simply hadn't thought the ridge would be quite so high and dry, devoid of springs or snowmelt. This cruddy little pool was full of gunk, volcanic ash, and algal clots, but the signs of wildlife told me there was no point in looking further. California and Milbert's tortoiseshells sipped minerals from fetid mud scribbled over with hundreds of animal tracks. The liquid looked awful, but I reckoned it would filter all right. The days of carefree reliance on clean water in the wild now long past, every sensible hiker carries a water filter or other means of purifying water sources that might be contaminated with the cysts that cause giardiasis or other ills.

The water, shallow and silty, proved very difficult to gather and to filter, but I managed to secure a quart or so. Looking back at the pale green pond, I decided I would boil as well as filter the water.

The climb back up to the ridge below Sunrise Peak was abominable — steep, steep, steep, and all deep motorcycle ruts. Much of the trail was eroded as much as three and four feet below grade! The best alpinist would find it difficult to maintain balance while crawling up this slick trench, lubricated with choking dust like graphite. I took to my hands and knees, especially where the water bars and switchbacks had been ruined by knobby tires. My maps gave no hint of the difficulty here. Without the artificial erosion, it would have been merely the stiff climb that the map contours had led me to expect. As it was, the route proved next to impassable. As I struggled and swore, I scrawled a memo on my memory to the forest supervisor. Subject: BAD MANAGEMENT!

- - -

Reaching the top of the worst pitch, I sat on the edge of the rut with my pack against a fir and thought about what I'd just been through. My stinking, soaking shirt bore a portrait of John Muir among pine boughs and cones. The landscape I hiked in was the Gifford Pinchot National Forest. Neither John Muir nor Gifford Pinchot would have countenanced for a moment building a trail on shallow and fragile soils at great expense, then inviting smelly, noisy, and dangerous machines to tear the hell out of it. Somehow, in trying to please everyone, the managers of this forest were totally blowing the concept of conservation, and the land itself was suffering.

Not that Muir and Pinchot shared a common sense of conservation. Pinchot founded both the U.S. Forest Service and the first forestry academy in the United States, at Yale, to supply foresters for the government. Having traveled to Germany to observe the science of silviculture in action, he aspired to build a whole new practice of scientific forest management for the country's immense public forest holdings. When I attended Pinchot's forestry school at Yale, he was still held in high regard. After all, his basic principle of using the resource while maintaining its value and future usefulness could hardly be questioned. For many his tenets are still the foundation of the conservation canon.

But earlier I had studied at the University of Washington's College of Forest Resources, where I had learned about John Muir, founder of the Sierra Club. Muir, a Scot who had come to California via Wisconsin, was transfixed by the "Range of Light," as he called the Sierra Nevada. He believed, as Pinchot did, in the concept of intelligent resource use — but, he believed, for some places that meant no use at all. Just as Pinchot's ideas put into practice led to the Forest Service, Muir's writings and actions resulted in Yosemite National Park and the National Park Service.

The two men, sharing a common disgust over bad management in the western woods, tried to work together at first. But after a chance meeting in Seattle's Olympic Hotel, when Muir attacked Pinchot for his duplicity on an important matter, they never spoke again. The issue was Hetch Hetchy, a spectacular valley in Yosemite National Park. Pinchot supported damming it for the use of San Francisco, a position that contradicted park philosophy and law; Muir thought it a travesty to thus betray the new park. As he put it, "These temple destroyers, devotees of ravaging commercialism, seem to have a perfect contempt for Nature, and instead of lifting their eyes to the God of the Mountains, lift them to the Almighty Dollar."

Pinchot responded, "Regarding the proposed use of Hetch Hetchy by the city of San Francisco, I am fully persuaded that the injury by substituting a lake for the present swampy floor of the valley is altogether unimportant compared with the benefits to be derived from its use as a reservoir." And there you have the essential bicameral nature of the American "conservation" movement, right and left brains locked in a perpetual battle between the so-called preservationists and utilizationists.

Pinchot won, Hetch Hetchy was dammed, and Muir soon died. Relations between the Forest Service and the Park Service and among their various supporters have been strained ever since.

John Muir never came back to the Dark Divide, but perhaps he gazed this way when he climbed Mount Rainier 102 years before my trek. His guide was Seattle school superintendent E. S. Ingraham, a Rainier authority. The normally staid Ingraham had a remarkable experience on one of his ascents, perhaps brought on by oxygen deprivation after sleeping in an ice cave at the 14,411-foot summit. As described in Paul Dorpat's foreword to *Washington: A Portrait of the Evergreen State,* he reported a grotesque crawling and glowing creature that he dubbed the "Old Man of the Crater." The Old Man somehow transmitted knowledge of an "ancient race of humanoids that lived within the mountain," which Ingraham named the "Sub-Rainians."

Dorpat believes that "the Old Man of the Crater is surely a variation of our popular legend, the shy Sasquatch" and that "there is only one way to approach these demure and delicate chimeras, the Sub-Rainian and the Sasquatch — as poetic go-betweens. Through their eternal wanderings, Washington's past meets its future." He concludes that "if Washingtonians continue to treat the Big Foot kindly and preserve for it a private place in their enchantments, *this Washington* will step lightly into the future." John Muir apparently failed to encounter the Old Man on any of his Rainier ascents. But he could have agreed with that premise: treat the world well, and it will treat you well later. If he were here now, he would see that we have not been so gentle, so far. We have not stepped lightly in this land.

My fellow forestry students in Seattle were split into Muirians in the wildlife and recreation programs and a Pinchot faction in the traditional log, pulp, and paper curricula. As one of the former, I leaned toward Muir's values. We tried to blend the best of both men's teachings but found that they often conflicted. In 1975, a hundred years after its founding by Pinchot, the Yale facility changed its name to the School of Forestry and Environmental Studies. In so doing the faculty hoped to reconcile the old divisions in a common practice of conservation allowing for many uses of the land, including protection, all based on solid science.

Progressive foresters have been working to balance fiber needs from the forests with recreation, water, wildlife, and mineral uses, as well as wilderness. Finding the proper formula is never easy. One thing certain is that even the use-minded Pinchot would be scandalized by many of the practices now followed in our timberlands. Struggling up the shattered grade, I had recalled Pinchot's ideal of "the highest and best use for this and future generations," and I knew that this wasn't it.

I had no idea whether Sasquatch dwelt within the Gifford Pinchot, as its believers claimed, but I certainly saw abundant sign of humanoid apes that day. Leaving their colonies below, they stormed the steeps on their greasy beasts of burden. Once on the ridges, they tore back down again, having shredded the plants, the silence, and the thin soils along the way. This advanced behavior shows a degree of intellectual and aesthetic development somewhat lower than a monkey's but approaching that of a larger portion of *Homo sapiens* than I like to admit.

Months later, at a restaurant in southwest Washington, I found myself seated for dinner next to Harry Cody, district ranger in charge of the territory I'd traveled. A fishing-trip guest of a dairying neighbor of mine, the ranger was affable, intelligent, and apparently as concerned about the health of the ecosystems in his care as I was. He expressed frustration at having to allow a larger cut of timber than the land could stand, thanks to Congress. I asked him about the impact of dirt bikes, especially on Juniper Ridge. He said that the damage I'd seen was from an annual motorcycle race on the trail. I was incredulous that the Forest Service would allow such an activity on erodible backcountry land. He said he had some concerns about it himself, so he'd pulled the race off that trail for the following year. I was relieved — until he told me that he'd shifted it to the next ridge west. Langille Ridge was so rugged bikers had seldom gone there: hence, it was pristine. He liked it, so that's where he was putting the bikers to relieve the pressure on Juniper Ridge. As for the trail I'd hiked, he planned to rebuild it for motorcycles.

Readying myself to climb again, I wolfed water. It ran down the front of John Muir's face on my T-shirt, mingling with the H_2O I was sweating almost as fast as I drank it. At that moment I'd have given half my remaining water to have Gifford Pinchot show up, just so he could see the vast eroded clear-cuts in the distance, the roads punched gratuitously up steep and wild valleys below, the motorcycle ruts in the soft and shallow skin of the land. "Behold, Mr. Pinchot," I would say with wry respect, "what your doctrine has become in practice in the national forest that bears your name." Then I would ask if he'd care to discuss Hetch Hetchy.

- - -

I set up camp near where the Sunrise Peak Trail took off. I dumped my boar of a pack at a good spot on Juniper Ridge much like the first night's but wider. The tent went up on veg, not just ash. Then I walked unencumbered to view the next day's pull, which looked down-up again but not so bad, then a *long* up-down to Dark Meadow, the first place I could trust to have water.

I decided to use the scuz-pond water for dinner and breakfast and save the last of the good Gray's River water to drink on the trail. Filtering and boiling the holy water of the filthy pond, cooking curry lentil stew, and making coffee took an hour of pure leisure. In the late sun I was pleasantly warm, like a country bun. If only I had more to drink! Now I was really feeling the lack of water and could think of little else for long periods.

As I stretched out in my REI Volcano bag, a soft cloud somehow confected of recycled pop bottles, I became intensely conscious of my body. My throat felt like a dried weed. My shoulders, legs, and back were old rubber bands, threatening to cramp tight if I stretched the wrong way. My feet were aware of where they'd been and where they were going. These conditions got me to thinking about the state of my body in my mid-forties. I lay there and took inventory.

I had an osteochondroma on my knee like a golf ball on a tee; a torn muscle in my back from a long-ago toboggan ride on Mount St. Helens that liked to make a charley horse whenever a masseuse was not at hand; hay fever; and the first hint of a hernia. I had wrestler's knees, weight lifter's knuckles, and discus thrower's elbow. I enjoyed an abscessed tooth, temporarily packed; a sebaceous cyst on my head that I could feel against my air pillow, and a calcium lump on my mildly arthritic wrist. My bursitic shoulders were bruised, my Morton's toes were squeezed, and I had jock itch for lack of bathing water. My sinuses, even as dry as they were, provided adequate proof of the indifferent universe. I was dehydrated and thirty pounds overweight, down from forty when I'm not dried out. Altogether I felt pretty good.

It occurred to me that Sasquatch, if corporeal, must be prone to many of the ailments that we suffer, with no medical care and with constant exposure to weather, danger, and rigors that we routinely avoid. Is this not a remarkable ape? Except that in these respects it is exactly like every other wild animal, and we are like no other. Supposing Bigfeet are much like humans at our dawning, except very much better at surviving in the wild? I don't suppose they lie awake at night counting their hangnails.

As the moon rose, I watched the ghost moths at their brief evening's work. Back in the tent I read a bit of Wendell Berry's *What Are People For?* and a bit of Peter Byrne's *The Search for Bigfoot: Monster, Myth, or Man?* It seemed to me that the two were not so very far apart in their intent. Berry is always looking for ways to better situate people in their surroundings. Byrne writes of an animal, in which he earnestly believes, that could not be better situated to its place. Perhaps the desired state lies somewhere between the two apes, one fitted but fading, the other seeking a fit before it's too late. Lying up against my tent mate, the Sherpa, I thought of other large beasts elegantly suited to their lifeways: the bears.

I was concerned about black bears because of my food. I knew that you should hang your supplies out of reach and never stow them in your tent. But in the subalpine, where the tallest tree is a ten-foot switch, hanging food out of reach is next to impossible. Besides, I didn't want rodents (or bears, for that matter) tearing up the Sherpa. I remembered a traveling pack of Boy Scouts still asleep while their gear and supplies lay shredded and distributed for thirty yards around their coastal campsite. Nearby a couple were trapped in their tent by a bear who sat patiently before the flap. I also recalled, from a trip to Katmai National Monument in Alaska, that the only brown-bear casualty they'd had in that bearful locale was the mauling of a man who had taken his bacon to bed. Considering these mixed signals, I brought my pack inside the tent and slept with bears on my mind.

Sometime around midnight I awakened with a stiff hip and saw that I was still intact. I reached out through the tent flap and plucked a bunch of huckleberries for the moisture they afforded my dry throat. I realized that the bears were probably gorging on the abundant fruits and little interested in my ramen. I settled down and allowed my bear-thoughts to change shape.

Here is a beast at least as unlikely as Bigfoot. But because many people have encountered bears in the wild or semiwild, and almost everyone has seen them on television, in zoos, or in magazines, we believe in them. We are surrounded by bear rugs, stuffed bears, teddy bears, begging bears, zoo bears, and dancing bears; by Yogi Bear, Smokey Bear, and Care Bears. We even hunt bears, kill them, and eat them.

The practice of chasing bears with hounds ended in Britain back in the fourteenth century, when the last one was killed off. In Washington State, this barbarism survives, along with bearbaiting. Overall, bears have adapted surprisingly well to our insults and haven't yet dropped out of the American landscape, except where big timber companies and hunters have systematically hounded them out of large tracts in the West or where we have removed every vestige of the sustaining wildness they need, as in much of the East. More and more bears are being killed for their gall bladders to satisfy demand for Asian pharmaceuticals. Yet bears survive, and no one doubts their existence. That is, unless the conventional wisdom says that they are not supposed to occur in a given area.

Grizzlies, for example, have long been considered extinct in Washington except in the extreme northern Cascades. When people have reported grizzlies outside that zone, the official response has been dismissive. Yet as André Stepankowsky pointed out in the *Longview Daily News,* more and more grizzly sightings have been reported well down the Cascades, even into Skamania County. When biologists have bothered to follow up, they have found some accounts to be genuine. Yet as grizzly biologist Paul Sullivan told me, interviews he conducts elicit a fairly high proportion of grizzly statements from "civilians"; virtually none are from officials. This has a remarkably strong whiff of Bigfoot about it.

In bears we have a beast of huge proportions who demands prodigious amounts of food, whose habits are mostly secretive, who is threatening in reputation if seldom in fact, intensely mythologized by our culture and many others, and far more often spoken of than seen. All these things might be said of Bigfoot — except that bears definitely exist. Apart from that minor detail and their very different genealogies, bears and Bigfoot seem to differ in one major respect. Perhaps Pooh put it most delicately when he called himself "a Bear of Very Little Brain." The fact is, *all* bears are bears of little brain, at least compared with any large primate.

So when you think of an animal superbly fitted for its circumstances, able to forage zillions of calories off the rough land, remain mostly hidden, threaten its adversaries, lift boulders, break trees, cover great distances in a hurry, and weather all elements and dangers other than high-powered rifles, traps, and hounds, think bear; then add two or three times the cranial capacity, a grasping hand, and twice the weight, length, and strength — and you have to ask:

If bears, why not Bigfoot?

At least, that's what I asked myself before drifting back to sleep beneath Sunrise Peak, no longer worried about bears.

5

The Saddle

A secret land they guard
high wolf-country windy cliffs . . .
where a mountain torrent
plunges down crags
under darkness of hills
the floods under the earth . . .
— *Beowulf*

I AWOKE TO WIND. Clouds came out of nowhere and licked away the orangey cream cone of Pahto. In the west another dark cloud hung low over Loo Wit. I didn't take it for much, but it made me nervous. As soon as I got the tent down, lightning crackled over the Dark Divide. In about the time it took me to recognize the danger, the storm swept toward me across the valley. Heavy rain clouds broke water over Juniper Ridge.

I threw everything into the pack as quickly as I could, hoping to avoid both a soaking and a shock. I was out on the highest and most open spot for a long way around. The wind hooted like a woofer on all sides, and the rain fell like flams on the drumhead of the day. The summer and fall, the hills, and I had all been so dry, I hadn't figured on this. Water was all I wanted; now here it came in sheets and I had no way to catch it. I wanted just to stand and soak it up, to drink it from the sky with my mouth open, dumb to the heavens.

I couldn't get my pack on, so I dragged it down into a fir copse, pulled garbage bags over it, and humped it onto my back using a rotted stump as a prop. The lightning paid no attention. I'd had it strike closer, near a Colorado aerie on my thirtieth (and nearly my final) birthday, but not by much.

I hustled as fast as I could, graceful as a gravid tortoise, up and down the ashy trail. The pumice gravel didn't go to mud the way a finer sediment might have, but it was slickery all the same. Under plastic and Gore-Tex I steamed, for the storm hadn't brought much cold with it. I exulted at getting beyond the storm unstruck, but I was unnerved by the lightning and my vulnerability to it — something I should have anticipated from Colorado summers.

Finally I rounded the western flank of Sunrise Peak. I had hoped to take a packless side trip to watch the sunrise from the summit of Sunrise, but I hadn't gotten up in time — just as well, or the lightning storm might have caught me on top. Now a detour of several hundred feet straight up the rain-slicked trail, without water, seemed pointless. The trail dropped to the flat below through a cycle slot so narrow and deep that I had to place one big foot in front of the other all the way down, my offended toe complaining at the indignity and the pressure. If 330 pounds supported on a human pedestal exerts 3,300 pounds per square inch, that toe was the inch. As I watched the rainwater gutter down the dirt-bike ruts, carrying away what was left of the trail, I took turns cursing my thirst and the bikers.

When I wasn't grumbling I was stuffing my mouth with sweet blue beads. Huckleberries are even better wet with rain, which washes off the bike dust. I imagined myself a foraging ape, which I was, nipping out of the brush to snatch sustenance from the shrubbery, then ducking back before the stinking, helmeted hornets-on-wheels appeared. Had I the strength of Bigfoot, who is reputed to toss oil drums about at will, I might have lain in ambush as I gorged and liberated the path from a few noisy invaders. But I could barely heft my own backpack, and as it was midweek, my victims / tormentors never actually appeared.

I chewed berries and leaves indiscriminately. The moisture was reviving, and under the circumstances the berries were breakfast. The problem was that they had another effect, one whose issue drew more moisture from the body than the berries contributed. The evidence lay along the trail in the form of every sort of purple scat imaginable.

The shapes of the spoor betrayed the denizens of the ridge. I was right in thinking bears were around, feasting on every bush. Their leavings heaped the trail with scarcely digested, sometimes intact, berries. Coyote scats, normally agouti-gray and bone-shirred, ran to lavender, almost furless, and more formless than the usual tapered links. Many other local mammals had left their deposits, and the birds had swabbed the stones with grapy stains.

At last I could stretch out my stride on the big, broad Saddle at the junction of Trails 261 and 262 below Sunrise Peak. By now the rain had stopped and the morning was pleasantly cool. There was a chance of finding water at this pass of sorts, where streams might originate from springs at the head of steep valleys. I offloaded my pack on the thronelike stump of a rotted-out conifer and went in search of water. The Saddle was a plain of cinnabar-leaved shrubs. As I roamed it, I gobbled huckleberries to satiety and beyond. Inexorably, the time came to recycle. Walking past a big patty of purple bear poop, I retreated into the skirts of a fir and kept close watch for bruins. With your pants down around your ankles, a black bear surprised on its berry grounds might be dangerous.

Taking part in the cycling of the earth's goodness is as good a time as any to contemplate weighty matters like "If bears, why not Bigfoot?" One of the most frequent objections to the existence of a large primate in the West is raised by those who wonder what it would eat. Some biologists have doubted the ability of the backcountry to nourish such a big, active animal. Working out energy budgets for a mammal of its proportions, they challenge Bigfoot proponents to fill in the blanks in the menu.

Such people are probably not foragers. Euell Gibbons, after all, was no anorectic. Several primary plant converters, from Roosevelt elk to mountain goat, attain prodigious size in these hills. Throw in a little red meat, fish, and insects, and bears are possible. Yet the resources are scarcely exhausted in most years. Consider the amount of *Vaccinium* pulp consumed that season, for example, as evidenced by all the violet piles; yet there were still plenty of berries for me, a large primate. As I was to find in the coming weeks, the amount of nutritious material in the wilderness is greater than most people begin to imagine, and much of it is composted uneaten. This suggests that additional animals might be supported.

Of course, every species has other limiting factors besides food supply. Population biology consists largely in naming these factors. Bigfoot might be subject to any number of limits. But looking around me as I took part in the great circus of energy's revolution, I doubted that Sasquatch could be ruled out by food alone.

The Saddle, largely open due to a great fire in 1923, was good for huckleberries. But all of Juniper Ridge had once been lightly forested with slender candles of noble and subalpine firs before the fires gave it an alpine aspect. Now, decades after the latest blaze, the blueberry bushes were gaining height, and firs were coming up in blue, spiky clumps. I couldn't see very far on the ground; a bear could easily be hidden by the undergrowth. I considered that as I hung back from a fir branch by one hand. And when I heard sharp sounds nearby, I nearly pulled up my wool pants beforetimes. That would have been a mistake. These were only people, not bears, and a bit too distant to be embarrassed.

The night before, perched on a scapula of the ridge with ghost moths brushing my beard, I had seen a campfire far down the slope at the head of a logging-road spur. A couple of trucks were nosed up to the blaze, and I could hear the far yodel of voices on the rising warm air. At first I felt intruded on in my "wilderness experience," then I summoned a mild sense of companionship with some of the few others spending the night in these remote districts. Now the party I'd seen below me had come to stalk the wild huckleberry on the high Saddle.

With my binoculars, from the shelter of the fir-bough privy, I ogled the interlopers, as if I were the bear in possession. There was a stout Indian man with a two-year-old astraddle his neck; a five-year-old child excitedly running about; a young mother with stiff auburn hair in a ponytail, carrying two-gallon berry buckets; and a young man with a short black beard and long black hair, intense dark eyes, and a vest with no shirt. The men wore clumsy old wooden pack frames, and one carried a rifle, probably to protect them from bears. When I emerged from the brush, I made lots of noise and coughed as little like a bear as I could.

We chatted, which is how I learned they were the people from the camp below. "What's that, a butterfly net?" asked the man with the child on his shoulders. They were interested in Marsha and why I had her, though a butterfly net seemed to me much more normal than a gun. After I explained that I liked to tally the butterflies I saw, he said, "Yeah, sounds like fun. But I don't think it'll do ya much good against bears." Others have said the same thing, substituting "Bigfoot" for "bears," one of many reasons that I seldom mention the subject. I said he was no doubt right and went off in search of water.

I found a fairyland of reds and yellows and blues and a menagerie's worth of mauve manure. I found an indigo and scarlet arrangement of huckleberries and mountain ash, a pastiche worthy of Pat O'Hara or Art Wolfe and their most sensitive films. But I found no water, even at the head of the drainages east and west, where the grass retained a pale green tinge and moisture couldn't be far beneath the surface.

I was very thirsty and almost out of water. I showed the early signs of dehydration — lightheadedness, heavy-footedness, tingling fingers. I thought hard. The next section involved a long, rugged traverse of Jumbo Peak's north and west sides to Dark Meadow. There *might* be springs along the way; there *should* be ponds at the meadow. But what if there were none? For all I knew there might not be any surface water between here and Quartz Creek, a long, steep two-day hike away. So far, all expectations of replenishment had proved false.

There was no telling how badly tattered by bikers the steep-pitched Jumbo trail would be, or how thick the dust that worked like fuller's earth to suck moisture from my mouth, throat, and nostrils. I recalled the high mortality of insects following the Mount St. Helens eruption: populations over a vast area where ash fell had been devastated because of the abrasive nature and absorptiveness of the ash. It would score the insects' cuticle and then wick them dry of critical body fluids. I remembered watching the slugs cross the road by my house the morning of the eruption, struggling with the desiccating ash. Now I was beginning to feel like that or like a worm when the pavement dries out after the rain.

I'd been eager to tackle the grade up Jumbo and down to Dark Meadow, but the lack of water, with no promise of more, the cycle ruts, and the threat of more lightning on the exposed top and sides of Jumbo finally convinced me to change my plan. Not that the decision was easy. Just because I'd aborted long walks in the past didn't make it routine. But I'd never believed in carrying on for its own sake — that had always seemed a destructive and silly attitude. When my father said, "Don't be a quitter," as all the dads did, I shrugged. And when I quit football because of a bad case of mono, he was glad, and shrugged with me. Later, when I quit wrestling (which I didn't enjoy) in order to lift weights for discus throwing (which I really cared about), the coach was furious. In his favor, I had been less than forthright about it. Mr. McGuire, an Olympic medalist at 138 pounds and still in perfect condition, faced me down in the hall after school and called me a cherry. I felt bad — but not because I'd quit wrestling.

Plan B has always seemed an honorable alternative if conditions argue for a change of course. Still, I'd planned this trip for so long, talked about it so much, and based so many things on its completion that a detour was not a light matter. A couple of day hikers heading for Jumbo offered me some of their water, but I knew they'd need it themselves. The man urged me on, but the woman, alert to the danger of persisting against prudence, shrugged. Marsha and the Sherpa, lined up on their stumpy perch, said, "We can go either way." So we turned onto Trail No. 262. I might have resembled Sisyphus, but I was headed downhill.

- - -

The route down the mountain was as beautiful as it was brief. I stepped as lightly as a small Indian elephant carrying Jackie Gleason. The bikers had evidently not used this side path much, for it had no ruts. The smooth sand trail, the intense reds of the huckleberry leaves and mountain ash berries, the pink of the fireweed, the sweet smells of the rain and the mountain balm bushes made the descent heavenly. My sadness at no longer climbing the skies fled before a firm conviction that flashed like a lighted billboard in my brain: there is more than one way into the Dark Divide.

I encountered two Indian women berrying on the trail. To the first, after she recovered from her surprise at running into a laden behemoth carrying a butterfly net, I said that the picking was much better up on the Saddle. The second, with one hand in a bandage, had blue teeth already and a nearly full pail. She told me that this was the best huckleberry harvest in years. I realized I was dealing with professionals and that my advice was redundant.

Before the final descent into the managed forest, I doffed my penance and took a lunch of sharp cheddar and homemade crackers, soft yellow apples from home, and the last of the water. If nothing else, I could stick my head in the Cispus River within a few miles. My perch was a small prominence over its valley, so only thin air stood between me and the East. Mount Adams sat nearly in my lap. On the other side of the trail a big mixed feeding flock of migratory songbirds thronged a mountain ash hanging from an outcrop. A female warbler on a rowan bough spread her softly yellowed wing, reaching past the brighter yellow leaflets for a fly on a bunch of fire-engine berries; beyond, the blue spire of a young noble fir was decked with juncos and warblers. We take trees and berried greenery indoors once a year and hang dead ornaments on them in honor of the season. Each season honors us the better, if we attend, with living decorations such as these.

The trailhead for No. 262 was at the end of a rocky logging road, and several vehicles were parked along the road. I took up a post on a log beside a small clear-cut. It was still several miles down that loopy log route to Forest Road 23, the thoroughfare that follows the Cispus River to the Dark Divide and drops down the other side to the Lewis River, and the day had grown hot. I wasn't eager to tackle those stony switchbacks without water. I decided to wait and ask for a lift from the first returning party of the three I'd met.

The first group to come down was the one I'd seen first, with the youngster tumbling down the steep last bit and the infant still atop the strong young Indian's shoulders. Among them they had five gallons of huckleberries. Had they seen a bear? They had not, and the rifle had remained on safety the whole time. Since they had two trucks, I thought I had a chance for a ride. But they planned to camp there another night, so they politely turned me down. At least I figured I could bum some water if necessary.

I sat dozing on my log, but the gray jays calling from the edge of the uncut forest awakened me. Noble fir seedlings coming in among the pearly everlasting in the clear-cut pleased me, enriching the Douglas-fir monoculture of most replantings. Orchid fireweed and a late penstemon the color of Concord grape jelly hummed with bees. I picked blackcaps and blue currants, a welcome change from huckleberries to moisten my thick tongue.

An array of autumn butterflies hovered over the soft white clouds of everlasting, sucking up the last of the summer's nectar: sulphurs, skippers, coppers, and some tiny gossamer-wings swooping a pas de deux. When one finally perched, I saw it was a russet hairstreak. I netted it with Marsha to confirm the identification for the first Skamania county record. Its rich chestnut forewing displayed a black stroke called a stigma, identifying it as a male. When I looked again, its courtship perch had been filled by another.

Just then the two Indian women came down the trail. We chatted about berry yields, and I asked for a ride to the bottom. They were nervous about me and reluctant, but Marsha and my sticky, thirsty voice convinced them I was harmless, merely in need of water. With my gear and their berries we barely fit into their car. As soon as we were under way, they passed back their water bottle, and I drank deeply for the first time in many hours. I hadn't figured on being in a car again so soon, but I was grateful.

Dolores, a Suquamish from Olympia, was maybe fifty, solidly built, with Coast Salish features. She worked for a state agency, and her left thumb was in a splint because she had overworked a tendon while handling big data tapes. Helene was in her late thirties and spoke with a mild accent. A Tulalip, she lived in Tacoma and worked in retail in Seattle. Dolores drove a fairly new Dodge and wore a T-shirt with a slogan from a television show I didn't know; she said she hadn't been to a tribal meeting in years. A Bible and a *Plain Truth* lay beside me in the back seat, badges of belief no more or less comprehensive in their revelation of personal creed than my John Muir T-shirt, though we are quick to judge.

As they found their ease, they spoke of Indian canoe races and honky bluegrass festivals (they attended the former but had more fun at the latter); of jobs, husbands, and the time their borrowed pickup truck was buried when a load-it-yourself gravel dispenser wouldn't turn off. They laughed and asked me to tell them about butterflies and what it was like to write for a living. They said it sounded a lot like fishing, and I didn't disagree.

As the maple curtain of the Cispus swept by, I asked the women if they knew any Suquamish or Tulalip legends concerning Bigfoot. "I know others have stories like that," Dolores said, "but we're 'city Indians.' We don't know those stories."

Yet they weren't strictly city Indians. They had spoken about favorite berry patches and the season's fishing and how to cook the salmon and the berries in the old way. In this wild place, far from the city, they seemed more at home than I. And Helene wanted to go up to Mosquito Meadows to see the country and the berries. "I only like them right off the bush," she said.

So they had nothing to say about Bigfoot. I've learned that a direct query seldom evokes Sasquatch talk among Native Americans. It's as if the stories are not their own to just give away. And yet there is no shortage of knowledge about hairy giants among the native people of the Northwest. I would learn this again and again when I wasn't so abrupt.

I'd expected to be dropped at the bottom of the long, steep logging road, where I could filter water and hitch somewhere — maybe to Trout Lake, where I could stay with my Forest Service friends until I got reorganized. But the car turned left at the bottom and kept going north along the Cispus all the way back to Tower Rock Campground. Long before the sun went down and the goats came out on the bridge, I was once more ensconced in the campsite Thea and I had occupied several nights previously. The cold, clear water ran abundantly from the pipe nearby, and I was whole after walking Juniper Ridge with its bike ruts and lightning. I felt this might be more than I strictly deserved and that it was not, all in all, a bad start.

- - -

In the late afternoon I walked to the nearby Cispus Environmental Learning Center. I'd once lectured at the center, and I hoped they might let me use a shower. Bathing on the trail had been impossible, of course.

Along the road in old homestead fields flitted ocher ringlets and cocoa-brown wood nymphs, butterflies I call the satyrs of September for their family affinity (Satyrinae) and their late flight among sere grasses where their larvae once grazed. Satyrs — another woodland creature once thought to be real — shared with Bigfoot, along with their mythic qualities, a reputation for a strong smell. Any doubters walking downwind from me might have had their faith restored in those rank rustic deities of old.

The shower was sublime. Afterward I called Thea, who was surprised and a little nonplused at my change in plans. She'd been looking forward to the reprovisioning reunions.

Outside, refreshed in the late afternoon warmth, I met a teenager blowing leaves off the sidewalk. Josh Haney disliked the smelly, noisy leaf-blower as much as I did, agreeing that it seemed out of place at an environmental center. Then, to my surprise, he launched into a creditable lecture on logging practices. "Come over here," he said, and I followed him to the edge of a construction pit, where shallow Douglas-fir roots poked through the soil profile. "Look at that," he said, pointing to the thin layers of humus and topsoil. "It's no wonder the forests don't grow back the way they used to, when you see what logging does to the soil."

He expanded on what he saw as poor forest management and the cupidity of the giant timber companies. Maybe sixteen, with longish dark hair and single-minded eyes as sharp as a Douglas squirrel's, Josh was precociously articulate, and his attitudes about the woods were remarkable for a country lad. He was a better talker than a listener, but he did listen too. I had a hunch we'd meet and converse again. I planned to loop back to the campground by a different route, so I took my leave.

I walked to the Cispus River's confluence with Yellowjacket Creek and crossed, holding my trousers and sandals overhead. Picking my way over stones, logs, and glacial sand, I reached the woods. By my map I had to be very close to the road and Yellowjacket Ponds; but as I battled what Josh called "viney maple," thistle, dewberry, and stinging nettle, I thought I'd never get to the edge. In the middle of the thicket I stumbled onto an enormous cedar stump. A great two-chambered hollow, it would make a fine bear den.

In *The Search for Bigfoot: Monster, Myth, or Man?* Peter Byrne says that the most common objection he hears to the existence of the animal is that there is simply no place left for it to hide. Yet here I was a few yards from a state highway, near a campground, a picnic site, and the old CCC camp-turned-ecocenter, in a spot where a woolly mammoth could quite handily hide out for a week. And who alive had ever seen this stump but the man who last logged around it? In his chapter "No Place to Hide," Byrne contends that there are *lots* of places to hide. As Edward Cronin wrote in the *Atlantic*, "The irregular topography would . . . help conceal a large primate. In the best monster tradition, [it] could disappear among the numerous gullies, canyons, cliffs, rock shelters, and varied slopes. A two-dimensional map tends to disguise the enormous surface area that exists in the three-dimensional terrain. . . . The slopes fold back and forth upon themselves to include a prodigious amount of land." Cronin was writing about the Himalaya and Yeti, but he might just as well have been speaking of Bigfoot in the Dark Divide. People simply have no concept of the complexity of the countryside.

Josh agrees. I ran into him again a little later on a forest road leading down to the closed bridge opposite the campground. He was excited, having come from a very old fire circle he'd recently found. His father, Bruce, judged from the stratigraphy that the charcoal predated the latest ash eruption of Mount Rainier, some eight thousand years ago. I asked Josh what he thought about Bigfoot. He said he believed in it outright.

"How many spotted owls do people see?" he asked, rhetorically but relevantly. Josh has his own theory about the decline of the celebrated northern spotted owl. He believes that Douglas squirrels increase with second-growth forest and that they drive the owls from their nests. "But the owls survive in there," he said, nodding toward a substantial chunk of old-growth forest behind us. "And so does Bigfoot."

Josh told me that a local hermit he knows shared that opinion, based on a lifetime in the backwoods. He was not at all sure that the hermit would talk with me or that he could even be found. The man turned up now and again for a hot meal or when he had a story to tell. He believes that as the old trees go, so goes Bigfoot, though a few of each are still around.

I completed my loop walk across the old, goat-pellet-paved bridge. At the other end I passed the goats. I got back to camp ten minutes before Thea arrived from the lowlands with small, lean steaks, home-grown kale, and a good zinfandel, all welcome after trail food. I related my experiences and my new plan. Before bed we walked to the bridge to watch the river by moonlight. Leaning against the cables, we listened for night noises.

Suddenly, out of the river mist loomed the Horned One — the greatest of all the Cispus River billies. With a beard as long as his wicked horns, weird yellow eyes luminous in the moonglow, and a randy reek, he might as well have been the arch-satyr himself. There, on Pan's Bridge, I crossed for a shimmering second that sheerest of membranes between the insubstantial and the solid.

Now, across the span of months and miles, I hear his bleat, and it sounds as if he's saying, "There are more things in heaven and earth, Horatio . . ."

And who am I to argue?

II - HEART OF THE DARK DIVIDE

6

Of Ouzels and Old Growth

Trees are guardians of the Earth, and we are the guardians of
trees. We rely on what we know of them, how well we see their
dominion over the planet. They spin our breath into being,
giving it in little slips. They scatter shale and literally hold the
mountains together with their roots.

— Kim R. Stafford, *Entering the Grove*

THE SAME SATYRS of September that flitted below Tower Rock
when I'd come down from Juniper Ridge were on the wing in
Dryad. Unexpectedly reunited, Thea and I spent a day at Brenda
Boardman's cabin on the Chehalis River. Brenda, Thea, and their
friend Lucy Suzuki relaxed and shared the harvest sun while I worked
out the next stage of the journey. Dryad: the evocative name, the
whim of a railroad official in 1890, might have been drawn from the
image of the three women in the rising morning mist as they walked
the long-grass meadow among the waking wood nymphs and ringlets.
This was pleasant, but I had to get back up into the hills before
comfort set in and the edge wore off the alpine scent. After a brief
regroup and recoup at our own farmstead across the Willapa Hills, I
went back to the Cascades.

When I returned to the Dark Divide I took my car, but I did not
leave my boots behind. I had a new plan. Instead of making a single
hike across the forest on footpaths and game trails, I would work
laterally, both driving and walking. Since the region had already been
sliced and diced by the Forest Service and logging companies, I might
as well take advantage of the ways laid open by the process. Some
would call me hypocritical for falling in with a pattern I had criticized.
But as I see it, my use of the roads is simply a partial payback for the
invasion of the wilderness.

In forestry school many years ago I took part in a wilderness policy seminar. The instructor, a noted researcher in public attitudes toward wildlands, administered a sort of test of the students' preferences in outdoor recreation. One of the questions asked whether we enjoyed driving small dirt roads in the hills. Prowling back roads has always been a pleasure of mine, so of course I wrote yes. That one answer resulted in my being rated as a "weak wildernist" — a designation I, as a committed advocate for wilderness and parkland, hotly resented. I wish the roads hadn't been built. Without them I would have covered less ground but I'd have seen it more thoroughly. Since the roads *were* there, I saw no reason to ignore them.

I would still walk fragments of the former forest but also drive the small and larger roads by day and by night. In this manner I would experience a broader slice of the land. I would try to make up for the loss of solitude and self-reliance on my longer hikes. As it turned out, some of the roads stretched my resources as fully as any of the trails.

Since Thea and I were to have met where Quartz Creek comes out of the Dark Divide to join the Lewis River, I decided to make that my point of reentry. On a clear, warm day I took off at noon with Bill Munro and Hank Williams on the radio. At Cougar I bought coffee from a seasoned waitress whose look told me what she thought of bird watchers or whatever I was. The café was full of mountain lion art and landscapes painted on crosscut saws. Polaroid portraits papered the door — on one side, drivers and their tractor-trailer rigs stacked with old growth; on the other, hunters hoisting trophies of bucks and bull elk. I did not bring up Bigfoot.

The next morning, in a campsite at Lower Lewis River Falls, I awakened not to the sound of water but to logging helicopters. After breakfast I hiked to nearby Middle Falls, where the sound was the river's. Water ouzels danced on the rim of the broad water slide. These slate-gray relatives of wrens, also known as dippers, are synonymous with pure mountain waters. As I watched, one dipper repeatedly plunged its head into the oncoming water, making great fountains over its head and back at metronomic intervals. Another, closest to me at fifty feet, picked and stabbed more gingerly in shallower water, pointing downstream as often as up. Paler, less sure, slip-sliding down, it was likely young and inexperienced. A third worked upstream at the base of a satellite cascade some fifty feet across and four feet high. It dove in, bobbed, swam, flew under water, and shot over runnels and little flumes repeatedly. I wondered if dippers ever rode, or got washed, over the big fall. The lead-pellet birds maintained their individual behaviors for the quarter-hour I watched. The only constant trait was their perpetual dipping.

Tatterdemalion maples and lacy cedars overhung the falls, dripping gold and lichen, as alder leaves peppered the water and rock. Water ran white over churns, then brown over shallow stone before plunging green into the deeps between. What a place to swim! But the day was too cool. I picked red huckleberries — watery and tart — just below the dippers' run. A mountain biker dressed in turquoise spandex rolled by on the Lewis River Trail as I climbed back toward my camp.

This place, with its helicopters and bikes, is not very wild until you get a few feet into the forest across the river or into the night. But it is idyllic. I could be a faun, male cousin of the dryads of the Chehalis to the west. In dappled sun on the edge of old growth, I had my lunch of kipper snacks where Quartz Creek crosses Forest Road No. 90. Here a dipper worked the quiet water in yet another mode. A kingfisher rattled like my cursor running along a line, and a lazy Lorquin's admiral floated overhead. Kinglets wittered in small firs. My original plan had called for arriving upstream on foot, but I was here just the same.

One advantage of enlarging my scope was that I'd be able to walk in a variety of woodland leftovers, which are widely scattered and cost a lot of prowling to find. To have any hope of penetrating the twinned tangles of the old-growth debate and the Bigfoot puzzle, one must spend more than an afternoon's saunter in the woods, and in more woods than one. For the facts of these matters grow out of the very mat of moss and needle and fern that cushion the feet of those who go forth to seek them. They do not spring solely from trial records, newspaper accounts, or barroom hearsay; those who seek the truth in such sources alone are doomed to secondhand conclusions and ir-resolution of the muddiest sort.

- - -

Quartz Creek chuckled under dappled sun, oblivious to the droning helicopters. The place reminded me of Bluff Creek in California, site of the famous Patterson film. Here was another place where hairy giants were said to walk among the trees and rocks and waters. Near the trailhead a rustic birdhouse fashioned of cedar slabs topped a signpost from the forties. Vanilla leaf and false Solomon's seal wove the groundcover, lady fern sent crepe streamers in from the sides.

Hemlock needles showed through the broad, backlit leaves of devil's club. Thick, mossy cedar planks bridged each rivulet of limpid spring water, green with the reflection of vine maples. Up a little way the stream spread out over dipped strata into red whorls of iron oxides, terraced and hued like the turkeytail fungi spackling the path. Already I was among big trees in a diverse conifer forest with most of the middle-elevation species — true firs, Douglas-firs, hemlocks, cedars. It was the time of shedding for the hardwoods; their leaves took tortuous passages down runnels, became beached, refloated, and traveled on.

Finding the trail washed out below a clear-cut, I realized how narrow was this envelope of old growth. Platinum Creek, farther on, had been scoured and piled with overburden and slash from another clear-cut upstream. Steeply up the other side, pipsissewa and twinflower wove the soil before the trail plunged right into the clear-cut that had caused the problems below. The young Douglas-fir reclaiming the space might someday embrace the soil against the storms and allow Platinum Creek to run metallic-clear again.

The trail climbed through middling timber, and far below Quartz Creek ran liquid crystal. Stretching up the opposite side of the canyon, maybe a thousand feet from creek to ridge, the big trees masked a clear-cut over the top. The wooded band narrowed on my side. Is this a big corridor? Compared to what? Like every other fragment, it looks great in the context of the shaven whole, but it's just a patch on the pelage of the former forest. At least from here on the creek was mostly free of logging all the way to its headwaters high in the Dark Divide.

An apple beside the trail showed that others had come this way recently, though I had the illusion of solitude. Old caddis-fly cases, cemented with sand, then dried out, barnacled the rocks. A bumblebee approached my purple pencil and yellow notebook, ignoring the red dead nettle blooming among the rocks. Such "lesser lives" surround us always, yet when big birds and mammals fail to show, a place is likely to be called lifeless.

In the Quartz Creek deepwood, between Platinum and Straight creeks, all I could hear was the breeze and needles dropping. A yard-tall stalk of last year's pinedrops caught the sun and mirrored the red of a nearby rotting snag. A vanilla snow of its seeds rode the zephyr — so why aren't there pinedrops everywhere? Because those seeds are packets of protein for millions of invertebrates and because the ground isn't right everywhere and because and because . . . All my life as a naturalist, I've been fascinated by questions of what's where or why not. Patchy distribution of habitat is one of the most active areas of study in ecology, especially now that the patches are getting fewer and farther apart. Endangered species are the result of habitats grown a little too patchy, snows of seeds and sperms without issue.

The silence couldn't last. A jet, then chain saws, roared in the north. But quiet fell when I came upon the Sue Hollenbeck Memorial Bridge over the third tiny, dry, mossy stream. I wondered who Sue was and who loved her enough to build a bridge for her. Golden-crowned kinglets tinkled over the bridge, some of the still widespread bits of life that must pass this spot a few million times a season, like larger seed snows, piping in a language not far from the songs of pollen. I'd settle for such beatitudes sung daily over my bridge.

Rising to the rim of the deep, steep canyon, I could hear but not see the stream below. A big windthrow clogged the trail, and I realized how difficult it would have been to backpack through here. Sasquatch is said to vault thick logs in stride, and I've known long-legged hikers who do the same. But for those of us with twenty-nine-inch inseams, scrambling over downed logs can be a crotch-stretching challenge. Over or under, with a backpack, is a killer.

Doug-fir needles hanging from cobwebs right before my eyes caught me up short more than once. Big orb-weaving spiders positioned themselves at face height across the trails. Their black-and-white banded legs broke up the pattern, making them barely visible. I've shed the arachnophobia that plagued me as a youth, but I still bridle at big webs and bulbous bodies in my face without warning. These didn't get me, thanks to practice with the fir needles.

I came to the juncture of Straight and Quartz creeks, a small spectacle. Straight Creek, anything but, meandered down from the north in a green mossy cleft over onyx patterns of oxides in its bedrock. Just above its mouth a single huge log spanned it, hewn on top for foot-tread. Quartz Creek flowed just below, down a broader canyon with ancient forested sides. The two merged in a pair of drop-pools before their combined forces plunged around a natural rock dam, beneath a bleached and slanted log, and down a twenty-foot waterfall into a blue pool. Even at this season, long past snowmelt, the fall was a white cataract; below it a third arm of the stream made its own broad, gentler fall. The shared mouth of the two creeks debouched into lower Quartz, broad from the force of erosion, staked with big and small trees and downwood, and scarped with green walls of maidenhair and moss. Bonsai hemlocks occupied a ledge above the falls. The slanted afternoon sun caught the cedar trunks and ruddy cliffs up and down the gorge, turning it into a foundry cooling from the day's melt.

A big flock of Vaux's swifts, like slender dippers, streaked through the canyon below the confluence. Dun birds of the air and the ancient forest, swifts lose their nesting places when the snags are cut or fall. Looking away from their sickle-winged flight, I saw earthbound fungi rimming the path — golden boletes, cherry russulas, peachy chanterelles. As the swifts screamed their last for the day, I returned to a supper of mushrooms and hash, washed down with good ale from the village of Kalama on the Columbia.

In the gloaming I walked up Quartz Creek to wash dishes where arnica and aster made pale moons midstream on a mossy rock. Fir needles plastered a gray chunk of granite in a sandstone bowl of its own making. Grass-green tresses of algae waved below the water line, blackening with the coming dark. An ouzel dipped in alarm at seeing me, then shot past to the rim of a falls. Who would credit this plumbeous slug as a bird, so fishlike at times, so versatile in making water work for itself? One might ask whether Dipper, in all its shades and ways, is more or less believable than Sasquatch. Or Swifts, scything the sky with all the elegance of an ouzel underwater, making nonsense of gravity itself.

A pygmy owl chink-chink-chinked on into the campfire hour, which I spent with Alan Cossitt, a Portland photographer I'd met at the previous campsite. He told me of tracking and photographing old growth in hopes of stemming its decline. As an autumn hatch of maple thorn moths, stoneflies, caddis flies, mayflies, and wasps buzzed his Coleman lantern, we swapped stories of forests lost and found. Then I slept, in a circlet of five old-growth firs and cedars.

- - -

What is this thing called old growth? We used to call it virgin forest or forest primeval; lately, the terms primary and original forest have been used. Textbooks speak of climax communities, bioregionalists refer to the temperate rain forest, foresters speak of overmature stands, and conservationists rally to the battle cry "Save the Ancient Forests." Overall the term *old growth* prevails. By whatever name, these woods are the nexus of the bitterest battle in the environmental history of the Northwest. Not Hanford and its radiation, not the Columbia and

its obstructions, not fish, not offshore oil, not growth management —
nothing has aroused the fear and loathing, spit and hiss, loyalty and
love that old growth elicits from those who wish to cut it and those
who do not. The story is complex and will change ten times before
this book goes to press: the details do not belong here. But in its
essence, the struggle is about the future of the remaining one-tenth
or less of the Northwest forest cover that still resembles the condition
of the whole before the arrival of ferrous metal saws.

Some say a quarter or more remains, counting high-elevation,
subalpine smallwood. Others insist we're down to a twentieth or less.
While some scientists and managers contend that any stand more
than a century in age should be called old growth, other ecologists
reserve that term for trees at least three hundred years old, and still
others contend it is a matter of disturbance history and forest structure, not age as such. Tree size and spacing, soils, component species,
amount of deadfall, slope, and climate all influence how older forests
behave and when they qualify as "late successional," the latest label
applied by the Forest Service. I think of old growth as woodland that
harbors all or much of what a biologist traveling with Lewis and Clark
would have found. And by that measure, one-tenth of the original
growth is a very generous guess.

A disinterested observer would find it astonishing that we could
remove the last part of something as grand as old-growth coniferous
forest. But hardly anyone is disinterested. As soon as they experience
ancient forests, almost everyone becomes interested. The currently
trendy term for those who engage in public conflicts is "stakehold-
ers." Certainly most of us who know the woods at all consider ourselves that, for we do have a lot at stake in these trees. In public
forums, so-called facilitators try to forge consensus among stakehold-
ers. But common cause seldom arises from joint stakeholding, because we share few goals. Our values differ radically — and where
they overlap, our stakes get in the way of dialogue even more than the
facilitators do.

Big old trees are board feet, specialty products, stumpage, jobs in
the woods and the mills, livelihoods for families and communities
and cultures; or they are holy groves, grand spectacles, guardians of
unduplicated diversity, homes for spotted owls and swifts and wood
roaches and thousands of other rare species, sites of unrivaled inspiration, and an inviolate trust. Individuals can hold shades of both
views, but when they do, they either fail to apprehend the absolutism

of the other side or they become speechless from guilt and confusion. Log-town folk who love the trees love young ones as well as old, love regrowth and promise, think that the big trees already protected are enough; or they don't know or don't care about the breadth of life forms that are at risk. If a feathered vertebrate arouses ridicule and hate, a forest moth or midge will get no sympathy.

On the other shore, conservationists come largely from the city, don't know much about life in one-show mill towns, and either don't believe all the little green THIS FAMILY SUPPORTED BY TIMBER DOLLARS signs or don't care. Often they have little sympathy for timber towns or ridicule them outright. Three regional portraits published nationally, Bill Dietrich's *The Final Forest,* Sallie Tisdale's *Stepping Westward,* and Tim Egan's *The Good Rain,* singled out Forks, Washington, as a true-blue logging town. None of these writers felt comfortable in Forks. Dietrich tried to portray the plight of displaced timber workers with fact and compassion. Tisdale likened her immersion in Forks to going home to her native Yreka, California, or to any other small town: "If I am an interloper in Forks, I am an interloper . . . in my own childhood." Egan, in his otherwise laudable book, wrote that "Forks is to the Olympic Peninsula what a butt rash is to Venus." Such an egregious remark made me wonder if Egan temporarily forgot the source of the paper his books were printed on. But even if they are more sensitive to someone else's hometown, sometimes it must seem to the good people of Forks as if the writers of the world are lined up against the workers in the woods. Upon reading one such broadside, one of the most gentle people I know — a fine writer and a conscientious timber worker — said to me, "It makes me want to kill these people." It was more an expression of frustration than a hateful threat. But in the face of a vanishing resource base and tighter restrictions on all sides, it is no wonder the folks of Forks and their ilk react with venom to what they see as the urban environmentalist mafia.

So this fight will never be reconciled; it will just wear out, as the Clinton timber plan — acceptable to neither side — or some judicial or congressional Yalta draws the "final" lines on the Balkans of the western woods . . . lines that, like those on any map or landscape, can always be changed.

- - -

The outcome of the battle for the old growth clearly has everything to do with the ultimate nature of the Dark Divide and indeed the entire

Gifford Pinchot and Pacific Northwest. I've found it to be widely assumed that if Bigfoot exists, it must depend on the ancient forest; that as ancient manifestations, they must be mortally linked. Thus the fate of the forest seemed to embrace the future of Bigfoot, if indeed it had a past. I am an advocate for every last stick of old growth, a believer that future forestry must get by on the cutover lands (for reasons I detailed in my book *Wintergreen*), but the emphasis in this book on big trees depends on that presumed linkage between them and Bigfoot — if there is no such link, I should change the subject.

I hadn't questioned this connection until a member of my writing group objected to the position I expressed in an early draft. A member of a timber-dependent family, she suffered from the sense of persecution that all logging communities feel these days. The spotted owl and marbled murrelet seemed enough to contend with, and here I was trying to pin a rap on her people for wiping out an animal that isn't even known to exist! It was too much. The U.S. Fish and Wildlife Service, when petitioned to list Bigfoot as a precautionary measure, thought so too: how can you designate critical habitat for a myth?

I acknowledged my friend's frustration at what might well be a fatuous attack on a beleaguered industry. She went on to ask, "How do you know that Bigfoot even prefers, let alone requires, old growth? Maybe it's perfectly happy in second growth, like deer and bear." She had a point, and my mindset, already wobbly in this matter, slipped a notch.

Well, what about it? Bear, deer, and elk are all said to thrive in the productive second- and third-growth "reprod," as foresters call it. This can be true *if* those woods have not been intensively managed with slash burns and herbicides to encourage the worst — least-varied — kind of forest monoculture. Sprayed zones, meaning much if not most of the logged acreage, lack the vigorous and varied shrubs and herbaceous growth that ungulates and bears exploit. Even sprayed plantations, if they are allowed time to mature before the next cut, may in time acquire some variety of life forms. But as cutting cycles get shorter to provide quick pulp chips instead of sawlogs, diversity dies. When you cut the regrowth in thirty years, little wildlife value accrues; then, if you spray the leavings to prevent alders from competing with conifers, the next potentially useful period is lost as well. This is one reason the timber giants clamor for federal old growth: having logged off their own estate and converted it to pulp rows, they need our mature trees for the lumber mills.

Even if blacktail deer and blue grouse do frequent the secondary forest, a great many other species do not and cannot. The disruption of soil structure, hydrology, and microorganisms, the alteration of ground cover and canopy, the simple removal of biomass, not to mention the depletion of carbon and nitrogen — all these inevitable changes make it impossible for many animals and plants dependent on those features to survive or recolonize. Even if the land can restore itself, species will not return unless sufficient nearby habitat remains — thus the curse of the fragmented forest.

Many people are familiar with the short list of protected birds that cannot survive outside the old growth, or at least big, mature, interlinked stands. Not ten people on the West Coast can list the almost countless other species dependent on old forests. Largely plants and invertebrates, these species are not figured in the political mix, and decisions about logging are made on the basis of a few "keystone" species that might or might not represent the rest. Even when so-called lesser forms of life are brought to light, conversants tend to dismiss them. "When I raise the question — do we need to consider the slugs and snails and lichens? — people are just appalled. They just can't believe it," said Chris West, vice president of the Northwest Forestry Association, as quoted by the *Chinook Observer.* Yet without mollusks and lichens, the forests as we know them could not exist.

Now, as forest practices change toward the rough rubric and rougher concept of "new forestry," one begins to hear of "green-tree retention blocks" and other fancy terms for old-fashioned selective logging. The hope is that by leaving some live trees standing and others dead as snags or on the ground, a logged forest will approximate some of the function of old growth while still providing a crop. Some politicians have jumped on this approach to save their skins in split constituencies.

Certain companies have embraced the idea of new forestry also, at least in name. For example, Plum Creek, Inc. — guilty of appalling logging practices along the highly visible I-90 corridor over Snoqualmie Pass, as well as in Montana — now advertises itself as a practitioner of "Environmental Forestry." Their ads, showing colorful artist's versions of diverse woodlands, go way beyond even Weyerhaeuser's time-tested and hyperbolic calendar pictures of fairy-tale forestry. Acknowledging Professor Jerry Franklin as the bringer of light and giving a simplified ecology lesson, the Plum Creek ads ask, "What is Environmental Forestry?" The answer: "Created by us, it's an innovative man-agement plan that goes beyond today's standards to recognize that forests are complex ecosystems, not just stands of trees." Of the plan's "ten principles," one is to "protect and enhance all wildlife species." Bully for any corporation that actually practices a less destructive form of logging — but in fact the companies still spray their cuts with herbicides, killing thousands of nesting songbirds and other life forms.

New forestry — environmental forestry, green-tree retention, what-ever you want to call it — is not the same as old growth and never will be. The Forest Service has adopted the stunningly hubristic phrase "ecosystem management" — implying that they, too, will save all the pieces of the forest puzzle. In fact, many species will fall through the cracks in the plan and will be lost, and with them the fabric of the forest will unravel.

Does Bigfoot belong to the guild of the adaptees or the fellowship of the forlorn? At least one Bigfoot researcher, Jim Hewkin, takes the position that the animal not only exists but thrives in disturbed sec-ondary habitats. As a retired Oregon Fish and Wildlife biologist, he deserves a hearing when he says that the kind of landscape produced by human uses is exactly what this adaptable ape likes. Perhaps he is right. To find out, all we can do is examine what we know about what and where such an animal might be, then guess.

First it might help to take a look at adaptation, the lingua franca of evolution, the Rosetta stone of inheritance, the sine qua non of sur-vival. In the old-growth and logged-off lands of the Dark Divide, I encountered one of the most striking examples of adaptation I'd ever seen, and it made me think.

Sometime after Quartz Creek, hiking below Dark Mountain, where a noble fir forest used to be, I heard a pika call from the clear-cut rubble! As I walked up a Cat-track on the south side of a clear-cut "unit," one pika called nearby and two others farther off. I was amazed. I'd know a pika's voice anywhere. But no rockslides were visible. Pikas without rocks seemed about as probable as woodpeckers *sans* trees.

Pikas, sometimes called conies, rock rabbits, or boulder bunnies, are lagomorphs — relatives of rabbits. Small as a Netherland Dwarf bunny, compact, agouti-gray and rust, with little round ears and promi-nent whiskers, they look about as cute as an animal can. Yet pikas are tough, competent organisms of demanding environments. Instead of hibernating, they harvest and dry plants to make the hay that sees them through the harsh winter season on the talus slopes or scree. Pikas occupy alpine rockslides around the northern hemisphere. I was used to seeing these small, geeking beasts in the high Rockies and the North Cascades. But here, where were their rocks?

These pikas seemed to have colonized logging slash! The closest one led me a slow chase all around the slash pile (or "cull deck," as the Forest Service fuels crews call them), sometimes right below my feet but always escaping. We exchanged calls, as I've so often done in arctic-alpine locales: "Squeek?" "Geek!" I gained one or two fleeting glimpses but no definitive look. The call was unmistakable, and the behavior was just like that of pikas on a rockslide.

When I thought about it, I saw that the structure of the log dump was not so different from a rockslide. Crumbling white plastic netting covered the little-burned slash of mostly large, broken logs. These culls involve much biomass, and of course it doesn't all burn. I'd seen scores of slash piles covered with slick black plastic in recent weeks. I shook my head to see that they sometimes burned the plastic along with the slash, releasing not only scarce nitrogen but also toxins to the clear, high air.

In the afternoon I again walked past the unit. Hearing no pika calls, I threw a stick and exacted a few geeks, which led me to the creature's haystack. Beneath a slanted log two feet across, providing protection overhead but open to the northeast sun, lay the herbaceous mound. It was about a yard across and a foot deep and composted on the bottom. It was probably several years old. I recognized the plants in it: lots of pearly everlasting flowers, stems, and leaves; bunchberry dogwood; sword fern; fireweed; oval-leaved huckleberry; a little noble fir. Also salmonberry, alder, and willow. The harvester had urinated atop its stack. Concerned weets sounded at a distance, moving around me as I examined the hoard.

Following a little stream some fifteen yards away to the north, I found a secondary stack under a log with the same orientation, containing mostly bunchberry strung out in a line. A varied thrush strummed in the distance as the light softened. I got a flicker of a sighting as a pika dashed beneath the charred gray logs. More than one report has described Bigfoot shifting rocks, catching pikas, nibbling their heads off. It would have to be a *very* clever creature to do that.

That slash pile should be acceptable pika habitat for a long time to come. Nothing much was growing there, and what was, they were eating. By the time these trees rot there should be another clear-cut to move into nearby. That part was depressing, since the unit next door comprised the finest noble fir forest I'd ever been in.

Over an ale at my camp, I pondered this adaptive shift. I'd seen pikas among basalt boulders near sea level, down at Beacon Rock on the Columbia, so the altitude didn't surprise me as much as the substrate. Later, in a dusty junk and book shop in Carson, I checked the pika entry in Victor Calahane's *Mammals of the World*. He wrote that pikas have been known to live in sawmill slab piles or logjams in streams. Even though I'd studied, watched, and written of pikas for years, I didn't know this. Clearly, this dun little critter has a broader ecological amplitude — more ways to live — than I'd appreciated. This rockslide specialist seems to be one of the few creatures that has made an adaptive shift to take advantage of at least some kinds of logging. As the pikas retired beneath their logs, what I knew to be true expanded.

- - -

If a lagomorph most often identified with alpine granite can thrive in sea-level basalt and mid-elevation woodpiles, what does that say for a primate's chances of switching from forest to scrub? Any beast that has lasted this long in our busy midst would have to be fairly adaptable. And some of the most convincing reports of Bigfoot come not from dense forest but from the lavalands and shrub steppe east of the Cascade Crest. These reports argue for a creature that could tolerate second growth or even embrace it, as in Jim Hewkin's view.

However, Peter Byrne counters convincingly that Yeti was never a "snowman," abominable or otherwise, except on rare occasion; he believes the Himalayan Bigfoot to be a forest dweller who occasionally climbs the heights. If he is correct, our animal might logically be construed as a woodland species too. Most signs of Sasquatch have been found in the deepwood and along roads and streams penetrating it. And there is the question of food. As I saw over and over in my journey, a matrix of old and young forest, with meadows and blowdowns and burns, provides a more abundant and varied diet for a foraging primate than clear-cuts and plantations alone. But for me the strongest argument in favor of big apes staying with big trees has to do with cover and privacy. Every animal needs cover, and the bigger the animal, the more cover it needs.

Can you imagine a landscape of seedlings and Christmas trees concealing a viable population of apes larger than ourselves? I can't — particularly woods worked often and well known to the workers who cruise timber, survey boundaries, build roads, and fall the trees, plant, thin, and fall them again. Whereas a matrix including large tracts of little-trodden older jungle — for jungle it is — could easily conceal some great beast, especially a smart one that knows how to move and how to hide.

In the end we must fall back on imagination. The question then becomes not whether Bigfoot needs old growth but what kind of a forest we can imagine Bigfoot living in. I don't doubt they could adapt to some degree, employing the brush and the clear-cut, even the doghair reprod, as elements of their home range, faces of their potential habitat, not without rewards. But I can't see Bigfoot taking to the cut-over land as well as those pikas have. Instead I can see it doing *just* as the pikas do as a species — using the highlands, the lowlands, the lavalands, the forest floors, and even the cuts — but as a shifting population, not as isolated colonies.

This won't satisfy my friend who wondered if Bigfoot preferred second growth, except in knowing that I have considered her point carefully. But allocating the remaining old growth based on Bigfoot's needs couldn't be any more arbitrary than the traditional method. What is the least form of forest that could conceivably harbor working members of one primate species and foraging members of another that has more use for wild cherries than chain saws? A lot to gamble on a whim? What previous plan has done any better? If we believe in owls but hold them in contempt, perhaps we should adopt a standard that few believe in but would hold in awe if they did. Unable to reconcile the desires and needs of our own species, perhaps we should appoint Bigfoot as arbiter, a species so fabulous that we couldn't help but take it into account if it ever cared to reveal itself. In this way a maybe-imaginary cousin could serve as an emissary between two family branches with little language in common.

- - -

In the early morning I walked back to the first mossy brook on the Quartz Creek Trail to filter a gallon of water. A cool green pleasure, this chore — to lie on my belly on the cleft-cedar footbridge with devil's club and old growth overhead, wild ginger, inside-out flower, and violets all around, ferns and moss buffering the brook. I tried the filter's drinking-straw attachment so I could sip directly from the stream, a delight long denied. The water was cold, clear, fine — better even than the good Kalama ale. And for breakfast more chanterelles along the trail. Across the creek a water ouzel piped in the day, drowning out the helicopters.

7

Monty West and the

Well-Adapted Ape

In this respect man resembles those forms, called by naturalists protean . . . having thus escaped the action of natural selection.

— Charles Darwin, *The Descent of Man*

W HEN I DECIDED to include a car in my travel plans, I realized
that I would have to devote a certain amount of time and
resources to keeping it on the road. My venerable Honda, Powdermilk, had never given me trouble in remote places, and I had faith. It
was rewarded: the worst that befell me was a weak battery when I left
Quartz Creek. On hills, with the little 1,300-cc engine, I've been
accused of having hamsters under the hood. This time, when I checked
the battery I found a rodent all right — a pregnant mouse stuck in a
hole in the frame under the hood. The hole was half an inch in
diameter, but her broad belly was at least an inch across. She'd gotten
her big-eared head, forelegs, and chest through the hole and then
became stuck. I'd found evidence in the auto of her nibbling before,
but what was the attraction of a hole with nothing on the other side?
Whatever her plans were, they'd gang all to hell a-gley.

I thought she was dead. Checking, I found her not only alive but as
agitated as you might be under the circumstances. I tugged her by the
nape as gently as I could, unable to imagine her belly and pelvic girdle
fitting through the perforation in the metal flange. Weakened from
the struggle (all night long?), she squeaked but did not resist. Eventually I got her through with no obvious damage. Her hindquarters
were wet and numb. I placed her, all sleekit and cow'rin', on a stump
with cheese and crackers, and she came around. Soon, fully restored,

the mouse scampered into the woods, and I coasted to a start down the hill.

I thought about this odd but minor incident, which interested me for several reasons, as I cruised the Lewis River road. First, I was struck by how quickly my attitude toward mice could change. I've always loved mice, but at home we trap them because of their fondness for crapping in the stove, the dishes, and the food, for making nests in the kitchen linens, and for nibbling wires. With the spread of the deadly *Hanta* viruses, the reasons are more than aesthetic ones. Yet the same creature I would have trapped at home I here had struggled with great care to release from a trap inadvertently set. How relative are our attitudes toward animals!

Second, this was a deer mouse *(Peromyscus maniculatus)*, the same as our home mice — arguably the most numerous and successful mammal in North America. One way to define something you're not sure about is to define what it is not; in their numbers and range, you could say that deer mice are the opposite of what we imagine Bigfoot to be. Even if this individual was showing no great talent for survival, on the whole her species has fancy-danced so well to natural selection's jig that it is the last candidate for endangerment on anyone's list. Deer mice are also the quintessential generalists, betting their adaptive marbles on reproductivity rather than on specialized gadgets or behavior. Any habitat will do, from hemlocks to houses to Hondas. Not total camp followers like house mice, they do prefer the north-temperate wooded locales; our own habitats are just one option.

Third, I was reminded that deer mice are part of the likely answer to everyone's biggest question about Bigfoot's existence: why don't we ever find a body? In fact we don't often find the bodies of any big animals, because bears, coyotes, and ravens strip and scatter the bones, and deer mice recycle the calcium in the bones in no time. So these little rodents help us quantify the traits of a large, rare specialist; point out the slippery slope of our own animal ethics; and tidy up the landscape of Bigfoot bones and other litter. That fortunate, wee and tim'rous beastie stuck with me.

- - -

I stopped at the North Wood Store at Eagle Cliff to try for distilled water, which they did have. As I paid and went out to refresh my battery, a parade of costumed men alighted from large trucks and came into the store. They were dressed in camouflage jump suits, and their faces were painted black in stripes and blotches. New trucks, big men, my age — Vietnam Rangers holding a reunion, or perhaps survivalist gun nuts? I shut my hood as they filed out of the store bearing candy bars and jerky sticks. "Let's do it," barked the leader, and they pulled out with a roar and much agitation of gravel. An impressive display of macho so early in the morning.

I spoke with Kevin Landacre, the proprietor of the North Wood Store and Eagle Cliff Cabins for the past eight years. Dressed in jeans and a green alligator shirt, Kevin was balding, with a brown fringe of hair and a short beard, and relaxed. Single, he obviously enjoyed talking at length with folks in the store. Some things still had him buffaloed, though, as when a kid rolled up on a bike and said, "Uh, Kevin, somehow the toilet's got overfloating." He told me it was hard to make it with the downturn in logging caused by overcutting on the south side of the Lewis Reservoir, as well as by federal timber withdrawals for spotted owl protection. Even so, he felt that the remaining lowland old growth should be saved — a rare outlook among timberland merchants. It was clear that the forest meant more to Landacre than making a living, as vital as that was.

I asked whether he'd heard any reports of Bigfoot sightings. "Not myself," he said. "But I'm open-minded about it . . . I'd love to see one." He said there had been wolf and wolverine sightings in the area, contrary to the beliefs of local mammalogists, and that a wolverine had been found as a roadkill by the Wind River maintenance crew two or three years before. So, he implied, why should we rule out Bigfoot? I agreed that seeing a wolf or wolverine, long thought to be gone from southern Cascadia, might be even rarer than spotting a mere Sasquatch.

Before I left, Kevin told me that the guys in camouflage were bow-hunters. I had heard that some Bigfoot hunters from Vancouver, Washington, pursued their quarry with large trucks, camo, and big guns. I was relieved to hear that these men were merely out to skewer grouse and deer. Kevin excused himself to give careful directions and suggestions to a woman in a rental car who was eager to see Mount St. Helens but was scared of being in "wilderness." That reminded me I had places to go. "Let's do it," I said to no one in particular and pulled out, with only a weak murmur from my charging battery.

I wanted to see something of the much-remarked Clear Creek corridor, the longest uncut stand of Douglas-fir in southwest Washington. I headed up Clear Creek as far as the road went, then turned onto Spencer Meadows Road and on up into the mist. The day was cloudy, cool, and damp. Scraps of old growth dripped with sodden traceries of short, wispy lichens, like moldy green tinsel. The paved one-lane road had not been built for people to view the Pacific yews, gleaming red in the rain; it was the result of years of fat Forest Service road-building budgets. As I climbed through a patchwork of clear-cuts, I viewed the raison d'être. Unlike the Willapa Hills, my home ground, here the clear-cuts were relatively small and not all contiguous. This showed the attempted restraint of the Forest Service compared to the private companies who hold total sway in my back yard. Some snags had been left, and some of the cutting was selective. This was not forestry at its worst, but I doubted it was the worst I would see.

The only car I'd seen for miles was parked at the Spencer Butte trailhead. An oldie, its bumper stickers read TEST PEACE — NOT NUCLEAR WEAPONS and THIS IS NOT AN ABANDONED CAR. It did not belong to the archers. Having heard of parked cars bashed for their owners' views as expressed on bumper stickers, I had never adorned mine. When the road rose at last into lodgepole pines, a golden-mantled ground squirrel expressed loud opinions that probably weren't far from my own.

Lichen-swaddled noble firs stood by the Cussed Hollow Trail. Clear-cuts followed, and young plantations of noble fir. Light rain fell from a cold gray sky whose dull light slowly strobed as I passed from mountain hemlock and noble fir to clear-cut and back again. At Spencer Meadows the pavement ended. I struck left toward the headwaters of Clear Creek. Now came the steep-slope clear-cuts, bleeding with erosion. This was just about as bad as Willapa, the difference being that trees had been left standing between the scars. The sense of fragmentation became acute, with vistas of ancient-forested mountainsides on the west side of Clear Creek facing slashed and burned foreground on the east. The road ended in the devastation of a partly burned clear-cut with intact forests on all sides.

I parked the car near the headwaters of Clear Creek, below Shark Rock, in the western reaches of the Dark Divide. The rush of water behind me, the soft drip from the trees, ravens gronking far off — these were the only sounds I heard. Driving up, I'd been listening to a tape of natural sounds from the temperate rain forest sent by my friend Gordon Hempton. Known as the Sound Tracker, the Emmy-winning Hempton has rambled the world in search of settings devoid of noise pollution where he could record the native sounds. At just this moment — no saws, no safety horns from a logging job, no engines or airplanes or voices — I felt I was in the middle of Hempy's tape. I recognized the rarity of the moment and enjoyed it for all it was worth.

A strange kind of amphibian, the tailed frog, occupies high, cold streams in the Pacific Northwest — except where the land has been so denuded that the streams silt up and rise in temperature. The tadpoles have suckerlike mouths for holding on to rocks, and the adult male has a cloacal tail to facilitate mating in fast currents. The tailed frog's nearest relatives, the leiopelmids, live in New Zealand — a much greater biogeographical leap than that represented by a great ape in the New World.

I'd never found the tailed frog and decided to investigate this high tributary of Clear Creek. Into the afternoon I searched the steep little stream, climbing among the stones and chill cascades. Large trees had been felled across the creek from one side, blown down from the inadequate buffer strip on the other. For the cut to follow the creek, more or less, seemed unusual. Nowadays large woody debris is sometimes left in the water for riparian structure to benefit salmon, but this was just the random result of the cut line.

I found no tailed frogs, though I had an unusually good look. Crossing a log, I fell face first into a pool from a little height when the rotting wood gave way. I continued my search for a while, probing the habitat on the frog's own level. But soaked and pretty cold, I had to get out and dry off. I went back to the car, stripped, toweled, and was about to don dry clothes and leave when a different impulse took over. The rain had stopped, and the air temperature was in the fifties, comfortable enough for a denizen of the coastal rain forest such as I.

Nude, I walked a little way and climbed a stump. In the dropping light and leaden cool, I regarded the woods around me in a complete circle, peering into mists in the crowns of firs and into the deepest recesses of the forest. I wondered if my naked, furless, puny body was being watched and remarked with wonder. And that's when I remembered Monty West.

West was a professor of anthropology at the University of Washington when I was a student there in the late sixties and early seventies. While many of the faculty reeled before the rising counterculture, Monty West embraced, even defined it. If his colleagues were intimidated, confused, or repelled by the coming wave, Monty West rode its crest. But he was no poseur. Naturally antiestablishment, Monty West did not have to affect hipness; his time had simply come.

Curious about this respected academician, who shared many of the values I assumed my generation possessed, I enrolled in a course of his on world folklore, imagining a pleasant romp among trolls and tales. But I quickly dropped it: I'd never encountered a reading list as intimidating or a syllabus as rigorous as his. So I never really got to know West, but I tuned in to the folklore surrounding him. Recently I tried to track him down, but he was nowhere to be found. Historian and photographer Paul Dorpat, a contemporary of mine at the University of Washington, lived near West in the Seattle neighborhood of Wallingford for years and used to see him frequently. Once Monty showed Dorpat a cave he had dug beneath a cherry tree in his back yard.

"I took a magnificent picture of him," Dorpat told me. "Wild, flying hair, still lean and athletic." Monty said he was going to live in the hole or else head up to Whidbey or San Juan Island, where he had "a place to go." A little later Dorpat saw him, for the last time, riding a bicycle, his famous Land Rover long gone (West said its mileage was always in proportion to the price of gas).

The story that came to mind on my solitary stump was his most famous adventure: Monty West's month-long sojourn in the wild Gifford Pinchot — in the nude. Sometime in the autumn of 1970, the story goes, West was dropped off at the edge of the wilderness. His plan was to enter the wilds entirely unequipped — no matches, sleeping bag, food, clothing, or other gear — and to live that way for a month. The point was to experience a state of mind like that of an aboriginal human being, defenseless against the wilderness. With no particular skills of woodcraft, he wanted to see whether he could survive, stay reasonably warm and nourished, and come back to tell about it. His particular desire, as an anthropologist, was to feel what primitive people everywhere must have felt as they confronted the world on its own terms.

The version I heard first, from one of West's acolytes, had him curling at night around a tiny fire made by friction. That part is not too different from what John Muir did in the Sierra, though he wore clothes. West supposedly ate wild foods, lost weight (he was already a beanpole), and survived. Eventually he came out — wild, hairy, and naked — to a forest road, where he waved down the first car he saw.

By this account the driver stopped, picked him up, took him to a rendezvous, and never mentioned his unclad state.

Now, as I stood shivering on the stump, I thought of Monty, skinny and cold and hungry and scratched up, trying to cover ground barefoot while keeping his energy up and his fear down. When I fell into that frigid creek, I was wearing boots and was close to warmth, dryness, shelter, and food. Even if I had been injured, I probably could have made it out; my car would have tipped off a logger, hunter, or hiker before too long. We have to work pretty hard to put ourselves in real jeopardy out in the roaded forest, free climbers and gonzo archers excepted. But unless I caught an arrow in the ass from some wannabe Robin Hood who mistook it for an elk's rump, I was at little risk. I could fall in the creek with impunity and come out laughing.

Now imagine the same scene with me nude (you can skip the details) and unshod, with no towel, heater, woollies, or food cache around the corner. Night coming, temperature dropping, in tangled and sharp-edged country. Maybe a broken bone or a bad sprain. I had a lot more insulation and stored calories than West, and those advantages might have gotten me through a few days. But humans under stress and out in the cold are notoriously susceptible to hypothermia. Essentially, if I'd been in West's situation and had fallen into a mountain stream at dusk in the autumn at high elevation, I might have been done for.

That modest adventure gave me pause. For just a moment I sensed the fragility of the body against the hard, hard land. And I realized that if Monty West did go into the woods and return, he was a lucky man. Most of us would not be very good at such an undertaking. If we didn't starve, freeze, or freak out, we would probably succumb to blood poisoning, tetanus, or sheer fear. If we didn't give up and come out within a few days, we probably wouldn't come out at all. Long, long ago we lost our adaptability. As the naked ape, we sold our ability to live unfettered in order to buy civilization. Hence the age-old fear of (and repugnance for) the wilderness. People who still know how to live well there don't hate the wilderness, but there are few such people left.

Those we used to call primitives, or aboriginals, knew how to derive sustenance, shelter, and security from their surrounds. It was no rare skill — everyone had it or died. But it was a great skill, and when it passed, something of eternal value was lost. Now when we go into the wilderness, as I did from time to time in the Dark Divide, we go armored in rip-stop nylon and Gore-Tex, shod with Vibram soles that shield our tender feet from the very earth. We go with matches, freeze-dried food, gas stoves, water purifiers, and all manner of comforts. We follow well-traveled trails, which we reach in motor vehicles. Some even take to the trails with motors, shattering any last pretense of wilderness encounter for themselves and everyone within earshot.

And then there is Bigfoot, if there is Bigfoot. Like the American Indians or any other native people, it travels well among the rocks and trees with no thought of escape or salvation: what it knows is the world as it is. Even native people take skins from other creatures to protect themselves from cold and abrasion, make fires to cook with, and build shelters from the elements. Sasquatch does none of these things. Maybe that is one reason Indians regard Sasquatch with fear and suspicion as wild men even more self-reliant than themselves.

A little way down the road I had noticed substantial rock-cleft caves in the stony slopes above the clear-cut. Perhaps Bigfoot makes use of natural shelters such as these. Many stories tell of finding moss-and-lichen beds fashioned like those made by great apes. Only one or two reports mention deerskin capes or other adornment. Essentially, if we have a beast here at all, we have one whose needs are met entirely by its wits and its muscle in concert with its habitat.

If Bigfoot falls into a stream, it's no big deal. If it breaks a leg, maybe it lives, maybe it doesn't — several of the best-known tracks show signs of a healed injury. Do parasites and disease enter the life of Bukwus? Does Dzonoqua get hungry when wild foods are scarce? If this is a mortal animal, these conditions must apply. And yet here is an ape that reportedly covers ground (even nearly vertical ground) at a rapid rate, that negotiates all kinds of rugged countryside, that shirks no sort of weather. Only one set of conditions seems to deter Bigfoot from living vigorously and well in the wild, the same ones that took away our ability to do so: human civilization.

It would be a hollow indictment that failed to recognize the astonishing adaptations represented by that same civilization. The most churlish Luddite could not help but marvel at the densely acronymic toy shop that defines our comfort, ease, and entertainment: TV, VCR, PC, ROM, MTV, CNN, V8, 747, VRT, et cetera. Technology has lifted our Western lives so far from the nettles and the mire that we cannot imagine going back. To the extent that these tools enhance life and reduce mortality, they could be called adaptive.

Yet another set of initials expresses the downside of modern life:

IRS, FBI, CIA, HIV, AA, CFS, PCB, PMS, STD, PC, ICBM, et cetera. Of course, not all of these baleful conditions have arisen directly from technology. Our numbers, our mobility, and the stresses peculiar to our age certainly exacerbate their effects. I don't know if anyone would give up the first set of initials to get rid of the second. It's too late, anyway: as a species, we are fully wedded to our electronic assistance. There is no going back to the woods — unless under population pressure or disease and strife or environmental change, our systems collapse under us, thrusting us into the primitive condition once again. If that were to occur, I wouldn't give a lot for most folks' chances, minus their microwaves.

The high concepts now are "interactive media" and "virtual experience." I, like others, look upon such amazing ideas with awe. What can be bad about instant communication around the globe, easy access to all the information in the world, and helmets that take the place of Yosemite or Yokohama?

Still I wonder. Take the chips away, and what have you got? When function depends upon form, and form is far removed from common experience, function ceases to be common — and surely shared experience is one field mark of civilization. It's hard to say how many people will ever participate in the upper strata of technology. But one thing is sure: as the number grows, so does our separation from the physical world. CD-ROMs may be interactive, but what they interact with is not the land; in virtual reality, virtual means exactly that — it ain't real. We see only what we need to see. When our needs are completely met by pixels on a screen, we will cease to be interactive with the world. When virtual reality does the job, who needs the real thing? And who will know what to do when the real thing appears?

Desmond Morris notwithstanding, we are not the naked ape. We're seldom naked, and when we are, we are even more defenseless than usual. Bigfoot is the naked ape — clothed with hair but naked the way Monty West was naked: equipped with nothing but his own resources in the face of nature. I don't know how Monty's experiment came out. He seems to have dropped out of sight in recent years. Whether he achieved the state of mind of an aborigine is a matter of sheer conjecture. Even if he experienced the early human's terror before the universe, I doubt that he felt the sense of mastery and confidence that must mark the competent native everywhere. But he interacted as few of us ever will; there was nothing virtual about his adventure.

Naked on my stump, I felt the flimsiness of our security in contrast to any wild animal's perfect fitness to its situation. And I understood a truth that had been tracking me ever since I'd set foot in the Dark Divide — that Bigfoot is the better beast. When Bigfoot enthusiasts gather, they debate whether the subject of their attention is a "primitive" hominid or not. In fact, insofar as it is powerfully fit for life in the world in a way that few humans today can even imagine, I would say that Sasquatch represents the advanced condition, that of the superior ape.

- - -

The black remains of burned logs lined the way as I drove away from Clear Creek through a cut called Backside. The timber sales, also called payment units — a frank phrase for what a forest comes down to in the end — are all named. The names exercise the imaginations, and sometimes the irony, of the Gifford Pinchot planners. I remember one called Glabella, the species name of the yellow violet that was probably common there prior to the cut. "Backside" seemed appropriate, for I felt I was indeed traveling the backside of the world as I descended into a mist like mountain-goat fur. A moss cushion as thick as a good comforter, incredibly soft and plush to the touch, lined a rivulet by the road. I felt I could fall into it and never come out.

Down at Craggy Trail I passed a stolid bunch of archers in semipermanent plastic camps, sitting around rotting in the rain. Careful — your greasepaint will run! It's a sure thing they wouldn't last long naked, bows or no. They paid me no heed. I rolled across a montage of different-aged cuts to where the pavement began. The light faded into a foggy, pearly dusk. At a place where erosion below the road had torn out the underpinnings of a clear-cut, some sort of yellow foam had been sprayed to hold the slope. Nothing grew there. Beargrass and bracken poked russet among the blue nobles on gentler slopes, where the soil had stayed. Logging leaves a litter-storm of tapes, tags, ribbons, and paint stripes across the countryside. But the soft scarlets of vine maples, huckleberries, and the eye of a towhee outshone all the harsh reds of the ribbons.

Dropping through the fog above Quartz Creek, I came once again to the place of the mouse. Assuming she had indeed recovered fully, I doubted that she'd traveled fifty yards that day. I'd gone well over fifty miles, yet I wondered which of us had learned more. I hoped that the mouse had learned to keep her twitchy nose out of small holes, though I knew she'd probably do it all over again. As for me, I'd learned (as Whitman said in "Song of Myself") that "a mouse is miracle enough." And I'd learned that I probably shouldn't go naked into the forest.

When Monty West did just that, I wonder what he learned. An amateur among pros, a skinny, naked ape afoot in the territory of bigger hippies even hairier than he and better suited to life on the land unadorned — what miracles were vouchsafed to him?

We're not likely to find out, since he has disappeared into the wilds of Wallingford or the San Juan Islands or somewhere. But I feel certain that one night, curled up against the cold in a moss-and-beargrass nest of his own making, his hunger dulled with berries and mushrooms and miners' lettuce and cold water, as alone as he could ever be, Monty West discovered one pure thing: what it is to be both human and animal at once. He might be one of the very few among us to know such a thing, for we have long tried to forget how to be animals. Out where Bigfoot walks, it is the only knowledge that counts.

8

Legends of the Dark Divide

I'm still frightened of that dark divide
will I gain entrance or be denied?
— Patti Scialfa, "Spanish Dancer"

THE DARK DIVIDE is not the first range I have prospected for its stories. I've written of the Willapa Hills in the southern part of Washington's Coast Range, where I live. A lumpy muddle of ridges and ravines, the Willapas plug a virtual ring of rivers above the lower Columbia. I could have plumbed these hills in search of a sense of Sasquatch. After all, why not work close to home?

I had thought of doing this, but the arguments against it prevailed. First, there's not much Bigfoot history here: a deputy with a footprint cast at Gray's Harbor, a logger/fisherman with a sighting up North River, a few tales from early Indian days near Cathlamet, a vague incident at Vader — but nothing like the rich lode of lore north of the Chehalis River in the Olympics, or east of the Cowlitz in the Cascades. It's as if the tall tales went out early with the tall trees.

Second, the Willapas have lost their wildness, at least in the sense of what had been there. If rain-forest apes lived anywhere in the Northwest, I cannot imagine that they didn't live in these once dense, deeply forested hills. But now, with thousands of acres of doghair regrowth, it's as hard to imagine Bigfoot here as in a Seattle mall. Well, not quite; a modest number of smart creatures could still hide out in these shaggy damps; I have, after all, seen a puma slinking through the algal green of the alders. But the Willapas are too diminished to easily support even my most willing suspension of disbelief and the desire to track the beast in the wilds of my own mind.

Third, I'd already "done" my home ground. Not enough, certainly not completely, and someday I shall revisit Willapa in writing. But for

Bigfoot, I wanted to explore country I did not already know. I'm surprised every time I step outdoors, but if you want to be surprised every moment you're awake, you head to fresh territory with your eyes open. I wasn't in a position to practice Powell's Law (Jerry Powell, a Berkeley lepidopterist, contends that "no systematic entomologist voluntarily works on insects that occur within 1,000 miles of his home laboratory"), but I did intend to take this investigation well away from my doorstep. And since the Himalaya, the Tien Shan, and the Amur were all out, the southern Cascades of Washington seemed a good bet.

Besides its rich tradition of Bigfoot reports, its essential wildness, and its novelty for me, the Dark Divide has another quality that never hurts when your subject is a mysterious one: mystique. This it gets from reputation (word of mouth, mostly); its isolation (too many forest roads penetrate it, but they are relatively little traveled); its appearance (black, toothy knobs running crosswise to the main range of white-capped volcanoes); its deep forests (Clear Creek and Quartz Creek sustain the longest and broadest Douglas-fir old-growth corridors outside the national parks) contrasting with open slopes above, the result not of altitude as much as of historic forest fires; and its very name.

- - -

It was a rainy night in the middle of September, somewhere beneath Dark Mountain. Instead of bedding again at a damp campsite, I took a long drive in rain and fog. My route — Forest Roads 90 and 23N — took me over Babyshoe Pass at 4,350 feet. Here the Dark Divide drops off the shoulder of Mount Adams, near the headwaters of the Lewis River. Through fog as tight as the Robert Johnson blues on the tape player, I traveled past Takhlakh Lake and Takhtakh Meadow, along the western border of the Yakama Indian Nation. Middling firs, tightly lichen-draped, crowded the narrow road — picturesque or spooky depending on your state of mind. Blue fingers of noble firs reached out to play the washboard road.

I crossed Potato Hill, a kind of Rubicon, past Trail No. 2000 (the Pacific Crest Trail), where horses slept in trailers. This is the border of the reservation — non-Indians can't go in without a permit. I remembered a conversation with a Yakama woman about her youth, when Bigfoot figured in every berry-picking expedition to Potato Hill, a handy bogeyman to keep bored children from wandering too far.

All the books tell stories of Sasquatch sightings along back roads at night. My ramble over Potato Hill produced one mouse. Later two little deer materialized near Orr Creek. I stopped to mark some territory I was unlikely to revisit soon, along Forest Road 56. The night was so silent, only a stream's breathing, so softly fragrant, so dark. The fog had lifted into a dove dome that broke up to show three stars to the south. Towering trees, tent poles of the night. Where Forest Roads 23 and 21 met, I found myself just east of Juniper Peak, along the Cispus River — only two miles from my campsite on the ridge of the ghost moths. A white alder wood leaned in toward the road, pulled back again where the Dark Meadows Trail took off beside three gargantuan firs.

Fighting drowsiness after many miles of dusty road, I listened to a radio drama called "The Brain." Nothing like an audio monster movie to send the night sinister, but it didn't. I felt only the calm of the wild dark and a growing desire to close my eyes. A bit after midnight I turned on to tiny Forest Road 2325 and followed it to the end, just a mile of ruts and rocks. I camped on the border between a clear-cut and big trees. Not far away the voice of Dark Creek talked me to sleep in no time.

- - -

I have to admit that I was attracted to the Dark Divide at least as much by its name as by its other qualities. "Dark Divide" — an evocative label naming two traits bottomless in implication, endless in association.

The "divide" part of the name is no mystery. This ridge serves as the watershed between the Cispus and Lewis river drainages. As for the "dark" part, I'd assumed the name derived from the black basalt of the region's most prominent landforms — Hat, Shark, and Kirk rocks, Dark and Snagtooth mountains, Craggy and Badger peaks — or perhaps from some tenebrous history I did not know. But it turns out that Dark is a patronymic, as I learned from Keith McCoy's book *The Mount Adams Country: Forgotten Corner of the Columbia River Gorge.* (McCoy is an insurance man, local historian, and third-generation resident of the Columbia Gorge country south of the Dark Divide.)

I'd noticed that one of the mountains west of Juniper Ridge was McCoy Peak. It was named for Keith's grandfather and uncle, Will and John McCoy, who arrived in 1882, working on the Oregon Rail and Navigation Line as it punched its way out the Columbia River slot toward the sea. Both left their jobs as engineers to plant orchards and build mills in the White Salmon Valley, but in the winter they mined gold up north in the black rock heights then called the Niggerheads. They had a mining partner by the name of John Dark, and it was he whose name stuck to Dark Mountain, Dark Meadow, Dark Creek, and eventually, the Dark Divide. In time the term became a descriptive and acceptable alternative for the old name, now rightfully considered racist.

Even as Dark and his partners were panning gold, the area that would be sprinkled with their names became a part of the Mount Rainier Forest Reserve — "created," as McCoy wrote, "by a far-off Congress in 1897 for future division into national forests of manageable size." Had the entirety of that set-aside become a real reserve, broken wilderness would not be a question here. There would also be few towns and little population for many miles around. Instead, large areas were given to the railroads, thus entering the private estate (mostly flowing later to the large timber companies), while the remaining public land was indeed divided. In 1908 President Theodore Roosevelt carved out the Columbia National Forest, and in 1949 Congress changed it to the Gifford Pinchot National Forest — establishing the long-term landlord of the denizens of the Dark Divide.

For a far longer term, perhaps 20,000 years, the Klickitat and Yakama Indians roamed these punctuated lands. The poles of their universe were the Cascade volcanoes — Tahoma (Rainier) to the north, Pahto (Adams) on the east, Wyeast (Hood) to the south, Loo Wit (St. Helens) in the west. The mountains themselves became personalities in their pantheon; Loo Wit and Wyeast were said to have been frustrated lovers whose forbidden tryst caused the collapse of the fabled natural arch known as Bridge of the Gods, where a steel span now crosses the Columbia. Particular bands made strongholds near each of the peaks.

The Indians traded among themselves — salmon from the river, obsidian from the Oregon deserts, shell from the coast, mountain-goat horn from the Goat Rocks, east of Tahoma. The crosspiece of the Dark Divide made both a highway between the Pahto country and the lands in the shadow of Loo Wit and beyond and a barrier between Tahoma and the big river. This natural pathway became indented long before the Forest Service designated it Boundary Trail No. 1 — boundary because it is a border between the ancestral Columbia and Mount Rainier national forests, No. 1 for the primacy of the route. On the western flanks of Mount Adams, Council Bluff furnished a gathering point for local bands and all who passed through. A settlement at Council Lake, at the bluff's base, was long ago abandoned, some Klickitats say, because of numerous Bigfeet near there.

As the local culture and lands shifted from Indian to white, Asian, and Hispanic, and sometimes back again when tribal lawsuits succeeded in enlarging reservations (such as the Yakamas' on Mount Adams), people of all colors were drawn to the valleys beneath the peaks. Villages sprang up along the Toutle below St. Helens, the Cowlitz under Rainier, the White Salmon down from Adams. Farms replaced camas-lands, muzzleloaders took the deer and elk instead of arrows. But through it all, the black-capped highlands between the peaks remained remote. Except for a few prospectors like Dark and the McCoys, the odd trapper and hunter, and early graziers following sheep and errant cattle, next to no one penetrated the Dark Divide.

Then a succession of land routes — two sets of rails, a scenic highway of mossy masonry, finally an interstate freeway — made their ways up and down the Columbia Gorge. Dams pooled the river and blocked the salmon, even as they let barges pass for the first time to the Snake River and beyond, and the great trees fed mills as they became something more than obstacles to farming. Hood River, Washougal, White Salmon, and The Dalles; Stevenson, Underwood, and Carson; Morton, Randle, and Packwood; Woodland, Cougar, Toledo, and many other settlements grew into more or less permanent towns along the lower flanks of the southern range. Several new types of anthropoid apes began to roam the old Indian trade route and the high valleys springing from it: the logger, the miner, the grazier, the homesteader, the hiker. And then a great power, the United States Forest Service, dedicated but confused, began to divvy up the Dark Divide among them.

Camping on a line between the land as it was and as it had become, I dreamed strange sagas of knives, trees tumbling among shaggy black rocks, and a land with a brain of its own.

- - -

I awoke to see Dark Mountain above me. Jumbo Peak bulked up to its right, and in between lay a lump with no name. I christened it Dumbo Peak, for the obvious reason and because anyone would have to be a Dumbo to be up there without water (as I nearly had been on my Juniper Ridge hike) and because to get up there it would be nice to have that esteemed pachyderm's ears. Mountain chickadees and dark-eyed juncos chipped open the day at my breakfast of banana pancakes, and a raven scouted over, flapping audibly. Two young grouse hunters from Amboy, a village on the far side of St. Helens, came by in a truck. One had a plug of chew in his mouth and wore a Woodland Logging Supply cap; the other wore a red hunter's cap. They'd seen one grouse, had a shot, missed. Chaw said you could get up the side of this unit to the Dark Meadow Trail — "It's nice up there." That's what I planned to do. I heard bikers' motors and hoped I wouldn't encounter them.

Dark Mountain projected a prominent visage: not too dark, scabbed with patches of yellow huckleberry and green willow, subalpine firs candling up here and there above the forest hem. Jet lumps of ragged rock cankered both shoulders beneath the gentle top, like dangerous moles. Well, that was one way of looking at it. In the morning's cool, clean light, I was more inclined to take the mountain as a mountain, minus the metaphors. Malice, after all, springs from our own kind alone. I had found it just possible to project a sense of the sinister onto the Dark Peak of the Pennine Mountains during a dangerous, boggy crossing of a waterlogged moor one sodden English March. But this Dark Mountain, actually rather bright in the September over-cast, seemed anything but malevolent.

I set off up a Cat-track on the south side of the clear-cut unit with gray jays following. They love these edges. Against my principles, I tossed a couple of crackers to see if the jays would take them, but the pearly corvids ignored my offering. How refreshing to find a flock of camp robbers unused to the camp. Perhaps it was just native curiosity that put them on my trail. A winter wren followed my "cherks" onto and around a slash pile. No bird carries a bigger voice or heart in a smaller package of feather and flesh. Talk about sophisticated micro-components: the tiniest chip will never match a winter wren's com-plexity or virtuosity. It was curious too, or maybe attracted to my T-shirt's logo of the Winter Wren Society, an unorganized band of Northwest nature nuts.

The turf at the edge of the cut was alive with the bright red berry clusters of the prostrate dogwoods known as bunchberries, along with tiny hemlocks, queen cup lilies, mosses, and huckleberries. Few of these will last without shade, as the sun becomes too drying, or with too much shade, as the young conifers come in thick. But for a time such edges can be prolific. The "edge effect" says that habitat edges are supposed to be rich in species. Citing this, logging apologists say we should furnish many more miles of edges through the regenera-tive process of clear-cutting. What they don't say is that overedging an ancient forest robs it of the ability to sustain populations of specialist species, which are far less likely to prosper on the borders than adventitious, generalist (and therefore quite common) animals and plants. So if you want a forest of jays, juncos, weedy grasses, and short-lived bunchberry, maximize the blunt borders of cuts. Soon you get to the point where it's all edge, as in the Willapa Hills. By then the dwellers of the deepwood are long gone — the spotted owls, the flying squirrels, the martens and fishers and swifts, the trilliums and mistletoe hairstreak butterflies — gone with the trees that sheltered them from the fecund generality of the edge.

The day was sunning up. I shed my wool sweater and headed up southwesterly through splendid wet old growth, mostly four-foot-thick western hemlocks and Douglas-firs five feet across. The understory was hemlock too, along with oval-leaved huckleberry, whose sparse blue fruits I ate. Big brown inchworm moths called *Triphosa* flitted through the shadows. Their larvae consume vine maple, whose green arches vaulted old clearings nearby. Slugs and squirrels had nipped the fleshy caps of mushrooms of many species. Elk had passed this way within twenty-four hours, their pellets still fresh.

Higher up the slope I entered noble firs, short-leaved and stiff, and white pines, with their languorous, damp brushes of long white-striped needles. A four-foot pine was a beautiful blue thing among the blue nobles and blueberries and blue lupines. Coming out of the forest I had the sharp impression of having indigo filters over my steamy glasses.

After two hours of climbing, I hit the flat ridge just below Dumbo Mountain. Beargrass, basket material supreme for the ones who went before, bound up the red, green, and blue huckleberries on the small-grained pumice of the plateau. Above, bikers raged, sounding like a motocross, then faded into the dominant silence. When I found what I took for the Dark Meadow Trail, No. 263, I saw fresh motorcycle tracks. My bearing at the point of intersection was 260° Dark, 340° Dumbo. There was a water bar with a log on its left, a short stump on its right. These details could be important if I wanted to find my car again that week.

After a while I hit good old Juniper Ridge Trail No. 261, by which I would have come here had I persisted in my original plan. It swung me around the hefty flanks of Jumbo. Up here it was cool, cloudy, autumnal, silent but for an exercised Douglas squirrel, an equally agitated chipmunk, a few birds tinkling or screeing, a quiet burble of water . . . So! I *could* have obtained water here when I was hiking — if I'd made it this far. Only one dark little brook was not dry, and this trickle was buried deep in brush, hard to reach. Mercifully, the cycles I'd heard were gone, headed down Boundary Trail No. 1. I reckoned the squirrel and chipmunk were registering their opinions of the recent invasion, though maybe it was me they were yammering at.

Dark Meadow consisted of grassy strawberry clearings littered with old logs and stumps from a great burn and studded with clumps of huckleberry, willow, and mountain ash. The openings were small, more willow flats than great meadowlands. Red vegetation climbed the nearby lap of Dark Mountain, facing east-northeast. The mountain's jagged basalt horns protruded above a soft-looking pelage of huckleberry underfur with patchy guard hairs of alder, ash, willow, and occasional fir. To the west it was lighter, rockier, almost arctic-alpine in aspect. Dumbo lay to the north beyond the pass, like a supine mammoth tufted with fir fur. Then came Jumbo, clothed with a heathy pelt rolling up to the jutting dome that from the north I'd seen as a great black molar — here it was more of a mastodon's hump.

Cedar waxwings probed the mountain ash berries, their thin "sweet, sweet" giving them away. One of the tufted birds, with cinnamon chest and cherry-studded wings, crowned a noble fir scepter — taking it for a cedar? Sprinkled along the rutted trail I saw evidence: bittersweet-colored berry skins. These pert birds ate just the seed and pulp. Eating was on my mind, too, as I watched the waxwings and criss-crossed Dark Meadow. I tried a mountain ash berry and found it tart and juicy, a little like rose hips, to which it is related. I chewed the tough seeds and decided ash berries might make a nice chaser to the surfeit of sweet huckleberries.

Behind my grandmother's house in Denver grew two stately mountain ashes, her favorites. When the thick clusters of berries came ripe, more orange, less red than these, my brother Tom and I would pluck bunches, take shelter, and pelt one another with the hard fruit. The riper ones made realistic red splotches on the target's skin. When one tree became diseased, Gram had a tree service come to remove it — but they took the healthy one instead. No more berry wars. A pallid, nonfruiting double cherry, useless to birds and to us, took the place of those treasured trees. I had never investigated the utility of rowan berries for anything but pellets. Now, nibbling, and seeing the bushels of berries of this and several other types all around, I was struck again by how much there was for an enterprising primate to eat.

I spotted a parsley fern at the base of a massive hemlock, its golden-fruited fertile fronds erect. Sedges and marsh marigolds greened the marge of a little pond, shallow and silty. A savannah sparrow, adaptee to this fire-sponsored savanna, called and showed in the willows. Where I turned back, before Trail No. 1 crossed Dark's lap and headed up over the saddle to the west, a field of corn lilies lay fading. Their seed-pods split out like many-legged beetles crawling down the stems, ready to green next year's meadow. Rattly in the afternoon breeze, brown and withered like tobacco leaves curing, they gave a deeply autumnal feeling to the place and time. Beside a dry ephemeral pond, a few blooms of Douglas spiraea — that most ethereal of flowers, with hazy pink puffs and ineffably sweet scent — stayed summer a bit. And down in the azalea scrub, one last white blossom survived among all the seed heads. Its scent was sweet too, pearlike and very faint, with a hint of gardenia. But the season was spent in Dark Meadow; the late afternoon chill said so. How the winter winds would howl up from Snagtooth and down from Dark I didn't want to know.

I picked a bunch of dwarf huckleberries, a species new to me, reminiscent of the wild blueberries of Maine. It was past time to head down. I found the point where I'd come up from the forest, more or less — though everything looked different going the other way, and the compass came in handy. I struck a route a little to the south so as to see new things, like the first Alaska yellow cedar of my journey. This is the tree whose wood has held so many carved and painted impressions of Bukwus and Dzonoqua on the totems and masks of the north, but these droopy specimens were barely big enough to make a rattle.

Coming down was much faster as I swung apelike through the old growth. I left it in the deep hope that it would not become a unit. I reached Powdermilk, opened an ale, and drank to the Dark Divide and its constituents: mountains, meadows, plants, animals, pikas, Big-feet . . . whatever. Everything but dirt bikes and chain saws. A varied thrush strummed in the distance. Jumbo was mist-swirled, Dark cloud-dulled, and a pale pink light glowed over Dumbo. The evening came on cool, but the sky blued into the dusk. There was nothing very dark about this wilderness.

- - -

Only it wasn't a wilderness. Not, at least, in the sense recognized by the U.S. Forest Service. The Dark Divide is the largest unprotected roadless area in Washington, hotly contested between those who would keep it that way and those who would road, log, and tame it. One view favors "productive" (that is, extractive) use of the public estate by providing for the well-being of nearby mills and the towns they support; the other outlook wants to keep substantial areas inviolate for the experience and stored wealth of wilderness and for the well-being of the society as a whole. The mill-town folks favor recreation, usually with motors. The city conservationists, with their livings elsewhere, want trails for their horses and themselves (and increasingly, for their mountain bikes). In a short time, in Klickitat terms, the Dark Divide has gone from an unknown smudge on a foggy skyline to a cause célèbre for wildly differing publics.

Both the original Wilderness Act of 1964 and the notorious 1979 USFS Roadless Area Evaluation known as RARE II somehow allowed the Dark Divide to fall through their filters. Wilderness advocates responded with their own proposal, hoping to have the divide included in a future Washington wilderness bill. But when such a bill passed in 1984, the idea of having three new wilderness areas in the southern Cascades — the Dark Divide, Trapper Creek, and Indian Heaven — was one too much for the congressional delegation to swallow.

Senator "Scoop" Jackson personally nixed the Dark Divide the first time around, and Senator Slade Gorton assumed the same position later. I remember gently lobbying his colleague, ex-governor and then-senator Dan Evans, about wilderness in southern Washington at a Nature Conservancy Christmas party. A long-time hiker and some-time environmental advocate, Evans was interested but skeptical about the chances that all three areas would be accepted. In the end Indian Heaven (with little merchantable timber and strong support from hikers and horsemen) and modest-sized Trapper Creek made it in, while Gorton prevailed and the Dark Divide was dumped again, despite the best efforts of the citizens' Gifford Pinchot Task Force.

More roads soon followed, fragmenting the area almost beyond hope for future designation as wilderness, which many believe was the federal intent. By 1990, when the Gifford Pinchot Forest Plan came out (a cumbrous document of which one reviewer said, "I speak seven languages, and this is not one of them"), the roadless area stood at 51,500 acres, down from 56,560 in 1963 and 55,000 in 1985. The plan's preferred alternative called for reducing this to 36,060 acres during the next decade.

The Washington Trails Association, seeking to protect at least the heart of the high country and its lowland approaches from roads and off-road vehicles (ORVs), proposed a "national hiking area." This would have sustained the essentially roadless core of the remains, with trails designated for hikers and horses, motors excluded, and protection from logging. The Forest Service responded, as I had discovered on Juniper Ridge, by keeping virtually all trails open to motorcycles.

Later the Randle District applied for funds from the Interagency Committee for Outdoor Recreation (IAC) to upgrade the Juniper-Langille Ridge loop to meet motorcycle standards. The application was rejected, and the Gifford Pinchot chastised for submitting such a controversial project. But when the forest supervisor and regional forester backed up District Ranger Harry Cody, the IAC changed its tune. A lawsuit seemed imminent when a coalition of conservation groups weighed in with a bold proposal: would the motorized recreationists relinquish use of trails in the Dark Divide Roadless Area in exchange for a much longer loop trail to be built around and outside the roadless area? In early 1995 a formal proposal was tendered the Northwest Motorcycle Association by the Washington Trails Association, the Gifford Pinchot Task Force, and eleven other organizations. The cyclists would gain a 132-mile ORV loop trail and forgo the use of eighty miles of trails, including Juniper and Langille ridges and Boundary Trail No. 1.

WTA vice president and volunteer lawyer Karl Forsgaard engineered the deal along with noted landscape photographer Ira Spring and many others from both user groups. If the initiative is accepted and the Forest Service and IAC both go along, a historic compromise will have been reached in an age when bitter confrontation rules most land-use disputes.

If cooperation won the day on the trails issue, dialogue failed in the matter of timber extraction. Only the courts brought logging to a temporary halt, giving the Dark Divide some breathing space. Gifford Pinchot managers were doing their best to "get the cut out," as Congress demanded. They planned to get a lot more out, much of it in the McCoy Planning Unit of the northern Dark Divide. Then Judge William Dwyer shut down the woods on behalf of the northern spotted owl and its old-growth community in 1992, finding the Forest Service not in compliance with the National Environmental Policy Act. The trucks slowed and mills went still as the Northwest awaited President Clinton's forest plan and Judge Dwyer's response. By the time Dwyer lifted his injunction on new timber sales at the end of

1994, complex new operating procedures were in place, involving such landscape categories as Late Successional Reserve, Adaptive Management Areas, Matrix (multiple use), and watershed planning units. Logging, which never really stopped altogether, will intensify, but unless the Republican Congress throws out Clinton's Northwest Forest Plan wholesale, Gifford Pinchot forestry will at least look somewhat subdued compared to the feeding frenzy of earlier decades.

Improvements in the trail and logging situations in the Dark Divide will beef up the momentum to finally protect the Gifford Pinchot's greatest remaining roadless area. It might be chopped up around the edges and up the middle, but a viable wilderness *can* be reassembled. As I wrote in response to the McCoy Creek draft environmental impact statement, "Planning should begin for the abandonment and removal of the McCoy Creek road and its spurs, in order to restore the wilderness character of the core of the Dark Divide." Establishment of a wilderness area here will be an uphill slog in slick motorcycle ruts, especially with a hostile Congress in power. But at least the effort will not have to labor under the name — the Amoeba Roadless Area — originally applied to the area by Forest Service planners during the RARE II roadless area survey of 1977.

Susan Saul, an award-winning and dedicated conservationist, shared this history with me. She wrote:

Sometime in late 1978, Charlie Raines, an activist with the Sierra Club Cascade Chapter, called me and suggested that we needed a better name than "Amoeba" for the roadless area if we were going to build public support for its protection. We discussed using geographic features that were distinctive and would identify the area in an attractive and memorable way. Charlie suggested "Dark Divide" — Dark for Dark Mountain, Dark Meadows, and Dark Creek at the center of the roadless area, and Divide because it draped the hydrographic divide between the Lewis and Cispus river basins. I liked the somewhat mysterious images that the name invoked and approved his suggestion.

When Susan wrote the Forest Service on behalf of the Willapa Hills Audubon Society, commenting on an inadequate USFS proposal for a mere 6,960 acres to be protected in a Shark Rock Scenic Area, she stated the group's support for a "Dark Divide Roadless Area" — the first time the name was used in a formal communication with the agency. Later Charlie Raines drafted a "Dark Divide Wilderness Act of 1979," but no sponsors arose from the state's congressional delegation. The Forest Service continued to refer to the area as Amoeba as late as 1985. "I have been told that the Forest Service agonized over what to call the roadless area in the draft Forest Plan," Susan wrote. "Some advocated sticking with the RARE II name while others pointed out the public had been consistently calling the area 'Dark Divide' for more than five years. It was hotly debated, but the public won." And so a Dark Divide Wilderness Area might someday appear on the maps of the Gifford Pinchot National Forest. Were its name still Amoeba, such an outcome seems unlikely.

All of these developments in the legal history of a landscape took place before anyone who wanted to watch. The onlookers were many and varied — conservationists, bikers, loggers and their families, everyone who cared about the future of the forest. And in the forest itself, perhaps watchers with beetling brows, narrow eyes, no neck, and huge feet stood by. None came to the hearings, scoping sessions, timber summits, or demonstrations. They offered no input to the Forest Plan but kept their peace, kept their distance, kept their council, and watched . . . as their land contracted around them.

- - -

Just what has been said about Bigfoot on the Dark Divide? Unlike the chapter and verse of Mount St. Helens lore or the detailed interviews recorded by Peter Byrne in Carson and The Dalles, the fabric of Bigfoot in the Dark Divide seems woven of gossamer flecked with vague intimations. Measured rumors and murmurs around campfires, mutters and brags in taverns, cafés, and kitchens. Reluctant reports from the field, sighs under the breath. Whispered dispatches from travelers, leaks from workers on condition of anonymity. Legends and traditions passed on in dance, art, smoky stories by the fireside. No one seems to know the beast, yet few seem willing to discount it altogether — at least among those who have had anything to do with the countryside.

There is the Indian abandonment of sites rendered taboo by Bigfoot. There is the nervousness of Indian children on the berry fields on Potato Hill. Just scary stories, or an atavistic sense of caution, like the fear of snakes? And there is the sheer common sense that if hairy giants survive anywhere, then the largest remaining roadless area in the heart of their storied ancient range should be where they live today.

Distilling the many fragmentary stories I've overheard around the edges of the territory, from Potato Hill to the Little White Salmon, from the Big Lava Bed to Spirit Lake, I like to imagine that John Dark himself was not without views on the subject of Bigfoot. The land was alive with legend when Dark and the McCoy boys took to their gold-holes beneath Snagtooth Mountain. There is little chance that they had not heard of the Indians' cohabitant of the hills. Like the miners a couple of decades later who claimed to have encountered a band of rock-throwing apes on the side of St. Helens, these young prospectors went into the wilderness with a tickle of interest in all things unknown and perhaps with a tincture of fear.

You can see them, the McCoys, huddled around a tin stove in their simple cabin as snow falls on the last night of the century. In comes John Dark, looking paler than the cold would account for. He's been hunting off to the east, along the old Indian trail. His eyes are strange, and he stammers as he takes off his snow-stiff coat and elkhide gloves. He isn't sure he wants to tell his partners what he's seen out there, where the black mountain meets the boggy tableland.

What will the others think? That he went snow-blind or has been too long away from people? But he gets the story out: a line of tracks, longer and broader than his winter boots and farther apart than he could easily leap, let alone step, and, strangest of all, barefoot. When he tells it, the McCoys admit they have seen similar tracks but haven't mentioned them for fear of derision. Encouraged, Dark says he followed the impressions for half a mile, then lost them in a creek. What does he think it was? asks a McCoy. The Indians talk about a beast — a giant hairy devil or wild man. They say it takes women and children. Dark throws another log on the fire, and the men crowd nearer as the night draws in. They raise a cup to the twentieth century and try to forget their fears. But they all retire with a shiver the whiskey fails to dispel.

When spring comes, they search the far side of the black mountain, and one day all three find a track in sphagnum mud by a meadow sinkhole. The mud is as black as the basalt above, the track as big as two of theirs. And there is a stink so bad they cannot linger. On the way back, Dark, in the rear, sees a muddy streak between two great blue firs. Something big, but no elk slinks like that. He says nothing, for it has already gone. And when he returns to the lowlands that summer, he stays.

Something was up there in the mountains, something dark, and it wasn't his name: he has no idea the countryside will one day be peppered with Dark this, Dark that. He marries into the Underwood family and has a family in the valley. Within a very few years both John and Will McCoy die as the result of accidents. Others take up the mines, but they don't last long. For a time both the miners and the Indians, by then much depleted, leave the Divide to the track-makers.

If John Dark ever did imagine such a thing, he was not wrong. Something of a dark nature imbues that land. But it isn't Bigfoot; everything we know about the American Yeti tells us that if it exists, it is infinitely more peaceful and nonviolent than the other great ape occupying the continent. Perhaps Bigfoot is something to fear in the abstract, because of our very nature and because we know the Indians feared Tselatiks. Not evil, however; not deserving of the epithet "dark," in the sense of malicious.

No, the shady chapters in the Dark Divide lay decades ahead of John Dark, when the Mount Rainier Forest Reserve was carved apart; when Congress skipped over such an obvious candidate for protection; when the Forest Service, driven by Congress and the timber lobby, axed the great noble firs, thrust roads into the valleys to get at still more trees, and opened the country so quiet in Dark's day to howling cycles, breaking the soil and trenching the fragile ridges.

If there is indeed anything shady about the Dark Divide, besides the eponymous pioneer and the color of the rock, it lies not in the haunting of the bogs and the groves behind Shark Rock and Craggy Peak. It may be found instead in the folly of the fragmented forest, in the dark history of the dismantled land.

9

Yellowjacket Pass

≈ ≈ ≈

The other, misshapen,
stalked marshy wastes
in the tracks of an exile,
except that he was larger
than any other man.
In earlier days
the people of the region
named him Grendel.
— *Beowulf*

THE DARK DIVIDE Roadless Area has been described as an octopus, with arms of wild country separated by roads and logged-off
zones. But as I viewed the land, from north to south, it more closely
resembled a short-torsoed primate. Two lumpy legs run down from
the Divide toward the Cispus and the Cowlitz, straddling the narrow
incursion of McCoy Creek's road, which reaches the crotch. Off to the
east extends the left arm, if the beast is facing away, across Summit
Prairie, with Council Bluff clutched in the left hand like a throwing
stone. The arm on the west encompasses the sinew of the divide
proper. Wildly mixing similes, I can see our model's sleeves studded
like Elvis's jacket with black rhinestones (Hat, Snagtooth, Shark,
Craggy, Kirk, and Badger), while his right hand lofts a great knobby
club like that of the naked and erect Cerne Giant, an English monster
carved into the chalk downs of Dorset. The cudgel is the Clear Creek
corridor. Quartz Creek is the carotid artery, running from the heart
at Dark Mountain up to the neck and the large head, which is capped
by the green fuzz of the Lewis River forest. The beast doesn't have
much of a middle and no neck at all. As for his feet, they're enormous.

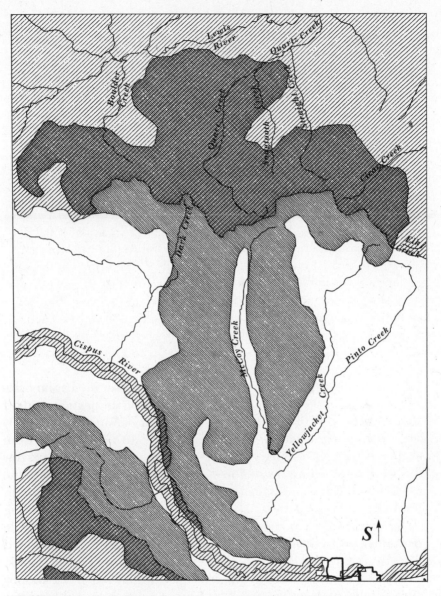

Outline of the Dark Divide Roadless Area. Note that south is at the top.
The Wilderness Society

The roadless area can also be likened to a maple leaf with deep lobes and a thick stem; or to an amoeba trying to cover a sea star; or to an octopus after all, missing a couple of legs, straddling the rough uses of the human landscape. Call it what you will, it comes to this: the Dark Divide has been chopped, logged, bulldozed, mined, biked, trodden, and tracked until it is only a skeleton of its former self. And yet the job has not been entirely completed. Something in the heart of this particular darkness, however fractured and imaginary, remains whole, wild, and very real indeed.

- - -

I'd come down from Dark Creek in the dark and camped tentless at Chain of Lakes below Mount Adams, north of big Takhlakh Lake. I was betting on no rain, and I won. The stars were like my Mountain Moo packet turned out into the sky. I awoke at seven-thirty with gray jays landing on my head in a cold fog fragrant with the terps and esters of high-elevation evergreens. Later I got up to a crisp blue sky, had crisp blueberries with my granola and Mountain Moo, and watched the jays — grays on the table, chary Steller's in a noble fir a few feet away. A frog croaked, kinglets tinkled; a red-shafted flicker hammered and yaffled.

About nine a truck drove in, and its occupants set up a racket of bangs, shouts, barking dog. The world is full of yahoos who (like flickers) seem to exist chiefly to make noise in national forests and parks. The gray jays, bored with me, moved off to where the action was, by the truck. The Steller's, more reticent and less enamored of the fuss, stayed behind in the forest fringe; when I went to the car, they moved in on some spilled granola. Kingfisher clattered, raven clamored.

Chain of Lakes was a golden meadowland of dried-up lakelets surrounded by candle-spire firs, green and blue, dead and alive, lichened and bare, with a willow-spiraea fringe. Juba skippers nectared on asters at the edge of the dried lakebed, while out in its sandy bottom a faun anglewing puddled. In spite of a sign that read "Closed to Motor Vehicles: The area back of this sign is classified under regulations of the Secretary of Agriculture to preserve its primitive environment / TRAVEL BY MOTOR VEHICLE IS PROHIBITED AND VIOLATORS WILL BE PROSECUTED," someone had taken motorcycles out into the lakebed and torn it up.

The yahoos by the lake turned out to be a tough, hard-working

USFS trail crew. They had a right to make some noise. One of the crew, a sturdy, young, permed reddish blonde wearing jeans, a red knit short-sleeved shirt, and a gold cross, came over to replenish the toilet paper in the john. She said they were building a trail around the campground to keep the bikers out. I mentioned that they had gotten into the meadow in spite of the sign. She said, "Yeah, we're not around to catch 'em, and they're cutting us seasonals off in two weeks, so they can do what they like." She told me that the biggest pond still had water and that Takhtakh and Muddy meadows were wonderful for plants. "Y'all have a nice time."

I lingered to see the pond, with firs reflected. A big blue darner worked the shore, hawking for smaller insects, which were scarce. As I watched it, one of the dirt bikers stopped to chat about lakes and fish and camps, and of course he was a perfectly nice guy. He nodded his red feed cap bearing the insignia of some airborne military unit and went on his way. An evening grosbeak called, and a ruffed grouse drummed, avoiding his pursuers in hunting season by existing on a Monday.

The sun was warm, though it felt as if autumn had arrived since I'd come down from Juniper Ridge, perhaps on the very storm that had caught me unawares there. Broken, unthreatening clouds sailed over the shoulder of Mount Adams. The gray jays, back with me, made weird, bell-like chortlings, as a Steller's glided down to flycatch in the sun over everlasting, saw me, and arrested, missing its prey.

From Takhlakh I detoured to Council Lake, lung-shaped, deep blue-green, deserted. I imagined the clinks from the Indian quarry and point knapping site that had been here. No finished points have been found, just bifacial flakes of flint, chert, chalcedony. But the site was abandoned after the Smith Creek eruption of Loo Wit 3,900 years ago. Why it was never resettled is the secret of ghosts, but in some stories, Bigfoot is implicated. Tah-Tah-Klé-ah is the Yakama Owl Woman Monster, another scary figure related to the giants and perhaps to nearby Takhtakh Meadow. A hermit thrush worked the chalcedony berries of a mountain ash, juncos probed the cherty perimeter of the lake.

From here Boundary Trail No. 1, a rutty road at the start, runs west all along the Dark Divide. I was bound for the wildlands far to the west, some fifteen miles via the Boundary Trail but closer to fifty miles by road, as I meant to go. Noon had come and gone. Lupines and pearly everlasting, many of them visited by an autumn hatch of orange sulphur butterflies, decorated the forest road as it crossed the eastern shoulder of the divide. In a gravel pit near the low summit of Babyshoe Pass, a patch of tiny, prostrate purple flowers looked out like an amethyst eye in a scarred face. The only vegetation for many yards around, the weedy, alien crucifer covered no more than a square yard, yet a brilliant male sulphur had found it and was nectaring for all it was worth. Just as the pikas of Dark Creek had adapted to bogus rockslides, so this sulphur managed to take advantage of a scarce nectar resource in a wasted habitat. Again my eyes were opened by an animal able to make do with the leftovers of a landscape in flux.

I stopped at Randle as briefly as possible. The loud trucks, one after another, the people . . . After the quiet, they were hard to take. I picked up the essentials — gas, beer, chocolate, stew, granola bars, cheese, Ak-Mak crackers — called Thea, and got out.

My way took me up Yellowjacket Creek, directly west of Juniper Ridge. The creek roared down in a deep canyon. Late sun slanted onto the second growth opposite, onto snaggy old growth above and below. The stream corridor was a beauty, but because of the road, there was human sign: painted trees; ribbons in stripes, polka dots, and solid colors; paper-plate signs tacked onto trees directing one party of hunters to another; a sediment of filter tips at every pullout. Does any other species mark its comings and goings as rudely as we do? What's wrong with urine and musk?

Marking a spot near Badger Creek, I spotted a banana slug crossing the dirty road, the first mollusk I'd seen on this trek. Battling dryness, it was heading toward the stream's moist edge. I helped it. I try to resist playing God, but the desiccating slug made me think of myself up on the Saddle, sucking the air and the dust for any spare mote of moisture.

My route away from Yellowjacket, Forest Road No. 2810, became an appalling route. Of the crummy hill roads I'd driven thousands of miles on in a dynasty of Volkswagens and Powdermilk, this was among the worst: strewn with big rocks, riven by dangerous washouts, with big downed trees hanging over the road, leaving just room to pass underneath. Trying to back away from a bad place between two washouts, I got stuck in the ditch on the inside edge of the "road." The few times I've been stuck I've picked great places to do it, and this was a doozie. The previous spring, way down a sandy track along the Columbia and many miles from help, Thea and I got out only by fashioning a corduroy road out of bitterbrush and sage. Here I had no such luxury. Remote and lonely, this could have been a hell of a fix, unless some great ape chose to assist me. In the end the ape within was barely great enough. After moving a lot of rocks, I put the hamsters and the front-wheel drive to their greatest test and ground my way out. Then I shook my head, laughed, turned around, had an ale, and camped.

Dinner materialized on the hood: beef stew, applesauce with fresh blueberries, Redhook Extra Special Bitter, and Cadbury's milk chocolate with almonds. The world was aright. I was perched in the heart of the Dark Divide, just a raven's mile or two from its toothy jawline. Craggy Peak, Kirk and Shark rocks carved up the southwest horizon with their sooty sawteeth.

Then, standing in a cleft near the broken summit of Craggy, Bigfoot appeared. His proportions were just as I'd imagined him. Big rounded shoulders, no neck, lump of a head on top. But he never moved: he'd been turned to black stone by mortification at what he saw below. Still he watched. Watching back, I saw the sun set over those time-tortured rocks. A great darkness preceded the coming of the stars. Then the Milky Way poured from a spout of black sky into the insatiable gape of the Dark Divide. Later, when the sky turned, that stone monster got up and walked.

- - -

Those who dismiss giant hairy apes from our possible fauna often point to the fact that Bigfoot encounters are never reported by experienced naturalists. It's true that most of the sightings come from hunters, frequent campers, and forest workers, all of whom may be considered naturalists of a kind. But no one trained in zoology, with a background of comparative and extensive study of animals in their natural surroundings, seems to see the beast. So I was fascinated to hear a first-person account from a good friend of mine who is a first-rate field biologist. Jim Fielder has a degree in biology from Central Washington University, twenty-five years of experience in teaching and nature guiding, and a life list of more than 1,500 birds.

I met Jim on the first Earth Day (April 22, 1970), when I was a graduate student at the University of Washington and he a biology teacher at Newport High School in Bellevue. Jim had asked me and Neil Johannsen, a fellow grad student in forest resources (now he has been director of Alaska's state parks for twelve years), to address his ecology class. When we arrived at Newport we found a tall, slim man in a black T-shirt, with long wavy chestnut hair and bushy sideburns and mustache to match, playing early Springsteen to a clearly contented class. Fielder was one of the most effective teachers I've ever known. The field trips he conducted for his devoted students became legendary for their ambitious scope, adventures, and lengthy bird lists. Highly envious of his students, I hitched along whenever I could. In later years, when Fielder left teaching and founded Zig Zag River Trips, we remained friends, exchanging nature notes and sightings from time to time. So I was not surprised when Jim called one night to share some news — at least not until he said what it was.

"Jimmy Field-trip," I greeted him. "What's up?"

"Bob," he said, "I've seen Bigfoot."

One late September night he was driving west on State Route 12, returning from Mount Rainier to a cabin at Packwood. "I was lucid and sober, Bob," he said, "under the influence of clear vision." About seven miles before Packwood, just past the turnoff to Backbone Lake, he was rounding a wide curve when he saw something in the middle of the highway about a hundred yards ahead. The object, down close to the surface of the road, looked dark and hairy. It is common to encounter deer, elk, and other wildlife on Washington roads, and Jim thought at first it might be an elk that had been wounded or struck by another car. He sped up to get a good look.

"At fifty yards," he told me, "it started to get up. At about twenty-five yards I thought it must be a bear — it was reddish-brown, the right color for that cinnamon-phase black bear you often see around Rainier. I braked and turned the wheel left to get it in my headlights, trying not to roll the jeep."

The animal stood up on two legs and with a deliberate gait lumbered off into the forest, taking at least ten steps upright, which bears do not do. "I rolled on past at about thirty miles per hour," Jim went on, "as it disappeared into the woods." I asked him what else he had been able to see. Used to making careful mental field notes, Fielder had gathered some details which, he said, he was careful not to embroider. From decades of identifying tricky birds and mammals, he knows how important it is to take note of subtle field marks without embellishing that which is actually visible.

"Whatever it was was no taller than me," Jim said, "around six or six and a half feet, but a lot bulkier. The arms were long, the hands about halfway from the hips to the knees. Unfortunately it didn't look toward me, so I got no facial features. Its walk was completely upright and seemed unconcerned. The feet were hairy and big, but not massive."

Struck by the brief but remarkable sighting, Fielder braked and turned back to investigate the spot. He found a steaming wet spot in the road, three to four feet wide, where he assumed the animal had urinated. "I was eager to get a sample," he said, "but I was dressed lightly and had no equipment with me. I decided to head back to the motel, change, pick up some gear, and come right back." But at the motel Jim received a message that his mother, for whom he was serving as caregiver, had had a medical emergency. He had to rush home to Seattle and wasn't able to return for nearly two weeks. By then there was nothing to see.

"I'm a cynic and a skeptic, Bob," he told me, "you know that — the last biologist in Washington who would believe in Bigfoot. But that night I went from a Bigfoot agnostic to a Bigfoot born-again in ten seconds."

- - -

Four years almost to the day before Fielder's sighting, I hiked into the heart of the Dark Divide. Two weeks into my month I was to cross Yellowjacket Pass. Full sun and chickadees joined me at a breakfast of broken granola bars and Mountain Moo (replenished, I could have sworn, from the Milky Way as I slept), tea, guava, and apricots. A pearly swoop of band-tailed pigeons circled the valley below. As they traded one island of trees for another, the morning sun picked out the pie-slice pattern of clear-cuts, designed for maximum fragmentation. The stone figure of Bigfoot looked on, stilled with the daylight.

Clear, hot sun rode a light merciful breeze with grasshopper songs on it. Beat fritillaries and bright anglewings nectared on everlasting at the trailhead. It was one mile to Boundary Trail No. 1 on Yellowjacket Trail No. 1A. The trail struck steadily up through the cool greenwood. Raspberry, starflower, twisted stalk lily, vanilla leaf, and bunchberry wove a thick green ground layer. Elk, deer, and coyote tracks churned the earth and pumice, making for pleasant walking. Sunlight spilled through, illuminating the yellow-rimmed black spots — like an eclipse with a corona — that appeared on almost every oval huckleberry leaf, little universes of leaf-mining larvae. Mulling minutiae, I look up in time to see the brown stir of large animals above me on the slope. From their many tracks and fresh dung, I knew I'd disturbed elk in their bedding place. The previous evening, taking a dusk walk at the end of the road, I'd bothered three deer, a doe and two yearlings, who bounded straight up the steep hillside.

Giant noble fir cones decorated the trail, half in tatters, like purple grenades that had begun to explode and then forgot why. True firs don't drop their cones intact, they fall apart on the limb. These trail bombs had been clipped off by chickarees, whose middens of seed scales, bracts, and cores showed the results of an abundant cone harvest. The cones were six or seven inches long and extremely pitchy. Their fragrance, like rarefied Pine-Sol, brought back my own brief logging days many years before, when I worked for a power-line clearing crew in the high Rockies. The noble fir bracts have a "tail" like those of Douglas-fir, but no "hind legs." So rather than a mouse escaping under a door (by which Doug-fir cones are remembered), these reminded me of a snapping turtle ducking under a frilly lily pad. More squirrel feed showed in a cluster of small brown mushrooms dug up with their caps nibbled and their stipes tossed about. A small, berry-filled bear scat gooped across the path, and in a sunny clear-cut at the top of the trail I saw the huckleberries it came from.

Here, on a flat shaded saddle, I hit the motorcycle ruts of Boundary Trail No. 1, which I followed south along the ridge. Some massive noble firs climbed up from French Creek. Loggers' graffiti branded logs with chain-sawed initials beside the trail — MT, MT / DA — and in a living tree, G and M crudely cut, as if removing the trees weren't enough of a signature upon the land.

A raven werted over toward Dark Mountain. As I faced west toward Holdaway Butte, the south end of Langille Ridge, I stood on the backbone of the Dark Divide. Looking east I could see the cone of Juniper, spiky Sunrise, the Saddle, and Jumbo — still a black molar perhaps, but from here its full mass was visible, like something out of the Beartooths in Montana. Before me too was Forest Road 29, scarring the McCoy Creek valley right up to the Divide, and the Boundary Trail, curving up to where I stood.

Varied thrushes and flickers called as I ate lunch beneath an Alaska yellow cedar, and for a change I couldn't hear the whistle of a logging show. Afterward, crossing a thicket of mountain azalea, small fir, cedar, huckleberry, and mountain ash, I entered a living oxymoron: a flock of Townsend's solitaires, which I'd never seen in numbers before. They were part of a huge mixed feeding flock of birds, including chipping sparrows, white-crowned sparrows, hermit thrushes, and cryptic autumn warblers; how many birds there were, the flaps and rustlings and chirps only hinted at. They were into the big fat huckle-berries, same as me.

Before rounding Hat Rock I turned and took a mind-picture of the panorama straight across the low point of the Divide to Dumbo, Mounts Rainier and Adams in peripheral view, the entirety of Juniper Ridge from Tongue Rock to Dark Mountain laid out before me. The country looked so big that I could imagine D. B. Cooper, Monty West, or Sehlatiks hiding out here forever.

A deep cleft took the trail through Hat Rock. In the cut I found a steep rock garden. The blossoms were mostly blown, except for laven-der asters, orange hawkbit, scarlet gilia, and yellow wallflowers. The incredibly sweet smell of the wallflower was worth a precarious kneel, and I didn't keel over this time. When I finished, an orange sulphur nectared on the same flower, followed by a hydaspe fritillary. A jay and a hunting wasp, both the blue-black of Superman's hair, worked the pumice for whatever it offered to eat. I passed a wallflower at nose level on the wall, as it should be, and breathed deep. The dense fragrance lingered like that of my grandmother's mock orange in the hose spray of a hot day.

I walked the very crest of the Dark Divide, ten feet across, through fir and western red cedar. One of the great black crags of the Dark Divide, Hat Rock raised its spire directly above me. Among caves and clefts, walls of moss and saxifrage and puny trees struggled up toward the bare basalt. In the lee of the north wall, hellebore was still green, the day was summery, and I'd stepped back a season. A nuthatch and a logging hooter both beeped, one near and sharp, one far and soft.

Just then my wild reverie was shattered as a jet fighter overflew the pass at a few tens of feet, shrieking like no voice that ever came out of flesh. Then the coyotes down the slope set up a great howl at midday, something I'd never heard. Did the unholy roar of those arrogant invaders hurt their ears? Or did they simply feel the need to protest, giving voice for us all?

Around the side of Hat, jutting promontories dropped sheer into Yellowjacket's headwaters. On my belly I approached the edge. Out of a sediment of blue juniper berries, quartz crystals shone from the black rock matrix. The dusky forms of Craggy, Shark, Kirk, and Badger loomed westerly, and Snagtooth was just around the corner to the south. I left the pinnacles and dove into the forest to reach Snagtooth Trail and Yellowjacket Pass.

Beside the trail rose a chiseled white snag like a Greek pillar with its capital missing. Trail No. 1 was indeed a thoroughfare! If the Indian traders were no more, a concatenation of tracks told of another commerce. In the mud by a new log bridge, the pugmarks of bobcat were going against me, coyote tracks my way, both impressed over last weekend's motorcycle tracks.

Inside the shadows of big Pacific silver firs, the orange fungus called chicken of the woods caught a sunbeam on a fallen fir's great trunk. Dwarf brambles trailed their triple lobes over the ashen soil among wintergreen seedstalks and leaves, a few late flecks of foamflower, a coral-root orchid, and a Twix wrapper, which I stuffed in my pocket along with yards of discarded pink flagging. Where the trail dropped steeply to the pass, the bikers had again trenched out the switchbacks and, what's worse, cut across them, exposing and injuring tree roots.

I passed Snagtooth Trail at two, arrived at Yellowjacket Pass a quarter of an hour later. It was not the meadow I had somehow conjured in my mind from the map but a deepwood saddle under mature true firs, hemlocks, and a few big Doug-firs. I found the little ponds, promised on the map, along the saddle just south of the pass, and they did lie among meadows wrapped in cedars. The surrounding forest was just open enough to see out of but not into. A pumicy trail, well traveled by animals, led along the side of the glade to the nearest pond. It drained via rushing brook into Straight Creek and thence the Lewis River, while the steep slope on the north side of the pass dropped into Yellowjacket Creek, then the Cispus River. At the midpoint of my journey I had crossed the Dark Divide on foot.

The pond, maybe a hundred square feet, was full of lazy skimmers (until my shadow hit them) and lazy efts of salamanders — like stretched-out tadpoles with baby feet. There was no sign of people in here, nor sound, except the occasional high plane. A chickaree, working the bark of a tree by the pond, freaked when it saw me. I settled on a log and took a late lunch of extra-sharp Tillamook cheddar, Thea's crackers with Ak-Mak reinforcements and bits of papaya, apricot, apple, orange, raisins, a Swede Park tomato, chocolate, and water. There were no mosquitoes, no yellowjackets. Only a few flies shared my bower of azalea and heather. Then one mosquito appeared and bit me on the temple — one of my least favorite places, like knuckles — but just one was okay; in June I would have been furred with mosquitoes, dive-bombed by deerflies.

Just then a long series of rapid whistles, or hoots, followed by one note, all on one high pitch, broke the stillness. Nuthatches piped in, as ever. Did I hear what I thought I heard? I listened for a long time but heard nothing more.

The air smelled Septembric. The sun lodged just off a blue hole. I didn't mind the prospect of a cool hike back, just so that big cloud to the west didn't spawn a rock-knocking, road-sticking storm before I got down.

I dipped my feet, smarting from the cycle ruts, and tried to catch an eft. The pond felt fine, especially the rich, wet moss at the edges. I caught an eft by hand but couldn't tell much from its mottled greeny skin, primitive eyes, toy hands. Released, it seemed no worse for the experience. One bird cherked, the first call since those whistles. I dried my feet on my headband, slid into the heavy boots, and prepared to walk out of the now sunny meadow.

I came to a pond the size of a back-yard swimming pool, full of both efts and tadpoles, with blue darners skimming the surface. A frog croaked, hoarse and uneven. Then I noticed frogs, minute and larger, in the wet grass, heading for the pondlets. I caught one that was under half an inch — a Pacific tree frog. The bigger ones must have been Cascades frogs. At least here was one place the acid rain hadn't yet scoured of its amphibious life.

A Cooper's hawk shot past me at the edge of the meadow. I heard a struggle nearby, and a squirrel scolding, as the rusty accipiter made a silent, quick kill just fifty feet away. Things still work here, I thought, in spite of the fighters and the logging booms approaching from down valley.

Rounding the biggest pond, I looked for salamanders and saw instead two intersecting lines of large tracks in the bottom. Very muddy and blurry, they looked to be about ten to fifteen inches long and half as wide, though they might have been inflated by the shifting mud. Little definition remained. The best one, near the edge, had a good heel impressed three inches, but no toes or claws. The step was something under a yard. The tracks led into tall grass, where they were lost.

- - -

Another autumn Thea and I would come to Yellowjacket Pass with two friends, Ann Musché and Alan Richards. We hiked in on No. 1A, they took Snagtooth Mountain Trail No. 4, and we met in the middle; remarkably, both parties reached the trail's fork at the same time. We saw anglewing butterflies sipping willow sap, aphid honeydew on noble fir saplings, coyote scat. Thea found the chrysalis of a zephyr an-glewing and an anise swallowtail larva. Ann basked in the meadow. Alan and I hung the food high away from bears. At night we watched constellations and listened to the great horned owls call. After camp-ing together, we swapped car keys and took each other's route and car back out.

When Thea and I hiked down Snagtooth, it was old growth all the way. The gray-fir woods were dressed with lichen, the ground with bark slabs, purple bracts of squirrel-felled cones, wintergreens, and pale saprophytes, coral-roots and pinedrops. From Snagtooth Mountain we could see from Council Bluff to Hat Rock, Juniper Peak to Dark Peak — a cross section of this old dentition. We saw no sign of Bigfoot or of anything our joint experience in the woods couldn't explain.

— — —

This time, as much as I wanted to explore the trail down Snagtooth Creek, there was no car waiting for me on that side. I turned back toward Powdermilk's parking spot, slightly unsettled by muddy marks and sharp whistles. Leaving Yellowjacket Pass, elevation 4,320 feet, in the late afternoon, I crossed the Dark Divide again and again, back and forth. I heard bikers like hornets in the distance: were they the yellowjackets of the pass's name? But then I spotted the spit-up paper nest of a *Vespula* in the trail and decided it belonged to the epony-mous wasp.

A redtail swirled around the upper headwaters of Yellowjacket. I wondered what it would be like to sail from Hat to Snagtooth, from Craggy to Kirk, and on to Shark, Badger, and Loo Wit herself with no thought of sore feet or sagging shoulders. Cool shadows settled as a Townsend's solitaire ascended Hat Rock.

If only it were so easy! My thick calves and thighs, so heavy with beefsteak that I sink in water, yet more marbled than when they were built for wrestling and throwing heavy objects, can get me to the peaks — but not like the solitaire, not like the hawk! Not like those three deer bounding straight up the slope. By many accounts, Big-foot, at two to three times my weight, climbs as effortlessly as deer. I found myself envious of all these weightless creatures as I plodded the steep trail back down. If gravity has a rainbow, I know only its dim reflection in the mud of the track below: gravity's anchor.

East of Hat Rock the trail leveled out. I strode along the Dark Divide and even straddled it at one very narrow point. I stood with one foot on each side and hugged trees on both slopes. Peeing demo-cratically, I shared my paltry contribution between two drainages with-out shifting position. I don't suppose any map, text, pass, or ridgeline has ever given me a keener sense of what watershed means than this small act. I was just twenty-five miles from where Jim Fielder would see a possible Bigfoot take a leak four years later.

One last handful of big plump huckleberries got me down the final mile. I held the last berry under my tongue until I struck the trailhead at six o'clock even. I reached my car just before sunset. A sunbolt shooting past Shark and Craggy illuminated Yellowjacket Pass and the entire Divide like General Electric or some other god.

The car bounced down the crummy road, past deep green and pink moss pads at rills, under the black gaze of the Bigfoot in the cleft of Craggy, back on watch. Pikas called from slash piles in the big clear-cuts. The dusk deepened all the way down to Eagle's Cliff. Once there, tired and dirty, I took a tiny cabin that General Electric had not yet blessed. In my little loft, lit by gaslight, I tried to read, but I was too tired. Instead, until sleep claimed the body of the rim-walker, I pon-dered the nature of divides.

It came to me that this trip was about many more divides than the physical one I'd just crossed. There was the great gulf between differ-ing visions for the future of the forest and the fine line separating the land of the living from that of the dead and gone. There was the murky border where history and myth meet and mingle. And always the boundary of belief. Everywhere I went, when the subject of Big-foot came up, people would ask me, "Which side are you on? Do you really believe?" More and more I saw that this was no sharp scarp, no razorback ridge between rivers.

Back in the meadows and ponds on Yellowjacket Pass: those were probably black bear prints. And the whistles I heard were likely some taunting dialect of the gray jay. Yet they had the tone and tenor of the whistles commonly described by Indians claiming to be familiar with Sasquatch. And the tracks and stride had the right dimensions, if not much detail. They were as "good" as many that have been claimed as Bigfoot's.

The workings of the solitary mind are a wondrous thing. There was nothing on Yellowjacket Pass that I, as a biologist, would ask anyone else to consider seriously as evidence for the presence of another primate. Yet just there and then I was perfectly prepared to believe: not to believe *in* Bigfoot necessarily, but to believe that the world is wider than we normally wish to accept. To believe that, yes, that *could* be the whistle of an ape; those *might* be the tracks of the whistler. That I might not be alone up there after all.

Thus muddled, I lost my footing on that other divide, with wakefulness on its bright side and slumber in the shadows, and rolled deep into sleep. Into dreams, where all the edges run together like mud in a mountain pond, disturbed by someone's footprints.

10

Grendel Redux: Snagtooth

And so I come through the trees and towns to the lights of the meadhouse, dark shadow out of the woods below. I knock politely on the high oak door, bursting its hinges and sending the shock of my greeting inward like a cold blast out of a cave. "Grendel!" they squeak, and I smile like exploding spring.
— John Gardner, *Grendel*

UP ON THE DIVIDE, the chilly mists of the low valleys dissipated in autumn sunshine. I returned to the forest creases feeding the Lewis River, hoping to get deeper into the old growth. On foot I followed Straight Creek over shaly steps and into the blue pools of hollows, heading for the confluence of Quartz and Snagtooth creeks. This took me down a steep, gravelly trail alongside a clear-cut, through young Douglas-firs. Chickadees and nuthatches led the way. Yellow-rumped warblers foraged in the second growth. It was spider season, and I used my net as a web wand. Even so, like the deer and elk with gossamer-strung antlers, I trailed yards of silky strands that tickled my forehead and forearms and crisscrossed my glasses.

I walked a line between radically different worlds. Bird's nest and turkeytail fungi were busy reworking the soil in the thinned stands as the plantation took on life. Environmental rhetoric represents the "reprod" as having too little life; foresters make it out to be too lively. The actual state of second growth lies somewhere between barren and fecund. Windthrow from the edges of the standing old growth increased the size of the clearing while adding some structure to its depleted community. At a corner where the land dropped a precipitous hundred feet into Straight Creek, the trail turned to follow the edge.

Sapsucker sign, punched out like a pegboard. Lush big red huckleberries, tart and crisp, took the place of blues, which I wouldn't see again until Indian Heaven. Quartz Creek Trail No. 5 appeared on a wooded lip of land above the canyon. Rounding the bottom of the clear-cut, passing enormous scorched stumps, I finally entered the best of the remnant Quartz Creek old growth. The greenwood muffled the sound of a helicopter logging across the Lewis River far below.

Pausing for water and dried papaya, I wrung out my sweatband in cool green shade. Vanilla-leaf parasols nodded beside me in a sunbeam; prince's pine and Oregon grape laid a deep green sheen on the forest floor. No more stumps! I appreciate stumps in their own right, but in this context the EarthFirst! bumper-sticker logic, "Stumps suck!" seemed appropriate.

Walking softly on the ancient duff, I bowed for windfall and to great trees and snags as a varied thrush silently wheeled through the boughs above. A mossy creek, a huge hemlock fallen down its middle, swaddled itself in lady fern. When I hugged Douglas-firs and hemlocks, I could reach just a quarter or halfway around. Yes, it's true . . . some of us do hug trees, including some reverent loggers I know. I think for me it's less a sentimental gesture than a measure, a recognition, an exposure of the full-frontal sensory skin sheath to the power and substance of these great green lives. Anyone who sneers and never embraces a tree is missing out on one of the finer sensual compensations for life in a mortal body.

Another pleasure is the rush that comes from recognizing the individuality of other life forms — the hit that naturalists, situated in the midst of the grand biological parade, get every time they meet something new. Few of us will ever know newness the way Linnaeus did in Lapland, when he first gave the boreal twinflower its lovely name *Linnaea* (and here it was, at my feet). But we know the sweetness of first encounter. The pleasure is deeply visceral; you feel it in your belly as well as your head. Sad, how few ever know this joy, for close observers are almost as rare as tree-huggers. If lingual illiteracy is advancing, natural illiteracy is already winning.

Professor C. Leo Hitchcock's university course, Botany 113, Local Flora, opened the world to me as few other ways of knowing ever have. Nature study was once commonplace in schools, and before there were schools a basic knowledge of flora and fauna was a prerequisite for survival. Now, with massive societal ignorance of our fellow animals and plants, we once again face the question of survival. Botany 113 should be a required course for life!

The black and spartan fertile fronds of deer fern poked up from the floor of an open grove of a dozen giant firs, recalling a scene from the redwood groves. Breeze and sun flickered across maple leaves. On an old mossy rockfall, pikas called from a swale of wood fern. The vine maples hinted at their coming red shift, not shouting it ahead of time as in the clear-cuts. The polished trunks of white snags rippled in sun and shadow. Artist's fungi climbed a tall snag, making balconies for squirrels. The messages of kinglets and red-breasted nuthatches carried like an aural semaphore.

Anyone with field guides has access to the common life forms. Yet the decisions about such forests are made by people who have no idea what the kinglets are doing in the crowns of the trees, who know nothing of the life beneath the forest floor. A field guide to old-growth life forms and lifeways should be required reading for all who go here.

I found myself wishing for a field guide to the colors of plastic ribbons. Everywhere I went in the Dark Divide the trees were flagged with a panoply of plastic ribbon — yellow, orange, red, pink, blue, polka-dot, stripe, and half a dozen others. Without knowing what the patterns mean it is impossible to know the intent of the invading flaggers. I'm sure many helpful marks are lost to vigilantes who routinely remove the flags of surveyors, developers, timber cruisers (who estimate lumber volume in a forest stand), and the like. Here orange-capped stakes and scarlet ribbons were scattered around. I suspect they were for a trail crew, but a well-intentioned vandal could mistake them for timber sale markers.

An aluminum plate stapled to a small hemlock bore messages official and otherwise: "RP/STA 170 + 77/DIS 20.0/AZ 210/8-22-88 SUS," neatly inscribed; and scratched crudely across it: FUCK YOU RAPISTS! The letters and numbers might denote a cartographer's baseline, a trail crew survey, or even a spotted-owl listening transect — but someone obviously thought it was a timber cruiser's tag, which it probably was. An additional message, likely scrawled with a Swiss Army knife, read LONG LIVE THE ANCIENT FORESTS.

I clambered under, over, and around the deadfall across the trail. It was just as well that I had not come directly from the Saddle, across Jumbo and Dark, and down Quartz from its headwaters south of Dark Meadow. Traversing many miles of these giants' pick-up sticks with a large, heavy backpack would have been torturous, taxing even the forest's powers of refreshment.

Such nurse logs these! Planter-dividers for the living rooms of the gods. Over time, under the hungry influence of the springing ferns, mosses, lichens, and seedlings, the logs break down, giving the soil its foodstuffs. In the standing snags, pileated woodpeckers carve honeycombs of rectangles. Dead wood, often thought wasted in its rich rotting, feeds all the small rotters and, through them, finally the earth itself.

Of all this life, maybe the fungi are the most obviously evolutionarily proliferated. Although the great fall 'shroom bloom was not yet out, russulas spattered the green carpet with patches of purple, red, and white. The inverted caps of *Russula brevipes,* a real steam shovel of a mushroom, must push up as much soil as worms do. Polypore conks, some two feet across, made chocolate shelves, white knobs, or gray, glistening knees and elbows. One conk capped the yard-broad butt of a log. The fungi came into their own in the slight slant light of September, which accented their subtle shades. The barbed blue trailer of a dewberry vine pricked me when I stooped to touch the viscid pearl cap of an agaric.

Scale becomes confused in the old growth. Bunchberry dogwood in fruit burst from the bark of a vast hemlock, while hemlocks no taller than moss thalli furred the stumps they'd both claimed. I was dizzy with the large and small of it all when I came onto a ridge with a high view of upper Quartz Creek and, it seemed, miles of unbroken old growth. The promontory was clothed in moss: a soft, flat landscape, its sharp edges buffered. For the first time, all things seemed as they should be in the Dark Divide.

At Snagtooth Creek in the midafternoon, I munched oblong rose hips that looked like the exaggerated peaches of a fruit label. They were neither sweet like peaches nor bitter, just another abundant wild food rich in vitamin C and beta carotene. A good little flow came down Snagtooth among signs that it ran much fuller and broader in spate. Off with the boots! The water was very cold, very fresh on my too-human feet. An enormous Douglas-fir curved up and over from the far shore.

In Snagtooth's sunny glade I sat beneath the waving cream racemes of goatsbeard and watched for rustic deities. Easily I imagined the Green Man, in one of his many incarnations, appearing here. The one I had in mind was Silenus — not the faun himself but the Silenus anglewing, a richly russet-and-black butterfly of forest glades and dappled streamsides in the ancient forest, unrecorded from Skamania

County. But the satyr of this glade turned out to be a winter wren, a natural Puck, cherk-cherking among the alders. Silenus did not appear.

Why did the early lepidopterists name so many butterflies after mythic entities? Probably because of their romanticism and classical educations as much as for the insects' sylvan habitats; the fritillaries include species named for Titania, Hippolyta, Aphrodite, Diana, and Cybele, and the anglewings include the faun, the satyr, and the zephyr, as well as Silenus.

Some have connected centaurs and satyrs, via the Wild Man, to Bigfoot. In *Beowulf* the giant Grendel descends on the mead hall and wreaks havoc by eating the heads of warrior Danes. John Gardner told the tale from the monster's point of view in *Grendel*, mixing malice and vengeance with remorse and envy in the mind of an unhappy creature who would never be human, thanks to the curse of God upon the offspring of Cain. I daydreamed about Sasquatch popping into the tavern down at Cougar, like his Nordic ancestor, Grendel, just to nip off a few feed caps and hardhats. God knows he's got a good excuse in the curse of the modern gods on the offspring of Selahtiks. Now that would be something for the tabloids. The world would never be the same.

As Blackfeet singer-songwriter Jack Gladstone told me, mythological themes are born of people's experience of place. Joseph Campbell called myth a public dream, and dreams private myths. By these measures my Bigfoot myth was growing each day I spent in the Dark Divide, each time I dreamed. Writer Kim Stafford described to me an Andean wise man who, when asked what the smartest animal was, replied that it was the animal we have barely seen and never found. That's Bigfoot for sure! Jack also spoke of a Blackfeet mythic teacher called Napi. Bigfoot has been my teacher here, my Napi; and that too is the name of a butterfly, *Pieris napi,* a white floater that frequents sunny patches in the forest such as the one I was basking in this late afternoon.

So Bigfoot and butterflies are both wrapped in myth. No butterflies bear the name of Bigfoot, but birds of the order Megapodes live in New Guinea, where they incubate their eggs in geothermally warmed soils, testing the temperature with their massive feet. Maybe there are unknown Megapodes on the backside of Loo Wit, consorting with Titania, but I doubt it. My sensibility doesn't allow for an easy blend of faerie and fauna. To me, despite their charming nomenclatural associations, birds and butterflies are material beings, very here and now and flesh and blood, or at least chitin and hemolymph. And if Bigfoot strides these heights, it too is physical: an animal with none of the magical properties of Greek deities, just needs and instincts much like my own.

My immediate need was a nap, a streamside drowse disturbed only briefly by a truly foul odor wafting through from somewhere. Was it something dead? Or something alive?

- - -

When I went into the Dark Divide, I hoped to enter the mind of the monster. I wasn't sure if that meant the working brain of a beast, the ethos of a fairy-tale phenomenon, or the intellect of the land itself. Maybe all three. At times I felt I succeeded. It would have been good to write about it then and there, when the feeling was fresh. But it always passed, and then there were the miles to be covered, the texture of the trip to record, the camp chores, the ten thousand personal preoccupations. When I made my field notes, I usually found myself trapped by the rusty steel jaws of my own brain pan.

Much later I tried to evoke the sensation of oneness with my subject in full-blown prose. The results convinced no one, least of all me. In one draft I emulated the high-flown language of Gardner's *Grendel*, at once blithe and profoundly sad. Another attempt took an Abbey-esque crack at a flip and profane world-view, excoriating loggers and mountain bikers alike for invading the territory of my speaker. One version told a short story involving Indians and Bigfoot hunters and ending with my animal on the door of the nearest tavern, ready for his date with a modern Beowulf in plaid shirt and pegged jeans. Yet another dropped the pretense of language as much as possible while still conveying the basic facts of a day in the life of the beast in a concrete litany of hard, monosyllabic words like shards of the stones themselves: "walk ridge crack rock scrape bark walk."

My friend and gentle critic Jenelle Varila, after hearing one of these labors in our writing group, got it just right. She said that I had entered Bigfoot, but then had taken over his mind instead of allowing him to overtake mine. "Bob Pyle's mind," she wrote me, "turned the crank in the mind of Bigfoot." She went on to pinpoint the challenge precisely: "It's incredibly difficult to release one's self, to allow the infiltration of another mind to drown the passion of our own." Indeed it is.

Others have written narratives from the standpoint of Yeti or Sasquatch with engaging results, but you know the author is still in charge; the creature might as well be Howdy Doody. Even the invention of a language or syntax, as some fantasy and science fiction writers have done, just serves to further screen an authorial voice that is, if anything, even more manipulative. The best fiction writers make you believe that their characters are in charge of their own minds and voices; but to me as a reader, the more transparent the magic, the more embedded I feel in the mind of the writer, though I may frequently forget it. Besides, most fictional characters are able to speak, so the challenge is not entirely comparable. As I found, it is damnably difficult to convey words, thoughts, actions, and perceptions for a creature that is, as far as we know, without language or speech.

What about animal fiction? Some fully engaging novels without people in significant roles, such as Richard Adams's *Watership Down*, simply endow animals with speech, as Gardner did with Grendel. Henry Williamson's classic *Tarka the Otter* and Daniel Mannix's *The Fox and the Hound* come as close as any books I know to placing the reader inside the skins of their characters without anthropomorphizing. But these third-person stories, masterfully steeped as they are in lutrine and canine sensibilities, are still drawn from the human intellect and conveyed with human conceits, tropes, and tools. Vladimir Nabokov, in an interview with Jacob Bronowski, said, "We should all remember that a lepidopterist reverts in a sense to the ancient ape-man who actually fed on butterflies and learned to distinguish the edible from the poisonous kinds." So I should have had a leg up on the process. If never quite reverting, at least I stepped inside the ape-suit — and, being there, found it ineffable. I don't know if anyone can give voice to the voiceless and stay out of it. As Jenelle said, "You must pull the shade of your own reasoning and peer deeply into the new territory." For most (if not all) writers, I suspect that shade is as stuck as mine.

Yet I did peer deeply into the territory. And at certain times I believe that I did intuit the Sasquatchness of the scene, that I left myself behind and climbed inside that great hairy headgear and felt the flapping of my massive feet against the rough pumice paths.

This happened at the mouth of Yellowjacket Creek when I imagined hiding out at the old hidden cedar stump as a hunted primate. It came to me again at Yellowjacket Pass when I peered into the meadow pool at efts and saw tracks in the mud that might have been made by my kind . . . and for a moment my kind was the clan of the big feet.

And on the dusky heaths of Juniper Ridge I was truly (if briefly) a cohabitant of the ghost moths.

The senses of Sasquatch came at random moments. How a pawful of huckleberries slaked my hunger and thirst at once with their feral juices; how the sun glanced off the fir boughs when it broke through Pahto's cloud cap, like the day's own promise of warmth; how the coyotes sounded Bigfoot's helpless rage, howling by day, when our — *our*— territory was invaded by the screaming fighters ripping the air just above treetop level. But nowhere did I feel the heart of the hairy ape leap in my breast more sharply than at Snagtooth, where all signs of change washed away in the waters of the canyon and the shadows of the old trees, and the odor I smelled might have been the musk of my own mate.

At these times I felt the joy of life that any superbly at-home animal of middling intellect must sense in its surroundings. I palped the tastes and textures and smells and sounds that make up the existence of a beast abroad on the land. And I perceived at least a spark of the short circuit animals operate on, when stimulus drives right into the base of the brain and from there to the limbs and the gut and the heart, wasting no time on needless thought. In these flickers of feeling I passed through the hide and into the mind and bones of the giant.

But I also sensed something of the confusion, fear, and outrage that a sentient creature must suffer when its providence — its habitat — is being overwhelmed by forces foreign to its ken. When these sensations came, Jekyll-like, I lapse-dissolved back into myself, for my own prejudices were showing through. Maybe Squirrel doesn't know about change, perhaps Puma doesn't care, and Sasquatch is immune. Yet I (now firmly back in my own brain) believe that if monsters walk, they need wildness to do it in. And after looking out at the forest from its red eyes, I see Bigfoot fading away like Tinker Bell. Dozing there by Snagtooth, I dreamed a great shape dissolving into the dim mosslight, trailing its fetid perfume behind it, diminishing, diminishing.

- - -

I awoke, chilled and stiff and hungry, to a vague emptiness. After losing her love, Edna Saint Vincent Millay described a place of sadness as that "where never fell his foot." That's how I felt awakening here. What if that big fat foot once fell but shall no more? Or, worse, has never fallen here or anywhere else, and my private myth is just a public dream after all?

Now the sun was sinking, and melancholy was a mood I could not afford if I wanted to get out of the forest by dark. So I said good-bye to Snagtooth. Wren song warbled far off, a woodpecker rattled like a voice inside. Then, as I rounded a bend, Quartz Creek muffled, the silence was palpable. A big downed log spanned eighty feet of the gorge, rising thirty feet to gain the far side. I declined to cross it. Would Bigfoot? Has Bigfoot?

This is so deep, I thought as I walked, so wild — no place to hide, my foot! After all, D. B. Cooper parachuted into these woods and was never found. And he didn't even know his way around. Nor did I, apparently. I lost the trail in the dimming green light after detouring around a massive log. All I had to do was work my way downstream to find the trail eventually. Even so, I felt a rare little sense of alarm. One *could* get lost in the big bush — and who wants to go orienteering in the dark?

A fly finished its day's flight. Quartz Creek glistened far below a bluff, cedar foliage far above, both colored Eliot Porter golds by the last sun. I passed the pika rocks, but the animals did not show; maybe they thought I was Grendel come to eat their heads off. Then the fern swale, smelling of good, sweet tea, erasing the memory of the putrid odor at Snagtooth. And so to the clear-cut and into the open again.

Then, discovering that I had lost the sweet-scented fern I'd collected for identification, I returned happily to the swale for more. Emerging again, I gasped, like a fish coming up for the second time, drowning in the open air. I didn't dare go back inside once more, or I might never have left the forest again.

III – DEVILS IN HEAVEN

11

Whistling with Bigfoot

The literature and art of nature and the myths of Indians are
the wellsprings of environmental sanity, leading back into the
earth itself.

— Ted Levin, *Blood Brook*

ON THE FIRST DAY of autumn I traveled up the Lewis River once
again, then south, beyond the Dark Divide, to the highlands
where Indians have gathered berries for thousands of years.

My brief time out had been hot and clear at Gray's River, but with
the equinox came the clouds. Fall expressed itself in the early reds of
maples and poison oak along the Kalama Bluffs. East of Woodland I
paused at the site of the Finn Hall, where in 1916 Finnish pioneers
founded a literary association (Kirjallisuus Seura) and a lending library. A grove of skinny cottonwoods surrounded the site of the old
hall, where all sorts of cultural events took place in the early days.
Only an interpretive sign reminds us of the rich Finnish culture that
so briefly flowered here. The generalized American mix absorbed it
in no time. In turn, and almost as rapidly, the mongrel European
advance displaced the native civilization that went before. Aided by
disease, the white wave swept over the Yakamas and Klickitats, the
Chinookan peoples, and the rest with a speed that must have seemed
miraculous to all.

Passing through, you could be forgiven for imagining that nothing whatever remained of the native culture — or for not imagining it
at all. Yet up the Lewis from Woodland, near the village of Ariel, a
pocket of the past resides in the compound of Chief Lelooska and his
family. Don Smith is a Cherokee who received the name Lelooska in a
Nez Perce adoption at age thirteen. Later he was also adopted by a
Kwakiutl clan. Don's studies of Kwakiutl ways go back forty years, and

for the past thirty-three he has worked to convey the traditional ways of story and dance to those who would know and respect them. When the dancers enter the cedar longhouse through a scrim of alder smoke, you might as well be in Alert Bay, British Columbia, before the British, before Columbia.

The winter ceremonies that Chief Lelooska performs for visitors mimic the old ways that were the mastic of Kwakiutl society. The villages occupied many green invaginations in the long coastline, abutting yet culturally separate from the many other native groups of the maritime Northwest. People came together in winter to perform and watch the Hamatsa dances, the youth-becoming-chief ceremonies that reaffirmed the lineages and myths on which their rainy salmon-and-cedar world was based.

Different families possess varying versions of the Hamatsa stories, but in many the cannibal spirit of the wild, Bokbokwollinooksiway, was central to the rites of passage. Familiars of the cannibal spirit might be the giant, Dzonoqua, and the ghost chief, Bukwus. Dzonoqua is Lelooska's chief crest, and he takes his three-part mask to potlatches to represent his family's history. To him Dzonoqua is a race of giants, certainly not all female, as one of his adoptive family's ancestors was said to have been seduced by a male Dzonoqua. Other clans think of Dzonoqua as the Wild Woman of the woods and Bukwus as the Wild Man of the woods, and they equate them with what we now call Sasquatch (from the Salish *saskehavas*).

On my way home from the coast of Vancouver Island after a long backpack one March, I visited the totem park in Victoria. There, in front of a cedar longhouse of the old kind, I came face to face with Dzonoqua in the bottom figure on a huge house pole of yellow cedar. As if emanating from her pursed lips, the winds whistled over the nearby sea cliff like the hoots and cries of the land and its spirit. I felt as Emily Carr, the noted painter of Northwest Indian land and culture, might have when she first came upon Dzonoqua on a Haida totem. In *Klee Wyck* she described this encounter in a remote village in the Queen Charlotte Islands:

Her head and trunk were carved out of, or rather into, the bole of a great red cedar. She seemed to be part of the tree itself, as if she had grown there at its heart, and the carver had only chipped away the outer wood so that you could see her . . . The eyes were two rounds of black, set in wider rounds of white, and placed in deep sockets under wide, black eyebrows. Their fixed stare bored into me as if the very life of the old cedar looked out, and it seemed that the voice of the tree itself might have burst from that great round cavity, with projecting lips, that was her mouth . . . I stood looking at her for a long, long time.

Looking into Dzonoqua's huge ovoid eyes, I remembered the magical lectures given by Professor Bill Holm at the University of Washington the previous spring, when I first learned of the winter Hamatsa dances and the role of the Wild Man and Wild Woman of the woods. Holm, of Scandinavian–Native American descent, was adopted by the Kwakiutl through the Hamatsa ceremony. He brought the color, life, and drama of the coastal dances to the receptive imaginations of his fortunate students. I will never forget Bill donning the heavy, yard-long black-and-white mask of the Raven dancer, its cedarbark fringe shaking as he emulated the footwork of the crouched dancer's exertions; or the jumpy black-and-white films he showed by Franz Boas of long-ago Hamatsas; and the foamberry whip, smoked salmon, and vile oil of the candlefish, called *oolichan*, at the end-of-course feast.

But my sharpest recollection was what Holm had to say about Bigfoot. Other figures, he told us, such as Tsitsiutl, the two-headed sea serpent (and thunderbird's harpoon, according to Lelooska), have been subsumed into the metaphor of symbolic myth. Yet among the people he knows in the many bands, especially those who still live on the coast or in the forest and who have contact with the wild, belief in Dzonoqua and Bukwus is still literal: they accept Bigfoot as they accept bear, wolf, and raven. Anthropologist Wayne Suttles, in a paper entitled "Sasquatch: The Testimony of Tradition," which he delivered at a major Bigfoot conference, suggests that the Indian zoology might be so different from ours that conclusions regarding literal belief are overstated. Even so, he says it is a mistake to consign native myths to the supernatural: "For the Coast Salish, the Sasquatch is part of the natural world."

- - -

Halfway between Ariel and Cougar, at Speelyai Creek near Yale, I stopped at Reese's Store. This was where, in 1969, a hairball of students from the University of Washington met the Reeses, a pioneer family who had agreed to guide us to the huge lava tube known as Ape Cave on the south slopes of Mount St. Helens. Harry Reese had come to the upper Lewis River Valley in 1933 and had been studying the caves and other natural features of the area ever since. The Reeses warmly welcomed this band of naifs, who knew little of their way of life and disapproved of what they thought they did know. Judgmental about logging and hunting, fans of federal set-asides and gun control, war resisters all, we must have seemed pretty alien to these men of the hills. But we were harmless — this was logging's heyday, long before the eruption, the Mount St. Helens National Volcanic Monument, the listing of the spotted owl. Reese was his own brand of conservationist, who taught the local Boy Scouts to respect the world and to live by its tenets.

As he often had with the Scouts, Harry led us up into the elfin lichen-and-lodgepole forest around Ape Cave. His gangly young sons, Len, Bill, and Bob, came along. One of them pointed out a number of tree casts — holes and channels in the ground made when lava cooled around trees and roots that then burned or decayed. These cavelets led into the underworld like tunnels; some continued for many feet or yards underground or intersected with lava tubes, where magma flowed away beneath lithified roofs. During their painstaking exploration of the lavalands of St. Helens, the Reese boys had actually crawled through the casts as far as they could before backing out. We were horrified and excited to hear of these rabbit-hole rambles in the dark squeeze of the rock. None of us would have done it.

The main object of our field trip with the Reeses, Ape Cave, is one of the longest lava tubes in the world, more than two miles in length. According to speleologist William R. Halliday, lava tubes are roofed-over feeder channels that conduct fluid lava (pahoehoe) to the advancing front of the lava flow. This one formed over a streambed during a lava flow from Mount St. Helens's summit some 1,900 years ago. As our eyes adjusted to the black hole in the black rock, we could see (if nothing else) how it might be the lair of creatures beyond our ken. Ape Cave had been named by Harry's Scouts, who were dubbed Mount St. Helens Apes once they had toured the cave and undergone a ceremony under their leader's guidance. Harry didn't share the procedure with us, but he did tell Bigfoot stories in the dark. We felt duly initiated once we emerged into the sun. My interest in Bigfoot dates from that day.

Now, twenty years later, I found Reese's Store closed, with roses twining over the rusted tin roof. An old register of Mount Saint

Helens climbers was still on the crumbly porch; tree-cast crawling was presumably never popular enough to require a register.

— — —

All the ape monikers came from the 1924 report of the miners' encounter with "giant hairy apes" in what came to be called Ape Canyon, seven miles to the northeast. Yet Mount St. Helens's connection with Bigfoot goes much further back. In his 1854 memoir, *Wanderings of an Artist among the Indians of North America,* Paul Kane wrote of St. Helens, "Indians . . . assert that it is inhabited by a race of beings of a different species, who are cannibals, and whom they hold in great dread."

William Halliday, director of the Western Speleological Survey, claimed in his 1983 pamphlet *Ape Cave and the Mount St. Helens Apes* that the miners' attackers were actually local youths, one of whom came clean in 1982. That made the third confession of would-be hoaxers, each with a different account, that I have heard. The incident inspired a fascinating response from a Native American writer. Jorg Totsgi, editor of the *Real American* of Hoquiam, Washington, and a member of the Clallam tribe, wrote in the *Oregonian* of July 16, 1924, that "the big apes reported to have bombarded a shack of prospectors at Mount St. Helens are recognized by northwestern Indians as none other than the Seeahtlk tribe of Indians. [We] have long kept the history of the Seeahtlk tribe a secret, because the tribe is the skeleton in [our] closet."

The headlines for Totsgi's piece referred to the "apes" as "Big Hairy Indians," "Mountain Devils," "Giants," and "Shaggy Creatures." He quoted several other Indians to corroborate his facts: Henry Napolean, a Clallam; I. J. James, a Lummi; and George Hyasman, of the Quinault tribe. Totsgi wrote, "Every Indian, especially of the Puget Sound tribes, is familiar with the history of these strange giant Indians." He went on to relate experiences and traditions passed on by Shaker Indians at a gathering on the Skokomish reservation, by Henry Napolean, by his own relatives, and by others in Oregon whom he visited during his research on the Seeahtlks. He reported a consensus among his informants on the Seeahtlks' huge, hairy bodies, their ability to kill game by hypnotism, and their gift of excellent ventriloquism. They spoke, he reported, the bear language of the Clallam, as well as the bird language. They could imitate any bird, especially jays, and had a keen sense of smell and night vision. Some Northwest Indians, according to Totsgi, believed that in changing from animal to man, the Seeahtlk "did not absorb the . . . soul power, and thus became an anomaly in the Indians' process of evolution."

Totsgi's informants agreed that the big hairy Indians were harmless unless antagonized but vengeful if abused, killing twelve Indians for every Seeahtlk who was killed. He related Henry Napolean's story of making a peaceful journey through underground trails to Bigfoot caves in company with a Seeahtlk he had come across. And in a tale told by Totsgi's grandfather, Kwaichtun, a group of Clallams took a young male Seeahtlk across Hood Canal in their boat after capturing him near Seabeck. The creature escaped, but that night "the Seeahtlk tribe came down and killed every Clallam there but Kwaichtun, who had moved his family across the canal."

Totsgi also reported that "Indians at times have been greatly humiliated by the Seeahtlks' vulgar sense of humor. The Seeahtlks play practical jokes upon them and steal their Indian women. Sometimes an Indian woman comes back. More often she does not, and it is even said by some northwestern Indians that they have a strain of the Seeahtlk blood in them."

This story was followed in that issue of the *Oregonian* by a brief account of the posse that investigated the miners' report, headlined "Apeman Hunt Broadening; Kelso Police Chief and Others Go to Spirit Lake." Chief George Miller had set out with Charles Palmer "for an outing," and they were followed by Bert Wall, James Foley, James Murphy, and Bud Edgar, to be joined by County Game Warden Leichhartd. The party firmly expressed its disbelief that "any such animals exist in that territory," but they went to investigate the story of "apemen" anyway. Just as true believers sometimes "find" things that aren't there, rock-solid skeptics often miss what is. In any case, the posse came back apeless.

The apes of St. Helens, hoax or no, are still remembered, though George Miller and Bud Edgar have long since entered the permanent purgatory of anonymity. Jorg Totsgi's reply to the incident demonstrated exactly what Bill Holm had told us: that a literal belief in Bigfoot is widespread among the native tribes.

The earliest known written account of Indians and apes is found in the *Diary of Elkanah Walker.* In 1840 Walker, a would-be missionary among the Spokane Indians, described "a race of giants" inhabiting a snowclad mountain to the west — St. Helens? They came by night, the natives told him, stealing people and salmon, leaving tracks some eighteen inches long. "If the people are awake," Walker wrote, "they always know when they are coming very near, by the smell which is most intolerable." Bigfoot-like accounts from Indian territory have proliferated ever since.

The names and details change, but the idea remains the same. Seeahtlk equates with Seeahtik, Seeahtkch, Sehlatiks, Salatiks, Seatco, and Saskehavas of other bands and tribes and with the more modern version, Sasquatch. The Coast Salish people of the Skagit Valley speak of See'atco or Kauget — One Who Runs and Hides. According to their legend, Sasquatch evolved from survivors of a raid on a Salish village conducted by a northern slaving tribe. Exiled to Whidbey Island, the villagers acquired night vision and the use of invisibility, as well as body hair, size, and strength. According to a caption under a print of the retreating See'atco by artist Frank Anton Woll, "with each decade the Sasquatch became larger, stronger, and spiritually more powerful, thus increasingly elusive."

Some of the many other names of beings that might be something like Bigfoot include Wampus, a legendary monster of the forests in the Oregon Cascades; Xi'lgo and Yi'dyi'tay, the Tillamook Wild Woman and Wild Man; At'at'ahila among the Chinookans; Qah-lin-me, devourer of Yakamas; and Omah, of the Yurok to the south. Most of these names and others have been compiled by Henry Franzoni of Portland, who has studied monster names with respect to Northwest geography.

A vast body of lore pertains to Ste-ye-hah'mah, also called Stick-shower Man or Stick Man. The Yakama word means a spirit hiding under the cover of the woods. Some say the "stick" refers to this habit, others that these creatures poke sticks into lodges to extract or harass victims, or rain sticks down upon them. In a recent Quinault story, women put out shallow baskets of salmon and other food, and See'atco takes the provender in exchange for firewood, which he places in the basket — another "stick" connection. Some Indians consider Stick Men to be spirits whose name should not even be mentioned; Don Smith — Lelooska — thinks the Stick Men have merely been conflated with Bigfoot.

The impressive fact, especially in light of the many versions with their seeming contradictions, is that all of the original Northwest people have a strong Bigfoot tradition. And this continues into modern times, if somewhat diluted by the cultural amnesia brought on by massive forced change. Eva Jerry of the Muckleshoots, near Seattle, told a wealth of Sasquatch stories until her recent death. And Fostine Lone Tree, a Puyallup/Quillayute from Port Hudson, Washington, told me that her mother, as a young girl at Muckleshoot, would hear Bigfeet whistling at dusk. She would whistle with them, and her mother would say, "You come in right now and quit whistling with Seeat-kos!" Fostine remembers that when her brother told of an encounter near Quilcene, she said, "I want a Bigfoot too!"

- - -

Miles and miles of desolate, road-gouged clear-cuts and stumphills lined the highway side of Swift "Lake," the third obstruction to the flow of the river named for Meriwether Lewis. The forests and canyons on the south side of the reservoir stared back, awaiting their fate. An embayment of logging slash, washed down from clear-cuts above, contained by log booms and policed by gulls, stretched for hundreds of yards: a delta of cellulose-bound nitrogen clotting the swollen limb of the phlebitic river. The boat launch at Swift Forest Camp (part of Puget Power & Light's mitigation for the reservoir) was no longer usable on account of slash flotsam. Some logs were being salvaged near the campground. I decided not to camp by that racket, even though the day was running down.

Across the reservoir gaped a big glacial hanging valley named Paradise, and the map showed logging roads into even that far redoubt. Paradise must have well described the Lewis River valley before the dams, before the roads. I can't help but wonder what a native from the paradise days would think of it now. If a Hamatsa dancer were to be swept from the longhouse into the present reality, could he even comprehend what he saw? Perhaps he'd think that Raven, creator of the universe, had lost his mind and was taking things apart again. Or that Trickster Coyote had made a great puzzle of the landscape just to confuse the People. Or maybe that Seeahtlk had run amok. Someone *has* run amok. All of us have.

I headed up Old Man Pass into a painting made of the vague colors of dusk, fog, vine maples, and lichen. The mist closing in made me wonder whether as many people think they are seeing bear when they see Bigfoot as the reverse. How good to be back in the fragrant, unpeopled silence! As the dark climbed the hill behind me, I made a dinner of pepperoni stick, Rainier Ale, cherry tomatoes from home, and a brownie and coffee from the Cougar Cafe. A varied hare tried to dart beneath the car, but missed by a whisker. Bach harpsichord inventions on the tape deck choreographed her footwork as she shot into the black wood.

Since the eruption, interpretive signs have sprouted like puffballs across the Gifford Pinchot. Outlaw Ridge Volcanic Viewpoint, with no other visitors, offered a fogscape. It seemed strange to see signs up here — Carson to the right, Trout Lake and the Sawtooth Berry Fields to the left. I went left and up out of the fog. Sunset glow lightened the sky, and a slender crescent moon rose on this first night of autumn, with a real twinkler of a star, rubies and blue, just off its horn in a halo. Pink stains and cotton rags filled the valleys below in a vague afterglow.

Mount Adams lay dead ahead, Rainier off to the left. As I drove a little farther on, Mount St. Helens, now blunted, stood out in clear silhouette against the light western sky. Lone Butte still had its old sharp shape. The buttes and ridges rode above the valleys on a woolly rug.

In the deep dark I came to the Sawtooth Berry Fields. A sign read "Huckleberries on this (east) side of the road reserved for Indians." Another sign warned of "congestion," but at 8:21 P.M. there was no one about but us Bigfeet. The road crossed the Pacific Crest Trail, where I stopped to stretch, listen, and pee. I felt as if Seeahtlks were close at hand, but I saw none. The stars, however, were fabulous over the church-spire firs. I realized now that the moon and its twinkler were actually setting; they had just seemed to be rising near Lone Butte because of the fog. Realities run muddy in the mountain mists, as I'd found many times before, but it was a lesson never quite learned.

I tried to pick a commemorative berry from the Sawtooth Fields (Anglo side), but the bushes were picked bare. How different this was from Juniper Ridge, where the bushes drooped under the weight of their fruits. The nightly low fighter flew over, a little higher here than over Yellowjacket, but still no great favor to the seekers after silence along the Pacific Crest Trail. I remembered the signs outside Oak Harbor, Washington, posted by the Whidbey Island Naval Air Station: "Excuse our noise — it's the sound of freedom!" and was reassured.

Near the Cold Springs Indian Forest Camp, I saw the green eye-shine of an animal by the road, slowed to spot it, and was surprised to find a pussycat, gray and white, longhaired. I thought it must be abandoned, but then I came upon a homemade double-decker bus with a collie outside. Wanting to see this better, I spent the night nearby. By daylight I could see clearly that this incredible bus consisted of two Volkswagen microbuses merged end to end on top of an erstwhile school bus, the three vehicles sharing a green hide. Tarps spread out from the main structure shaded dogs, cats, kittens, three bikes, even a small flock of chickens. There was no sign of folks about the place. It was the ultimate nomadic hippie home.

I wondered whether this out-of-the-loop family was mimicking the autumn lifeway of the Indians who moved to the berry fields for weeks in the fall to gather *olallie*. Or — I was vaguely disturbed by the thought — maybe this *was* what was left of the Indian encampments. But it was parked on the whites' side of the road.

Soon enough I came upon the real thing. The Cold Springs Indian Camp had the ghost of a traditional longhouse, an uncovered pole structure with no pretensions of prettiness. A sign read KAH-PUS-PAW / COLD SPRINGS LONGHOUSE / P-SOW-WA-SWA-KOTH / SAWTOOTH MOUNTAIN. Bedsprings, perhaps for drying berries, lay over pits full of trash. The methods have changed, but the point is the same. As Keith McCoy wrote in *The Mount Adams Country*:

> Most of the berries were dried on grass or willow mats spread in sunny spots. Others, by the age-old method, were dried on mats tilted toward a burning log so the heat of the sun could be bolstered by the heat and smoke of the elongated fire. The Indians had a code of honor which, it is hoped, persists these 50 years later. A berry field campsite, its drying log, and even its tepee poles leaned in a tree for the next year's use were never violated by another tribesman.

McCoy wrote that at the berry fields, baskets and bags, beadwork and buckskin, wapato and camas roots might all change hands in the brisk intertribal trade. If not such a traditional scene, I had hoped at least to find someone in residence at Sawtooth. But the camp was deserted. The berry season had peaked and the gatherers had gone on.

Nearby, at the Surprise Lakes Camp, some sites were still occupied. I saw some ponies but no people, except some white bow-hunters in camo and greasepaint walking on the dusty road. The Surprise Lakes were just that: little blue lakes tucked into the red folds of the huckleberry flats, mountain ash gold and orange all around, with Pahto peeking over the eastern horizon like an eagle's head looking away. Three female goldeneyes floated and dove on one of the ponds. The huckleberries might be gone, but wild strawberries were fully in bloom. Inspired by the strawberries and the psychedelic green bus, I wondered: Are these berry fields forever?

I looked for an answer in the Forest Plan for the Gifford Pinchot National Forest. The pole-frame longhouse at Cold Springs is used by the Kah-milt-pah band of the Yakama Indian Nation for yearly gatherings and ceremonies in honor of the huckleberry harvest. This is only one of many ways that the native inhabitants use the area. The plan reveals that members of the Yakama Nation (including the Klickitats), the federally unrecognized Cowlitz tribes, and the Warm Springs and Umatilla Indians have all used the Gifford Pinchot for a very long time. Today the sites they have frequented lie in several wilderness areas and more or less actively managed parts of the forest.

On June 9, 1855, Kamaiakun, on behalf of the Yakamas and many related bands, signed a treaty with Governor Isaac Stevens. The treaty guaranteed the tribes continuing rights to fish, hunt, gather roots and berries, and graze animals "at all usual and accustomed places." In recent years this and related treaties have been upheld in legal disputes about contemporary fishing practices, profoundly affecting relations between Indians and whites. Only now is the situation beginning to sort itself out as the salmon fisheries collapse for all, thanks to the dams. The berry wars have been subtler, with no large economic implications. But the gathering and drying of *Vaccinium*/huckleberries/*olallie* is no small matter to the traditional occupants of the uplands, for whom berries have always been important for winter subsistence. Even "modern" Indians, such as the women I'd prevailed upon to give me a lift from Juniper Ridge, consider berry gathering an important spiritual closure to the summer, whether or not they need the berries for nutrition. And it's not just huckleberries: according to the Forest Plan, traditionally used plants included nuts, bitterroot, camas tubers, other berries, and many other edibles; bark, roots, beargrass, and other fibers for weaving and basketry; and a wide array of medicinal and ceremonial herbs.

Before the dams were built on the Columbia and Lewis rivers, the berry gatherers made expeditions back and forth between Indian Heaven (as the entire huckleberry uplands were then called) and the main salmon-fishing spots such as Celilo Falls on the Columbia and Chickoon Creek on the Lewis. Dried berries and salmon pounded into pemmican went together the same way that whipped soapberry, eulachon (candlefish) oil, and smoked salmon did for the Kwakiutl.

Vast shifting gatherings took place as the people followed the ways of the seasons — berries to salmon, stories to games, campfire to long-house. As recently as 1911, more than a thousand Indians convened at Indian Race Track in the southern part of Indian Heaven, where the women gathered and dried berries and the men raced horses and gambled prior to the late autumn hunts.

It is easy to see why Washington's southern Cascades came to be called Indian Heaven. For the relatively few Indians who had survived the early onslaught of diseases and other risks, everything remaining of the good life they'd known could be found there. But the last horse race in Indian Heaven took place in 1928, and in the next decades the dams were built. The treaties' many loopholes allowed whites to acquire much of the best land within the boundaries of the reservations, and conditions changed in nearly all of the "usual and accustomed places" of traditional usufruct. As the Forest Plan modestly concedes, "Timber management activities generally result in some level of ground disturbance to a site." After logging, skidding, burning, spraying, and planting, nary a berry, beargrass clump, or sacred site is likely to be left.

To give them their due, the Gifford Pinchot planners attempt to take Indian needs into consideration these days. As they rightly conclude, "Native American values and value systems are inextricably linked with the use of Forest resources for both economic subsistence and sacred/religious purposes. For many, 'Indianness' is centered on the ability to carry out these activities and to obtain the resources necessary to do so." They seem sincere, if turgid, when they write of ways in which native religious systems can "potentially interface with National Forest management."

For example, in the 1980s the managers decided not to sell any more beargrass permits to whites in areas regularly used by Yakama basketmakers. And in 1932 the so-called Handshake Agreement set aside the eastern part of the Sawtooth Berry Fields for the exclusive use of Indians, thus diminishing the tensions arising even then between native pickers and recreating whites. But that area might not be enough now. Forest succession is rendering the old berry fields unproductive, and the number of nonnative berry pickers — whether arriving in homemade buses, motor homes, or mountain bikes — is growing all the time.

The Forest Plan says "the supply of berry fields is endless," yet admits there is likely to be increasing competition. And while it is true that "huckleberries grow well in disturbed and burned areas," not all forms of disturbance promote their fruiting. Herbicides, for example, used in many forestry operations, do not help. Recalling that Northwest timber interests once referred to the forests themselves as "endless," I would regard that term with circumspection if I were a Yakama. But then, if I were a Yakama, I would take *everything* the whites say with plenty of salt and keep my potential interfaces to a minimum.

- - -

Six months before Kamaiakun signed his treaty, Sealth had done the same for the Duwamish. Kamaiakun got five hundred dollars a year, a comfortable house, and ten plowed acres to be the go-between for his confederated bands and the government. Sealth (Seattle) got a city, a statue, and a famous eco-speech that he might or might not have uttered in some form or other. Eventually Seattle became a metropolis where American Indians make up the poorest minority. The Yakamas, though deprived of their salmon by dams and jailed when they tried to carry out the terms of the treaty, at least retain a substantial land base, berries and all. Also it is difficult to find a Duwamish Indian with any direct knowledge of Bigfoot, while the Yakamas, though reluctant to talk with prying whites, retain a rich Bigfoot tradition.

Marlene Simla is the great-granddaughter of Chief Spencer of the Klickitats. Now a Yakama child welfare specialist who works for a tribal agency called Nak-Nu-We-Sha ("we care"), she shared with me the story of Bigfoot as child-minder on Potato Hill's berry fields. Marlene knew two old stories of abduction. In the first a long-strided giant put pitch over a girl's eyes to take her away. Another time a baby on a cradleboard was said to have been taken at Potato Hill while her mother gathered berries. This tale has long been used to keep children from straying. The time came when Marlene told the story to her own children while berrying at Potato Hill. (Chief Lelooska says that these days the threat of Bigfoot is used to mediate squabbles over the TV.)

A friend of Marlene's, Mary Schlick, is a student of basketry who has her own Potato Hill story. When her husband worked for the BIA, she lived on reservations, and her enthusiasm for basketry began with dogbane-fiber hats made by the Warm Springs weavers. Then she discovered cornhusk bags made with dogbane and hop strings (but not cornhusks). One fall at Toppenish in the Yakama Nation, having missed the berry season, Mary "traded" dollars for a gallon of huckleberries. They had been picked on Potato Hill by Gracie Ambrose, and they came not in the usual ice cream container but in a beautiful coiled, step-design berry basket made of cedar bark and beargrass. Gracie told her to save the leaves and take them back to the berry fields so the harvest would be good the next year.

The First People respected many such traditions in their use of *olallie*. When the berries ripened, no family was to eat them until one designated house held the "first feast" — a ceremony with counterparts in the salmon harvest and other foods. Many names have to do with berries. According to Seattle anthropologist Eugene Hunn, writing in *A Columbia River Reader*, Indian Heaven was once known as *ayan-as*, or lovage place, for a medicinal root that could be gathered there. The Klickitats camped at *pswawas-waakul* (sawlike), now the Sawtooth Berry Fields. "All gathered," Hunn wrote, "to socialize, trade, and race horses at *Kalamat*, 'yellow pond-lily,'" a broad meadow astride the Klickitat Trail. These organic names evoke the folds and patterns in the blanket of the land. It is good to know that our own language can do better than "potentially interface with National Forest management." In fact it was on a national-forest nature trail in Vermont where I found Robert Frost's description of the berries whose "blue's but a mist from the breath of the wind."

As I dropped off the bushy heights toward Cultus Creek, I thought of the importance these high ghost-moth heaths have had in the lives of the native peoples. And I thought of how the "city Indians," as my friends from the Saddle called themselves, even if they come back for berries, have lost touch with the giant hairy Indians. Later, when I read Jorg Totsgi's account of the Seeahtlk of Ape Canyon, I was struck by the name's similarity to Seattle, or Sealth, also spelled See-alt, See-ualt, See-yat, and Se-at-tlh. Is it possible, I wondered, that the Emerald City, through its native namesake, actually honors Sasquatch?

- - -

The berry-field campgrounds I'd thought of using were all designated for Indians, and my English-Scots/Irish-German genes vastly outweigh my little scrap of Algonkian, so I went on to the Forest Service's big Cultus Creek Campground, which was empty. I took a pleasant site in a fir grove beside rustling Cultus Creek. When night came, it was all stars; there was no need for my tent. I fell asleep quickly but had only a light night's rest, with small animals mothing frequently about my head and a nightmare in which I was carried away by Bigfoot. The sound of the stream was in it, the only such dream I've ever had. I cried out, waking myself up. As I lay stretching my stiff legs, with deer mice dancing on my bag, I ran through the various stories I'd read of Bigfoot abductions. With a few notable exceptions, the victims have been females, which accords with the Indians' stories of Seeahtlks occasionally making off with their women. In that case I had little to worry about.

But the stars had shifted, and as I watched them and waited for either sleep or dawn, I couldn't help but think about the stories. How rich the Native American storehouse of Seeahtlk traditions! Few of them are found in books, since their owners are seldom willing to share the tales with Bigfoot investigators, after generations of exploitation by ethnologists, as they see it. I recalled my good fortune in hearing a dramatic and heretofore unpublished story of an encounter with Bigfoot.

The previous spring I had led staff and board members of the Portland-based Ecotrust, an organization devoted to conservation of the temperate rain forest, on an outing into an old-growth cedar reservation. After days of meetings, words, documents, and figures, the conservationists were eager to get out of doors to see something of the resource they were laboring to protect. I guided them up a closed logging road, then into the deep duff of the cedar wood, where giant candelabras of western red cedars punctured the forest roof and moss padded the floor. For a while we dispersed among fluted trunks as big around as redwoods, losing ourselves among their quiet mass.

On the way back out I found myself walking with Gerald Amos, a former chief of the Haisla Nation of coastal British Columbia. The Kitimaat Haisla were working with Ecotrust to protect the watershed of the Kitlope River, which they call Husduwachsdu. Kitlope, Tsimshian for "people of the rocks," embraces the greatest remaining Canadian rain forest. When the subject of Bigfoot came up, Gerald told me a remarkable story from his village. Later Alan Hall, grandson of the original teller, Billy Hall, recounted the story in more detail. I have his permission to share it here in his words, just as he told it by a campfire in the Kitlope forest.

— Welcome to our campfire. Tonight I am going to tell you a story about my grandfather, the late Billy Hall, how he encountered those hairy monsters we call Sasquatch. This is a true story. There is nothing mythical about what I am going to tell you, because it is a true story based on the experience that he had with these monsters. These monsters that we are talking about are real, as real as you and I who are sitting here.

My grandfather was preparing for hunting bears, when there was a good market for bear pelts. When my forefathers prepared to go hunting for anything, they went through a ritual of purification. They purified themselves by bathing regularly with devil's club, or whatever was at hand to use. My grandfather and his first cousin, Robert Nelson — these two guys were never separated. He and Robert were like brothers, really. They went through all this purification during the wintertime to get ready to go hunting bears during the months of April and May.

My grandfather owned a place just across from Kemano, a little bit further down the channel we called Muskook, a sandy beach there. And up above Muskook are three valleys. One is the Muskook Valley, another one is where sweetgrass grew and it was called Sweetgrass Valley. They ventured out to go and hunt there. My grandfather had an uncle named Kwabellish, who looked after the canoe down at the beach while they went hunting. So they went up, and Robert Nelson and my grandfather parted. Robert went up one valley and my grandfather went up to the Sweetgrass Valley. They broke a little sapling, and whoever came back first was to plant the sapling in the ground to let the other guy know that he had come down ahead of him to the ford.

My grandfather reached his destination. Where he went, at that place there was a great big rock. He had his oolichan that he used for broth, and he was eating it and walking around this rock, wondering if there was any significance to it. Then he went and sat down to finish his meal and looked across the river and saw what he thought were bears. They were black, and there was nothing unusual about them; he was going to go there and shoot them and skin them for their pelts. But as he went there and tried to sneak up on them, he had a hard time crossing the river. He wasn't sure which way he was going to shoot these bears.

It wasn't until he aimed and shot, at the instant of impact, that he heard these human beings howling. He knew it was a human being [that he shot]. Then he saw them start to run — and they were running upright. And he knew they weren't bears. But the one that he shot, he lived for a while and then he died. My grandfather started pushing the panic button, for he saw that these were not bears, and he saw one that never had any hair on the body at all, and it was a female. He saw that it had breasts just like a human female and he knew that he had done something wrong.

So he took another look again before he went into shock and he saw this band of Sasquatches and watched them pick up the dead one, and they were crying like human beings. Then he went into shock. He didn't remember how he came out of it and crossed the river — he remembered that he had a hard time crossing. He came out of the shock momentarily and he was up on top of the great big rock — he didn't know how he got up there! And through all the process, with the instinct of survival, he took stock of his situation. He felt something poking on the inside of his leg and he looked at it, felt it. He found out that his hunting knife was lodged there. He knew he had put that there for a purpose. Then he heard and felt the presence of some other beings close by him. He looked down and there were two of these big male Sasquatches. They were trying to get onto the rock with him, but they couldn't. He knew they were trying to communicate with him, but they couldn't. He told them, in our own language, that he had made a mistake. He apologized to them in our language, that what harm he had done was not done intentionally. The big Sasquatches seemed to understand him, and both turned and started walking away from him.

Since it was getting close to darkness, my grandfather told himself, "I'm going to make a run for it." So he climbed down from the rock and ran. He ran down towards the canoe on the beach. He ran tirelessly until he suddenly found out he had run past the place where he was supposed to set the peg, the sapling. So he ran back, got the sapling, put it in the ground so that Robert would know that he was down on the beach already.

He made it down to the beach, and before he reached it, he hollered to his uncle to launch the canoe, "I am in trouble!" By the time he reached the beach, Kwabellish had the canoe down the beach. When he got there, he told Kwabellish to get into the canoe. He looked back and saw the two monsters running down the beach after him. My grandfather told Kwabellish what had happened to him. So the old man started talking to these big beasts the way my grandfather had talked to them on top of the rock, telling them in our language that it was all a mistake. So the beasts turned around and went away.

Then my grandfather and the old man had to wait in the area until about noon the next day, when Robert came down. By then my grandfather had lapsed into a coma. He started to throw up, and what he threw up was saturated with the smell of those animals, and that smell saturated the canoe. They were able to go back to Kemano, but he didn't come out of the coma for four days.

My grandfather, when he came around, was able to do all kinds of things he hadn't been able to do before. He was able to communicate with other creatures. In those times they were waiting for the oolichan to come up the Kitlope River and it was during that time that he was sitting on the beach and he started communicating with all these creatures out in the sea. The oolichan told him that they were going to be there the next day, so the old man told his people to start off for Kitlope from Kemano. The oolichan, sure enough, came up the next day. He believed the spirit of a medicine man named Kolalli entered his body when he was in a coma. So he was able to perform the feats that the medicine man before him could do. . . . These are the things that happened during his lifetime.

- - -

When Alan Hall tells this family tradition, his campfire guests shiver. But they see that the stunning encounter, as terrifying as it was for Billy Hall, also brought him power. So it often is in the heartfelt tales of Indians meeting with giants. And the power continued into the next generation: when a giant logging company determined to log the Kitlope, the Haisla resisted with stronger determination. In cooperation with Ecotrust, they peacefully wrested an accommodation from the company.

In the summer of 1994, a year after Alan told his grandfather's story, the British Columbian premier announced that 800,000 acres of the Kitlope would be preserved without any logging whatever. The West Fraser Timber Company both received and gave praise for the unusually cooperative result. As the Kitimaat Haisla celebrate this amazing victory around their campfires with their Ecotrust friends, Billy Hall's story will be told again, along with a new story: how the greatest temperate rain forest has been saved for the people and all its creatures. In this battle of the Titans, Bigfoot wins, and everyone else wins too.

— — —

As I lay awake beside Cultus Creek, the story of the Kitlope Sasquatch came back to me. Although unique, in many particulars the story conformed with the others I had heard. One of the most distinctive features of the Indians' Sasquatch is that they are always represented as either devils or an outcast tribe possessed by demons — wild people. Rather than a different kind of animal, as we tend to conceive of it, Bigfoot appears to the natives of its territory as either supernatural or human — but beyond the pale of convention and acceptability. Some call them simply demons. Many place names in the Pacific Northwest that include the word "Devil" or "Devil's" have been connected with Indian myths of Bigfoot or other monsters: ten lakes in Washington alone, as well as a Devil's Slide, Devil's Washbasin, several Devil's Peaks, and Diablo Reservoir.

We shouldn't be surprised when Native Americans define the hairy creatures as something close to themselves, for every report confirms Bigfoot's hominoid traits. On the other hand, its enormous strength, night vision, and other unusual attributes could easily suggest a supernatural being. Nor should we be surprised that the obvious third option — a related species of primate, neither human nor spectral — does not suggest itself to Indians. This, I surmise, is because native North Americans are one of the few groups of aboriginal humans who have had no contact with primates other than themselves (and perhaps Bigfoot).

South American Indians have New World monkeys as neighbors. African and Indo-Asian tribes are well acquainted with Old World monkeys, baboons, apes, and orangs. North Americans, with no construct equivalent to "primate," would consider their own form unique in nature. A large, apelike animal would naturally seem a kind of giant hairy Indian; or, if it was too weird and perverse to be of the People, then a devil. Where there are no apes, all apes are humans, or spirits.

I read a similar interpretation in Roger L. Welsch's article "Omaha Dance Lessons" in *Natural History,* concerning Native American humor. Asked by a stranded traveler if he had a monkey wrench, an old Omaha man regarded his gamboling grandchildren and laughed,

"Monkey ranch? No, these are my grandkids." We can appreciate the joke since our kids are monkeys too. But among the Omahas this goes deeper: monkey is the trickster figure, Icktinike, and tricksters share their powers and vulnerability with children. "I have heard again and again from Omahas the story about the first time an Omaha saw a monkey in a nineteenth-century traveling carnival," Welsch wrote. "The immediate response of the Omahas was 'Icktinike!' Having never seen a monkey, having never seen Icktinike, they all agreed: the monkey is Icktinike; Icktinike is a monkey."

Certain artifacts suggest that some Amerindians were acquainted with *something* having the visage of an ape. A number of carved stone heads found in the Columbia River basin and masks from the Tsimshian and other north coastal tribes possess strong primate features. The resemblance was noted as long ago as 1877 by pioneer paleontologist Othniel Marsh, who reported to the American Association for the Advancement of Science, "Among the many stone carvings [from the Columbia] were a number of heads, which so strongly resemble those of apes that the likeness at once suggests itself."

These ancient effigies include prognathous, chinless faces with heavy brow ridges and in at least one case a sagittal crest. Their age is unknown, but they are considered prehistoric. Scientists who don't know where they are from usually call them anthropoid; those who do know say such a conclusion is preposterous. Such reactions reinforce the view of scientists held by many Bigfooters: that they refuse to see evidence that challenges their assumptions. As writer Rick Wiggin put it, "Preferring the comfort of existing dogma to the intellectual embarrassment of gross scientific error" — the error of having overlooked a large primate on their doorsteps. The relics do not prove that Bigfoot exists nor that Indians had contact with apes, but they do raise uncomfortable questions.

In the cosmology that many Indian beliefs describe, the border between the "natural" and "spiritual" worlds is a permeable membrane indeed. When I asked Lelooska whether Indians of his acquaintance considered Sasquatch real, I learned that it might be the wrong question altogether. First, he explained, even the Kwakiutl differ among themselves on many points of tradition. Second, reality for them varies and shifts in meaning. An elder told him that there are many ways of existence that whites know nothing at all about. To many coastal Indians Dzonoqua might be as real as a bear. But a bear might change its nature as easily as Bigfoot.

For this reason Marjorie Halpin, convener of the 1978 "Sasquatch and Related Phenomena" symposium, suggested "enlarging the context within which the Sasquatch phenomena are considered. Specifically . . . we should examine the full context within which the creature is seen, rather than continue to dwell almost exclusively on *what* is seen, on the object as a thing in itself." Or, as anthropologist Wayne Suttles said at the same conference, "While Sasquatch-like creatures may inhabit the real world of the Indians, this may not be relevant to the question of whether they inhabit the real world of Western science."

Once, on a horseback ride in Monument Valley, a Navajo wrangler named Harold charged our group of nature writers to "take your imagination out of your back pocket." That is good advice for all of us who spend too much time locked in a box we call reality. However, as Thoreau said about the imagination, "Give it the least license, [it] dives deeper and soars higher than Nature goes." I have no doubt that many Bigfoot encounters flow from soaring imaginations loosed from the back pocket or any other bounds.

As we confront questions that we expect to have answers, we are left perched awkwardly on a two-horned dilemma: do we accept the Indians' relative universe, where beaver and Bigfoot, magic and muscle, are all expressions of the same thing? Or do we stick with our own material tradition and demand an answer devoid of metaphysical paradox? You can take your pick. But if the stone heads and plaster casts of footprints are as solid as they seem, the day might come when we no longer have to choose — when the fur and the campfire smoke coalesce into something we all can call real.

- - -

Apes, demons, or great hairy humans, there have always been devils in Indian Heaven according to the stories. Now, as the river fish decline to the vanishing point and the competition for berries exceeds the provisions of the Handshake Agreement of 1932; as white affluence expands and Indian poverty just stays the same; and as the government in its wisdom parses the future of the forest that once was theirs, the Indians have cause to revise the stories. It becomes as clear as mountain meltwater just who the devils are: another tribe, all right, but not the giant ones. I don't doubt that the tribes would take Seeahtlks and Dzonoqua back in troops, if they could only erase the tracks of the manlike apes from over the sea.

12

"Bigfoot Baby Found in Watermelon, Has Elvis's Sneer"

≈≈≈

"A mysterious creature — that's news, Ishmael. The fact that people see it — that's news."
— David Guterson, *Snow Falling on Cedars*

THE LOGS IS A FINE old country tavern, a blend of modern tack and old wood and the reek of burgers and beer and smoke. Covered in creeper and striped with old mortar, it is built of green vines and conversation as much as the logs of its name.

Driving on a vanishing road that led dimly in the dusk to the forest of Monte Cristo, I turned back and dropped down to BZ Corner for a burger and a beer. Inside the tavern, piny walls held up Mount Rainier in a beer ad with illuminated animal figurines. Jolly photos of the regular patrons leered from laminated tabletops. As their neon logos promised, Bud and Rainier were on tap, but also Full Sail Ale from the Whitecap Brew Pub in the Columbia sailboard town of Hood River, down the gorge. A stuffed iguana and bowling trophies on the mantel of the great stone fireplace rounded out the decor.

At the bar, attempting a jocular tone, I asked about local Bigfoot reports. Most of the drinkers laughed it off. But one man, Hank, had grown up around Spirit Lake, where he'd heard many stories. A friend of his in Longview, a grandson of one of the 1924 Ape Canyon survivors, claimed to possess his grandfather's rifle, which was "twisted like licorice." "I know another guy," he told me, warming to it, "who came to work on a logging show and found fifty-gallon oil drums tossed off the landing like bushel baskets." He spoke of a Bigfoot sighting by a busload of people near Bellingham. "I won't discount it," said Hank. "After all — who's gonna call bullshit on it?"

Who indeed? No one can prove that Bigfoot isn't there. Perhaps we can say with some confidence that the last dusky seaside sparrow has dropped out and confirm to our satisfaction that there are no more passenger pigeons. Yet black-footed ferrets were found when all were thought to be gone, and ivory-billed woodpeckers are now known to survive in Cuba. Extinction, or absolute absence, is difficult to demonstrate. We can proclaim with confidence that there is no elephant in a given room at a given time. Lacking any likely fossils, we agree that minotaurs and unicorns probably did not walk the earth in the way that bulls and horses do. But proving the nonexistence of an animal with adequate fossil precursors in an immense area of wild and tangled character is a centaur of a different color.

The world at large might consider Bigfoot an intriguing possibility rather than a nutso folly if it weren't for the creature's enthusiastic adoption by the trashy tabloids. Whatever their entertainment value for bored shoppers queuing in supermarkets, these pulp purveyors of putty for drafty brains ensure that anything they embrace wholeheartedly (itself a dubious proposition) is sure to be regarded, by those who consider themselves sensible, as absolute codswallop.

I enjoy scanning the tabloids. Sometimes I pick a longer line (or ask Thea to take care of the checkout) so I can surreptitiously skim the more outrageous contents — the many resurrections of JFK, the omnipresence of Elvis, the obesities that make me look like a beanpole, the babies born with alligator eyes, the endless possibilities of impregnation. But as much as I enjoy the aliens ("Martians Take Over Wall Street"), the unlikely couplings ("Toddler Weds Great-grandmother"), and the wild hybrids ("Cat Gives Birth to Furred Frog"), I find myself wondering who really buys these things. Some sales go to sneering disbelievers drawn to the lurid headlines for their entertainment value. But many readers of straight prose must share my blend of fascination and horror that there are enough gullible or mindless people to keep these cynical serials afloat.

This is now the habitat of Bigfoot in the popular mind: the pages of sensational rags that trade on people's foolish hopes, real fears, and profound ignorance. How are we to consider Sasquatch seriously when his cohabitants are dead presidents, revivified rock stars, and pregnant pumpkins?

One rock "star" who is very much alive gave me some insights on Bigfoot and the tabloids. I'd enjoyed the songs of Mojo Nixon that I'd heard on the radio, such as "Elvis Is Everywhere" and "Debby Gibson

Is Pregnant with My Two-headed Love Child." One summer while teaching in Vermont, I met a singer and teacher named Bobby Parker, who is a good friend of Mojo's. The two had taken a cross-country bicycle ride some years before, during which, Bobby said, "Mojo found his name and his vision."

That vision is a sublimely twisted one of warm beer and love in old Impalas out beneath the power lines, no lost love for malls and banks, and rude romance ("My Baby Is Vibrator Dependent"). Mojo is not for everyone. But he has a remarkable handle on what makes people tick, especially people who buy the tabloids — like Don Henley's lyric in the song "If Dirt Were Dollars": "I was flyin' back from Lubbock, I saw Jesus on the plane . . . or maybe it was Elvis. You know, they kinda look the same."

When Mojo performed in Seattle, I went backstage afterward to meet him and to mention having met Bobby. But Bobby had beaten me to it; Mojo said, "Oh, yeah — you're the butterfly guy!" I wanted to ask him about Bigfoot. One of his songs, "The A-mazing Bigfoot Diet," deals with the cooption of the big fella by the tabloids. It begins "I married a Bigfoot, gave birth to my mother." Credulousness is one of Mojo's big topics. After his success with "Elvis Is Everywhere" ("You know what's going on down in that Bermuda Triangle?" asks the lyric. "Elvis needs boats!"), he installed a 1-800 Elvis line, at his own expense, to hear people's Elvis sightings and insights. Hundreds of people called in to relate their experiences with the King, exceeding even Mojo's expectations of the lowest common denominator.

"Yeah," he told me, "I figure a lot of the Bigfoot people must be like these Elvis cats."

"How's that, Mojo?" I asked.

"Well, with these folks," he replied, "it's not a matter of not having both oars in the water. They don't even have a boat!"

- - -

For a while now I've been collecting tabloid articles about Yeti-like phenomena. This not only gives me a chance to purchase the execrable items (a delicious act of virtuous slumming), but also expands my sense of how Bigfoot is viewed in these circles.

Many of the stories appear in the *Sun*, such as "I Am the Mother of Bigfoot Baby: Woman's amazing tale of survival in the wilderness." Debbie Bates was kidnapped and raped by an eight-foot Bigfoot, then escaped when he got in a fight with a grizzly. Debbie, described by writer John Coffin as being "ugly as sin," was shown happily bottle-feeding a young chimp. She shared the front-page headlines with a Civil War hero found alive in the South Carolina woods and an obsessive Presleyana collector who named his son Elvis and his home Graceland Too.

The *Sun* also revealed "Proof in Bible: Bigfoot Exists." John Coffin, something of a Sasquatch authority by now, reported on a biblical scholar's conclusion that the giants referred to in Genesis were the ancestors of Bigfoot. When the offspring of Cain bred with women, they begat the Neandertals. (This is actually not so far from Beowulf's way of accounting for Grendel.) If you turned the page you got the Terror Truck, a ghostly trucker who plays chicken with motorists on the highways of Tennessee; a dog-faced baby, and "Happy Hubby Makes 2 Sisters Pregnant 11 Times."

Another issue gave us the "First Ever Photos of Bigfoot: Mountain drama as brave climber meets 700 pounds of fighting fury." Climbing in Oregon, Leonard Morton came across a particularly fat, pear-shaped Bigfoot, with a head as big as its torso, and caught the image on his camcorder. Then "the crazed creature from hell chased the brave adventurer into a small cave, where it kept him pinned for a terrifying eight hours." Just for fun, Peter Byrne of the Bigfoot Research Project analyzed the photographs. He showed that two shots, supposedly taken some distance apart in space and time, were merely reverse views of the same pose. No surprise. William Rock's story appeared along with the genetic bonanza of a leopard girl who got a new face, a baby who glowed in the dark, a runaway boy who had a sex change operation, and a woman who gave birth to triplets of three races.

Wilderness encounters provide much of the *Sun*'s grist. "Bigfoot Captured Alive — He's Human (monster is gentle as a baby)" showed the Manitoba captive in a decidedly nongentle pose looking a lot like Lon Chaney, Jr., as Wolf Man. Of course, he escaped, so he was slightly overshadowed by the fat man who exploded after winning a pie-eating contest.

Another capture was reported in the *Weekly World News,* claiming "Scientists bag 7-foot creature in MONTANA!" Dick Donovan wrote the scoop on Dr. Leonard Owens's bagging of the beast with a tranquilizing dart. In this version the creature had the rheumy eyes, nose, and mouth of a down-and-outer captured for a makeup session and photo op outside the Salvation Army mission in Butte. The photo was as different from the *Sun*'s as a mouse is from a cat. A later issue reported his inevitable escape in the Vienna Woods, where he had been flown for tests; two armed guards were found with their skulls crushed. The lead story, even with its recycled photos of the wino from Butte, had to compete with the world's first potty-trained frog.

The *Weekly World News*'s next two Bigfoot stories had to do with babies. Tucked into an issue with a wax dummy of Hitler that cried real tears, a man who ate a live bat, and Siamese twins who fought over their boyfriend was "World's First Photo of a Bigfoot Baby." Dutch anthropologists in southwest China kidnapped the thirty-two-pound infant with six-inch feet from its screaming eight-foot mother. The baby was hairy all over except for its humanlike face. A later issue tells Katie Martin's story. Unlike Debbie Bates, Katie wasn't abducted; she met Bigfoot while hiking at Mount Rainier and fell in love when he brought her flowers and berries. Later she had his baby. The mother-son portrait showed young Kelly with ordinary limbs and a furry face with a mashed nose — just the reverse of the Chinese baby. Other stories in the *News* told of a terrified teen who touched Bigfoot in a dark barn; a hermit trapper with a Bigfoot friend who came to visit when UFOs were in the vicinity; a pair of Yetis who were air traffic controllers for a fleet of UFOs; and Chinese soldiers who shot "the world's last female Bigfoot."

Given this constant barrage of weirdness, is it any wonder that serious-minded individuals regard reports of a large, hairy humanoid with something less than openness and generosity of spirit?

- - -

What I find particularly compelling about the relegation of Bigfoot to the dregs of journalism — or to the heights of hyperbolic print entertainment, if you prefer — is the vast distance between the myth's honorable past and its present media purgatory. How did this universal archetype, whose likeness can be found in almost every culture and in whom great power has been vested for many centuries, become so degraded?

It might be valuable to review the ubiquity of hairy-giant traditions. We have seen how prevalent and enduring is the hairy-devil / wild Indian figure in West Coast Native American history. But similar entities are found among Indians all over North America, ranging from the Algonkian Windigo or Witiko, a cannibal man-beast of the

North Woods, to the Iroquois and Cherokee giants called Stoneclad. And the Pacific Coast Bigfoot figures continue north well into Alaska.

Martha Demientieff, a native Alutiiq writer and teacher whose family runs a river transport company, told me of a Yukon village deserted as recently as the summer of 1992 because of the appearance of the Wood Man, sometimes known as Neginla-eh. And on a recent trip to Homer, Alaska, I became acquainted with a rich lode of Bigfoot tradition on the Kenai Peninsula. The residents of English Bay tell of many encounters with Nantiinaq, who could change from Bigfoot into any other form. Some of the stories were collected in a magazine called *Fireweed Cillqaq*. "They said there used to be real ones before," wrote Kathy Kvasnikoff. "When you got close and tried to touch them like this, nothing would be there."

Bigfoot has several counterparts in Asia. The Yeti, or abominable snowman, is of course the best known. Yeti became international news when mountaineer Eric Shipton found a clear set of tracks near Mount Everest in 1951. *The Long Walk,* a 1956 memoir by Slavomir Rawicz, told of the wartime escape of five men from Siberia across the Himalaya. A close run-in with two seven-foot-tall, reddish Yeti caused them to change their route and lose a man in a crevasse. The *Atlantic Monthly* of November 1975 carried Edward W. Cronin Jr.'s account of snowman history and lore. Cronin, a scientist conducting an ecological survey of the Arun Valley of far eastern Nepal, became a believer when he discovered a long trail of prints similar to those in Shipton's photographs. The walker had appeared beside Cronin's tent in the night, then left the camp and crossed extremely steep terrain. And Peter Matthiessen, in *The Snow Leopard,* wrote of "a dark shape" he saw jump behind a boulder, "much too big for a red panda, too covert for a musk deer, too dark for wolf or leopard, and much quicker than a bear. With binoculars I stare for a long time at the mute boulder, feeling the presence of unknown life behind it, but all is still, there is only the sun and morning mountainside, the pouring water." Matthiessen returned from a later expedition to eastern Nepal with photographs of prints that he regards as good candidates for snowman tracks. And so Yeti lives on.

But Yeti is only one of the Asian Bigfeet. There is also the Alma of Mongolia, depicted in Tibetan natural histories, and the related Almasty, or Wild Man of the Caucasus; Yeh Ren, the Chinese Wildman, which has been reported for at least 2,500 years; and the Yeti-like Chuchunaa of Siberia. These creatures are taken seriously by many in

Asia, even considered mundane among Caucasian herdsmen. Peter Matthiessen has told me that both he and George Schaller have open minds about several Asian species. Large-scale Eurasian search efforts have been funded recently by organizations ranging from the BBC to the Chinese government. According to the London *Sunday Times,* a million-dollar Franco-Russian expedition planned to go into Kazakhstan. Led by Marie-Jeanne Koffmann, a twenty-year veteran of the chase, the high-tech team intended to "capture an Alma with the help of the local population. We want to take a mould of its face and specimens of its hair, skin and blood and then set it free with a radio tracer band. There is to be no King Kong spectacle of bringing it back." According to British archaeologist Myra Shackley, the Chinese have designated a portion of the Shannongjia forest as a Yeti reserve. Shackley believes that Asian man-apes might well represent surviving Neandertals or their descendants.

Ape-monster traditions come not only from mountainous regions but also from islands, deserts, and the tropics. They include the Cigouave, a voodoo-related Haitian forest beast; the Oreng-Pendek or Sedapa of Borneo and Sumatra; the Orang-Dalam of Malaysia; the Agogue of East Africa; and the Duendi of Colombia. There are swamp beasts galore, the Moth Man, the Gray Man of the Carolinas, and a wide array of troglodytes. Few cultures lack a human-faced hairy monster, giant, or wild man.

It would be a mistake to think that Yeti-like entities are the property only of "primitive" cultures. Woodmen and forest gods and goddesses loomed large in Hellenistic, Phoenician, and other proto-European societies. So prominent and diverse were forest, cave, and other wildlings in relatively modern legends and beliefs that the great Swedish taxonomist Carolus Linnaeus actually recognized and named several species, including *Homo troglodytes, H. nocturnus, H. sylvestris,* and *H. ferus.* Wild-man images lasted well into modern times in Europe, at least as an artistic footnote to the dominant culture.

Probably the best known of these figures is the Green Man. As explained by William Anderson in *Green Man: The Archetype of Our Oneness with the Earth,* "The Green Man signifies irrepressible life." The counterpart of the Great Goddess, he smuggled the pagan preoccupation with plants and the rest of nature into Christian tradition. Anderson's book shows images of the Green Man — vines, tendrils, and leaves sprouting from his mouth or entwining his head — decorating ecclesiastical architecture throughout Europe. Shades of the

Green Man may be reflected in Robin Hood, the King of the May, the Jolly Green Giant, and ultimately the botanist: a Green Man graces the main gates of Kew Gardens in London, the very seat of plant study.

So when I sat in the Quartz Creek greenwood looking for Silenus, satyrs, fauns, and zephyrs (all of which are anglewing butterflies as well as rustic pagan deities), Bigfoot might have walked in and sat down beside us and been in perfectly suitable company. If Sasquatch is not Pan, Puck, Silenus, Dionysus, Enkidu of *Gilgamesh,* and Robin Goodfellow; if Dzonoqua is not Diana, Demeter, Astarte, Gaia, Maya, the Great Goddess, and Mother Nature, then they are damned close to it. For what are any of these characters but embodiments of nature, the earth, and all that is green and contrary to control?

We live in an age when control — the grid, the boot, the gun, the nozzle, the law — has the upper hand. We have lost the wild repositories of power beyond the campfire, the mythic figures in which we might invest our fears, whom we might supplicate in pursuit of hope. Instead we have religions that rule behavior and perpetuate themselves through the application of order and conformity. For all of its values, contemporary religious life offers little of the all-embracing ardor of any "pagan" culture.

The secular world lacks even that pallid and weird mythical figure, the devil (whose medieval form was concocted from the repressed wreckage of the arch-satyr Pan). Reason and rationality have sought to replace the need for the superstitions that upheld nearly all societies of the past and still prop up many in the present. But we don't really behave rationally. Most of us have no sense of the stochasticity of the world — the natural history of chance — or of what cause and effect really mean. Churchgoers or not, people tend to behave deterministically, as if there really were such a thing as fate. Though the end of superstition might be an advance, most people still adhere to it, calling it luck or faith. In seeking to banish the terrors beyond the city walls, we have either subordinated our spirits to some "spiritual" system or traded them for the illusory comforts of the material world.

Now we are seeing a rebirth of the desire to combine nature and spirit among some earnest folk who value the religious impulse yet feel religion has resided too far from the real world for too long. Earth and Spirit conferences and celebrations, the Green Spirituality and Green Cross movements, the writings of Matthew Fox and Thomas Berry and other more or less apostate priests and teachers, and the emergence of neopagan followers of the "old religion" are all manifestations of this urge to reintegrate what many see as elemental urges too long in conflict.

As an interested heathen, I have watched various efforts to woo Gaia back into spiritual life, to rehabilitate the Horned One, to turn the considerable energy and resources of religion toward the problems of environmental conservation. The basic approach is heartening and infinitely more desirable than the contrarian practice of many fundamentalist institutions, which would banish nature altogether in pursuit of ultimate control.

A simple and reliable test of a creed's standing on these issues is to ask how its adherents regard the term "wilderness." Those to whom it is anathema, something to be avoided and subdued, are on a one-way track toward irrelevance. Religions that revere wilderness, however, as the home of our neighbors, as well as the place where devouts and prophets from Jesus to John Muir have sought enlightenment, may be part of the solution.

Unfortunately, much of the regreening movement is highly naive about nature and prone to confusing oatmeal with ideas. The head-long rush to embrace everything Native American (to the intense discomfiture and resentment of many Indians); the wholesale adop-tion of pantheism and animism without any awareness of their moti-vations, history, or special knowledges; and the conflation of the Green Man (who, like Dzonoqua, is sexually ambiguous) with the "wild man" of muzzy-minded men's groups all detract from the possi-ble potency of these movements.

This is where we get back to Bigfoot, for Bigfoot has much to do with potency. If hairy giants represent the same archetype as the Green Man and the Goddess, mightn't they also suggest a model for reintegration? As ethnologist Marjorie Halpin wrote in *Manlike Mon-sters on Trial,* whether as "'missing link' or as a quality of ba'wis [Tsim-shian for Bukwus-ness] manifesting throughout nature, the Sasquatch is a recognition of the connection between the human and the natu-ral." Or as permaculture guru Bill Devall put it in *Simple in Means, Rich in Ends,* Sasquatch is the "ideal man-nature being."

If the myths often regard Bigfoot as a bogey, they also invest it with serious and important powers. And isn't that the way with nature? The world is both scary and empowering. It is this duality of intimidat-ing force and becalming strength that made it necessary for many religious dogmas to edit nature out. Adam and Eve were not expelled from the garden; they turned their backs on it when their authors edited out the Goddess. As Joseph Campbell put it in *The Power of Myth,* "When the Hebrews came in, they really wiped out the Goddess. The term for the Canaanite goddess that's used in the Old Testament is 'the Abomination.'"

The Hebrews were not alone in relegating nature to the profane. As Campbell went on to tell Bill Moyers, "The Christian separation of matter and spirit, of natural grace and supernatural grace, has really castrated nature. And the European mind, the European life, has been, as it were, emasculated by this separation. The true spirituality, which would have come from the union of matter and spirit, has been killed. And then what did the pagan represent? He was a person from the suburbs of Eden. He was regarded as a nature man." Am I alone in seeing the shadow of Sasquatch at the gates of Eden?

Campbell concluded, "Spiritual life is the bouquet, the perfume, the flowering and fulfillment of a human life, not a supernatural virtue imposed upon it." Moyers then asked, "Is this what Thomas Mann meant when he talked about mankind being the noblest work because it joins nature and spirit?" Campbell replied, "Yes." And when Robinson Jeffers, in "November Surf," referred to the "two-footed / Mammal, being someways one of the nobler animals," he was hoping for a time when mankind "regains the dignity of room, the value of rareness."

As we seek such a state and names for the natural world to help us live with it instead of against it, could Bigfoot be an ambassador for a truly green spirituality? An icon with shoulders broad enough to accept our mortal dread, and honest enough to promise the earth as long as we both last, has a real appeal. Hardly a god, but maybe doing the same job if, as Campbell says, "gods are guides to the deep center of truth."

Unfortunately we may have gone too far in devaluing the thing we call Bigfoot to ever bring it back into respectability. Largely this is the result of a basic difference between how we view reality and how the Kwakiutl view it. To us something is real if we can see or touch it every time we look for it. To them it might be solid now and phantasmic tomorrow yet be equally real. The adoption of an absolutist or positivist view of the world, a figment of Western thought with roots in Aristotle, Newton, and Spencer, militates against appreciation of the Kwakiutl view. When the Greeks and Romans traded their old pantheon, what we've all grown up calling "classical mythology," for monotheism, they gave up all the sweet and maddening ambivalence of their gods.

They sacrificed, in short, a universe in which chariots pulled the sun and thunderbolts were thrown by pissed-off, imperfect gods, where mortals might marry gods and be blinded, killed, or eaten for it, then reemerge in another form. They traded whimsy and pregnant possibility for the idea of order, swapped all sorts of resurrections for just one. The new ethical order, if observed, was at least more humane, if no more rational. But in the deal they gave up the kind of relationship with nature that allowed the likes of centaurs and satyrs to romp.

You would think that the religiously mystical should be able to accept the possibility of transcendent states of existence, such as resurrection. But if a certain magic is not to be found in the scripture of a particular creed, it is out of bounds, in the realm of the Beast. For the so-called secular the scripture is likely to be *National Geographic*. If it's not there, it's not at all.

The old bestiaries suggested the existence of phoenixes and rocs and all sorts of weird organisms, even hippos and rhinos. That narwhals turned out to be "real" and unicorns "unreal" would have mattered little to the compilers, who were more concerned with recording what men *thought* was out there than documenting natural diversity. Nowadays biogeographers believe only in what they can be shown. I understand this impulse and act on it in my butterfly studies. But whatever we have gained through the objectivity of Western science, we have lost in the utility of rocs and phoenixes and all creatures beyond the pale of the cabinet or the cage.

The very fact that the word "myth" has come to mean in the common parlance an erroneous idea or mistake reflects our collective faith in one-dimensional reality. As Campbell and Moyers richly showed in *The Power of Myth*, a myth is simply a system of belief. And many of the most enduring belief systems do not have our myopia.

Now come the new cosmologists and the quantum physicists who, going Einstein one (or several) better, tell us that the world is a relative place after all. Interpreted in one way, modern physics suggests that the Kwakiutl could be right: Dzonoqua today might be here and rock-solid real and tomorrow exist on the other side of a dimension that hasn't been named or numbered. Of course, you won't find a physicist who really supports the notion of some Bigfoot enthusiasts (those without a boat, in Mojo's words) that Bigfoot moves between dimensions at will. Quantum mechanics tend to tinker at the edges of universes and in deep time and other imponderables, not so much in the here and now. But the point — and the irony — is that we seem to be coming back, kicking and screaming, into an intellectual environment where logical positivism has to scramble to stay on top.

Realities differ. I have a brother whose reality today is vastly different from the one he perceived prior to a head-on encounter with a cattle truck. A psychiatrist we once consulted told me that to try to change his mind about the reality of his "delusions" would be futile, that they are as real to him as asphalt or elm trees are to me. The membrane between reality and dreams was one of the tissues rearranged in his brain. Though Howard's wit, subtlety, intelligence, and vocabulary remained intact, his version of events and his apprehension of the world have changed dramatically. I have given up telling him that he was not the Ivory Soap baby.

In the same way, to those who see, in Chief Lelooska's words, "with Indian eyes," realities about Bigfoot (and many other entities) are relative. In a generous extension of this logic one might propose that to the readers of tabloids the stories are real. Perhaps they are the visionaries among us, the ones who are able to see past our heritage of Western objectivity into the rich realms of alternative realities. After all, some of the boatless people's narratives have all the imaginative flair and color of the wilder aboriginal myths. But I am not that generous. These people need help. The difference is that while Indian traditions are held in common by entire clans or tribes and are told with a mixture of respect and whimsy, these modern myths tend to be taken in dead earnest by particularly unconnected individuals. I wouldn't be surprised if it is their very alienation that drives them into the arms of aliens.

One person who heard of my interest in Bigfoot wrote, "I have been in contact with a starship commander and several specialists aboard his fleet for almost a year now. [They have told me that] Sasquatch has the ability to move from the 3rd dimension to the 4th, at will." Bigfeet live in sovereign, matriarchal tribes, communicate through shamans, heal wounds instantly, channel, and travel through mental projection. "My frustration," he concluded, "is knowing they exist, but being unable to assist them in protecting their habitat, since proof of where they live doesn't exist. And if proof was available, the area would become, I fear, . . . a shooting range."

Another correspondent predicted that I would have a close encounter based on the numerology of my name. "Your master numbers in all three names would cause a harmless resonance that the sasquatch crowd would recognize and respond to." He went on, "If we are 3-D, they are around 5-D. . . . About all a shotgun would do would pepper their aura field." A third enthusiast announced that "the world is going through an incredible transitional period that has to do with God (not religion), ETs/UFOs + Bigfoot. Prepare for survival in the '90's." I'm sorry; these are not the words of shamans.

The tabloidization of the world seems no different from the general spread of dross in the mass culture today. Examples abound: television almost *in toto*. Wal-Marts and malls instead of vital town centers. Vocabulary's decline. Bestseller lists. Lite music, food, and beer — oxymorons all. And architecture: I recently saw a historic photograph of a magnificent hotel, the Louvre, that once stood in Astoria, Oregon. On its site now stands a McDonald's. The barbarians are not at the gates; they're well inside.

Bigfoot has not escaped the march of mediocrity and tacky commercialization. As the late primatologist John Napier wrote in his important book, *Bigfoot: The Yeti and Sasquatch in Myth and Reality,* "Bigfoot in some quarters of North America has become Big Business, a commodity to be exploited to the full. It can no longer be considered simply as a natural phenomenon that can be studied with the techniques of a naturalist; the entrepreneurs have moved in and folklore has become fakelore." And that was in 1973. Since then the Oregon Tourism Division has featured a frame from the Patterson film on a flier labeled "Oregon Scavenger Hunt Item #17 (a direct-mail piece with gratuitous shock-value photo of Bigfoot)."

A silly-looking Harrison Bigfoot was the official mascot of the Washington State Centennial, and the Seattle Sonics have another version. The name "Bigfoot" denotes pizzas, monster trucks, and innumerable campgrounds and motels. Not only Willow Creek in California but also Harrison Hot Springs in British Columbia and Carson, Mount Baker, and Elma in Washington hold annual Bigfoot revels. These are all in good fun. But the foot races with big plywood feet, the clowns in gorilla suits, and the endless array of Sasquatch doodads encourage little real respect for a venerable myth.

The Northwest Indians, with their masks, totems, and tales, might be said to have commercialized Sasquatch first. Dzonoqua was sometimes involved in the breaking of a copper, one of the most important potlatch transactions. But as Lelooska explained it to me, Dzonoqua was a figure that impinged on many aspects of life besides potlatch — wealth, power, the chieftancy, forest mysteries, and so on. There is no such depth to the contemporary exploitation of Bigfoot.

Bigfoot became a staple of the scandal sheets when the Patterson film called attention to a possible monster in our midst, then left us wondering. It was inevitable. So was the movie *Harry and the Hendersons,* which was actually not an unsympathetic treatment. In the end we must ask, has popular culture devalued a great myth or given it new life? I think I know how Dzonoqua and the Green Man would vote.

But there are other, brighter signs that a respect for the old traditions might not be dead. Among the many sensational treatments of Bigfoot can be found a number of titles that treat the subject intelligently, with subtle humor and suitable respect, and with care for both the language and the importance of myth. Notable among these is David George Gordon's *Field Guide to Sasquatch,* published by Sasquatch Books of Seattle.

The small shelf of Bigfoot fiction is largely filled with rustic murder mysteries and salacious tales somehow involving Sasquatch as malefactor or local color. But lately several writers of stature have turned their attention to the big fellow. Scott Russell Sanders's *Bad Man Ballad* is the best of the Bigfoot novels I've seen. In his short stories "Bigfoot Stole My Wife" and "I Am Bigfoot," in *The News of the World,* Ron Carlson plays off the urban legend of predatory Bigfoot to probe restlessness from both sides of a broken equation. In *Bigfoot Dreams* novelist Francine Prose describes a trash journalist who identifies with the Bigfoot of her crazy stories. Both authors play off the tabloids and come to opposite but equally desperate conclusions. Carlson's bereft character says, "Believe it. Everything. Everything you read. Everything you hear. . . . Believe the small hairs on the back of your neck. Believe all of history, and every version of history, and all the predictions for the future. . . . Everything has happened. Everything is possible. . . . I gotta believe it." To Prose's Vera it's all false hopes. "Your dead ones aren't really dead. Cucumber slices will cure your arthritis. Elvis is alive and well on Mars. Your alien lover is at this very moment winging toward you via UFO. It's not true, Vera thinks. None of it."

Some distinguished essayists have also written memorably on manlike monsters. Doris Lessing's piece "The Thoughts of a Near-Human" is labeled fiction by the *Partisan Review.* It is an account of a Yeti distanced from its own kind through contact with humans, then driven to contemplate suicide by captors who fit it with a transmitter before releasing it. Told from the animal's viewpoint, the story has all the moral authority of the writer's powerful essays. In *The Klamath Knot,* a splendid exploration of evolution myths in southwest Oregon, David Rains Wallace treats forest giants in a manner worthy of their lineage. "The giants who left their tracks near Bluff Creek are eloquent mythic expressions of evolutionary uncertainty," he writes. "Are they competitive lords of the snow forest? Cooperative children of the ancestral forest? Are they human? Are they alive?" And Washington writer Wenonah Sharpe, in "Some Thoughts on Sasquatch Watching," speaks of our good fortune in having "an indigenous wraith, a shadow still dancing on the cave wall, a sylvan deity not yet vanquished by the inexorable march of science and universal education."

At least one fine Bigfoot poem has emerged. In her "Oratorio for Sasquatch, Man, and Two Androids," Margaret Atwood wrote: "Sasquatch: / A wound has been made in me, / a hole opens in my green flesh; / I see that I can be broken . . . to murder my pines, my cedars / is to murder me." Atwood, like Lessing, treats Bigfoot as a vessel of alienation and profligacy. Wendell Berry's "To the Unseeable Animal" can be read as a love song to the mystery of the beast beyond.

Sculptor Richard Cook has found the animal's humor. Cook describes himself as a practitioner of Beringerology, the study (and manufacture) of fake fossils, named for Dr. Johann Beringer, the victim of a notorious paleontological hoax. But he creates his pieces to delight, not to fool anyone. Working in clay from the Whiskey Creek beds next to his cabin near Port Angeles, Washington, Cook creates a wonderful array of extinct animals both hilarious and ingenious. These he gives wildly punning English and scientific names such as the Culture Vulture *(Omniverons)* and the antlered Sconcetron *(Candelabraferens),* a forerunner of Rudolph. Cook has done two species of humanoid giants: Big Foot *(Megalopodus),* whose black skull bears great tusks; and Quelbitrax *(Flagrantedelicto),* "a specialized sasquatchian cousin," whose teeth are like barbed spearpoints. They "must have made it a formidable biter," writes Cook, "though I should think it would have had a hell of a time disengaging afterward." Maybe that's why it's extinct.

A new and supple Bigfoot is emerging in music as well, in the lyrics of several singer-songwriters in Sasquatch country. The Dorsches, a musical family from Aberdeen, south of Washington's giant-rich Olympic Mountains, have recorded a lovely song called "Footsteps in the Wind." It tells the story of a young girl finding a huge track by the river and wondering, "Could Bigfoot have been here, or am I imagining he's near / Oh, I wonder if he's watching me, or if he might appear / Think I hear / Your footsteps in the wind." In the haunting harmonics of the repeated refrain, you feel the immanence of something large, important, and good.

J. W. Sparrow is a folksinger who lives in the Bigfoot territory of Mount Rainier's foothills. His song "The Man in the Mirror" tells of "a man up on the mountain, with his hair down to his knees," who is "standing tall for all of us who say that we still care / about this blue shining jewel we all share / A gentle voice whispering, 'Yes, compared to what,' / a message concerning the paradise we've got." Sparrow's refrain too is a compelling one: "It's the man in the mirror, the last mystery / The one you often hear about but very seldom see."

It is "the man in the mirror" who is the problem here, and if we go a little green around the gills at the realization, it will only heighten the effect. We must cleave to the Green Man, we must grasp the Goddess, however we try to avoid them. Someday we will discover interdependency, or else. The recovery of respect for "a creature that would understand forests in ways we cannot," in Wallace's words, will only hasten the day we take responsibility for our own footprint on the land.

In the meantime, what are curious people to think? Phil Bunton, editorial director of the Globe Communications tabloids, told the *Los Angeles Times,* "Our readers want to believe this stuff. The world is very boring."

The credulous public, caught between the cynical tabloids and the skeptical scientists, are unable to use the archetype's power to enrich their lives. Is there a third way to regard Bigfoot with a truly open mind — realizing that its flesh-and-blood existence among the deer and the ravens is an open question and at the same time that it clearly *exists* in the hearts and minds of many?

Dr. John Mack, Pulitzer Prize–winning professor of psychiatry at Harvard Medical School, believes that UFO abductees should be taken seriously. If he's right, aliens may one day graduate to the *New York Times.* Our methods of empirical observation need to be stretched, he says, to appreciate the experiences his patients have related to him. Echoing Lelooska, Mack says we have so constricted our consciousness that we cannot experience what the Indians call the spirit world. Carl Sagan regards the public credulity about aliens and other tabloid-type tales as evidence of widespread scientific ignorance. Considering the popular denial of evolutionary biology, I tend to agree. Unlike my correspondent who tells me that aliens are helping Sasquatch colonize prefab habitats in space ("they leave with great reluctance. After all, Earth is their home"), I don't believe that Bigfoot has the remotest connection to UFOs. But maybe both phenomena should cause us to reexamine how we judge the testimony of the universe.

For the world is *not* boring. The Green Man is coming back and will lift the scales from our blindered eyes. And who knows? Maybe this time he will take the face of Bigfoot, and the Goddess will don Dzonoqua's mask.

Will we rescue the myth from the gutter, restoring its green shimmer, its beauty, power, and potential? If we do, the habitat of the giant will truly become our own. Until then we will have to be content to meet Bigfoot at the supermarket checkout stands. For there he will surely be found, hanging out with the King.

13

One Hundred Hours of Solitude

≛≛≛

One returns from solitude laden with the gifts of circumstance.
— Wendell Berry, *What Are People For?*

I F THE ANCIENT PEOPLE of Indian Heaven had worn NBA-sized moccasins, this could have been one of their footprints.

On the face of a big flat rock jutting into Deep Lake, right where I stood, was a remarkably footlike impression. When I placed my wet foot inside the print, it looked as if a little boy had stepped in his big brother's track. I sat beside it, dangling my legs over the rock's edge and trying to decide what to make of the artifact. I'd seen much less impressive marks claimed as Bigfoot tracks. I was confronting something that I had to admit might represent an upright ape who, long before, had walked where I was now walking.

- - -

When the day came to hike into the Indian Heaven Wilderness Area, I awoke to see cottonwoods and firs overhead, five gray jays at breakfast, a day cool with high, heavy broken clouds. I devoutly hoped that rain would hold off until I was well up onto the plateau, for on this leg of the journey weather would make all the difference in the world. I waxed my boots to be ready for the worst and departed in the forenoon with the skies clearing, the temperature pleasant.

After registering at the wilderness boundary, I headed up the steep Cultus Lake Trail. I saw lots of boot tracks, but there would be no cycles, hooray! The troughs were wide, made by pack horses, and walkable. Rounding a hairpin switchback on the way to the top of the world, I emerged into an opening that seemed a doorstep for Mounts Adams and Rainier. In full sun the two snowy lumps, their valleys cloud-wrapped, rose like improbable painted backdrops in a low-budget version of *Paradise Lost.* Now the sky was clear, the air in the seventies, my fresh supply of Gray's River water more than welcome.

By one measure you have entered the wilderness when you've left your daily life behind. My field notes show I wasn't there yet: observations like "an anglewing skirts the edge, a pika calls from rocks below; Cultus Creek mutters under the breeze in the firs" alternate with jots like "ASK THEA: Dory's address? coffee? coffee cup w/specs!!? Howard & Caitlin's full names & address? + notch in belt? flea bath for Bokis? letter to KB?" Putting away my notebook, I resolved to put away the world as well, so that I could begin to really see the earth.

Soft fungi lined the trailside — puffballs, flocculated chanterelles, orange-peel *Peziza* — but they failed to soften the rocky path, which kept climbing for a long couple of miles. A white inchworm moth flew to a patchy fir trunk, chancing in its gyre to land on the right color patch. A Douglas squirrel, dismantling fragrant pink and blue fir cones for its swelling midden, darted up the backside of the same tree.

Then the first Indian Heaven meadows appeared, and I entered the palette of reds for which the tableland is famous. A little pond was a mirror framed in reds, pinks, yellows, oranges, greens, and the blues of berries and noble firs. A redtail did several silent doughnuts in the still water and overhead as well. Stalks of a long emergent grass, fringing the mere, lay limp against its limpid surface. If I'd gone no farther, I would have forever understood the enchantment of Indian Heaven.

Raven's coarse trill broke my silent arrival at Cultus Lake. A low barking in the east was likely another dialect of the multilingual corvid. When I found my campsite on the south side, facing Bird Mountain, the gray jays were already there. I knew it was my campsite because two contrails had crossed overhead, marking the spot with a big X. On a fairly level spot by a berry patch, away from the modest fire pit, I set up the camp that would be home for several days. Dragonflies hawked the clearing in the slanted sun as wrens inspected the action and golden-crowned sparrows teased a young Cooper's hawk.

Now came the challenge of the food cache. It isn't easy to suspend comestibles out of reach of scavenging bruins in the subalpine, where all the trees are small and limber. But unlike Juniper Ridge, where I'd given up and (against all advice) taken my pack into my tent, here there were trees worth trying. I tied the cord as high as I could between two firs, one lashed to another for rigidity, and pulled it taut.

Lots of effort to little effect. By sunset, after I had struggled with ropes and bags for an hour or two, my cache hung about six feet off the ground: a good gift height for bears.

I managed to filter a quart of water or so from the shallow, silty lake. As I began to prepare dinner, the Cooper's hawk was attempting to do the same. Investigating a thrash and a flutter, I found the cinnamon-breasted accipiter going after a small bird in a fir bough. The songbird flew, the hawk flew and twice missed. Between sallies it sat on bare limbs in full view, its head rotating left, right, up, down, looking for the vagrant prey. When the sparrow launched, the hawk followed but failed to make contact. It made an irritated pass at a chickaree issuing rapid, single-note alarm calls nearby; the squirrel freaked and lost its voice. In the fading light I could see the hawk's yellow legs, chartreuse bill with black tip, striped breast, banded tail, gray-brown mantle, white eyebrow, and dark eyes; what I couldn't see but easily imagined was its frustration and hunger. Finally the raptor flew off, having paid me no mind — unlike the noisy, nosy squirrel and the raven, who passed over with voluble comment.

Before it got too dusky I searched the forest margin for a granny stick, or clothesline pole, to bolster the hangline. The downed trunks and branches were all too heavy or short, but they furnished a plenitude of firewood. In the wood edge by the meadow, pasty white warts freckled the scarlet caps of fly agarics like clouds in a lurid sunset. The real sky was clear, cooling into mauve. I returned to camp, kindled a fire, and prepared my couscous. Before bed I walked to the upper meadow and saw the quarter-moon through mist and pines before it set. Polaris came out tentatively over Cultus Lake as I pulled into my tent and lighted my candle lantern. Bark-picking birds were still at work after dark. After the usual screaming low flight of fighter jets about eight-thirty, pure mountain silence. I was twenty-four hours into solitude.

- - -

Cold, clear, up at eight. Many a naturalist would be shocked, but for me that's an early start. I had coffee and granola bars, conserving my H_2O. I didn't think fluids were really an issue in this lake district, but the aborting of my earlier trek on Juniper Ridge was still too fresh in mind to let me squander water. I walked around my own lake and across to the next, just a quarter-mile to the northeast. Deep Lake shone the blue-green of an ocean bay in summer. Far out from shore a flock of ten ducks stippled the surface, all in the same brown eclipse or female plumage, maybe shovelers or mallards.

I intended to join the ducks, but first I shit in the woods. That's something "nature writers" seldom write about, but it occupies a portion of every day in the out of doors and requires close attention to your surroundings. I was glad to see Ten-Speed Press's publication of *How to Shit in the Woods* by Kathleen Meyer. It's astonishing how few people are adept at it and how few it takes to spoil (and actually pollute) a wild area.

During the time of enforced contemplation, I speculated on scat calling cards and the species who leave them. We are among the few animals that make an active effort to hide our feces. Many leave them purposefully to advertise their presence in the territory to potential mates or rivals. Exploring animals, as any dog-walker knows, eagerly seek and sniff the signs of others. Cats scratch, but they seldom bury their poop very effectively. As in so many matters, we do the opposite — we urgently avoid the wastes of our own kind. Those who mark the territory are seen as slobs, not interesting interlopers.

So what does Bigfoot do? When Sasquatch goes apeshit, does it hide the evidence as careful people do? Or, like some bad-mannered zoo baboon or human, does it scatter its crap around the countryside at will? If this is a beast that perceives its plight, caution would argue for concealment rather than advertisement. Some of the monster-hunters claim to have found Bigfoot droppings, massive mounds of excrement somewhere between human turds and bear heaps, usually less unformed than a cow pie. Bigfoot newsletters print photographs of lumps and reports of "specimens" stored at this or that laboratory or in someone's freezer. But coprolite researchers have not yet made a Bigfoot breakthrough.

There is an alternative to advertisement and concealment. I remember the mild shock I felt when I visited the Cincinnati Zoo a few years ago and saw the coprophagous behavior of the gorillas. I thought it must be a manifestation of zoo neurosis, like a fox pacing back and forth in the same interminable, stylized route. But Dian Fossey set me straight in *Gorillas in the Mist:*

> All age and sex classes of gorillas have been observed eating their own dung and, to a lesser extent, that of other gorillas. The animals simply shift their buttocks slightly to catch the dung lobe in

one hand before it contacts the earth. They then bite into the lobe and while chewing smack their lips with apparent relish. The eating of excrement occurs among most vertebrates, including humans, who have certain nutritional deficiencies. Among gorillas coprophagy is thought to have possible dietary functions because it may allow vitamins, particularly B12 synthesized in the hind gut, to be assimilated in the foregut. Since the activity is usually observed during periods of cold wet weather, I am inclined to relate the "meals" to instant warmed TV dinners!

In Bigfoot's case this behavior could be doubly adaptive, doing away with the evidence of its presence while recycling valuable nutrients. Of course, something has to come out in the end. But Bigfoot (who doesn't bother with toilet paper) must be better at hiding its scat than at least half the humans, judging from many a feculent roadside pullout and campsite.

Deep Lake was hemmed by a fir-and-huckleberry frieze, with Mount Adams rearing above the eastern shore. Emergent grass lay prostrate on the surface like threshed rice on a paddy, but this was no cultivated scene. Human sign was present in the eroded paths around the shore. Some of the erosion, like the racecourse to the south and the peeled cedars here and there in the national forest, might go back to the Indians. But most of the paths were worn by recent decades of use by hikers, riders, fishers, hunters, berry pickers, and beauty lovers. I was just the latest of these, but for now I had it to myself.

The soft mud of the beach bore signs of deer, big and little; dog, coyote, and horse; marten and bobcat; and an array of birds. I was thinking about how obvious a Bigfoot track would be among these lesser imprints when I came to the rock overhanging the water and spotted the foot-shaped impression stamped into the very stone.

The depression in the rock could have been an erosional formation, an old carving, or modern vandalism. But the stone was probably lithified ash rather than cooled lava (basalt), so it might represent a fossil Indian or Bigfoot print. It was thirteen inches long by about five at the "instep." The indentation was slanted inward, so the outer edge ran out, leaving no clear indication of width. I could imagine a sharp heel impression and a reasonable indication of the ball of a foot and a big toe. No other toe marks were evident, so if this was indeed a footprint, the foot had either been covered (as by a moccasin) or the detail had eroded away. I had not brought along my

When I approached the big flat rock on the shore of Deep Lake, I found an impression remarkably like a big footprint clearly engraved in the lithified ash. This was just a quarter-mile from Cultus Lake (*cultus* means

plaster of Paris from the camp, and I needed to obtain water and bathe. So I decided to study and cast the "track" later. If it had been here these hundreds of years, it could wait another day to be memorialized.

The surface of Deep was calm. Blue dragons hawked and rustled over the shores and shallows. Red crossbills swooped over, and the ducks circled the lake lazily. I hung awkwardly over rocks to fetch water until I found a perfect, butt-shaped perch like a tractor seat over deeper water. During the slow filtering process it occurred to me that this could be a Bigfoot butt print. I laughed at myself but ruled nothing out.

Bathing off the big rock, I recalled such a boulder jutting into Glacier Lake in Colorado. On childhood fishing trips it was one place

"bad" in Chinook), so named by the Klickitats because of the legendary abundance of Bigfeet in the area.

I took home a plaster cast of the curious impression I found at Deep Lake.
T. L. Pyle

we boys could dangle our lines where our jittery impatience wouldn't spook all the fish in the lake. Because of latitude, five thousand feet of elevation in the Cascades equals ten in the Rockies, and Deep was as cold as Glacier. Cringingly I immersed crotch, kidneys, nipples, armpits, nape of the neck. My danglers withdrew, demonstrating both the adaptive value of genital shrinkage in a sperm-threatening medium and the effectiveness of cold showers. Clouds of silt boiled up around my feet like mushrooms of dust before a rolling front of TNT. How many lives I destroyed, how many *Giardia* cysts I stirred up, there was no knowing.

As I stood there doing my best to acclimate, a ten-inch cutthroat trout swam up to my toes, nosed around, and worried something prismatic on the bottom. I saw its blunt bill, the pink stripe down its side like a streak from the huckleberry meadows. Then it departed with a flick and, later, a mild leap. I dove to fetch the rainbow thing, thinking it might be a lure I could recycle. It was a fish head. I returned it and knew where I would come fishing later on.

Airplanes contrived a constant caravan overhead. I'd naively thought that wilderness-area overflights were banned, but a low fighter (passing below me for a change, over the brink to the east) disabused me of that fairy tale. A small, low-flying plane made a hell of a racket, but mostly I heard the dull roar of jetliners. I thought of all the times I'd been in them, looking down at the wilderness, wishing I were there instead . . . and this time I was. I basked nude in the sun, alone on the level that mattered.

In the shallows of Deep Lake baby cutthroats probed the now-settled silt. A chartreuse-spotted darner dragonfly with tears and holes in her wings haunted a wet, rotted log, apparently ovipositing. Then a blue male came, grasped her thorax with his claspers, and forcibly hauled her off with a great rustle of wings. Entomologists try to avoid anthropomorphizing insect behavior, and the word "rape" is not one to be taken lightly in any context. But this was the most dramatic ravishment of a mate that I'd ever observed among insects, exceeding even the summary couplings of monarch and parnassian butterflies. A white-faced hornet gave me very close attention — it was hard to be still — and moved on.

A Clark's nutcracker split the sky with its raucous caws and swooped over the lake to the top of a tall dead fir, a pearly flash. A shiny amphibian jumped into shallow water, and I lunged for it. My eyes fooled by the refraction of the water-lens, I touched it but didn't go far enough. Later it swam near my feet, and I caught it with my net. Four to five inches long, it was fat like a toad, olive on the back with black spots and warts, a yellow belly, yellow spots along olive sides, a yellow mustache over and behind the broad froggy mouth, and a prominent gland behind the gape. It had a very long second toe and was a fairly slow frog, with a soft croak when struggling in my net. Upon release it floated in the water with its nostrils out, then sunned on a rock.

Circumnavigating the lake, I tried to sneak up on the ten ducks, which had drifted into a shaded bay, but the fishermen's trail was too exposed, and they moved off again. Four paddled across sunlit green water reflecting red bushes, then returned to the other six in the northwest cove. I thought I saw blue bars on a stretched wing; gray heads, maybe some green. Stocky ducks, some white in the uncurly tails, some reddish on the breasts, the biggish yellow bills held down.

These are the kinds of details a naturalist automatically records while admiring the creature on a different level entirely. I was able to pin down the first animal as a Cascades yellow-legged frog, the ducks as shovelers. When you can attach details to a creature, you can name it; with a name, it becomes someone you know and can recognize again.

Going through the process of field identification, almost a daily practice wherever I am, I thought of the "footprint" across the lake. If Bigfoot is ever to appear in the field guides, it's going to take a lot more knowledge than we have now: more field marks, more spoor than equivocal coprolites or a muddy mark in a rock. And that, of course, is why others are intent on catching it, just as I caught the frog. But this is no slow amphibian. It is not at all clear to me that they will ever succeed.

Back at my little lake, as dinner was cooking, I tried to improve the food cache. I got it up to almost eight feet with the granny pole balanced on rocks and wondered if it would last the night. Hearing a folderol, I discovered that the sounds came from two sources: gray jays swiping crackers I'd put out and pocket gophers working subterranean heather roots. I couldn't see the rodents, but from seeing their mounds and watching the ground ripple from this underground industry, I deduced what they must be. The ruckus stopped at my footfall. Bigfoot is said to dig up gophers for dinner, which seems at least as plausible as catching a Sasquatch in the clear, above ground.

After dinner I read Peter Byrne's vivid tales of campfires, tigers, black panthers, and Bigfoot in *The Search for Bigfoot*, by firelight. I almost felt Byrne was there to share my own campfire and go over the events of the day. A pale blaze lit up the western sky, mares'-tails flicked over the east, as my fire licked away at long-dead timber and I turned the pages.

Rarely can one enjoy a high-country campfire legally or in good conscience anymore. But here there was no shortage of fuel, no near fire danger, no oversmirch of smoke. Crackling t.p. and lichens had spread the fire in no time to the dried fir. It gave me hot tea, light to read by, and the same comfort in the night that everyone who has ever huddled around a fire circle knows.

Reading about monsters, however insubstantial or benign you feel they are, one can appreciate that comfort. I next took out Mel Hansen's valuable little book, *Indian Heaven Back Country: Trails, Lakes,*

and Indian Lore. On the morrow I would need his advice on trails and
lakes, but for now I looked to the lore. Hansen described the Ape
Canyon incident of 1924, the famous Skamania County Commissioners' 1969 ordinance, which would fine anyone who killed a Bigfoot,
and a possible encounter of his own when hiking near Darlene Lake.
In the course of his research for the book, he found that Cultus Lake
translates from Chinook, the widespread trade jargon, as "bad lake."
"I questioned why the Indians considered Cultus Lake to be bad," he
wrote. "Was the water unfit to drink? Was the lake devoid of fish? Was
the area avoided by the Indians and, if so, why?"

Seeking answers, Hansen asked Myrtle Overbaugh of White Salmon to interview her friend Bessie Quaempts, an eighty-four-year-old
Klickitat Indian, on the subject. Ms. Quaempts said that her people
often saw and spoke of Bigfoot, or Sehlatiks. "Did the Indians camp
and fish at Cultus Lake?" Hansen asked through Mrs. Overbaugh.

"No," replied Ms. Quaempts, "many Sehlatiks people there. Indians afraid of Sehlatiks people."

Hansen wrote that the Yakamas considered the Sehlatiks to be
"wild outcasts of the mountain tribes — evil spirits to be avoided."
Perhaps that was a reason for the designation of this splendid place as
"cultus." Another Chinook jargon word connected with Bigfoot is
"Skookum." Originally it referred to a place inhabited by "an evil god
of the woods," according to L. L. MacArthur's *Oregon Geographic Names.*
Though the word has come to mean "strong or stout," the many
Skookum Creeks and Skookum Lakes in the region might refer to
malign giants as much as to any other quality. There were many places
where the native inhabitants felt uncomfortable, judging from the
distribution of "cultus" and "skookum" over the landscape and from
the many dark tales emerging from shaded groves and hidden valleys.
If just a fraction were inspired by Sehlatiks, it could indicate a presence that once was widespread.

With the moon winking through the firs, its ecliptic low to the
south, I could scarcely connect the gentle pallor of the night with
anything evil. The fire ebbed; I poked it alive. The red coals of carbon
brought to mind the crimson amanitas so abundant here. Various
cultures have employed the alkaloids of the *Amanita muscaria* mushroom — toxic, but highly mind-altering if you survive ingestion — in
shamanic or religious rituals. Mythologist Robert Graves suggests that
Greek satyrs and centaurs were inspired by pantheistic or Dionysian
humans who ingested *A. muscaria* to enhance their sybaritic lifestyle

with heightened sensations, strength, and sexual powers. I don't know whether the fly agaric was used by Cascades Indians, but if it gave a connection to Pan, why not to Sehlatiks? Just as the ancestors of the Klickitats surely exploited the succulent king boletes that abound here, they might have at least tried the hallucinogenic red toadstool. A bad amanita trip could turn the loveliest place "cultus," could perhaps, even, call forth giants in the night.

- - -

The next day I was out of camp with the waking jays after fresh huckleberry granola, coffee, biscuits, and honey, fuel for a long day's hike. It was a heavenly day to explore the middle reaches of Indian Heaven — clear, blue, warm in the meadows, cool in the woods. As I set out, golden-crowned sparrows hopped about in the trailside vegetation. The touch of gold at their foreheads matched my terry-cloth sweatband, already seeing service on the uphill stretches.

The trail was a real thoroughfare, a raised bed lined with logs in places, with deep drainage trenches on either side. A trail repair order at the Cultus Creek trailhead, signed by Ranger James Bull, referred to a stretch called "the Turnpikes," and I figured this was it. Hardly wilderness, but I suppose necessary.

I heard a sharp "Geek!" as I came upon what Mel Hansen had called the "massive rock slide" at one end of Clear Lake, a much more suitable habitat for pikas than a slash pile. Clear Lake stretched away southerly toward a perfect rounded forested hill, which it reflected just as perfectly. The boulder bunny's head poked up from behind a boulder; it had a whiskered gray muzzle like mine, big ears, button eyes. Nuthatches tooted their plastic horns all around. The beepers and geekers together composed a comedy chorus that would break up the most jaded audience.

For only the second time in my current foot travels, I hit the Pacific Crest Trail, which bore no sign, in accord with USFS policy in the wilderness. Skirting little round Deer Lake, I passed beneath some giant noble firs. Long papery white bracts and purple-edged seed scales with pink stripes, from different parts of the cone, lay scattered all over the trail. I took one apart to see how it worked and ate two or three fir seeds — sweet and terpy-tarry, about as substantial as a sunflower seed. A grape-, pink-, and straw-colored squirrel midden on top of a log, a heap of nearly whole blueberries and leaves in the trail, likely deposited by a small bear. If you didn't know where they came from, the berries could almost go on your granola, they were so close to fresh. Others had noted *Ursus* in the area, for soon I came to Bear Lake, wooded, with isolated coves. On a long, alluring peninsula a purple towel hung in the sun, and blue tents peeked from the trees, but I got away without seeing anyone.

The white flowers, red, winy berries, and pawlike leaves of dwarf bramble crept over the forest floor. Rush Creek's bed, dry and full of vesiculated basalt cobbles, made a way through the broken forest as I left Trail No. 2000. I wanted to get down to the meadowlands and out of the forest that the new Pacific Crest Trail adhered to. Rush Creek quickly brought me to the *old* Crest Trail, which led northerly to tiny Acker Lake. Hikers on the new forest trail miss this lake and much of the meadows. I understood the management objective, but (selfishly) wasn't prepared to be bound by it. The meadows were, after all, what I'd come for; cruising through on the hikers' turnpike had nothing to do with me. And this was how I'd pictured Indian Heaven: beautiful blue lochs bounded by high firs and paint-box meadows, silent but for the breeze and the pipers and rustlers in the brush.

I traveled south into what has long been known as the Grand Meadow. Golden grasses and sedges filled a dried lake bed where grasshoppers sawed their last days away. A beargrass mound bore a dense mass of marsh violets with little rounded heart-shaped leaves and still one purple-blue flower. In a dry streambed two tawny California tortoiseshell butterflies, their tongues out, basked and puddled on dry basalt cobbles — for what reward? One left and returned, and they tussled, as if there weren't enough rocks for all. Then I made out that the "cobble" was a purple coyote scat. Male nymphalid butterflies often visit droppings for nutrients. They were joined by a faun anglewing, rich rust above, brown and jade beneath. They pumped their wings, fresh and bright, ready for hibernation. On a perfect fall day these brilliant russet butterflies are dazzling even with their wings closed, showing soft, striated browns, grays, greens, and blues. Spring side, autumn side, butterflies of the equinox. Later, when I arrayed my cheese, apples, and crackers on a log "table" left by horsemen, I was surprised to find a tortoiseshell immured in my raisins. This irruptive species had been all over the Northwest for two or three seasons, and this one had somehow found its way into the raisins, a fossil in the making.

Another bright fall butterfly, a male orange sulphur, flew up the meadow mimicking the old markers of the disused trail, which I now abandoned in favor of map and compass. The grassland reminded me of the Monarca Llanos of Michoacán, in Mexico — the high clearings where the migratory monarchs fly on sunny winter days — and the various orange butterflies gliding through completed the illusion. Water boatmen with inch-long oars worked the edge of a small lake, along with whirligig beetles and water striders; the aquatics alone could occupy you forever, I thought. The water's acidity must still be low to allow so many insects.

Huckleberry and heather hedged the trail. The meadows were dry until I came to an oxbow enclosing a saturated chartreuse mat of sphagnum studded with alpine wintergreen. In an elbow of the oxbow, an old purple bottle neck protruded from the moss, sign of former medicine, not of the Klickitat kind. The medicine worked for me when I lost a favorite mechanical pencil and, backtracking up and down grade, found it. The same purple as the bottle and the marsh violets, the pencil stood out in the hoof-ground mud.

Arriving in the late afternoon at Rock Lake, a boulder field with water, I was just three miles from a trailhead on the western side of the wilderness. I'd crossed Indian Heaven, from Cultus on the eastern edge to Rock on the west, in a day, meaning that the wilderness area is none too large. Fabled Blue Lake was too far for the remaining daylight, so I turned back on an old closed trail to Lake Umtux. This splendid route was granted me by Mel Hansen's blessed book. Since my three sets of backup maps — USFS, USGS topographic quadrangles, and Green Trails — differed in almost every respect, I could never have covered the ground I did without the late author's assistance.

Water, reflections, sharp and soft shapes and hues made up the fading day. Rabbit mounds, pronounced by red huckleberries, rose above the meadow grass. The lowest hucks were more purple, the higher bushes more orange; backlit by the dropping sun, both turned neon. A pea-green pond was backed by the entire red end of the spectrum. When I struck Lemei Lake after six, the sun still lit the harvest-hay meadows. At sunset six mallards flew off the last lake before my own. An old, vague route crossed a vast meadow below Clear Lake. I arrived at my camp in the dark after nine hours of hiking in heaven.

The night was almost balmy; I lingered up with the moon. A screech owl called, and bats flittered over camp. I closed my eyes behind a mental shade of reds, taxed by an overload of brilliance. As one often sees at night the images of the day in the mind, I saw a mosaic of scarlet bushes, blue lakes, and tawny meadows stretching away forever. I saw deeply rutted paths but no roads, no clear-cuts. And across the vague meadows, I saw forms that could have been elk, deer, or firs; could have been bears or bushes or Klickitat people, carrying baskets of *olallie* back to the race-track encampment. Could have been hairy monsters on parade. Might have been any of these, then changed into another. Such things happen in heaven, which, as Thoreau says, is "under our feet as well as over our heads."

- - -

I spent my last day in Indian Heaven close to camp. First business was gathering mushrooms. I don't know how anyone gets along in the woods without a stout butterfly net. I'd already employed Marsha as walking staff, retriever, plant vasculum, and yoke for carrying heavy water vessels. Now she carried a peck of king bolete mushrooms and a quart of huckleberries, gathered along the Lemei Trail close to camp. The boletes went into an omelet, and the berries into pancakes; I made hash browns with red and green peppers in case that wasn't enough. Of course I planned to share with the gray jays. By the time I finished off one of the best meals I've ever had with a mocha java, even the whiskey jacks were sated.

Then I returned to Deep Lake to cast the print and try for a fish for dinner. A shorebird was perched atop the flat rock as I approached it. It flew to a black pebbled beach, and I saw to my surprise that it was a snipe, a bird I associate with wet lowlands. I thought of all the times I'd heard the search for Bigfoot called a "snipe hunt," usually by people who had no idea that snipe are real birds. Now here was the snipe itself, smack dab where some might say Bigfoot once walked.

I mixed plaster of Paris and poured it into the impression on the flat rock. While it set, I tried to catch a cutthroat. I am no angler. I have not experienced the fly-fishing bliss that informs so much contemporary nature writing. When my father took me fishing, I always drifted off with my butterfly net. But pan-fried trout and fresh boletes sounded fine. I'd foraged in my father's old creel and brought along some line, hooks, sinkers, a red-and-white Dare Devle spinner (my boyhood favorite), and a lure with fake salmon eggs. With duct tape I rigged up the pole of my butterfly net as a rod and cast out . . . time after time. My father would have been amused, or disgusted. On the first cast I caught an unfortunate Cascades frog by the foot-web and released it. Then nothing. It would be leftovers for dinner, but at least I'd tried. The "track" cast came out rather better than the other kind, so I took back a nice footlike chunk of plaster, if no fish.

That night I was enjoying my last campfire in Indian Heaven when I heard a human call. I went up the trail to see if someone needed help. There I found a pair of night-bound hikers, a mother and her son. Karen wanted to go on and try to find her uncle's party, perhaps at Clear Lake. Max, tired and unnerved by the dark and the eerie calls of very near coyotes, wanted to stay by my fire. Offering to share the site and the blaze, I found, curiously, that I almost wanted them to stay. They went on, but a little later another group bumbled into my camp, thinking I might be Karen and Max. When the silence returned I was glad I didn't have them all as guests: just me, the fire, and the moon.

What was it like before fire and flashlights, on a moonless night? I love the dark and revere the night. Yet a night with no light at all is like eyes with no lids: too much of a good thing. I tried to let the stories of marauding hairy devils get me spooked to see what that might feel like, but the fire and logic kept the fears at bay.

In spite of Teddy Roosevelt's gruesome account of a trapper raked away from his campfire, *Beowulf*'s eerie tale of Grendel slaughtering thanes in the mead hall, John Gardner's bloodier version from Grendel's point of view, the many Indian tales of abductions, I can't manage to see Sasquatch as threatening. Of course some individuals could be, just as some people are. Monsters scare us whether they exist or not. Yet if it walks, Bigfoot is no monster, merely an animal. Animals can represent either allegorical, atavistic fear, like Dorothy and the Scarecrow's lions and tigers and bears, or actual physical threat, like grizzlies for hikers in Montana or Alaska. Bigfoot, like a big bear, could play both roles. But there is no recent reason to believe that it represents a serious threat to humans. In virtually every contemporary account, it only wants to get away.

And yet we are not the masters of our hearts in darkness. When my whistled "Clair de Lune" to the moon echoed across the lake, *something* didn't like it. A cry arose near the shore, like a cross between a heron disturbed at night and a crow's caw with massive amps. But as it receded to the northwest and repeated — it would call each time I whistled a phrase — it became a weird and harsh one-note call, like a scream or a roar or a metal sheet being whipped. And though I knew this must be an animal, one I couldn't place in the field guide of my mind, it managed to get me a little spooked after all. I left the fire well banked and crackling as I retreated into my tent.

- - -

My wild idyll ended in the morning. The previous night's phantom arrivals were just the vanguard. At the other end of the lake people were loudly comparing the merits and prices of real estate in the San Juan Islands and Ocean Shores. So why didn't they go there? I remembered why I whisper in the wilds.

As I packed, my colorful array of stuff on the tent's fly sheet made a truly appalling mass. Any Yakama of old would have doubled up with laughter at the sight of it. Of course I didn't *need* the books, the Therma-Rest pad, the changes of clothes, the air pillow, the candle lantern, camera, binoculars, butterfly net, maps, charts, journals, and so on. But I wanted them and was willing to be my own beast of burden. Apart from a lot less food and the transmogrification of my plaster from package to cast, the burden was the same I'd arrived with. I jerked my foot out of my boot at the feel of something foreign — my neglected watch. A friend fresh back from the Amazon had told me of shaking out his boot for no reason, only to dislodge a huge bird-eating spider. We react automatically to lumps in our shoes, just as we do to bumps in the night and whistles in the woods.

The watch said it was time to depart my tidy if slightly more used campsite. I left behind my impression, more clinkers in the fire pit, and a sliced *Boletus:* benedictions. Clark's nutcrackers whistled in a fir, and a sharp-shinned hawk, smaller than my resident Cooper's, skimmed three feet over my head. If there was anything cultus here, I hadn't seen it. I surrendered the lake to the party of eight that had captured the far shore.

The retreat went faster than the entry, thanks to gravity's assist. On the way out I mused on the nature of being alone in the wild, and in evolutionary time. In Indian Heaven I had known a hundred hours of solitude. On my way to Deep Lake for water early that morning I had met up with Allen Cossitt, the photographer I'd first met at Quartz Creek. Having spoken to no one but the jays, myself, and passing voices in the night for so long, I wanted to stretch out my solitude. Just entering his own, he understood. Now, wading the stream of weekend hikers, there was no escape from company.

When you encounter no other person for days on end, you begin to forget what you look like. In time you might forget who you are. This forgetting was part of the power quest during which Northwest Indians hoped to encounter, and survive, Dzonoqua and other power-guarders. Today, drowning in people, we too forget where we came from. But unlike the vision questers, we meet no guides.

Seeing nothing with which our kind recognizes kinship, no one to mar our sublime ancestral solitude, we come to believe we are unique on the planet. The next step is that well-known psychosis of solitaries: declaring ourselves God. Judging from our behavior so far, we're well on the way to doing just that. I believe the hubris of *Homo* comes at least partly from our assumption of uniqueness. The recognition of others in our midst who are not so very different might inspire a little humility. Perhaps the Indians are right when they speak of presences that only those with Indian eyes can see. Perhaps we are not alone after all.

14

Natural History of

the Bigfoot Hunters

This may very well be the destiny of the lonely Sasquatch, to be
perpetually obscured by those who try hardest to discover it.
— Michael M. Ames, *Manlike Monsters on Trial*

TWO PLASTER CASTS stand on my work table. One, bought from
the Western Bigfoot Society, was taken from a mold made in
1967 at the site of the Patterson-Gimlin film at Bluff Creek in northern California. Pressed in gray Mount St. Helens ash, this copy is gray,
fourteen inches long, six across, and obviously hominoid: a big footprint or a fake. The other cast is the one I made at Deep Lake. It is
about an inch shorter and narrower than the Bluff Creek cast, and it
lacks obvious toes, but the possible heel, big toe, and ball of the foot
aren't bad. To me it suggests the press of a primate foot: a big footprint or a feature of erosion.

So I was prepared to leave the matter until I saw in an issue of
Smithsonian an article by Richard Wolkomir on recent anthropological finds in the Americas. A photograph said to represent a child's
footprint preserved in Chilean sandstone looked strikingly like the
negative of my Deep Lake artifact. Recently I showed my cast to Grover Krantz, author of *Big Footprints: A Scientific Inquiry into the Reality of
Sasquatch*. Krantz regards the 1967 Patterson-Gimlin film and the
prints that came from the area as probably authentic. But he was not
impressed with my Indian Heaven plaster; it seemed to him too flat-
bottomed for a human footprint. When I compared it with the Chilean print, he said he didn't regard that as a real footprint either.

These bits of "evidence" — chunks of plaster, photographs, the
dents in earth or rocks — demonstrate one thing for certain: we have

At Bigfoot Daze in Carson, Washington, I acquired a copy of a plaster cast taken from a mold impressed in Mount St. Helens ash; the original cast was made at Bluff Creek soon after Patterson's adventure. *T. L. Pyle*

no common sense of what constitutes proof of existence, of what *evidence* really is. This is one of the major reasons for the lack of consensus among those interested in Sasquatch phenomena. But it is only one. Perhaps even more important is the sheer variety of method, motive, and mentality among those who go forth in search of hairy giants. As I began looking into Bigfoot, I found the natural history of the Bigfoot hunters at least as compelling as the animal itself. I soon realized, however, that the personalities and territories of the investigators would become the most time-consuming and trying aspect of the undertaking. None of them reveals his findings or theories unless he trusts that the inquisitor won't rip him off. (The male pronoun is appropriate throughout this discussion, since virtually all of the serious Sasquatch pursuers I've met are males.) All are ego-involved and proprietary when it comes to the fabled object of their pursuit, and each one is an individual, full of foibles and crochets and more or less obsessed — probably as it should be for seekers of grails. I was fully familiar with all these traits among the many butterfly enthusiasts I have known.

I have also found the Bigfoot hunters to be generous, kind, and helpful, though not usually to one another. Make no mistake: there is a competition going on here, a contest perceived by the participants as the most important possible, with the biggest stakes; the competitors intend to win if at all possible. Some show a spirit of collegiality and a desire to expand our knowledge. Individuality looms large in this enterprise, however, and friendships forged over Bigfoot may be short-lived or carry a tinge of shared suspicion. Except for their tendency to believe in advance of proof, this strange company resembles another idiosyncratic troop, the scientists.

Actually, they don't believe *without* proof; they simply accept a standard of proof that academic investigators are usually unwilling to allow. This brings us back to plaster casts and to Grover Krantz. A full professor at Washington State University's Department of Anthropology in Pullman, Dr. Krantz is the exception to the amateur status of most of the hunters. He is also much harder-headed than most when it comes to evidence. Even so, he is convinced that unnamed anthropoids walk the woods. Or, rather, one named anthropoid: he thinks Bigfoot is probably a species of *Gigantopithecus*, the enormous apes of the Pliocene and Pleistocene known from tooth and jaw fossils found in Asia.

I visited Krantz on a June Sunday when the campus was bare of students and my steps were the only echoes in the halls of the handsome old anthropology building. My visit was not a guaranteed success since, in an essay on the ethics of the Bigfoot hunt in *Washington* magazine, I had written:

> Professor Krantz may resent the professional opprobrium he receives as a Bigfoot believer, fallout that simply demonstrates the pre-Copernican attitudes of many scientists. He doesn't deserve their close-minded contempt. But if Krantz dislikes the appellation of crank, he would appreciate even less that of murderer. For if he kills, or causes to be killed, a hominid, then a murderer he will surely be in the minds of many people.

Nonetheless he greeted me civilly in his laboratory, which was lined with shelves supporting plaster casts of footprints as well as more conventional human and pre-human fossils. A lanky man, Krantz wore blue jeans and a gray work shirt with lots of pens. His hair and beard were the color of his shirt, the hair a thick, trimmed tassel, the beard short on the chin, long on the neck. He flopped in his chair and lit a cigarette ventilated by a device of his own making. Behind specs his eyes warned that he was weary of mindless and repetitive Bigfoot interviews.

In his book Krantz analyzes the available physical and other evidence for Sasquatch and speculates from an informed position on the ecology, biological traits, and evolutionary affinities of this and related putative animals. Respect for this rogue anthropologist, who dares to speak seriously of such matters, has generally increased since the book appeared. He believes that his career and reputation have suffered to some extent because of his warmth for the subject of Bigfoot, but his recent promotion and his colleagues' newfound interest suggest to him that they may be coming around — if not to acceptance, at least to a desirable open-mindedness.

But then, Grover doesn't want people to *believe* in Bigfoot, at least not the way they once believed in unicorns. He says that believing is something you do because it makes you feel good. At one time he did believe, which he equates with hope. Later he came to *know*, which is something quite different. "I don't *believe* in Bigfoot," he told me. "I have certain knowledge that causes me to *conclude*." What is this knowledge? Chiefly the tracks, as he explains in his book, and the Patterson film. I asked to see one of the tracks on which dermal ridges and pores clearly appear, authenticated by forensic pathologists. The print was impressive, yet, he lamented, it did not satisfy the scientific establishment, which is why he insists on the need for a Bigfoot specimen.

Just before I left, he showed me his reconstruction of the skull of *Gigantopithecus*. Known and respected for his work on *Homo erectus*, Krantz has received both praise and derision for the model. In their 1990 book *Other Origins: The Search for the Giant Ape in Human Prehistory*, Russell Ciochon, John Olsen, and Jamie James engagingly describe their search for fossils in Vietnam and their belief that Giganto (as they call it) cohabited with early man. But they give both Krantz and Bigfoot short shrift. Ignoring his *Gigantopithecus* model, they call his theory that Bigfoot and the extinct ape are identical "threadbare" and dismiss him as "a fervent believer" who "has stepped outside the bounds of science."

As a self-described intuitive iconoclast, Krantz is used to it. He is happy to see minds opening, and one senses that he anticipates the victory being all the sweeter when it comes because of the mockery that has gone before. By his own confession he is no woodsman, and his ultralight helicopter sits grounded in his garage, so Krantz is unlikely to make the discovery himself. But as far as he is concerned, he already has the evidence, and it is up to the others to catch up. Even so, no one will be happier than he when the type specimen is safely lodged in a museum. It is Krantz's insistence on a specimen that makes him controversial and that brought about my earlier indictment of him.

Grover Krantz may be unusual in being an academic on the track of Sasquatch, but he is not the only scientist to treat the subject seriously. Myra Shackley, lecturer in archaeological science at the University of Leicester, stated in her book *Still Living?* that Mongolia's Almas might be a surviving Neandertal and that Yeti and Bigfoot probably exist. Geoffrey Bourne, the former director of the Yerkes Primate Center, wrote in his *Gentle Giants* (1975) that *Gigantopithecus* "may indeed have survived to the present day in very isolated areas" and "might be the animal that is responsible for the *Yeti* and Bigfoot sightings." And John Napier, the late former director of the Primate Biology Program at the Smithsonian Institution, concluded that a hoax sufficient to explain the facts was even more unlikely than the animal itself.

The symposium "Sasquatch and Related Phenomena," at the University of British Columbia in May 1978, brought together twenty professors in various fields along with several serious laymen to consider the mythology, ethnology, ethology, ecology, biogeography, physiology, psychology, history, and sociology of the subject. All took it seriously, and while few if any accepted the existence of Sasquatch outright, they jointly concluded "that there are not reasonable grounds to dismiss all the evidence as misperception or hoax."

- - -

So while it is not true, as often asserted, that science has willfully ignored the phenomenon, far and away the greatest number of Bigfoot buffs have been nonacademics, if not antiacademics. It is common at Sasquatch gatherings to hear vicious derogations of the academy for "repressing" information or for blindly ignoring the obvious and thereby pulling the rug out from under the worthy ranks of the dedicated amateurs. These charges, however naive and lacking in empathy for the scientific method, are not without basis. Many tenured or tenure-hopeful scientists have pooh-poohed the topic without any critical attention to its substance. Grover Krantz and the BC Twenty can thus be seen as courageously bucking the tide, sometimes to their detriment.

The amateurs (true lovers of the search) have no such tethers on their enthusiasm. Nor do they labor under the restraints of experimental protocol. This results in a vibrant output of opinions, publications, and theories that run the gamut from brilliant to disturbed, from cleverly intuitive to sloppy and gullible, and from helpful to hopeless.

Most of the Bigfooters begin by gathering all the information they can find, then rejecting those reports or references they deem groundless or unsupportive of their biases. A few of the major players apply certain standards to weed out the more vacuous or obviously fatuous data. Others build great middens of material, like Grendel's bone pile in the mere, where chaff and kernel compost together. Ray Crowe, the big, voluble, white-mustached director of the Western Bigfoot Society, is the model for this catholic approach. His periodical, the *Track Record*, is a repository of all things Bigfootish, from obvious dross to genuinely intriguing gems. Ray says of his all-embracing approach, "Always read with your skepticals on."

Of the many cataloguers, one of the most thorough and opinionated is Danny Perez of the Center for Bigfoot Studies in Norwalk, California. He has published an odd, detailed critique of the Patterson-Gimlin film in his *BigfooTimes*, as well as a very useful bibliography of ape-man publications entitled *Big Footnotes*. Perez is also one of the most outspoken advocates of gunning down a Sasquatch and is known for attempting to do the same to his friends and colleagues in verbal exchanges. In action he is like an impatient terrier, yipping and nipping.

Crowe and Perez typify two morphs of the Bigfoot searcher, in fact two poles occupied by obsessives of all sorts. Sticking with the corvid theme of Ray's name, you might say that they are both jackdaws, gatherers of all kinds of glittering objects. But while Ray is more the lumbering, deliberate raven, issuing occasional barks or good-natured hoots, Danny apes the jay, forever squawking in a high-pitched and aggressive manner around the eyes and heels of all the other creatures in the wood. Most of the other giant-hunters more resemble magpies — also acquisitive and endlessly curious, but querulous rather than declamatory in their statements and retiring by nature. These several seekers after Sasquatch tend to be very serious, and I began to wonder whether any were in it simply for the fun. When I met Ray Wallace, I found one who was.

Along with the footprint casts on my desk squats a round stone about the size of a high school shot but weighing some four pounds instead of the twelve we hefted when we put that steel ball. The stone was a gift from Ray Wallace, who presented it as an example of a missile that Bigfoot routinely throws to kill deer. To him the existence of round concretions (common formations in sediments) provides perfectly adequate evidence for the presence of hairy monsters that hunt deer. Or else he was having me on.

Shortly after my interest in Bigfoot became known, I received a letter in a childish script from Toledo, Washington, a logging town in the Cascade foothills. It was from Wallace, a Toledo patriarch and, in all senses, a character. He enclosed a couple of snapshots of someone in a gorilla suit, in one photo sitting on a log and in the other tugging at an elk carcass by a stream. He claimed to have encountered Bigfeet often and to have many still photos and motion pictures of them performing various activities. "Let me know what you are interested in and maybe I can help you out, as I have built roads where these giant sized people have roamed for over 300 years and the only people sees B.F.s are people like me that's running these big yellow Caterpillars as that's what the B.F.s are interested in as they will follow a cat around all day and watch us build roads."

I was surprised to learn that a roadside zoo I remembered along old U.S. Highway 99 (before Interstate 5 was completed) — white deer, bison hunching in the rain — had been "Ray Wallace's Free Zoo," a landmark for a generation. That was one of the first things I found out when I went to visit Wallace. The door of his Toledo home was open, and Ray, a big, craggy man in high-waisted dungarees, red Loggers World suspenders, and flannel shirt, with mussed white hair and stubbly jowls, was at ease in a tilted-back La-Z-Boy. I took up a place beside him, and for the next four hours he told me stories.

Wallace was born in Missouri in 1917, and in 1919 his family came west; he was raised on the Cowlitz River, where Indians camped and taught him to track when he played hooky. Ever since he has plied the trades of the woods up and down the West Coast. His specialty was building roads into the wilderness, but he also speculated in gold, platinum, oil, beefalo, and Bigfoot.

I had a hard time keeping him on the topic at first. He seemed more interested in telling about UFOs, which he claimed to have seen regularly all around the St. Helens country. One of the first he saw was "back when the Russians put them Spudnicks up . . . it was a-foolin' around a star. At Thelma Sorenson's place up Salmon Creek, she 'n' her husband got a divorce and she wanted to sell that flatbed truck . . . We went out there and saw three flying saucers come by, and boy, you talk about moving!" Since then "them dawg-gone flyin' saucers is all over the place." Everybody else around there has seen them too, he maintained.

As president of the Yellow Creek Logging Company, Ray held Forest Service contracts in northern California in the fifties and sixties. It was reports of disturbances to his road-building crews that first drew attention to the Willow Creek area, which has since become "Bigfoot Town, USA." Huge tracks and equipment vandalism, found by worker Jerald Crew and Ray's brother Wilbur, led to extensive newspaper coverage nationwide and attracted the noted cryptozoologist Ivan Sanderson to investigate. Sanderson told the story in detail in his book *Abominable Snowmen: Legend Come to Life*. He described Wallace, who was righteously upset about the meddling monsters' interference with his contracts, as "hard-boiled and pragmatic . . . a professional skeptic" — hardly my impression.

Later Ray became involved with Tom Slick's Pacific Northwest Bigfoot Expedition of 1960, bringing in a couple of trackers with dogs. Always on the lookout for opportunities, whether in timber, minerals, or monsters, he and his partners offered Slick's operatives a look at a captive Bigfoot for cash up front. When they asked to see the animal first, Wallace claimed it had sickened and been released.

Ray's hearing has been damaged by constant bulldozer work, and he tends to speak loudly. Much of what he bellowed to me, punctuated by dawg-gone's, had to do with saucers and giants. He played a record he had helped to produce, an LP of ballads by a Johnny Cash–type country singer named Don Jones. Cut in Nashville, the disk included a Bigfoot song mixed with Bigfoot screams that Ray had taped by lowering a microphone into a hole he'd dynamited out around a trapped Sasquatch. The high-pitched shrieks could have been anything, but Ray maintained that a "government counter-intelligence machine . . . declared these screams to be no sound of any known animal in the world today."

The LP jacket photo, taken by Ray and clearly staged, showed a Bigfoot and a mountain lion placidly sitting together after sharing a deer kill. The Bigfoot was saying "Zuki, zuki" to the puma, which is what you're supposed to say to pacify giants. Bigfoot runs with cougars and bears, Ray said. He once told Bob Titmus, a noted Bigfoot tracker and taxidermist, who was tanning cougar hides, "You shouldn't kill Bigfoot's pets."

As hokey as Ray's pictures were, he called the Patterson-Gimlin film a fake: "I know exactly which Yakama Indian was in that monkey suit," he said. He also claimed Patterson, "a cagey guy," stole his screams. The record played on: "Scientists call him the missing link, some people think he is extinct." Ray said the single "got down to number ten on the scale of things . . . ten more points and we'd 'a' got a gold record." It used to be for sale in a shop called Cowlitz Landing, where Ray's writings could also be had in a tabloid of the same name. "You could hear it there too," he said. "But that dawg-gone nickelodeon durn near wore it out."

Elna Wallace came in to turn down the record and asked me to stay for dinner. She did not seem amused that yet another Bigfoot buff was egging her husband on. Then Ray told me about a diary he'd bought written by early California gold miners, red-hot with Bigfoot stories. He was sure a movie would be made of the book, once it was written. If I'd write it, he offered, I could have a half interest. I steered the topic back to Bigfoot. "I've fergot more about Bigfoot than most people ever knew," he said. "I worked where they lived. You don't move fast around 'em when they're standin' there with a dawg-gone rock in each hand."

Ray doesn't claim to have been attacked by a Bigfoot, but he has been hurt in the woods. He broke his back when a whistle punk (signal man) screwed up, then wore a body cast while he set chokers for four months. In a bad crummy (crew bus) wreck, he broke his hip, "three lombards," five ribs, and a knee. But he was cured by an Assembly of God preacher overnight. He also puts stock in "choirpractors," raw garlic, and lemon juice, which cured his arthritis in two weeks.

Before I left, Ray told me that he actually believed that the Bigfeet were aborigines wearing bearskins. This didn't square with his pictures or the reputed dimensions, but consistency did not seem to be a major roadblock for Ray. According to folks I talked with on the Hoopa Reservation who remembered him, it never has been. There are those, in fact, who believe that Ray began the entire series of modern northern California episodes himself. He appeared on the scene immediately after the tracks were found near Willow Creek. And he says he knows who was in the "monkey suit" at Bluff Creek when the Patterson-Gimlin film was made.

Perhaps Ray has seen something, perhaps he hasn't. But of course

NATURAL HISTORY OF THE BIGFOOT HUNTERS

he is without credibility in the Bigfoot world. The serious searchers will be surprised that I have spent so much space on him. Yet by himself Ray Wallace embodies the diversity of traits found throughout the guild: intelligence, cleverness, cupidity, guile, wit, judgmentalism, hyperbole, and genuine curiosity. It is clear that he once had the latter, even if it has since been bulldozed under his own mountains of bullshit. He was a significant figure in the early-sixties stories out of California, and he has popped up in Bigfoot lore ever since.

Driving out of town, I was stopped by a policeman for having a taillight out. He turned out to be a former student of mine, and I asked him about Wallace. Ray had donated the land for the town high school, the young officer said; he was "a pillar of the community."

On my way out, Ray had kindly handed me the concretion. He hadn't a clue where they came from, but he knew they were "Bigfoot's bullets." And then he gave me one thing more. With the winning, confiding smile that Sanderson had noted, this bulldozer of a man winked at me and said, "Don't waste your time looking for Bigfoot."

— — —

Who are the "major players," the serious Bigfoot searchers I referred to? Six names come chiefly to mind: Ivan Sanderson, Bernard Heuvelmans, John Green, René Dahinden, Peter Byrne, and Grover Krantz. Bob Titmus could be added to the list, but he has not been recently active. One cannot take a close look at the North American hairy giant without taking each of these men into account. The late Sanderson was a prolific author of natural history and long the world's leading student and raconteur of animal mysteries. Heuvelmans, a much-respected Belgian zoologist and "the father of cryptozoology," wrote the encyclopedic *On the Track of Unknown Animals*. Green, Dahinden, and Byrne are the leading trackers in North America. Green and Dahinden will have nothing to do with Byrne, and they have not spoken to each other for fifteen years; Byrne advocates a more collegial approach.

It was Byrne whom I had met at his Bigfoot Information Center in 1975 and had subsequently brought to Yale for the seminar that turned several academic heads. Byrne, born in Ireland, became a tea planter in India, then a tiger hunter and safari guide. Most of his kills,

- 191 -

he told me, were to finish off wounded animals left by his drunken and idiot clients. Later, convinced of the need to protect the wildlife he had formerly tracked to shoot, he helped found the International Wildlife Conservation Society and originated Nepal's first tiger preserve. He recently assisted with a water project there.

As early as 1948 Byrne found a possible Yeti track in Sikkim and began searching for the maker. Ten years later he was recruited to the Himalayan Yeti expedition supported by the charismatic and much-loved Texas oil heir Tom Slick, who was influenced by Heuvelmans's book to pursue the elusive snowman. Byrne proved instrumental in having part of a possible Yeti hand shipped from Nepal to England in the suitcase of the willing (and amused) actor Jimmy Stewart, who had been visiting a maharaja. Later Byrne was summoned by Slick to California to head up the Pacific Northwest Expedition, on the heels of the Willow Creek footprint findings.

It was in this period that much of the current animosity originated. Byrne, Dahinden, Green, Titmus, and Wallace were all involved in the expedition, at Slick's expense. The friction of egos and the resentments spawned then have never quite healed. Canadians Dahinden and Green (still speaking at that time) hied themselves back to British Columbia to carry out a satellite investigation for Slick. And then, on October 6, 1962, Slick was killed in the crash of a light aircraft. All the expeditions he had supported came to an abrupt halt, and the Sasquatch search's one strong bonding influence evaporated. Byrne returned to Nepal and led river expeditions out of Katmandu, among other activities, for the next few years. He recalled that his first American period was bracketed by a pair of eerily connected events: hearing Marilyn Monroe sing "Happy Birthday" to Jack Kennedy at Madison Square Garden when he first arrived; then, back in the Nepalese bush, hearing of JFK's death from a village big man, who told him, "Your Big Man has died."

In 1971 Byrne, back in the States, founded the Bigfoot Information Center in The Dalles. He and Dede Killeen edited *The Bigfoot News*, a mother lode of information. In 1975 he published the best campfire read of all the Bigfoot books, *The Search for Bigfoot: Monster, Myth, or Man* (foreword by Jimmy Stewart). In 1979 Byrne and Killeen suspended the project and returned to Nepal and India to work on Asian elephant conservation. In 1991 Byrne's *Tula Hatti: The Last Great Elephant* was published. Back in Oregon, Peter's interest in Bigfoot was rekindled, and he founded the Bigfoot Research Project in 1992.

Well funded by the Academy of Applied Science of Boston, the Project is described as "a benign, scientific investigation designed to prove the existence of a large, bipedal, hair-covered hominid believed to be living in the forested mountain ranges of the Pacific Northwest." With a staff of three, equipped with four-wheel-drive Blazers and Bell Jet Ranger helicopters; sophisticated computers and software designed for tracking serial killers; digital global positioning equipment; motion, sound, and heat sensors; radios, cellular phones, and night-vision scopes; and a widely known contact line (1-800-BIGFOOT), Byrne feels he is finally poised to find the animal if it exists. But rather than raking the countryside, as he did in his youth, he is concentrating on computer analysis of his database to construct what he calls "geo-time patterns" — integrative models that will predict where and when Sasquatch is most likely to occur. Then, he believes, the team can go forth into the field with a much greater likelihood of success. The full-time team includes Tod Deery, director of field activities, and office manager Deborah Wolman, who copes with the many serious, flaky, and obscene calls on the 800 line.

Byrne is the object of resentment by the other big names for several reasons. His suave and handsome appearance, enhanced by his Oxbridge accent, pressed khakis, sweat-stained safari hat, and silk cravat they see as a pose to further oil his considerable charm. That a young foreigner would have a position of leadership in Tom Slick's California operation never sat well with the others. His unorthodox conclusions — that Bigfoot is shorter than often stated, quite intelligent, and entirely unthreatening — contradict their own. His insistence on a peaceful approach to the creature, eschewing guns and attempting contact and communication, strike the other searchers as unrealistic, sanctimonious, and troublesome for their own methods. He further makes them look bad by (at least in public) rising above the disputes, taking the high road, and pleading for cooperation, while they kvetch and point fingers.

Under the title "Carpe Diem" in a recent *Track Record,* Byrne wrote that "Bigfooters, especially those who tend to spend time in the rascally and useless trade of chastising their competitors, would do well to keep the time factor of their trade in mind." He goes on to state that we are "literally no further forward than we were when Tom Slick and his merry men . . . were scrambling up and down the pineclad slopes of the Six Rivers National Forest, the rugged mountains of the Trinity Alps and the dark ravines of the Marble Mountain Wilderness." In other words, let's get with it, chaps!

The greatest source of resentment against Byrne and his undertakings, however, must be his substantial financial support. Not since Tom Slick, who was devoted to Byrne and vice versa, has there been a financial angel for Bigfoot research like the current Academy of Applied Sciences commitment. Sasquatch hunters have been notoriously poor, always scratching for money for gas and plaster. Bob Titmus worked as a taxi-driving taxidermist in Kitimat. Roger Patterson promoted his film through public appearances, multiple rights sales, and any other way he could (Robert Gimlin is said to have never profited from it). The entire field has scrambled for cash, so it is understandable that Byrne's success (again) at gaining sponsorship would rankle. Then there are charges of dishonesty and double-dealing — but in this poison-pen fraternity I look at all personal attacks with as much skepticism as I apply to sightings of hairy monsters.

In spite of the calumny I have heard, I like Peter, as do most people who are not his rivals. And I don't think I'm just charmed by the khaki and the accent. I've known plenty of two-bit expatriates, has-been white hunters in tropical tuxedos, left behind by the Raj or its equivalents in some steamy outpost, living on image and foreign aid. Peter isn't one of them. I take him for a committed conservationist, a fine writer, and a genuine gentleman explorer, a species as rare today as any Yeti. He may take some shortcuts on the way to knowledge, but he has a better chance of getting there than most, and not just because of his bankroll.

I have yet to share a campfire with him, but we have sat around fireplaces in both our homes, sharing good ale, chenin blanc, or single-malt whisky, trading tales from Nepal or New Guinea, comparing signatures of Tenzing Norgay — his from personal correspondence, mine an autograph garnered in my grandmother's postwar rambles. Our conversation tends to focus on the possible phylogeny of wild men and on how they might be contacted and how conserved. I've seldom heard Byrne utter an unkind word about his colleagues. He respects Krantz, though he disagrees with him about killing a specimen. Once Ray Wallace's name came up, and Peter called him a nice and good fellow. "But he's a joker," he said, recalling certain incidents from the Slick era involving an alleged trapped animal and a demand for more money for Frosted Flakes to feed it. "Don't waste your time with guys like Ray." How oddly this echoed Ray Wallace's own words to me, "Don't waste your time looking for Bigfoot."

- - -

In May of 1994 I attended Sasquatch Daze at Harrison Hot Springs, a mountain resort town in British Columbia's Fraser River Valley. This annual event capitalizes on the area's long history of Bigfoot associations, which were first written about by J. W. Burns, a teacher on the Chehalis Indian Reserve in the twenties and thirties. His articles popularized the name "Sasquatch" and brought notoriety to the region, leading to the first Sasquatch festivals. In 1959, for British Columbia's centennial, a "Sasquatch Hunt" was mooted, then dropped. As John Green wrote, "Perhaps never before has a tourist resort achieved such publicity without actually doing anything."

The modern Sasquatch Daze, including art exhibits, Bigfoot races, and a series of forums, is an attempt to build on the town's old reputation to enhance tourism while throwing light on the Sasquatch mystery. Steve Harvey, the beleaguered organizer, was troubled by the weather, which had turned cool and rainy after a banner weekend for Canada's Memorial Day. The town was nearly deserted when I arrived, the usually thronged promenade wet and lonely, the lake undisturbed except by wind. Inside the massive old Harrison Hot Springs Hotel, however, the forum was well attended. Mostly by males — the only women present were wives and friends of Bigfooters, a trio of Bigfoot promoters from Elma, Washington, and a couple of tanned and scented blown dandelions on vacation who had just dropped in: "We're into the supernatural, Bigfoot, all of it," said Shirley.

I took a seat in the back of the room. The first speaker, freelance zoologist John Bindernagle, related his own track finding and explained that his experience made others feel free to tell him of their own. He thinks that many wildlife agency employees privately believe but are afraid to speak up. Bonnie West of Elma agreed. "When I placed an ad calling for Sasquatch experiences," she said, "I was overwhelmed . . . two to four calls came in daily." Her booklet, *Bigfoot! He's Still Out There*, relates the sightings of a sheriff, a policeman, some moms, loggers, and a woodsman named Tall Tom.

A spirited discussion followed about certain recorded calls and sounds well known among those present, which a morose fellow behind me said with no if's, and's, or but's were the noises of hogs and coyotes. Another tape was played, and a gruff voice from a man in a plaid jacket in the back said, "We know where that tape came from — Ray Wallace!" "Trash, then," someone responded.

The next talk, "The Muddy Whites of Their Eyes," was given by Donald Hepworth, an Englishman who works in animal welfare in Canada. Traveling through Idaho, he watched a pair of young Bigfeet climb a bank. In the dusk he took them at first for "Negro children." One was clearly female, he said, and someone asked if her breasts were pendulous and drooping, as in the Patterson film. "No problem there," he replied. "They were really quite firm and perky." When pressed, he said he was used to seeing women equestrians and noting their figures beneath all the riding gear.

The compact, crouching form of Danny Perez sprang up and doggedly attacked the Englishman's report on several points. A tall, spare man who had been quiet pulled him off, saying that Mr. Hepworth sounded to him like a good observer and that either he was a liar or he had seen two Sasquatch where he said he had. Hepworth went on to suggest that Bigfoot was an underutilized natural resource, and he proposed Sasquatch safaris to employ displaced loggers. I was reflecting on how well this would go down in my depressed loggers' town when Sally Newberry, who plans her own Bigfoot festival for the diminished timber village of Elma, announced that her travel agency intends to conduct expeditions into the Olympic Mountains to see sites of Bigfoot encounters.

As this was being digested, Perez barked back, demanding to know what experience Hepworth had with primates. Hepworth replied that as an SPCA inspector he had rescued a gorilla. "Its owner dined in the nude with the gorilla," he said, "while watching roller derby." Hepworth confiscated and nursed the gorilla, but it died, "probably killed with rat poison by the owner's psychiatrist boyfriend." So this is Sasquatch Daze, I thought, and settled in.

The bitchiness at Harrison Hot Springs is nothing new. When the International Society of Cryptozoology held a Bigfoot symposium in Pullman, Washington, in 1989, their newsletter described the results as "colorful." But the *High Country News* headlined it "Bigfoot Researchers Go Ape," and the *Longview Daily News* described it as a "big flop meeting." The "colorful" incidents included death threats, an arrest, a night in jail, a restraining order, and a shadow meeting held in a motel room by the "flakes" (paranormal types), who were not allowed to raise their concerns at the meeting. An anthropologist was admitted after agreeing to keep mum about his earlier assertion that three Yetis had astrally projected themselves into his Milwaukee bedroom. Danny Perez ranted, Paul Freeman walked out in protest of all the backstabbing (and of his own dismissal by many as a hoaxer), and Grover Krantz struggled for decorum — all par for the course in a field described by ISC member Forrest Wood as "characterized by much bickering, feuding, and backbiting."

- - -

The ones I'd really come to hear were the man in the plaid jacket and the tall, spare man, John Green. At the break I managed to speak with Green, one of the famous Sasquatch-hunter residents of Harrison Hot Springs (the other is Bob Titmus), as well as its former mayor. Probably the most prolific writer on the subject and holder of the largest database, Green is considered Mr. Sasquatch by many. He was a journalist and publisher of the weekly *Agassiz-Harrison Advance* at the time of the 1950s goings-on in California. After getting in on Slick's expeditions there and in B.C., and later following up on Patterson's film, he continued his investigations in Canada.

John Green was holding forth on one of his favorite themes, the stubborn failure of science to address Sasquatch. "A serious university or wildlife agency research effort would be win-win, whether they found it or not," he maintained. "Why doesn't it occur? Because our science is based on either/or and cannot afford to take chances on a perception of 'maybe.'" But, he said, scientists often do take that chance on other matters. Besides, the parsimonious interpretation — that the beast exists — is clearly better than the alternatives, such as a widespread and elaborate hoax.

Green doesn't talk with the Indians much anymore, partly because they don't distinguish between concrete and other realities. Nor does he talk with Peter Byrne or René Dahinden. He claims that Byrne is a con man who will say anything for financial support and use his information in any way that supports his preformed conclusions. Yet when Green described his hopes, they sounded curiously like Peter's. By computerizing his many reported events (examples of which appear in *Bigfoot: On the Track of Sasquatch* and his other books), he hopes to enable others to see patterns and apply them to their disciplines. His interest in the where/when/why of the animal sounded much like Byrne's geo-time patterns, and I wondered whether this might be a source of their enmity. He said he could not use Byrne's data because he couldn't count on their accuracy, though others have found Byrne to be very cautious in accepting reports, one of the traits that impressed the scientists at Yale.

As for Krantz, who was also at Harrison, Green said he was "gullible" but clearly liked him. Ray Wallace, he said, was either "bats or having a hell of a good time, telling anything and believing nothing." The real Bigfoot hunter, according to John Green, was his neighbor Bob Titmus, who was too ill to attend. Titmus is an expert hunter and tracker with a splendid array of casts, all of which he has taken himself. (Much of Titmus's field work was carried out in the Kitimat district, not far from the scene of Billy Hall's story of the Kitlope Bigfeet.) The primary splits in the field, Green said, are "kill/no kill" and "share/no share"; the latter is one of the sources of his celebrated schism with Dahinden. Green claimed that what René cares about is *who* finds Bigfoot, and it had better be him. So when Green shares data with people who haven't "earned" the right, he angers Dahinden.

Green said, convincingly, that his circumstances were such that he could walk away from Bigfoot tomorrow without losing anything other than a matter of interest to him. He is not invested in personally making the discovery, at least not in the way that Dahinden (and many of the others) seem to be. I believed him. I had known this face — combed-back, wavy silver hair, deep expressive wrinkles around tired, intense eyes, and a hard, thin, but not unfriendly smile — in a younger form, looking out handsomely from the jackets of his books of the seventies. It impressed me as the face of a man with a certain rigidity, born of long embattlement, but also with an authenticity of spirit. If that spirit is not equally generous toward all of his former coworkers on the Slick expeditions, I suppose he has his reasons. Clearly the hero of this meeting, he is nonetheless exactly what he claims Sasquatch is not and will never be — deeply and obviously human, for better and for worse.

As John Green and I parted, the man in the plaid jacket strode past, sucking on a pipe and looking straight ahead. It was Dahinden, Green's former field companion and close collaborator in the early studies. Shortly after my Guggenheim Fellowship was announced in 1989, I received an evening telephone call from a man with a strong, gruff European accent. Identifying himself as René Dahinden from Canada, he wanted to know if I was on to something and what my plans were. I assured him I did not plan to look directly for Sasquatch, and he soon rang off.

Having read about Dahinden, I felt I was looking straight at him when I saw the movie *Harry and the Hendersons,* in which a dedicated and well-armed Bigfoot hunter is parodied. Now I was standing with René under a roofed kiosk, watching the Bigfoot races in the rain. A team comprising the good people of Elma, where rain is the usual state of affairs, was undeterred, but the group was having a hard time coordinating the four-person feet and was losing soundly to the Canadians.

Dahinden is a tough, compact man, stocky but trim. He wore a blue short-sleeved shirt that showed arms still well muscled when he doffed his lumberjack plaid to look for matches, a navy T-shirt, and worn blue jeans. He too had gone gray since the Tom Slick expedition. Raised in Switzerland, René came to Canada in 1952 and heard about Sasquatch from a farmer who employed him. He has been on the track ever since. Many of his findings are colorfully reported in his book *Sasquatch: The Search for North America's Incredible Creature,* written with Don Hunter. Unlike many others, he proclaims his skepticism. "How do I know it's out there?" he asks. "I've never seen one."

Dahinden, with his jowly red face and short hair that looks trimmed with lawn clippers, has an impish demeanor, but his talk at Harrison Hot Springs was salty and dismissive: "I'm telling some of the people in this room," he said, "that they'd better learn about footprints, or they should just take their buckets and play in the sand." He has no patience for hoaxers: "We'll all get thrown in the same damn pot with morons and their damn fakes." He is irritated with those who give credence to what he sees as obvious hoaxes, as he believes Green, Byrne, and Krantz did in certain Washington State cases at Bossburg and Walla Walla. "Why fuck around with that shit when you've got a big case somewhere else?" he spurted. He interviews everyone he can and bases his strong opinions on a combination of exhaustive knowledge and hunches that "hit him in the head." A bombastic elder gnome, he is both respected and resented for saying exactly what he thinks.

René laughed and cursed over the peccadilloes of forty years spent on the spotty trail of what might be a wraith. He of course has opinions on all the others. As he has written, "The search for the Sasquatch is a bit like looking for the Holy Grail, except that it is performed by very unholy people." He blames John Green for mistakes in interpreting the Patterson film, but he doesn't let himself off either. After Patterson died, "We did so many dumb things." This unleashed a bleak soliloquy on Dahinden's interest in that storied strip. He acquired rights to the film, but having failed to ask the right questions at the time, he and Green had to rely on Gimlin's word. A convoluted and vicious course landed him in a legal and financial morass involving Gimlin, Patterson's widow, and many others. I got the feeling that Dahinden would much rather have spent the time searching for Bigfoot, but the grail was elusive and the film was there. It wouldn't be the first time celluloid had stood in for flesh and blood.

Dahinden chuckled at the races, pipe smoke swirling through his gappy teeth, and pointed out an osprey overhead. His eyes lingered on the high valleys where he'd spent happier, younger days. When he came back, I asked him what finding Sasquatch would really mean to him. Puck spoke up through a wide smile: "I'd appoint myself Bigfoot's attorney and spokesman. We'd go to the government and say Bigfoot was there first, according to the Indians. They drove him out, and now we'd demand they throw the fuckin' Indians off the reserves so he could go home!"

He looked weathered by the rain that now came hard, but he was far from finished. As he said in his book, "I just have to keep on going — and I will do — until one of these creatures is found, dead or alive."

Sasquatch Daze was winding down. The folks from Elma spoke better than they raced. Fred Bradshaw, a jovial retired police officer, recounted his impressive encounter with a huge upright creature in the southern Olympics whose odor burned his nose, "like feces and sweat." Then Robert Milner gave accounts from the Rockies and played videotapes of interviews, though the one of a person who was under the influence of *Psilocybe* mushrooms at the time of his experience did not inspire confidence.

Scott Herriott, a professional stand-up comic, told of an encounter with a Bigfoot near Willow Creek. It had bioluminescent eyes "as red as the light on the camcorder" that didn't get used because his companion was weeping with fear. They said, "Soka, soka," to the beast, á la the famous Sasquatch abductee Albert Ostman, and I recalled Ray Wallace's "Zuki, zuki," which he said he had learned from a Yurok. Herriott finished with part of his comedy routine, which was received better than the straight part.

Next came the small, bearded Danny Perez, who wanted to know why Herriott hadn't carried a gun and blasted the thing? Danny's talk, though histrionic, was interesting, and his main premise — that we are conditioned to think that something that cannot exist does not exist — was apt. After saying a few rude things about his collaborators and avowing his lack of respect for credentials and books, he announced that he planned to publish a book of his own in 2000, "because I get a kick out of this." He admitted that he is "blunt and nasty for accuracy's sake," and that he discounted certain Russian reports, partly because "my contact was an asshole." Then he returned to his attack on poor Donald Hepworth, questioning his reliability because he'd been married twice.

Grover Krantz took the podium to speak on the challenge of what to do if one actually had a specimen, qualifying his comments (and getting a laugh) by saying he might not be reliable since he'd been married four times. Even those who disagreed with the idea of taking a specimen were intrigued by the challenge of what to do with three hundred to five hundred pounds of rotting flesh that smells bad to start with and that represents a scientific H-bomb, a huge media honeypot, and a legal tar baby.

The group dispersed. All the worthy hunters went their ways to imagine their answers to the questions Grover had raised; to watch for red eyes and black shadows as they drove the rainy roads; to picture their canonization or enrichment or apotheosis or honorary degrees, should they be the lucky one; to suck on their resentments and beefs and blandishments like so many sore teeth. I settled into a long wet drive back to Gray's River, where John Green, René Dahinden, and Grover Krantz were but names on a sagging bookshelf.

I found myself thinking about the taxonomy of Bigfoot hunters Krantz presents in *Big Footprints*. He recognizes six categories: hardcore hunters, novices, tranquilizers, recorders, and "professionals."

The hard-core hunters are after a body or, more specifically, the first body, because as Krantz says, "There will be no second prize." He discerns four main motives: fame, money, personal vindication, and scientific knowledge. Given the stakes, he feels it is entirely natural that little sharing and lots of prevarication go on. The novices, he believes, are naively bumbling along in the belief that they will find a Bigfoot and that the world will happily believe them. They either graduate to another category or drop out of the search. Tranquilizers want to capture an animal for proof and study but believe it should be done with tranquilizing darts instead of bullets. Krantz gives a reasoned argument of the impracticability of this approach, which is based, he says, on a dramatically false set of assumptions.

The recorders gather information and, not being hunters, usually distribute it freely. Their data vary widely in quality, and some really collect accounts the way others might collect stamps. They publish periodicals such as the *Track Record, BigFootimes,* the *Monthly Bigfoot Report,* the *Bigfoot Record,* and dozens more. A few recorders become chroniclers, chief among them Green, Heuvelmans, and Sanderson; one, Perez, has produced a "respectable" bibliography. Krantz eliminates all those who mix UFO and paranormal information with hominoid reports as irrelevant or in the category of wackos and what he calls the "lunatic fringe."

Grover's final (and least favorite) group are those he calls "professionals." These investigators, he maintains, "*do not* want the sasquatch to be proven to exist." They have made a profession, or at least a reputation, based on the beast and stand to lose their standing (and, for some, their livelihood) when it is found. This group can include the UFO/supernatural types if those themes further their purposes; in other words, they are calculating opportunists. Some "professionals" are simply out for any publicity, something real Sasquatch investigators try to avoid whenever possible unless it might advance the search.

Krantz's nomenclature is a helpful accounting of the types and motives of these wraith-trackers, but it leaves out the academics and scientists who have taken a serious interest, such as himself. Since virtually all the other investigators scorn mysterious and monolithic "Science" for its uninterest, those scientists who pay attention deserve special note. Nor does Krantz's list account for serious investigators who disavow the use of guns or darts.

Perhaps another subspecies should be recognized: those who root around for big apes in less likely (because they are open or densely populated) areas such as Iowa, South Dakota, and New Jersey — as some people do, nearly full time. And an appendix might note the range of day jobs held by these night watchers: a physicist in New York, an environmental planner for a Washington tribe, a carpenter in Michigan, an Omaha English teacher, college students in Indiana, an electrician from Bremerton, a pycnogonist (sea-spider specialist) employed by a primate laboratory . . . there seem to be no demographic limits to the field except, apparently, gender. And there are more of them than anyone might suppose.

I have several times been approached by men mad for Sasquatch who in their driven fervor seem to fall outside all categories. One of these was Ken, who called me from the local store one autumn afternoon. I brought him home and talked Bigfoot with him over an ale. A big, paunchy man of fifty-two, he wore a plaid poly shirt open to sweaty black chest hair; his green poly pants shed threads where they'd been shortened. The Goodwill effect was warranted: a broke Texan, he'd just driven down from Alaska in an old truck with a U-Haul trailer attached with a homemade hitch. The expression on his creased, shaven face flickered between speculation, obsession, and exhaustion. He was tired of getting "Mexican wages" working construction. One good photograph, he said, and he'd have it made.

Ken's Indian girlfriend in Alaska had seen a Sasquatch at Iliamna when she was five. He'd been up there, spending eighty dollars a day at a lodge, going broke and weary. He figured that by following leads he could find it; had just returned from a fruitless look around Mount St. Helens; hoped I could give him some tips. I wanted to shake him and tell him to get a life, or a job. I did the next best thing: I told him to go see Ray Wallace. I wasn't sure if it was unkind, and if so, to which one? But I figured they'd have fun, and if Ken was lucky, maybe Ray would give him the same advice he'd given me.

— — —

So what is it, finally, that drives this compulsion to associate with monsters? To give up jobs, homes, sometimes wife and family (as René chose to do after his wife gave him an ultimatum), for a date with frustration? Is this passionate pursuit mainly a matter of looking for the main chance? Clearly fortune is an important lure, as is true for Ken. For others, notoriety: René told me he would have liked to play the Sasquatch hunter in *Harry and the Hendersons,* and he didn't mind a bit if the character was modeled on him. One of the other speakers at Harrison, Cliff Crook, had been humiliated as a boy by his father for telling about an ape encounter; his hangdog demeanor and hurt tone, as well as his words, suggested he'd been trying to vindicate himself in his father's eyes ever since, even though Dad was no longer around to prove it to. Cliff uses the bitter memory to fuel his Bigfoot Central, an investigation center in Bothell, Washington.

Danny Perez said he got a kick out of the search, and this motivation may be closer to the mark than most excuses. Almost all the hunters recall a time, often in their adolescence while reading Sanderson or Green or watching the Patterson film or some hokey Yeti movie on TV, when they were "grabbed" by Bigfoot — like the unhappy camper snatched by the beast from his fireside in Teddy Roosevelt's gruesome tale. Whatever the root cause, hundreds and maybe thousands of men have chosen to gamble family and livelihood, respect and reputation, even their very sanity, in pursuit of a prize that might not even exist.

If there is one common trait among this odd bunch, it is that they all belong to the species Roger Patterson called "the eternal individualist." And if they share a single urge, I think I discovered it during another talk at the forum in Harrison Hot Springs. The speaker was Jim Hewkin, a retired fish and game professional from Oregon. He spoke about Sasquatch as a real animal with real needs and traits. In his camel sweater, dress shirt, and pressed slacks, Hewkin looked the part of the genial grandpa. But his voice was that of a man who has spent much of his time out of doors in rugged situations — the same kinds of places that Bigfoot loves. His talk took on an incantatory tone, and the account became a beguiling litany of beasthood:

"He's a monster, he'll eat anything, alive, dead, fresh, rotten. . . . He's a survivor . . . mobile, quick, fast, and strong. . . . Anybody who sees a slow Sasquatch is not in the ball park. . . . He's got no limits, climbs any mountain, swims any river. He's got no barriers. . . . Not an endangered species, that's *us*. . . . He can pull down big game on the run or by stealth, like a cougar. . . . He can lay down a light track or spring like a deer. . . . Has a lot of humor, yet restraint. . . . Rocks cars and cabins, but lets folks go. . . . We agonize, he couldn't care less. . . . An opportunist at the top of the food chain, in great shape — he's got it made! Adapted to the cutover lands, lives a good rugged existence. . . . He's got no need for wages, lives off the fat of the land, and pays no taxes!"

The room was hypnotized.

And suddenly I realized: these guys don't want to *find* Bigfoot — they want to *be* Bigfoot.

15

Back to Earth

Giants seem to have originated as a way of giving human form
to all that is titanic and inchoate in nature.
— David Rains Wallace, *The Klamath Knot*

AFTER INDIAN HEAVEN I tried — and failed — to remember
another time in my life when I'd gone so long alone. My extended backpacks have all been with mates or friends. When I lived
alone, I never stayed in by myself for that long. And even if I had, it's
not the same as being alone in the wild, where you cannot pick up a
telephone or walk to a neighbor's. Yet in some ways you are not as
alone in the woods as you can be in a city. There are the nuthatches,
the pikas, the ravens, the fat slow frogs, and the trees. They might not
give much back, and they don't care about you; except for pets, other
species seldom reciprocate our ardor. If anything, they'd probably
just as soon you weren't there. But if you're aware of them, you know
that you are a member of a community that makes a crowded suburb
look vacant. Knowing this, you never feel lonely.

Dropping off the berry-lands plateau of Indian Heaven toward the
lavalands below, I had miles and hours to think. What came sharply
to mind was another journey into a solitude of a very different kind.
The previous January I had traveled south by rail to visit the Hoopa
Indian country in northern California, the location of the notorious
Bluff Creek encounter, which resulted in Roger Patterson's film of
1967. I wanted to see the country that had generated the best-known
piece of Bigfoot "evidence," where so many of the Bigfoot heavies had
teethed; and I wanted to speak with the people who had hosted
generations of giant-hunters.

After taking the *Coast Starlight* to Redding, I spent the night in the
Shasta Lodge. In the morning I rented a weathered Tempo from

Rent-a-Wreck and set off westerly into clouds of blue manzanita, then into snow at Buckhorn Pass. Dropping down and out of the falling flurry I wound among pines and oaks of many stripes clothing the thirsty, drinking hills. Weaverville was all Gold Rush brick and doodads, with a pub in an old brewery that was not one now and served no good beer and a Forest Service office where I gathered maps of the Trinity Alps. Over Oregon Summit, then down the wild, green Trinity River canyon. From mossy knolls sprang live oaks of darker green and digger pines with long, droopy blue needles. A snow-peppered forest lay behind and above the greens, and wet red madrones sprang from moss pads down canyon. The redbuds for which the route is noted were not yet in bloom, but a yellow swarm of willow tips and hazel catkins glowed against the black oaks and dark rock. Where the canyon deepened into a dog-legged chasm, ancient rusted cable cars were poised where they'd once crossed over to camps on the wild side.

Eventually I came down to Willow Creek, a.k.a. Sasquatch City, and checked into a cottage at the Willow Inn in the fern woods outside town. Large humanoids were encountered between here and Happy Camp in the 1890s. Bigfoot prints were again reported near Willow Creek in 1938, then again twenty years later by Ray Wallace's road crew, and sporadically ever since.

After dinner I spoke with the resident family: a young mom, her mother with a bouffant, a loquacious ten-year-old boy. They told me all about recent local sightings and tracks, giving no clue that they did not believe in earnest. The local attitude was apparently one of acceptance. The boy said he had seen one track when he was with a group. "I'd love to see one . . . it . . . him, her — them?" said his mother. They mixed up the names of Bigfoot and a local striped wolf-beast the Hoopas are said to believe in ("The Indians believe in a lot," said the older mother), and the boy further conflated both with werewolves. I decided not to consider these folks my primary informants.

I spent the evening driving the upper reaches of the Hoopa Reservation and visiting the Bluff Creek area, since my time was short and I would be less likely to encounter others at that hour. Foggy curves took me up to the confluence of the Trinity and Klamath rivers on the road to Happy Camp. I crossed Bluff Creek, a roaring torrent below a concrete high bridge. When I hit snow at a little above 2,000 feet, slid, and skidded to a stop, I got out, smelled the snow, and spoke to the perpetrator of the local mania: "Hello, Sasquatch, Dzonoqua, Omah. I come in peace and mean no harm. Zuki, zuki." I recalled Ray Wallace's peaceful password, debunking the Patterson film: "I know just which Yakama man was in that monkey suit." Whether he knew any such thing, there is a lovely irony to it: it was Ray's reports of Bigfoot ravaging his road-building operation in these hills back in the late fifties that helped bring the Bigfoot rodeo to Bluff Creek.

Among the pilgrims were two men from near Yakima, Washington, Roger Patterson and Robert Gimlin. Patterson, a slight but handsome horse breeder, sometime rodeo cowboy, inventor, showman and small-time promoter, had been captivated by Bigfoot since reading an article by zoologist Ivan Sanderson in a 1959 *True* magazine. Part Indian, he was encouraged by the beliefs of older Yakama Indians who were his neighbors and began to search widely for evidence of Bigfoot. A number of what he called "pre-expeditions" produced impressive and consistent plaster casts of tracks from Bluff Creek and from Woodland, Washington. When hunts at Ape Canyon on Mount St. Helens proved fruitless, he recruited the assistance of Gimlin, an experienced tracker. Part Apache, Gimlin was a cattleman skilled at tracking from horseback. In 1966 Patterson's Trailblazer Research, Inc., published a little book documenting his progress to date and reprinting newspaper clippings of reports from throughout the Pacific Northwest, illustrated by his drawings of the reconstructed events.

In the fall of 1967 Patterson, then thirty-four years old, and Gimlin took their search back to the Trinity River country in Del Norte County, California, the origin of so many tracks and sightings. After days and nights of nothing, their big break came in the early afternoon of October 20. Approaching Bluff Creek, they spotted a female Bigfoot on the other side, squatting by the bank. When the horses saw her, they bucked in fear, and Patterson fell with his horse. He grabbed his rented movie camera from a saddlebag and ran after the retreating ape. While slipping on the rocks of the stream, he captured 952 frames of jumpy sixteen-millimeter film which, if genuine, is of stunning importance: the soundest evidence yet for the existence of what Patterson himself called a "ghost from a long-dead day."

The film, part of which settles down into reasonable focus, shows the subject walking away, turning around with a swing of her massive breasts and a rippling of muscles in shoulders and thighs, and retreating into the far forest. Afterward Patterson exploited the film for modest gain while continuing the search, until he became ill with Hodgkin's disease. Convinced he could be cured if he had enough money, he made a last attempt to fund an expedition to Thailand to

In October 1967 Roger Patterson and Robert Gimlin surprised a female Big-foot bending over a stream in northern California's remote Trinity Alps. Patterson's horse shied and fell, and by the time he recovered and grabbed his movie camera, he had to run after the Sasquatch to film her. This is frame 352 from his film, which has never been convincingly debunked.

obtain a manlike ape that was supposedly being held captive in a monastery. He died at thirty-nine, remembered mostly by Bigfoot buffs and doubted by most scientists who have seen his film.

In the nearly three decades since its making, the Patterson-Gimlin film has been viewed by millions on television and in lectures and cinemas. The subject of vituperous rights battles, it has been denigrated and mocked, and held up by advocates as the best evidence for the animal's existence. John Napier, Peter Byrne, John Green, Danny Perez, British and Russian experts, and (most recently and thoroughly) Grover Krantz have all analyzed the filmstrip. Byrne gives it an 85 percent chance of being real, and Krantz concludes strongly in its favor. I have watched a first-generation copy many times, and I find it highly intriguing: not definite proof but also not dismissible. In all the scrutiny, it has never been definitively debunked. Universal Studios said that its production as a hoax would be almost impossible, and the Disney folks said no one could have manufactured it except them — and they had not.

- - -

Now I was near the spot on the road where Patterson and Gimlin had had their dramatic encounter with whatever it was. The light snow on the road was ideal for tracks, but I saw none of any species. Hundreds of footprints have been recovered in the Bluff Creek drainage since Patterson's film was shot. I was not looking for tracks but rather for the spoor of the beast on the breath of the night: a sense of the place that spawned this particular case of mass delusion or rich encounter. At the moment I didn't particularly care which it was.

I drove a number of other roads in the vicinity, most of which did not exist when Patterson and Gimlin traveled in on horseback; they have been built since for logging access. At one point, mildly stuck in the snow in the reliable but decidedly not off-road Tempo, I sat and listened to the night. Suddenly I heard a long, falsetto moan followed by yips, both far off and not at all like coyotes. Then it sounded nearer, as I listened intently. I shifted, it stopped; I shifted again, it called. As I moved back and forth, it yipped rapidly. It was the air escaping from the foam back of my seat! I felt like an idiot, but this confirmed how little it takes to make suggestions to the suggestible. I remembered Idaho writer Clay Morgan's account of hearing horrible shrieks he was sure belonged to Bigfoot but that turned out to be lake ice cracking in the sun. That made me feel better.

Rolling back down through the reservation, I saw a raccoon, an opossum, a cat, and three deer and had a good look at the valentine visage of a barn owl as it flew to and from a telephone wire. I could easily see how that particular face had spawned a thousand ghost stories. The rest of the eyeshine in the night came from the new geology — bits of broken yellow center-line cat's-eyes, roadside reflectors, and bottles — except for one silver-green gleam at about six or seven feet that I caught in a corner of the brush before it disappeared. (Bigfoot is always reported to have red eyeshine.)

No Indian bars were open on the reservation, so I went to Bub's Place in Willow Creek. I was glad to have a red, billed feed cap with me, recently received as a bonus for buying a pair of Redwing boots. Every man in the tavern, save the cowboy-hatted bartender, wore a red feed cap. Midwestern seed-and-feed companies were among the first to give out these hats as promotions to drivers and farmers. They have since hybridized with baseball caps to become the national head-wear of the rural American male. Instead of cotton duck, like baseball caps, feed caps are made of polyester in front and sweat-net in back. The forehead panel is always padded with foam to make it stand up aggressively, or maybe to mask the absence of anything behind it. At the back is a plastic snap-tab closure. There is almost always a company logo, a sports motif, or a crass aphorism on the inflated pate. In this bar almost every red feed cap read "Forty Niners."

I'd hoped to pick up on some loose talk about my beast, but I heard none. There was pool, shuffleboard, and swearing over country music interlarded with Tom Petty and Bruce Springsteen, a fair amount of drunkenness, but no Bigfoot in evidence. Most of the patrons were white, though a few Indians sat off to the side. Finally I mentioned the subject offhandedly to the bartender ("Anybody seein' that Bigfoot lately?"), but he scarcely seemed to know what I was talking about ("I don't know nuthin' about that"). The Indians heard but looked uncooperative.

I was about to leave when an attractive Indian woman down the bar caught my eye, smiled, and walked over. I thought, Great, an informant! (Then, wryly, Right — me and Franz Boas.) But I never had a chance to ask the woman what she thought of her giant hairy neighbors. As she approached, her smile faded into a distinct frown and then a full-blown smirk. "Redwing shoes!" she spat, and everyone at the bar looked my way. I might as well have had on earrings and a T-shirt saying "I love spotted owls." A red feed cap by itself just wasn't good enough. There, in the midst of wannabe cowboys and real Indians, I felt more alone than I could ever be as a solitary interloper in the wilderness.

- - -

The next morning the leaning, hollow Douglas-fir outside my cabin, thickly upholstered on its north side with mosses, lichens, fungi, and licorice fern, dripped in the light rain. The general feel of the area was that of a semi-arid land, but this was a rain-forest tree. I could see why these northern Californian hills are considered a borderland between two bioregions.

I breakfasted on a fry of chicken chunks, onions, peppers, and cheese, along with biscuits, honey, and coffee, at a place called Mountain Annie's Skillet. Only mildly piqued by the coincidence of the

proprietor's handle with that of a character in the novel I was writing,
I didn't let it spoil the great breakfast. As I finished my biscuits and
coffee I could see out the window, some twenty yards away, the poste-
rior of the famous Willow Creek Bigfoot, carved from a sequoia stump
by Jim McLarin: neckless, hulking, ape-faced, long-limbed, furred in
the furrows of gouged and weathered redwood. Two ladies in the
next booth read a paper called the *Kourier*, which had a Bigfoot with
tracks across the masthead next to an American flag — the apotheosis of myth in small-town USA? I asked the waitress, youngish, pretty-
ish, heavyish, with brown longish hair, dressed like Mountain Annie
in a plaid shirt and jeans skirt, if local people generally believed. "Yes,
oh yes," she said. "Around here, lots of people believe there's something definitely out there." She steered me to Hodgson's store, across
the street, for postcards and info.

Al Hodgson, a slender, balding man with a storekeeper's demeanor,
had been the first person to talk with Patterson and Gimlin after their
historic encounter. He agreed with the waitress that many people
locally were believers in Bigfoot, though not everyone. As for himself,
he was cautious but thought it likely. He carried a good line in Omah
postcards, books, and paraphernalia. "Some tracks were found late
last summer," he told me. "We were accused of faking them for Labor
Day and Bigfoot Days." He knew all the major Bigfoot hunters. His
favorite was Peter Byrne; Ray Wallace, he said, was "hokey." As for the
Indians, they were reluctant to talk. One 104-year-old Hoopa man
had told him that there *were* Omah around in his youth, "but the
recent stuff is all fake."

At nearby Roberts' Mercantile, Mary Roberts carries Hoopa crafts,
including the splendid work of Dolores Clark, whom she suggested I
contact. When I asked my standard question, she smiled and shook her
curled honey hair in mock exasperation but concurred that "there's
something up there, and most locals think so." She mentioned fresh
tracks found at Tish Tang Campground in September. "I have a warm
feeling about him," she told me. "He never hurts anyone — maybe turns
a few things over. I don't like the idea of him being shot, drugged,
captured." Then, with a sweet-natured shrug, Mary said, "I like to
think of Bigfoot where he is."

I drove to Hoopa. The language of the Hoopa (or Hupa), an
Athabascan variant, allies them with some northern tribes. They are
thought to have come south about a thousand years ago. Hoopa
tradition refers to an early epoch peopled by a race they call the

Kixunai, whose satyrlike leader, Lost-across-the-Ocean, was their progenitor. About a thousand strong when first contacted by whites in 1850, the Hoopa had 1,100 enrolled members in 1970. Though change came fast with the gold rushes, their 87,000-acre-square reservation, the largest in California, preserved most of their traditional homeland.

I saw the museum, with its phenomenal collection of basketry, and purchased Dolores Clark earrings for my stepdaughter, Dory, and niece, Heather. I asked the clerk if anyone was likely to talk with me about Omah. "Talk to the man out there with the cowboy hat," he suggested. "His name is Jimmy."

Jimmy Jackson, at eighty, looked sixty-five or less. His hard-worked hand with gnarled yellow nails was surprisingly soft and warm to the shake. He was watching people pulling punch-tabs in the concrete-floored gambling hall between the bingo parlor and the museum. I thought, If this isn't contemporary American Indian culture as wrought by treaty and appropriation: baskets and bingo side by side! Jimmy and I worked slowly into conversation, talking about the rain, the lottery, and so on. His sister, Mrs. Badgeley, asked me, "Where are you from, sir?" That gave me an opening to pop the question, but it was a little abrupt. I should have taken a week to get to it, or a year.

I spoke clumsily, jabbering about Omah, myths, and legends. Jimmy didn't get my drift or didn't want to, said they had their own problems, too. "Bigfoot," I said.

"Oh! Bigfoot!" Omah, he told me, is a Yurok word, not Hoopa at all. (If there is a truly Hoopa name for it, I never learned what it was.) Jimmy said he was not a believer, though he possessed a footprint cast. His womenfolk, however, all believed.

"My wife and daughter saw tracks on the reservation, but I wouldn't go look," said Jimmy. His mother, still alive at 102, had told him there used to be people — human beings — out in the woods who made the big tracks, but no one ever saw them now.

"What about the young?" I asked Jimmy. "Do they go into the forest to look around?"

"Nah," he snorted disgustedly. "They're not interested in anything but . . ." and he made a sniffing gesture. "They don't care about the old ways on the land or anything — don't even ask."

I crossed the street to the post office, where I elicited giggles. I'd been operating under the belief that the Northwest Indians still accepted Bigfoot literally, even though most whites laughed it off. Here almost the reverse seemed to be the case. Yet what Jimmy had said echoed in my mind: he didn't go into the forest, what was left of it, nor did the young people. Maybe Jimmy's mother was right, and Bigfoot was a thing of the past.

Next I dropped into Honeybunch's Café. There I had coffee and a butterhorn that I hardly needed; between Honeybunch and Mountain Annie, I would soon roll off the rez. Two Indian women, undeterred by my presence, were speaking of Dolores and her six husbands. When it seemed polite to do so (though I knew profoundly that none of this was remotely polite) I butted in and asked if that was Dolores Clark, the artist of the earrings I'd bought. No, it was the sister of one of the ladies. But the other one, who turned out to be Honeybunch, was Dolores Clark's sister. And the conversation evolved, somehow, to the point where I learned that she was also the former sister-in-law of Ray Wallace!

Honeybunch insisted that Bigfoot was a creation of Ray Wallace and Yellow Creek Logging Company, that they had trumped it up in the sixties. "The Indians didn't have it before, and they pay no attention to it now," she said. None of the women present claimed to be believers, including Honeybunch's daughter Tessie, who kept the café these days. When her kids came in with report cards, I wanted to ask their thoughts, but Jimmy had said, "Don't even ask."

Honeybunch told me that Willow Creek and the whites benefited from Bigfoot. That was obvious from the Hodgsons and the Robertses and the Bigfoot Campground not far away. "But not Hoopa," she said, "and hardly anyone here believes." She laughed at the idea — but she was open to that of flying saucers, which was also an enthusiasm of Ray Wallace's, I recalled. "There were six mills in Hoopa when Ray Wallace was here," she said; "and now there are none." Just baskets and bingo and 90 percent unemployment. The hospital closed and the BIA moved out when "big forestry" shut down the mills. Feelings ran deep here, and I suspected that most of them had little to do with Bigfoot.

Recently, listening to a radio broadcast of President Clinton's Timber Summit in Portland, I heard a statement by Margaret Powell of the Hoopa tribe. She said that Indian reservations were going through a healing process. The Hoopas, by practicing enlightened timber management, were continuing to harvest logs *and* attract spotted owls while national forests and private timberlands on all sides struggled with closures. She felt that the Hoopa approach could serve as a model for many of the issues being discussed at the conference.

This was a different story from the one I'd heard at Honeybunch's. Either things had really picked up since I was there, or I'd been snowed. Either way, it seems that some members of the tribe are much more involved with the woods than I had gathered from my informal visit. And that would not surprise me. When a fundament of your tradition has been co-opted by white adventurers and businesses, why even discuss it with another curious Anglo?

I have since spoken with Stephen Suagee, a former Hoopa tribal attorney who worked on issues of fisheries, water quality, and forestry. A member of the Cherokee Nation of Oklahoma, Suagee now works for the Colville Confederated Tribes in north-central Washington. The mills closed, he told me, because the former levels of timber harvest under BIA management could not be sustained — a theme familiar on the Gifford Pinchot too. Now under Indian control, the tribal timber business is gaining health as the Hoopas seek sustainability and economic diversification. Of course, forestry is subject to community debate.

Similarly, the mix of attitudes toward Omah varies. Suagee had the sense that some Hoopas construed Bigfoot as flesh-and-blood animals, while others thought of it as more of a mystic entity; he wondered whether "belief" might be the wrong question. He mentioned having heard the term "forest Indian" used for Bigfoot, in contrast to the culturally developed people of the valleys. He felt that if something didn't want to be found in that incredibly steep, remote, dense country, it needn't be. "These hills seem enchanted," he told me, "with the possibility that anything could be there. In spite of the logging, it's still wild; that feeling survives."

Before I left Honeybunch's, one of the women offered that she really wasn't sure about Bigfoot. Tessie asked her, "Well, would you go out in the woods alone?"

"NO!" she replied emphatically. But, she said, some of the older women who still gathered herbs did. And they were the ones who believed.

In 1811, when explorer David Thompson crossed the Athabasca River in Canada, he found huge tracks, fourteen inches by eight, made by a biped in the snow. Some trackers-in-time, reading his description, have marked them down as more likely Bigfoot than grizzly. When the Hoopa left their Athabascan territory a millennium ago, did they leave Bigfoot back in the northern Rockies, only to find the Omah of the Yuroks waiting for them in the Trinities?

If Lost-across-the-Ocean knows, he's not telling; nor is anyone else. Maybe there are secrets here. But thanks to some twenty-five feet of film, the creature is out of the bag. Whether giants ever set foot in Hoopa, Bigfoot and its fans are here to stay.

- - -

Back in Willow Creek, trucks rumbled past like giant Tonkas with Lincoln Logs, and still-forested hills tumbled down to the untidy strip of small-town commerce. The Bigfoot books are full of Willow Creek tales, like Ivan Sanderson's account of two MD's who nearly struck a seven-foot Sasquatch while they were driving just east of town. But today the jumbo effigy was the most exciting thing in town. It was high time to follow its tracks back to the redwoods, where it came from. For not only had the effigy originated from a bole of a big tree, but the legend had its modern beginning among the sequoias as well. The first recorded reference to a manlike giant in California came from the vicinity of Crescent City in 1886.

Down the Pacific slope from the Hoopas' back lot in the Coast Range, I entered the shaggy landscape of badly barbered *Sequoia sempervirens*. The species name means living forever, but appallingly few of the precontact coast redwoods have made it this far, after living for many centuries. What's left of the world's grandest forest is there only because of the several state parks, the Redwood National Park, and the Save the Redwoods League. I recalled the stories of Georgia Pacific cutting around the clock to sabotage plans for the national park, as I scanned the cutover stumpland.

My mother owned a palette-knife rendition of redwoods in thick oils, now hanging in my sister's home at the southern end of the big trees' range. It shows the massive pink-barked pillars holding their own behind a pasture fence that seems to protect them from the settlers. As a child I always pictured the world's tallest trees that way . . . like the dark woods of fairy tales poised beyond the pale. Only in fairy tales the forest usually represents the malevolent; I'd never understood the fairy-tale admonition "Don't go into the deep dark woods." I saw the woodland border as the beginning of the good place.

Later I served as a ranger naturalist in Sequoia National Park, the Sierran headquarters of the other species of California redwood, *Sequoiadendron gigantea*. Walking daily among the world's most massive trees, I gained an even greater sense of the deepwood as the abode of what is truly good in the world.

Fear of the forest is deeply ingrained in all the mythologies of forest ogres, trolls, lustful satyrs, and giant hairy apes. Greed-driven Georgia Pacific logged with a vengeance, as if by cutting everything they could rid the redwoods of evil spirits (as well as trees). Now, coming back to redwood country, I wondered whether the monster myths penetrated the shadows of these deepest of all woods.

I paused in the rain at Prairie Creek Redwoods State Park. Stepping among the simian hulks of redwoods and the dark shadows they cast, picking a wet and pungent way through the thickets of tanoak and peppertree, I got the feeling that great beasts could easily secrete themselves here. A giant standing still in this company would be just another venerable tree; or it could merely step behind another and disappear, just as Ishi, the last of the Yahi Indians, hid himself from white eyes in northern California for much of the early twentieth century.

In my conversations up and down the redwood coast — in the college-and-mill town of Arcata, the cafés of Eureka, the taverns of Crescent City, the campgrounds in the parks — I heard a lot more about the monstrous behavior of GP's successor, Louisiana Pacific, than I did about Bigfoot. This was in the twilight of the passionate and violent Redwood Summer of 1990, and LP was talking about shipping jobs and raw-log redwoods to Mexico. Both the environmentalists and the workers were unhappy, and some were beginning to seek common ground, trying to find what the poet W. S. Merwin has called the "forgotten language" that will "tell what the forests / were like."

With forest fragments on everyone's mind, mythic monsters seemed a trivial distraction. I wondered if that would be the case if 98 percent of the trees were left, instead of 2 percent. And yet something I heard on the sodden northern California coast would reverberate with the rails all the way back to Washington, and it wasn't just the mumblings of moss monsters lurking in the burlwood.

When I needed to return to Redding to turn in the Tempo and catch the northbound train, the snow had accumulated so thickly on the road over the Trinities that I couldn't go back the way I'd come or by the next several passes to the south. In the end I was obliged to drive all the way south to Ukiah, then east across the Clear Lake country to pick up I-5 back north. It was a long drive, but I had enough time. I passed into darkness in the steely loops of the Eel River, somewhere beyond the looming Humboldt redwoods. As I left the big trees for a countryside of hops and grapes, I realized that I would pass quite near Hopland. This most aptly named hamlet is the home of the esteemed Mendocino Brewing Company, California's first microbrewery and a bright star in the zenith of the good ale revival, whose center of diversity is the Cascadian bioregion.

Of course I stopped in at the brew pub. Mindful of the drive ahead, I sampled the fresh, cask-conditioned Redtail Ale only in modest amounts. If I'd had the leisure to stay overnight in the inn across the street, I could have paid better respects to the rich, coppery, magnificently hopped brew. Instead I sat and merely sipped at the new oaken bar beneath the stamped tin ceiling of the old original tavern, watching the publican draw pints from the six superb hawk's-head beer pulls cast in brass, and enjoying the company of a cluster of brewery workers, retired hippies, and loggers. There was a fair smattering of feed caps, as well as cowboy hats, braids, and bald heads. I felt a lot more welcome than I had at Bub's Place in Willow Creek.

The off-duty brewers all cautioned me to avoid the steep and winding Route 175 east out of Hopland, each outdoing the other with tales of its meanness. They strongly recommended the main highway out of Ukiah instead. When the time came, we parted with promises to exchange microbrew T-shirts.

As I was leaving, a tall, slim, weathered logger with a massive black mustache approached me, having overheard a snatch of the conversation. He put his arm on my shoulder and leaned near. He was neither drunk nor aggressive, and I wondered what was coming. He glanced around, then looked me in the eyes and said, "Bigfoot lives." That was all. He returned to his pint, and I closed the door on the sweet-and-sour scent of hops, malt, and men.

Of course I took the road they'd advised against. It was wild, curvy, and narrow, but my Rent-a-Wreck Tempo came into its own and tamed the terrors of the infamous 175. I'd finally managed to make the tape deck work, and with the help of Robert Johnson, Tom Waits, and David Lanz's seven-minute version of "A Whiter Shade of Pale" played over and over, I made it across the Coast Range, past Clear Lake to the interstate, and all the way north to Redding, with two hours to spare for my three A.M. train.

I waited cold on the platform. When the train came, I settled into the warm car and sleep. I slept all the way under Mount Shasta and Castle Crags, past snowy Klamath Lake, and most of the way to Eugene. Again and again I dreamed of a lean face peering through the frosty window, a great black mustache, and its owner's eyes; and over the organ strains of "Whiter Shade of Pale" and the clacking rails, I heard his two plain words: "Bigfoot lives." But it was Omah speaking.

IV – FOOTSTEPS
ON THE WIND

16

Northern Spotted Bigfoot

≈≈≈

> The trees crowded to the very edge of the water, and the outer
> ones, hanging over it, shadowed the shoreline into a velvet
> smudge. T'sonoqua might walk in places like this.
> — Emily Carr, *Klee Wyck*

HAVE THE UNITED STATES Forest Service and certain timber
companies collaborated to suppress Bigfoot sightings?

This seemingly bizarre proposition became worth asking after I
spent some time among people whose working lives are lived in the
shadows of the tall firs and the open glare of the clear-cut. In asking it,
I explored other large questions about our fundamental view of the
forests' future.

When I left Indian Heaven, I dropped down to Goose Lake on the
northern edge of the Big Lava Bed. In the lake, snags poked through
a scum of dust and needles. I'd heard of a set of hand prints supposed
to be preserved in lava at the end of this lake. I joined some picnickers, a couple of families from White Salmon, who were talking about
the prints. The legend, they told me, said that the hand prints (now
submerged) were those of an Indian woman who had fallen while
escaping a lava flow.

I thought of my "footprint" casting from a little way north, and
asked one of the men what he knew of Bigfoot. He stroked his small,
sandy mustache and patted his paunch. "When I was younger and
skinnier," he said, "I built a bridge to log a sale up the Lewis River. I
went on foot in there for fifteen miles, spent days and days, and saw
no sign of that Bigfoot." He'd logged all over that territory, he said,
and he noticed every broken twig, every bit of bear and elk sign: "I
think it's a hoax."

Then, as I was leaving Goose Lake for points south, he called after me, "I wouldn't worry about Bigfoot."

Goose Lake floats between the bottom of Indian Heaven and the top of the Big Lava Bed. I could have taken a straight shot into that great petrified pudding, but I decided to approach it from several points around the edges rather than attempt a north-south transect. No landscape in the state is more forbidding for the traveler on foot, and it seemed to me that a multipronged approach would give me a wider perspective on the big flow than picking a narrow path down the middle, which might not even be possible. But first I had business in Trout Lake, a ranching, logging, and Forest Service town about fifteen miles to the east.

Trout Lake grew up at the head of the wet camas prairies draining Mount Adams's glacial meltwater toward the Columbia. Pahto looms to the north when its snowy buffalo hump breaks out of the clouds, and the Yakama Nation unfolds to the northeast. From here it isn't far down the White Salmon River to the "spandex ghettos" booming on the back of sailboarding in the Columbia Gorge, and it's a short hop to several wilderness areas. As the headquarters of the Mount Adams District of the Gifford Pinchot, Trout Lake has become a desirable posting for young Forest Service workers, as well as an outdoors mecca.

The town was full of Indian-summer butterflies and the season's last tourists. When the late sun dropped, I dowsed a meal at an old country inn on the river. The White Salmon was likely without salmon, but it was surely white in the harvest moon's light. I found the Forest Service village and searched out the cabin of my friend Howard Bulick. He was out, so I let myself in and I spent the evening reading David Quammen's "Natural Acts" essays from *Outside*. In one he wrote that "the essence of travel is relinquishing full control over the texture and path of your own life — and one aspect of that relinquishment is a chronic shortage of decent reading."

The first part of the quote certainly seemed right at this stage of my journey. As for decent reading, I'd carried Peter Byrne and Wendell Berry in my backpack, but it was a delight after the weeks away from my own glutted shelves to dive into Howard's books. I fell asleep over poet Robert Sund, whose "Ish River Country" reminded me that before the pioneers and the Forest Service came the people whose names grace the land — all those names with "ish" on the end, like the Salish country Sund was writing about. Here, away from the soft, wet valleys, on the edge of the hard lavalands, the names have lots of k's — Klickitat, Yakama . . . Selahtiks.

On the last morning of September, a Sunday, Howard and I shared Thea's granola, his bananas, and coffee. I showed him my plaster cast and asked if he knew what the Forest Service felt about the Klickitats' wild Indians or hairy devils. He called a coworker who had an interest in the matter. Al was home and free, so Howard invited him over. Al was currently working on spotted owls for the Mount Hood and Gifford Pinchot forests, a specialty just then coming into its own.

In fact, the Trout Lake Forest Service camp was in total disarray over this modest spotty lump of a bird. With the federal listing of *Strix occidentalis* as an endangered species and Judge William Dwyer's ruling that the USFS was in violation of federal law until they took the owl fully into account, chaos reigned. Most timber sales had been shut down until the owl populations were surveyed and a new plan approved for their protection. Of course this involved the entire old-growth question, not just owls, but they were the lever that could jack the system open to change.

The huge timber cuts formerly demanded by Congress had begun to look like a thing of the past. The Multiple Use Act of 1960 stated, "It is the policy of the Congress that the National Forests are established and shall be administered for outdoor recreation, range, timber, watershed, and wildlife and fish purposes." However, as everyone knows who knows the woods, the third-named commodity has driven the show. Mel Hansen, in his book about Indian Heaven, quoted a retired forester who had spent twenty-two years in the USFS:

> If one has aspirations to eventually become a U.S. Forest Supervisor, he must plan to advance through the ranks of timber management. Somewhere along the line he may work with some other branch for a short time, but no other branch offers him a chance to build himself a small empire in the district or become a staff member in the supervisor's office. Timber is adequately funded while other branches are not. The Forest Service is pressured from Washington, D.C. This pressure is first exerted on the Regional Office and in turn to the Regional Forester and then down through the District. The ever present message is, "The economy of the country depends on timber."

Hansen might have mentioned that Congress has consistently pressured the Forest Service to produce nonsustainable levels of harvest. With Senators Mark Hatfield and Bob Packwood of Oregon and Slade Gorton of Washington, among others, calling for four or five or six billion board feet of timber per year — which kept the mill towns humming and the votes coming — the rangers were always under the gun to "get the cut out." When I had discussed the trashed trails on Juniper Ridge with Randle District Ranger Harry Cody, he lamented the impossibility of managing the forest properly under that dictum. Many service professionals realized that the national forests were being hammered, and a nucleus of them formed AFSEEE (the Association of Forest Service Employees for Environmental Ethics). Regional Forester John Mumma became a cause célèbre when his career was wrecked by his superiors for his resistance to overcutting in the northern Rockies.

The Mount Adams District was reeling under the court order. District Ranger Jim Bull (known locally as the Big Bull) had recently informed employees that at most the allowable cut on their slice of the Gifford Pinchot might approach half of what it had been. Everybody from timber sales personnel to biologists were scrambling to realign their jobs to meet the requirements of the judgment, while still selling some timber to help the balance sheet and the local mills and loggers.

Al was one of the Forest Service people detailed to learn more about the whereabouts and needs of the spotted owls. He had been a student of Grover Krantz's at Washington State and spoke highly of him. Roger Patterson had worked for Al's father at Hanford, and his dad vouched for Patterson's integrity. Naturally, with Krantz and Patterson in his background, Al was interested in Bigfoot.

I related to Al what Ray Wallace had told me about his road-building contracts with the Gifford Pinchot National Forest; the contracts said, in effect, "If you see Bigfoot, don't tell, or we will cancel your contract." One official told Wallace they just didn't want anyone to be killed. Considering the source and Ray's many apparent flights of fancy, I questioned the existence of such a clause. But he was adamant and consistent in the telling of it.

Al said he had heard the story of the Bigfoot contract clause, but he couldn't say if it was true. An old-timer told him he had worked under similar restrictions. Al was familiar with other bizarre on-the-job conditions, for example a Canadian deal whereby a big logging union required workers who saw an owl to shoot it or be fired. Later I heard other rumors and whispers about Bigfoot clauses in forestry contracts but never saw one. I suppose someone who cared could pursue a Freedom of Information Act procedure to unearth an actual document. But I found the mere existence of the folklore illuminating: no one would invent such a rumor if there was no concern about the consequences of Bigfoot's discovery.

Related stories exist concerning the timber companies. Grover Krantz has written of "people whom I suspect may be paid by the timber industries in the Pacific Northwest." He thinks that these people are fabricating elaborate and unbelievable accounts of bionic or supernatural Sasquatches that cause people to dismiss the topic out of hand. "There is no hard evidence that this is actually occurring," says Krantz, "but the behavior of some individuals is otherwise difficult to explain." One pipe dream he heard of concerned monsters fashioned from titanium. "The best way to make sasquatch research look ridiculous," he maintains, "is to make outlandish and absurd claims of this kind, with as much publicity as possible, and try to associate yourself with the scientists and laymen who are doing serious research. By this means the whole subject of the sasquatch becomes tainted by association, thus making the government, most scientists, and much of the public think it is all fantasy."

Grover told me that the rumor mill consistently turned out stories of forestry workers, both government and private, being instructed by their superiors not to reveal any Bigfoot evidence or intimations they came across in their work. I have heard such accounts also. If true, they could help to account for the paucity of reliable Bigfoot reports from the industrial woods. On the other hand, some of the most titillating tales have come from foresters who think for themselves. The loggers of my acquaintance tend to be individuals who would not be likely to abide by any higher-up's embargo on tall tales. But if a code of silence was seen as protecting jobs and timber sales, they might go along.

The meat of the allegations is that Bigfoot, or even the suggestion of Bigfoot, would be bad for logging. The middling owl hardly brought a mighty industry to its knees or "crippled a regional economy," as they like to say — timber corporation profits have never been higher (for example, Weyerhaeuser's 1994 profits were up 86 percent over 1993), and both Oregon and Washington are booming. But it did tie a massive public lands bureaucracy in knots, and it tied up a lot of timber. So think what a big new ape might do. *Sasquatch would make the spotted owl look like a gnat.*

The northern spotted owl has not begun to do the things it is blamed for. Overcutting, mechanization and automation, union-busting, foreign exports of raw logs, and the belated and reluctant recognition of the need to conserve the diversity represented by older forests — all have contributed to the timber downturn. The fiber-mining boom could not have lasted much longer, even if all the old growth was allowed to be cut. The owl, as the listed representative of the ancient forest fauna, simply became the key, the tool, the wedge: the stalking horse and the scapegoat.

Even so, the owl has been powerful. The slowdown required by Judge Dwyer while owls and old growth are properly surveyed has given advocates of ancient forests time to regroup and marshal their resources for the final battle. Suppose an unrecognized species of anthropoid ape was discovered on a national forest . . . or a hominoid, which would raise questions of our evolutionary singularity and perhaps even call up issues of human (or near subhuman) rights. Even if the beast were an ape along the lines of chimps and gorillas, its animal rights position would be volatile; but the pressure to protect a much more manlike creature would be irresistible.

The Endangered Species Act would have to either be immediately enforced or be altered to omit the new creature in favor of continued timber harvest. The Republican reluctance to reauthorize the act is driven in part by the fear of finding new endangered species on public and private lands. The unquestioned discovery of Bigfoot would justify that fear in spades. Forest management in the Pacific Northwest will never be the same after the spotted owl. After Bigfoot, Gifford Pinchot's agency and its mission would have to be entirely reinvented.

For example, the McCoy Timber Sales Draft Environmental Impact Statement (which would allow logging of more old-growth hemlock and noble fir in the heart of the Dark Divide) will have to be completely recast in light of Judge Dwyer, President Clinton's Timber Plan, and the owls, which turn out to be more populous in the inner Divide than elsewhere in the forest. Logging is taking place there now and will surely go on in the future. But it won't be the same show as before. If the Forest Plan had a new overlay for its maps, showing the suspected range of Bigfoot, it would not be a whole new ball game, it would be completely out of the park.

Given such a prospect, grim from the standpoint of those whose present and future depends on the flow of logs from the public lands, is it so surprising that Bigfoot is considered bad news? I can imagine — for imagining might be all it is — the timber lobby closing ranks behind closed lips, uttering nothing of what they know perfectly well to be up there, whether flesh or fancy. This attitude was typified in an article entitled "See No Sasquatch" by Bill Palmroth in the Winter 1992 issue of *Oregon Fish and Wildlife Journal*. After relating an experience that "was enough to convince me of Sasquatch's probable existence," Palmroth wrote, "If you were to report it, there's always the chance that the federal government could suddenly become interested in Bigfoot. If so, your logging operation probably would be suspended indefinitely while the Feds took time to study the creature's habitat requirements." He went on, "That would leave you in a real fix. What's more, any habitat study by the government would very likely lead to a Bigfoot recovery program necessitating additional forest set-asides."

Palmroth's final paragraph, framed on the magazine page by ads for contract logging companies, encapsulated the flavor of the rumor I'd heard: "Your smartest option," he wrote, "is to keep any future Bigfoot sightings under your hat, especially if you're on public land. As my grandfather used to say, 'Say nothing and saw wood!'"

I was surprised, then, to learn that timber giant Weyerhaeuser Company had actually solicited sightings. A notice headed "Anyone Seen a Sasquatch?" appeared in the November 1969 issue of *Weyerhaeuser News,* the in-house organ, asking any employees who had seen or heard of Sasquatch to report their stories. This was accompanied by a cartoon of a huge, grinning Bigfoot wearing a Weyco hardhat and standing behind two men, one of whom asks, "Where did you say that new guy is from?"

A follow-up piece appeared in February 1970. The substantial, unsigned article contained a survey of the Sasquatch situation in a rather flip voice, an interview with Roger Patterson, photographs of him with casts of prints, and a frame from his film. It also included several employee responses to the prior query. Helen Upperman of Tacoma sent a wonderfully apropos quotation from Cavafy: "It is night and the barbarians have not come, and some men have arrived from the frontiers and they say that there are no barbarians any longer and now, what will become of us without barbarians? These people were a kind of solution." Tom Adams of Fontana, California, suggested that Bigfoot, like gorillas not so long ago, might be thought mere figments because they have "not been *seen* by civilized men from the *intellectual* world."

The other responses were joky and distinctly less inspiring. The Aberdeen foreman (mercifully unnamed) sent a letter that today would not get past the transom, or he'd be out over it: "Here is a picture of my secretary. Do you suppose she is really the Sasquatch? There is quite a resemblance to the picture . . . If you think there is a possibility this is the real thing, please let me know so I can make arrangements for a new girl."

Finally, the December 1974 issue of *Weyerhaeuser Today* (as it was renamed) carried a column headed "Employees to Be on Lookout for Sasquatch." Peter Byrne, then at the Bigfoot Information Center in The Dalles, had appealed to the company to put its 57,000 employees on the alert for sightings. John Hauberg of Seattle, identified as "a long-time member of our board of directors," gave his support. "It seems to me," he was quoted as saying, "that Weyerhaeuser might lend a hand through the many hundreds of our people who live in the Douglas-fir region in areas where sightings have been claimed."

This hardly sounds like a company trying to suppress knowledge of Bigfoot on its lands or on public lands where it logs. On the other hand, nothing seems to have emerged in the twenty years since this request, even though loggers routinely account for a large percentage of reports. A cynic might ask, what better way to prevent information getting out than to call it in to HQ? At least that way it could be monitored for any alarming details that might prove threatening. A more generous interpretation would take Weyco's reputation as a relatively progressive company at face value and assume that it truly intends to share any monster data that come out of its woods. We'll not know until the day they hold the press conference.

What about Bill Palmroth's allegation that the feds would lock up the woods once a good report came in? And what has the official response been so far? I am aware of only two. The U.S. Fish and Wildlife Service was petitioned to list Bigfoot as an endangered species on an emergency basis at a time when armed expeditions were at a peak. The Portland office failed to advance the petition through channels, reasoning that it did not contain substantial data and that the Endangered Species Act did not provide for the listing or study of cryptids (unknown species). This was probably the correct response in legal and biological terms, although one might have hoped that

FWS would query serious searchers and examine the literature and available evidence. But until the species is demonstrated and named, the feds will not touch it. This should give some comfort to "wise use" types who believe that the government is doing backflips to list everything in sight in order to undermine the economy and ruin their livelihoods.

The other governmental response to Bigfoot actually emanated from the sedate Army Corps of Engineers. Long known for their massive concrete works, including a large number of pork-barrel dams, the corps began to change its mission and its image in the 1970s. One of their projects was to prepare environmental atlases of certain states, Washington being one. Under fauna the corps listed Bigfoot and said: "Reported to feed on vegetation and some meat. The Sasquatch is covered with long hair, except for the face and hands, and has a distinctly humanlike form." It called the Sasquatch agile and strong, with good night vision and great shyness, "leaving minimal evidence of its presence."

While the army did not come right out and say that Sasquatch occurs in Washington, it discussed the subject seriously at some length and included a map of sightings. The compilers, with the U.S. Army's imprimatur, classified the animal's existence as not unlikely. The $200,000, five-year atlas project surprised many by its open-mindedness. Bigfoot researchers found it refreshing that an agency concerned with the most concrete of matters could also attend openly to hairy giants. Conspiracy or not, the U.S. Forest Service has shown no such willingness to discuss the animal in official publications.

- - -

In ninth grade, when I was called upon to write a career report (and thereby to declare a career choice), I chose forest ranger. I had no idea that district rangers spend much of their time and energy administering timber sales, and when I finally got to college and looked into the forestry school, I quickly changed my mind. I later pursued three graduate degrees in forestry, but in the nature interpretation and ecology branches of the field, which provide a counterbalance to the timber beasts both in and out of the forestry schools.

One thing I learned was that people enter forestry for many jobs and reasons, but they all start out loving the woods — or the idea of the woods. That many of them end up sacking the woods for a living is no different from the fact that many professional entomologists, who begin with a love of bugs, spend their careers broadcasting toxins to deal with "pests."

The Forest Service offers as diverse a collection of people, with as wide an array of motivation, background, and outlook, as any resource agency. From firefighter hotshots to rare-plant mappers, from backcountry rangers to timber cruisers, from tree fellers to tree huggers, the Forest Service has been home to all sorts of men and women enamored of the woodsy life.

Perhaps none of Gifford Pinchot's club of individuals has struck me as more of a one-off, break-the-mold guy than Captain Gutz-Balls. Back in the late summer of 1987 I received a handmade postcard that read in part: "Just finished Wintergreen as did my parents . . . and the retired forester in the Winnebago three spots down. I was born in Skamokowa where my father tot 3 yrs. at the deceased school. . . . You can tell you're an out of stater as you love slugs and us Warshingtonians hate them almost as much as Caliphonians. Just remember that progress is the development of more machines to provide more people more time to be bored in." It was signed "Capt. Gutz-Balls."

This sounded like my kind of guy. I wrote back, and from time to time I've received bizarre missives from the captain. Most of them are color-Xeroxed old-fashioned postcards showing dinosaurs stepping out in various beauty spots — *Tyrannosaurus* rampant at St. Petersburg, *Pteranodon* over Santa Cruz and Skamokawa, Washington, *Brontosaurus* on the capital's mall at cherry blossom time, *Triceratops* balanced on a high gorge bridge in Oregon. Or they might depict the good man himself — his top-hatted visage winking out of a crèche, or at attention in a ranger suit with Smokey hat or hardhat, standing guard before the Gray's River Covered Bridge, a ranger truck with Bart Simpson at the wheel, or the erupting Mount St. Helens from various perspectives.

Packets might come with enclosures such as prehistoric sharks' teeth from Florida, Woodsy Owl or EarthFirst! stickers, Smokey Bear patches, or a Capt. Gutz-Balls Fan Club sticker with a spaceship motif. An envelope might be addressed to "Mr. & Mrs. Robert Pyle Family, The Butterfly Folks, Gray's R. Covered Bridge" and bear the return address "On the road — Trapper Cr. Wilderness Area & Carson Hot Springs" or "From the Hollowed Halls of the Mt. St. Helens Gonzo Gallery."

The captain's Christmas message one year was a typical mix of nonsense, self-pointing fun, and cryptic aphorisms. "I'm sending this processed tree carcass now because I'm horizontally challenged and a person of torpor and motivationally deficient . . . but that's what I get for being a uniquely-fortuned individual on an alternative career path, or a person with temporary unmet objectives! So how come by the time we've made it, we've had it?"

One pastel card from the fifties showing *Stegosaurus* at Balboa Park informed me that Gutz-Balls had "started our sentence for the gov . . . thru typo my Uzi training was changed to 'squeegee' and I am in the midst of a 4 week refresher seminar at the Cougar Condo & Bar facilities for the governmentally infirm and insane! Yours, Ranger Rance" (one of his aliases, along with Ranger Rex and Ranger Rocco).

By an astonishing coincidence, I had a chance to find out first-hand what he meant about the squeegee. That fall Thea and I drove up to the Boundary Trail access above Yellowjacket Creek for a hike. We had just turned off the Yellowjacket road and were starting up the abominable Forest Road 2810, when we encountered a green Forest Service pickup. The driver stopped and so did we, to ask conditions and chat. He looked familiar . . . slender, fair, mustachioed, ranger suit . . . it was Captain Gutz-Balls! His FS duty for the summer consisted largely in cleaning outhouses (he and his colleagues refer to themselves as "turdbusters"), hence the squeegee reference. He was as surprised to see us up there as we were to encounter him.

Now here was a Forest Service guy who was out there to be out there. (We were a long way from any toilets, as far as I could see.) He clearly didn't buy the timber-trimming rationale for the existence of the agency. And as for Bigfoot, he reckoned it was a matter of time until it came home to roost for the USFS.

How refreshing it was to find someone with a truly weird sense of humor and a protective attitude toward trees who had burrowed into an agency known for too little of either. The captain reminded me of the presciently named Owl Party's 1968 candidate for commissioner of public lands, Washington's elected official who manages some six million acres of land. When asked what he intended to do if elected, Richard "AC-DC" Green said, "I plan to go forth and fearlessly commission the land." Somehow I feel that we'd hardly be worse off with guys like Gutz-Balls and AC-DC Green in charge than with the "get out the cut" professionals who have left the state and national forests in tatters.

With a wave, a mock salute, and the promise of more crazy postals, Captain Gutz-Balls took off for the next outhouse as we trod toward our rendezvous at Yellowjacket Pass.

Though few can rival the captain in uniqueness, many Forest Service employees hardly fit the mold of the chain-saw dervish, the career-climbing yes-man, or the agency desk drone. I have known a strong woman who works backcountry assignments in summer and lives in a tree house in winter; a raft of full-timers who took early retirement rather than toe the line; and a pack of biologists who comb the woods for rare and vulnerable species of plants and animals, then buck the bosses to try to keep those habitats safe. Many of the most interesting people, like the captain, have worked as seasonal employees. This gives them some insulation from the pressures of government service and perhaps greater freedom to be themselves.

Paul Freeman of Walla Walla, in southeastern Washington, was a Forest Service watershed patrolman in 1982 when he had, he claimed, a dramatic sighting of Bigfoot. He said it outweighed his 325 pounds by at least 500 pounds and stank like something spoiled. His colleagues called the event a probable hoax. Hounded by reporters and anonymous threatening callers, Freeman left the service and moved away. Later he returned to the area as a meat cutter and a devoted Bigfoot hunter, intent upon clearing his reputation.

With his son Duane and fellow Bigfoot enthusiast Wayne Summerlin, the big, bearded, fifty-one-year-old Freeman unearthed a remarkable amount of putative evidence from the Blue Mountains on the Washington-Oregon border — rock art, tracks, sightings, films. These vary wildly in quality, from interesting to inept, and they seem to appear only when Freeman is around. On the whole his evidence has not enhanced his stock among the fraternity, except with Grover Krantz, who feels that some of the tracks are genuine. Freeman says the giants hole up in the Wenaha-Tucannon Wilderness Area on the Wallawa-Whitman National Forest. Forest Service officials remain dubious about their former employee's stories. As perhaps the only one from their ranks to become a vocal Bigfoot convert, he is treated circumspectly at best.

Another former Forest Service part-timer, whose scientific data are beyond reproach, is Bob Pearson, a resident of a timber town on the hems of the Dark Divide. In his work on the Gifford Pinchot he came to realize that the formal spotted owl surveys were failing to record all the birds in some densely forested areas. He has since conducted his own survey, on his own time and expense and un-officially. He has detected an unrivaled density of owl pairs on lands designated as "matrix" rather than as owl preserves in the Timber Plan. Matrix designation equates with the old "multiple use" management that will probably amount to timber business as usual. Bob's work demonstrates how faulty any plan can be when it is based on inadequate field work. The difference between his work and Free-man's, aside from rigorous technique, is that the owls actually appear when he calls them — they don't leave mere wingbeats on the wind.

Acutely aware of the motorcycle sacrifice zone (photographer Ira Spring calls it an ORV playground) that Harry Cody seems bent on making out of the Randle District, Bob has conducted a second survey. He has documented hundreds of miles of foot trails in the forest that have been abandoned or obliterated — many of them since the reign of a former district ranger whose kids liked trail bikes. By now the remaining trails have been increasingly turned over to motorcycles.

- - -

The yeoman foresters of the Gifford Pinchot have been outdoing themselves in soliciting public input and informing us of their management process. It is almost as if, having been slapped silly by the courts and Congress, they are appealing to the people to validate that they are doing something right. In the past few years I have received a steady stream of mail from the Gifford Pinchot managers. Here is a list of some of what I've saved:

- The Forest Land and Resource Management Plan ("Forest Plan"), a massive document detailing all aspects of future management, dense and rendered largely redundant by Clinton's Timber Plan
- Decision Memos for amendments to the Forest Plan, concerning the management of noxious weeds and unwanted vegetation, scenic and wild rivers, reforestation, monitoring of goldeneye and wood duck as indicator species, snowmobiles, cattle and horse grazing allotments, and so on
- Annual monitoring and evaluation reports and a long errata list for the Forest Plan
- Watershed and landscape analysis reports
- Integrated Resource Analysis input requests and position statements
- Access Travel Management questionnaires
- Various "scoping" documents for future projects

- McCoy Timber Sale and other draft environmental impact statements
- Position statements on specific timber sales
- Findings of No Significance for various actions
- Invitations to open houses "to get to know you" and to "identify any concerns you might have" about Indian Heaven and recreation, timber harvest, silvicultural, and wildlife projects
- Invitations to town hall meetings about the president's Forest Plan
- A six-page memo entitled "How to Work with the Forest Service," which asks the reader to "share your vision with the land manager"

In addition, a series of newsletters arrives at frequent intervals: *Pinchot Perspectives,* headed by portraits of the young and old Gifford Pinchot himself, asking "What's happening with the Forest Plan?"; *Pinchot Projects,* with a female field worker on the cover, which summarizes all National Environmental Policy Act–related projects on the forest, an impressive catalogue of activity; *GPNF Wilderness,* using as a logo a songdog howling at the moon, explaining changes in methods and goals for monitoring and responding to wilderness damage; and *DEMO Newsletter,* on the Demonstration of Ecosystem Management Option Project, a scheme to find out whether the "new forestry" (later called "new perspectives") really works. The newsletter plans to compare "silvicultural options for maintaining, enhancing, or re-creating late successional characteristics in managed forests in the Douglas-fir region of the Pacific Northwest." In other words, how many trees can you cut down, and in what ways, and still have some of the benefits of older forests?

Finally, there came to my mailbox a brochure titled *The Reinvention of the Forest Service: Charting Our Course.* In keeping with the Clinton administration's task of "reinventing Government . . . we on the Gifford Pinchot National Forest are asking you for your ideas on how we can be reinvented." The Gifford Pinchot Task Force of concerned citizens would love to take the managers seriously. But according to some Forest Service critics, it's too late for that.

Although they consumed enough paper to keep at least one pulp mill busy, and staff time that could have done a lot of good on the ground, all these efforts to keep abreast of public desires and to keep the public abreast of their intentions seem laudable. How likely is it that the dialogue will truly affect policy?

Undoubtedly the manufacturers in this paper mill include many

dedicated individuals who mean what they say about public involvement. But some forest users are convinced that when all the questionnaires are sifted and newsletters recycled and memos revised and
open houses closed up, the Gifford Pinchot will go ahead and do
what it wants to do. Some footnotes may be added to the Forest Plan
based on popular comment. But as Randle District Ranger Harry
Cody has demonstrated with trails and motors in the Dark Divide, and
as the timber sellers have showed again and again, bringing about
meaningful reform finally rests with the courts. Now, with the adoption of the frightening phrase "ecosystem management" in all its
staggering arrogance as the service's slogan, many feel the USFS is
beyond redemption. As Andy Kerr of the Oregon Natural Resources
Council said at Clinton's timber conference, "I hear ecosystem and
the forester hears management."

In a September 20, 1993, editorial titled "It's Time to Clear-cut
the Forest Service," *High Country News* publisher Ed Marston por-
trayed decades of empire-building, nonresponsiveness, and "roguish"
behavior on the part of the service in Colorado and elsewhere. He
pointed out that in addition to John Mumma, "nine of the 13 Northern Region forest supervisors" who had signed a letter in 1989 saying
the agency had lost its sense of mission were no longer on the job.
Instead of taking the letter as loyal criticism, Forest Service brass had
treated it as treason.

Marston maintained that environmentalists should resist Clinton's
Option Nine forest plan because it involves experimental forestry
instead of outright no-cut zones, and "we know the Forest Service
can't implement a policy that requires good science and ecological
integrity." He went on, "Given how the agency has isolated itself from
the ground and from communities, and given its contempt for science, there are no options: The Forest Service . . . should be abolished." Though difficult, "abolition . . . wouldn't be as impossible as
reform. And debate over how to replace the Forest Service would
invigorate the West."

Of course, the service isn't going to be abolished. And I'm not
sure that it should be. When Clinton appointed Jack Ward Thomas, a
respected scientist, as Forest Service chief, conservationists hoped
the agency might be poised for meaningful reform. As the leader of
the original spotted owl study that led to the defining crisis in Judge
Dwyer's courtroom, he was an unlikely, exciting choice for chief. If he
would chain-saw the logjam and light a fire under the decadent dead-

wood of the bureaucracy, Thomas might be the man to save the service. But his ratings during his first year (1994) were poor in all areas except FS morale. Furthermore, in a June 13, 1994, memo from Thomas to regional foresters, he showed himself as no friend to de facto wilderness areas such as the Dark Divide: "Unless these roadless areas are removed from the timber base through forest plan amendment, you should proceed in an orderly fashion to enter more such areas and manage them." Is it any wonder environmentalists fear that Thomas might turn out to be another casualty of pulp politics?

- - -

Orlo, subtitled *The Bear Essential,* is an apostate environmental paper out of Portland edited by folks who would feel at home with Captain Gutz-Balls. The summer 1994 issue helped Smokey the Bear celebrate his fiftieth anniversary. "This amiable symbol of fire-as-evil-force," Charles Little wrote, "has turned on his masters and helped to create today's 'forests of torches.'" Little called this "Smokey's Revenge." The issue also included a section called "Bigfoot among Us," with an article titled "Believing in Bigfoot" by Michelle Allen, and "Bigfoot Speaks!" a mock-tabloid interview with the big man by Samuel J. Freehold. As the satirical piece begins, Bigfoot lights a cigar and taps the ashes into his paw. The interviewer reminds him that it is a non-smoking room. "I know, I know," Bigfoot retorts. "It's just that Smokey is always getting on my case about smoking in the field."

Maybe it's time that Bigfoot gets on Smokey's case instead. As recent tragedies in fire management and the parlous condition of Western forests attest, the day of this gruff but pleasant ursine archetype may be past. Perhaps the next half-century should have a different front man . . . hairy like Smokey, but a lot smarter.

What would the discovery of Sasquatch mean for the United States Forest Service and its motley band of managers? If the Gifford Pinchot, just to take one national forest of the many involved, seems to have generated a paper storm over owls and martens and pileated woodpeckers and timber sales and trails and rivers and roads and cows and elk and meetings, meetings, and more meetings, imagine the parade of pulp that Bigfoot's arrival on the scene would inspire. As the greatest anthropological, zoological, and evolutionary discovery of our time, the animal would elicit a "management mandate" that would — or should — completely unseat the reigning model.

"Ecosystem management" terrifies disinterested ecologists precisely because it assumes that people have the godlike ability to "run" something as complex as an entire biophysical system in nature. As a former land manager, I would be the first to say that no combo of science and mechanics exists that can begin to do this. All the Forest Service can do is to make decisions based on the best available knowledge, then see what happens. This is merely monkeying around; it is hardly managing the ecosystem.

The Greater Ecosystem Alliance, a nonprofit organization devoted to maintaining the international ecosystem of the North Cascades, takes a radically different approach. At first glance, its goal of "integrated ecosystem conservation" might seem just as presumptuous as the Forest Service slogans. But the humility of the Alliance attitude separates it from the Pinchot perspective.

The editors of *Cascadia Wild* tell us that "land managers and citizens need new norms that take them toward an ecosystems future . . . They must be based on what we know nature produces, not on what we desire nature to produce for us." This set of "biological and ecological limits that must guide the setting of new ecosystem conservation standards" is something the Forest Service has never really understood.

— — —

Biologists Arthur Sullivan and Mark Shaffer have described the unruly collection of life on earth as "the megazoo." To a large extent, the Forest Service is the keeper of the Cascadian megazoo. Will it remain a many-ringed circus under a nurturing big top, or will it fade into a more and more tawdry carnival?

I remember a small itinerant circus coming to our tiny community a few years back. As I drove into Naselle, I saw a tethered elephant grazing by the roadside — perhaps the only elephant ever seen in Willapa. But as I gazed in mild shock at the unconformity in local fauna, a carny with a mahout's hook came over and smacked the beast cruelly to get it back to work hauling lines to erect the tent. The poor pachyderm was so threadbare I could almost see the patches. Is this the sort of attraction the Gifford Pinchot will become — ever more shabby, as it attempts to serve everyone's demands *ad infinitum?*

Michelle Allen, in "Believing in Bigfoot" says, "I fell for Bigfoot — hook, line, and sideshow" when she attended the Mid-South Fair in Memphis as a child. "There he was — on the far side of the fair — glass encased and scantily clad in a loin cloth. A recorded message told how Bigfoot had been captured and shot. I fell for it." Perhaps Bigfoot has no more substance than a bogus freak-show attraction. And perhaps it has. When the creature steps out from the glass case into the full sight of ranger, chief, and president — that's when the show would really begin at the megazoo.

Will the ringmaster be some overworked ranger — maybe a Harry Cody, inviting everyone with a motorcycle to trick-ride the untrodden trails, or a Big Bull, negotiating the maddening tightwire strung between the demands of Congress and the courts, with no net for his career? Will it be a Pinchot man or a John Muir type? Or maybe an Earth Mother, evolved from one of the many young female professionals treading the Forest Service midway, women like Mary Bean of the Gifford Pinchot, who, while her colleagues were laying out timber sales or sending memos, worked to obliterate roads in and near wilderness areas. It isn't likely to be a clown like Captain Gutz-Balls, swept up from the loo crew to the supervisor's chair.

Yet somehow I feel that if Smokey is to survive another fifty years, it will be under the guidance of leaders with a different sense of mission. The Forest Ranger will never be the Green Man. But if enlightened leaders somehow emerged from the flow charts of the USFS, its career foresters could become like the hereditary Order of Verderers, who care for the ancient wood known as the New Forest in England: dedicated to the trees, to the land, through the generations, for the ages.

There are some bright signs. On a field trip in the Olympic National Forest a few years ago to locate a rare butterfly in a stand of old growth designated for sale, I was accompanied by half a dozen biologists and District Ranger Kathy Snow, all of whom were hoping for an excuse to manage the stand in a better way than by balance sheet alone. We didn't find the butterfly, but the stand remains: an anomaly in a district that has given up more than its fair share of fiber.

The brightest light I have seen in the forest came in the form of an elegant poster for a conference called "Managing Ecosystems for Biodiversity." Not yet free of the hubris of ecosystem management, it nevertheless got the purpose right. The powwow was cosponsored by the Okanogan and Wenatchee national forests and the Pacific Northwest Forest Sciences Laboratory, Jack Ward Thomas's old shop. The poster depicted a footprint on the forest floor, made up of elements of natural diversity: a monarch butterfly at the heel, a fishtail in a pool, a skink, oxalis and violets, pebbles and pine needles, feathers and ants and fungi; in the instep a bumblebee visited bunchberry;

and the toes were an egg, a rose, an alder leaf, a true bug, and a pine cone. This sweet and whimsical image told of a fresh path into the woods, where we might all step more lightly than we have. And without any doubt it was a Sasquatch track.

Protecting all this diversity while working with affected communities to provide the products and jobs we need on lands that can still be productive, all under the new ground rules, will jog the rangers into the twentieth century — possibly even before it is over. But I can think of nothing that would present the Smokeys with a brighter new day than the arrival of that big footprint right in the middle of the Forest Plan.

On at least one occasion the Forest Service actually invited Bigfoot to stop in and visit. When prospector Perry Lovell found eighteen-inch tracks on his claim in 1969, North American Wildlife Research of Eugene, Oregon, applied to the Applegate Ranger District for a special-use permit to construct a Bigfoot trap. The ten-foot steel cube stood baited and set from 1974 to 1980, catching in that period one bear and one hippie. After a dream visit from the intended quarry, the caretaker left and the trap was sealed open and abandoned. To this day it may be visited as an interpretive attraction.

So the foresters have not always shut out the possibility of hairy giants. Whether or not they ever scuttled the evidence of such a print, they can no longer ignore it. And whether or not it is ever shown to be "real" in the sense of spotty owls and smoky bears, management for Bigfoot might mean better forests for all.

17

Lost in the Big Lava Bed

━━ ━━ ━━

Stuck in the ruts to the who knows where . . .
— Jack Gladstone, "The Roman Road"

WHEN I LEFT the foresters' encampment at Trout Lake, I began the last formidable leg of the Dark Divide passage: the Big Lava Bed. When you cross the pine- and dogwood-strewn landscape of the Mount Adams country, dark hulks rear up and surprise you through the scrim of green. These are the lava deposits that flowed from dikes and pipes in the volcanic system, expelled from the magma pool that underlies everything here. Cooling, they froze into pillars and lobes and layers of stone. Now the jumbled basalt lies about like leftovers, a bowl of gelid black-bean chili overturned across the tableland.

Fall colors claimed the shelterwood along the forest roads, chiefly vine maple and dogwood in versions of vermilion. I took a detour, signposted "Natural Bridges," through a mixed dwarfish forest of lodgepole and ponderosa pine, Douglas-fir, and larch, the larch going yellow. Mountain box and mountain balm wove the field layer, lemon-drop leaves of dogbane among kinnikinnick and long-blown beargrass made the ground layer.

The Natural Bridges of Klickitat County are superb landforms whose existence, a hundred miles from my home, I'd never guessed at. The formation consists of long, sinuous, open-roofed lava tubes, some thirty to eighty feet across from rim to rim, spanned by lava arches that look remarkably like ancient mossy human-built bridges in Cornwall. The tubes' bottoms are bunched up with boulders from rockslides. One rim supports dry old forest; the other, recent Doug-fir plantation. In a bouldery hollow, vine maples billowed in a red swell like molten lava.

I ventured under the eaves of one bridge whose egress was plugged

- 240 -

and found something I'd never seen before: moss stalactites, the wispy growths of two or three species of moss bonded together to form long inverted cones. Hundreds of these green icicles, some as long as six inches, drooped from the lintel. Some were blunt, others quite sharp, many web-slung. As a child I carried a passion for stalactites but a phobia for webs — finding these would have been a dilemma indeed. I had studied stalactites and stalagmites in every cave or limestone mine I could visit, and later, as a ranger-naturalist leading walks in Sequoia National Park's ornate Crystal Cave, I reveled in them. But I had never heard of mosses gathering into long plaits at the dripping doorways of caves. Coming across a natural feature of which I've been utterly ignorant throws me. I wondered how long these all-moss formations had taken to grow and what they could tell me about who had come before.

Layers of lava sills one to six feet thick receded into the low cave. Greenish-pale lichens shone almost phosphorescent. Crinkly sheets of gray foliose lichens hung down like wings, and pale agaric mushrooms pushed up from below. One ruby-red and one bright yellow crinkled leaf lay before the entrance on the needled, mossy mud. The green curvy wands of the maples fended off would-be entrants. Old gray leaves lined the floor beneath the trees, whose living leaves were grass-green near the cave, butter in the shade, scarlet where they reached out into the canyon's sun. It was cool in the lichen-light, the vine maples' shade, the cave's gape.

But not quiet. People picnicked nearby. "That's a good buy, eight of these for a buck. Shoulda got twenty-four of 'em." Most of the visitors seemed preoccupied with getting the "best shot" of the bridges on their instant cameras. But that's interpretive sites for you. People don't come to these places to marvel at moss stalactites or to find silence. They're taking a break from jobs and television, malls and movies, and it's their forest as much as mine. Their method of enjoying it should not concern me. Still, I found myself shrinking into my cave, Grendel-like, thinking rude thoughts about people who discard filter tips willy-nilly and wishing someone would please bite the heads off these nice, yammering folks.

I retreated to the eastern end of the site. The biggest of maybe six or eight bridges was here, farther into the young plantation, where few would look. I heard two or three pikas among log-strewn boulders — a training ground for living in slash piles? But this was not just pika and golden-mantled ground squirrel habitat. There were several elegant Bigfoot dens — at least until the place became a logjam, a picnic spot, and a photo op.

Stumps of old-growth Douglas-fir stood around, the culls dumped into the ravine, no doubt for the benefit of pikas (I reasoned ironically); why else would the Forest Service allow logging right up to the edge of a prime geological interpretive site and the dumping of logging waste into the middle of it?

— — —

Roads ring the Big Lava Bed, but none have been built into it farther than a long stone's throw. My plan was to spend a few days in the area, roaming its rim roads and venturing within wherever I could find a wormhole. I drove down the east side in the late afternoon. Dry Creek was double-dry; Lost Creek disappeared as promised. South Prairie, grassy openings with boggy bits and aspens on its western edges, hosted more cows than any other visible form of life.

Up under Little Huckleberry Mountain the road followed the very edge of the Big Lava Bed, all the way to the south end. Humpy lava poured right down to the verge. On foot I followed a hunter's trail a short way up and in, finding it very difficult to negotiate. The place was both incredibly beautiful, with vine maple glowing red in green grottoes, and incredibly rough, with holes and traps and turgid tongues of wicked dark rock poking everywhere.

This was no place for backpacking! I knew that I'd been wise (if cowardly — not an infrequent match) to choose several penetrations of the Big Lava Bed over a single long traverse. As the Gifford Pinchot Forest Plan says, "Due to its size and the roughness of terrain, exploring the Big Lava Bed requires initiative, independence, and stamina"; it is "infrequently explored by hikers" — both understatements.

That same document describes the Big Lava Bed as having been "formed by a relatively recent (less than 3,500 years) volcanic eruption from a cone and crater which produced one or more flows of lava." An elevated lava platform near the crater of the big cinder cone, however, has been carbon-dated at 8,100 years. The *Seattle Times* called the bed "one of the largest and most impressive sheets of recent lava in Washington" and said, "This waste of basaltic lava covers 12,500 acres . . . posed in a wild array of disorder and violence." About nine miles long, the bed varies in width from one to four miles.

The Forest Service once maintained two trails across narrow sections of the flow, linking fire lookouts, and strung a simple telephone line along the northern crossing. These were abandoned in the forties. Where I first poked my way in might have been the remains of the Little Huckleberry–Red Mountain telephone trail. The area has since been undisturbed except for a modest mineral claim in the southern end for ornamental lava and rare visits by hunters, botanists, and geologists. As the Forest Plan puts it, possibly indicating a bias, "recreation activities include hiking, hunting, sightseeing, hunting, and plant study."

The planners were also a little confused about the fauna of the area. "The lava flow and its vegetation are used," they wrote, "by a variety of rock-dwelling insects and other mammals." Bigfoot has often been called a bugbear (*Webster's:* "an ogre, something that causes needless terror"), but never an insect. Perhaps the Forest Service has bugbears in mind when they speak of mammaliferous insects. Certainly the lava beds furnish niches, in both senses of the word, for many mammals *and* insects, and for at least one big hairy bugbear.

On the first day of October I made my way to a point where I figured I could penetrate the Big Lava Bed on its northwest flank. A red pumice face that had been quarried for gravel made a deep coral angle of repose by the road. It hinted at the complexity of the igneous history of the area, for anyone who thinks it's all just a uniform black-rock mess. I passed the pumice shortly before coming to Crest Camp, an old base for horse packers with hitching posts and a loading ramp. Here I was only about three miles from the Indian Racetrack in the southern extremity of Indian Heaven, near Red Mountain. It made me wonder whether the Indians who gathered for *olallie* and salmon and stories and horseracing up on the plateau, and who surely used Crest Camp too, ever spent much time in the lavaland to the south and east. With the thoroughly inviting open meadows of Indian Heaven so near, why would they want to?

A turkey vulture flew up from beside the road into a lichen-draped fir. I could see sky through its nostrils, see its hood — useful on this chilly morning — up around its bare and lurid neck. Extra lymph glands in their warty wattles lend vultures immunity against the septic substances they love. Investigating, I found the attraction — a road-killed coyote. It was fairly new, yet a mass of maggots writhed beneath its face, and it was very ripe to the nose. A rotting road-killed Bigfoot, which is supposed to smell horrible to start with, would take terrific dedication to deal with.

I drove to the top of a spur road off the eminence of Crest Camp.

It should have offered a great view over the Big Lava Bed, but dense fog swiped the scene. Lots of logging loomed, and in the mists in the burned clear-cut below, lots of Bigfeet roamed, but all the apes had roots. A sign read "LYNX Evaluation Plantation Cowlitz Tree Improvement Co-op. Established 1988 by Wind River Ranger District. Funding Provided by Batesville Casket Co. Batesville Indiana." With a product like that in mind, this should be truly sustainable forestry. A second sign, with a routed tree design, noted "Site Preparation by Wind River Fuels Crew 1988."

The coffin-wood project bordered the Pacific Crest Trail on its far side. I planned to cross a low saddle to link with the trail, then follow it northerly to the edge of the lava bed. The firs whipped, cold mists blowing through their limber tops, as I set out into the stormy woods.

The "saddle" seemed to be a steep hill of open second-growth hemlock with beargrass and bunchberry below. It made pleasant going at first, but the terrain rose more than the one contour line indicated on the USGS map. Then I plowed through some hundred yards of bucked-up blowdown, a bitch to cross, and emerged on a ridge, clear-cut on top.

I was way west of the lava bed, *not* where I wanted to be. I struggled through the clear-cut to a line signed "Boundary of Partial Cut," which was none too partial. There I found a logging road and a boom landing that I certainly hadn't expected. Juniper, hazel, and Rocky mountain maple fuzzed a beautiful beargrassed ridge. When the sun came out, I felt hot and sweaty in my wool and Gore-Tex. The cold wind shifted into the treetops, and I hoped for no more windthrow today as I timber-bashed my way back down to the car by a guessed route that got me there.

I realized I had totally hosed up, taken the wrong "saddle," and ended up in a logging-road system south and west of where I wanted to be. People say compasses don't work well around the Big Lava Bed, and I was inclined to believe it. At least it made a convenient excuse for my poor orienteering.

From a spot a little farther along the road I could see the impressive crater in the north end of the Lava Bed. Orienting on it, I was able to find the true saddle, not far from my earlier takeoff. In three minutes I hopped over the low rise and landed on the Pacific Crest Trail on the edge of the lava.

Chilly wind and bright sun made a nice combo for exploring. The PCT runs along the Big Lava Bed for about two miles after dropping from the racetrack and before darting west toward Panther Creek. The land had been logged right down to the prime trail of the West; the trees in the little buffer area had, predictably, blown down, entailing much bucking for the trail crew and a not-so-pretty sight for hikers.

I worked my way maybe a mile into the bed, lit by late slanted beams. My feet found a very complex texture of broken basalt, sills, caves, chunks, boulders, layers, and screes; then I reached fairly flat terrain covered with dense, small lodgepole pines, giving way to grottoes, chasms, caved-in tubes, and bridges. There were no picnickers. Dark firs and pines contrasted with the deep reds of vine maple in crevices. Chipmunks worked a wonderland of lichens, mosses, creepers, and gone-over beargrass plumes. Porcupines stripped bark. Douglas squirrels took hermitage in grottoes lush green with moss. A pika sounded in the distance, over vague thunder. Coyotes, by their scat, gave away their endless pursuit of the others. This place should truly be a pika paradise, unless Seeahtlk munches off their little harelike heads. There were geeks aplenty, but no nuthatches for harmony — a rare occasion for this trip, as was the utter absence of aircraft overhead.

Pileated woodpecker's rectangular sign showed in snags. Ravens ronked under an east-facing ledge. Under another overhang I found an enormous, four-foot pika haystack. Almost all beargrass, it really looked like hay, bound with a sprinkling of maple leaves and pine sprigs.

The bugaboo question, "What would Bigfoot eat?" comes up often in discussions of the animal's actuality. Biologists and hunters debate whether it should have a potbelly like a gorilla because it must eat so many greens, or whether it hunts or scavenges. Some state dogmatically that the ecosystem simply could not support another large forager, especially in winter.

But as I repeatedly found, large stores of foodstuffs filled the landscape — berries, mushrooms, small mammals, and so on — largely unexploited, getting ready to rot and recycle. As an ecologist I am not so sanguine in this matter as to believe that the land can support an infinite variety and number of consumers. Resource availability is indeed one of the major limiting factors in animal distribution. However, I saw plenty to suggest that a large, uncommon omnivore could find something to eat here more often than not. One of the menu items might be pikas.

In the fall of 1967 Glen Thomas, an Oregon timber worker, reported watching a family group of Bigfeet hunting small animals among rocks near Tarzan Springs in the Cascades above Estacada. The impressive hole dug by the male is still visible, according to members of the Western Bigfoot Society who made a recent field trip there. "He brought out what appeared to be a grass nest, possibly some stored hay that small rodents had stored there," according to Thomas, as quoted in John Green's book *On the Track of Sasquatch*. Then the mama, papa, and baby Bigfoot gobbled several of the unidentified "small rodents." Thomas was no mammalogist — Green quoted him as saying, "They ate it skin, feathers, and all." From the habitat and the hay, I would guess that the animals might have been pikas.

Peter Byrne visited the site in 1972 and found thirty or more holes where boulders weighing as much as 250 or 300 pounds had been dislodged. Marmots dwelled among the rocks. It would certainly be easier to catch a deep-sleeping woodchuck than a wide-awake pika. Bigfoot would have to be fast to grab the skittering creature, all right, but perhaps a rock-popping Sasquatch can actually pin a pika down. Others have reported such behavior both in granite rockslides and in basalt country.

Here in the lava bed the little lagomorphs have endless tunnels for escape, too small for any pursuer but a weasel. Yet the big haystack I found was under the rim of a large overhang, and an animal capable of negotiating the rocks better than I could probably find many such. Nice, fat, hay-fed pikas might even offer a resource specialization to primate dwellers of the stony black-lands. In this and other ways, the Big Lava Bed undermines the "nothing to eat" objection to Bigfoot, just as its many hidey-holes destroy the "no place to hide" fallacy.

You think you're making progress crossing this place. Then you come to unpassable arches and gaping maws, shadowed casts and lightless shafts, trap doors and detours. These many holes — how deep do they go? Marsha's four-foot handle easily went all the way down many. One black orifice led down to the center of the earth at least. Is Lost Creek really running somewhere down there, as local legend suggests, only to emerge at the south end?

My camera, set at a slow speed, went off like a cannon in the silence. It was five-thirty, darkening, my boots imbrued, the blue of juniper and firs going bluer. Crimson caps of British-soldier lichens spattered the rocks alongside vine-maple leaves, but most of the colors were somber now. I'd come as far as I felt I should.

Was I observed? It was easy to imagine it as I picked my way carefully through the minefield. I arrived back at the saddle trail at six, emerging into hemlocks and Douglas-firs, which don't seem to grow in the lava bed, and a good big stand of native rhododendrons. Had I not misread the map I'd have had another two hours in the forbidding beds. But I'd had a good peek in and anticipated a deeper probe.

— — —

Instead of weathering the rigors of the Big Lava wilderness overnight, I took the easy hospitality of Stuart and Mildred Chapin in White Salmon. Mildred's family has a long history in the area, and Stuart was at that time a member of the Columbia River Gorge Commission, which oversees the management of the national scenic area. Because of the different visions of the various gorge interests, from hikers to lumber mills, fishermen to dam operators, wind surfers to barge companies, developers to the surviving Chinook and other Indians, a place on the commission is a permanent hot seat. Stuart took the heat in good grace, and he and Mildred made their love of the big river abundantly clear in their big old house perched on one of the larger lava flows of the gorge.

In a snug room full of books and family pictures, I read most of a recent *Oregonian* series called *NW Forests: Day of Reckoning* by veteran forest reporter Kathy Durbin. The USFS had adopted the Jack Ward Thomas spotted-owl report, if obsequiously and temporarily. But four years later Durbin would be sacked by the newspaper's new owners, who were afraid of alienating powerful timber interests. For now, I was excited that the topic of future forests was receiving such a thorough look.

Laying the pulp aside and snuffing the light in my cozy den, I conjured up an image of the Big Lava Bed by night. Camping there would be a wild delight if you could find a flat spot for your tent. But I would not like to be lost and picking my way around after dark, when a broken ankle would be almost as likely as nightfall itself.

Over breakfast in the morning, Mildred told me of gathering small native cranberries in the South Prairie bogs for sauce at Thanksgiving. We enjoyed homegrown ripe tomatoes, hazelnuts, and chestnuts with conversation of forests and gorges, which led into Stuart's question: Could Sasquatch survive out there? I thought hard. Though still not coming to any conclusions on Bigfoot's physical existence, I felt I could answer yes in terms of the possibility of survival. Still. For a bit. If the timber plan works.

When Stuart asked me to expand on that, I said I had demonstrated to myself the abundance of wild food in these forests, at least in the fructuous fall. I mentioned my lepidopterist friend Karōlis Bagdonas, who found that grizzly bears in the Rockies forage vast numbers of miller moths roosting among the talus; the fat-rich insects furnish a major part of the grizzlies' summer diet. Insect eating has not been widely reported for Bigfoot, but why not, especially during insect outbreaks? We know that chimps probe for termites with sticks.

I'd seen clearly that adequate, or generous, denning and hiding places survive, at least in the ancient deepwood and the Big Lava Bed. A fast-moving, deeply secretive, and reasonably smart ape could remain generally hidden. The not-infrequent sightings are evidence that it screws up now and then, as all animals do. Yes, the woods are big enough for Bigfoot. But fragmentation is its bête noir, and another couple of decades of road building and cutting like the past two could void that conclusion for me.

With no strong feelings about Bigfoot, Stuart and Mildred were open to my ideas. From his efforts at guiding the Columbia Gorge between development and conservation interests, Stuart was well aware of the complexity of the ecological conditions I was posing for a potential ape. Their attitude was emblematic that the time was past when one could scarcely mention the subject of Bigfoot in sensible company without fear of derision.

Outside a fresh rain had put a rainbow over the gorge. The sun emerged, and we watched salmon-colored painted ladies nectar the zinnias of their butterfly garden, while crows and ravens arranged a field-guide page over the black cliffs. I took my leave, thankful for the fruits of the season, the comforts of a good home in a fine place, and an intelligent sounding board for thoughts too often held in solitary confinement.

- - -

The Little White Salmon road took me to Big Cedars County Park, where I recycled my coffee among fair- to middling-size arborvitae. A light rain fell. Perched under a cedar umbrella I realized it was almost time to head home. But I was fully in the thrall of the Big Lava Bed. I took one of the few short roads into the area and came soon into a scrub of manzanita, silk-tassel bush, ocean spray, mock orange, and cascara, tough shrubs that can take the rocky, well-drained "soils." The road ended in a clinker field softened by small ferns. Plant collectors had been there, leaving their sign of broken flower pots. A cold breeze wheezed under plumbeous skies. I continued on foot, intending to locate a roundish plain indicated on the maps to determine what it was. But I found that I'd left my compass back at the Chapins', and my sense of direction was on its own.

Back in White Salmon that morning I had wanted to pick up some Rainier Ale. The old gentleman of whom I'd asked directions to the state liquor store gave them to me clearly, then handed me a Southern Baptist gospel tract entitled *I will abstain.* About to enter the maze of the basalt boulder field without a compass, having just consumed a strong ale with lunch, I suspected he probably had the right idea.

The beds looked different here, with tall wild raspberries, mountain box, and elderberry. But as I left the clinkers, pines replaced the hemlocks and the terrain changed back to shelves and grottoes. The road had not, in fact, touched the interior. A narrower old track carried on a little farther to a sinkhole full of water, the first I'd seen in the lava beds. A circle the size of a wading pool, it was rimmed with grass and duckweed and saxifrages. Water striders made clear dents in the surface with their six pontoon bubbles. Whirligigs too had found this remote oasis. A wild wind came up, bending the toothpick pines that looked fit for tepee poles alone.

Deer tracks registered in silty spots moist from rain, but the coyote scats were full not of fur but of the fine purple seeds of the raspberries. There were also Havoline and Prestone bottles, a back-road cliché, the plastic spoor of the idiot-mobile. Furry rosettes of a composite plant caught water poolettes. Away from the sinkhole a creature would have to be able to catch rainwater or know how to tap into the underground streams to slake its thirst. For an animal able to work the pipelines of the Big Lava Bed like a subway system, life here might be rewarding. I imagined an interstitial universe beneath my feet, populated by dim-sighted salamanders and waterbears.

At the end of the old haul road, I cut south to find the big open ellipse shown on the topo map. Moss stalactites grew here too, under the eaves of lava windows. At four o'clock I remembered that it was midnight in Berlin, and Germany was about to become one nation. What a different scene it would be at the Brandenburg Gate! Here too rose high stone arches, but I was the entire crowd. And these thick walls of basalt might stand forever, keeping no one in and almost everyone out.

Orange chanterelles trumpeted from damp moss patches. Some

white chanterelles and a small cauliflower fungus showed up too, both uncommon delicacies, and big boletes raised their brown pelted caps. I plucked red huckleberries, sweet salal berries, and sour Oregon grapes. This stark space was not without its nourishment. But the salal foliage, a jade jungle, would not let me see the ground, making travel over lava mounds and mossy cobbles treacherous. It also signaled a change in the substrate.

I had made it to the map's oval, a slight depression with deeper soil and vegetation more like that of a "regular" forest — thick salal and bracken, pipsissewa, trillium, twinflower; Douglas-fir, heavy maple, and a bit of white pine among the diminished lodgepoles. I believe it was an old lakebed. But it wasn't much more walkable than the jumble outside. Deadfalls and salal made crossing the oval almost as rigorous as picking through the lava fields. Without my compass, which might or might not have worked here, I navigated by the sun and my native sense of direction to get to the other side.

In a small, open stand of blue huckleberry lay some old bear poop. Bear denning spots are unlimited here, if bears like rocks. Even people can learn to like rocks if that's all there is — ruins of Anasazi pueblos in the slickrock of the Southwest show this clearly. More recently a renegade band of Modoc Indians took up residence in a habitat not unlike the Big Lava Bed — except a lot drier and less vegetated.

As the Smithsonian's *Handbook of North American Indians*, volume 8, notes, some precontact Indians lived in "barren flows of lava. The edges of the geologically recent lava flows were important as hunting places for . . . marmots, an important food in spring; and they also served as fortifications or refuges for the local population."

The Modoc of California have a history with Bigfoot and with life among the rocks. Tawani Wakawa (as quoted in the *Bigfoot News*) told of his grandfather's first encounter with Matah Kagmi, as he called it, one evening in 1897 on a deer trail near Mount Shasta. "Grandfather made a motion of friendship and laid down the string of fish that he was carrying," Wakawa wrote. "The creature eventually understood this as it quickly snatched up the fish and struck out through the timber nearby."

"Let our motto be extermination, and death to all opposers," railed a Yreka, California, newspaper in 1854. White fervor to wipe out Indian opposition to their expansionist plans peaked with frequent genocidal raids on the Modocs and others. When the Modoc people were all consigned to a reservation on Klamath Lake, a band from the Lost River country to the south resisted. Settlers invaded their homeland, and troops came to force the last Modocs out. Under the leadership of Kintpuash, otherwise known as Captain Jack, the band resisted with arms, then retreated into what is now the Lava Beds National Monument, south of Tule Lake on the Oregon line. For the next seven months they lived like pikas among the rocks.

According to the *American Heritage Book of Indians,* Captain Jack's band "consisted of perhaps 250 men, women, and children, with perhaps 70 or 80 men of warrior age — most of the men were well-known to the whites, under such monikers as Humpy Jerry, Shack-nasty Jim, or Curly-headed Doctor." Somehow this community eked out a life among the hot rocks. I wouldn't be surprised if adept parties crept out to Tule Lake, returning with water, ducks, and other provender. But in the time they lived there the Modocs became the masters of the black badlands. "Attack after attack was trapped and shot to pieces in the nightmare lava beds," says *American Heritage,* "total Army casualties running to over 100 killed and wounded." When a peace talk took place, Captain Jack (possibly suspecting a trap) turned on General E. R. S. Canby, army commander of the Department of the Columbia, and killed him. After that he wore Canby's uniform.

President Grant would have no more; he ordered General Sherman to bring Kintpuash out. Sherman, never accused of being an Indian lover, replied, "You will be fully justified in their utter extermination." Artillery was brought in, and the Modocs were shelled out of their lava hideout. Captain Jack and three others were hanged, and the rest were banished to a pestilent reserve in southeastern Oklahoma, where most soon died. Captain Jack's rebellion was doomed from the start, like all the other Native American acts of resistance. But for a time his followers lived independently in a wild labyrinth of lava.

I suppose that the natives around the Big Lava Bed knew its innards as well as Jack knew his lavalands. Some of the edges, as at South Prairie, furnish the resources of wet savannas anywhere. But given the rich plateaus north and east and the great river to the south, they mightn't have had a reason to explore the lava bed. At least they were never driven into the lava bed as a last resort. Had Captain Jack come here, he would have found a land with fewer clues for orientation.

Given the tumbled topography and the monotonous cover of pines, it is extremely hard to set a course and keep to it. You could walk around and around for days and never come out.

When I found my way to the far edge of the old lakebed, I did not know where I was. I could see no horizon and no sun under a sky that ran to blue holes and black patches. I wasn't unduly worried, but I was more than ever aware of the absence of my trusty Silva from its accustomed pocket. Searching my maps for clues that were not there, I rested on a squirrel midden that barely softened the lava. The chickaree-in-residence ran up a pine with a mushroom in its mouth. Around the edges of a blue and green moss-and-lichen fairyland of a crater sprawled the big nests of bushytail woodrats, spilling seeds and coppery manzanita sticks.

But my immediate concern was finding out where the hell I was. I knew I was only half a mile from a road on the northeast or southwest. But if I meandered roughly northwesterly, I could go almost ten miles without seeing any landmarks. The landforms outside, the mountains and ridges, ought to facilitate orientation, but frequently they were invisible through the forest cover. The big cinder cone was far to the north, and I wouldn't see it until I was on top of it. And it was nearing sunset. I hadn't carried bivouac equipment with me on this ramble so close to the car. I was beginning to see how one could become stranded in a place where blind wandering at night could be fatal.

After another hour of deliberate forays this way and that, hoping for inspiration, I started to worry. What was the worst that could happen? Hypothermia was possible at 2,000 feet in October, but I could probably fashion some sort of shelter to keep warm enough. My fat reserves were good for a month, if not a year, and there were plenty of berries and mushrooms and other plants to keep the edge off. With luck I might come across another sinkhole full of water, the lack of which debilitates the lost hiker much sooner than lack of food.

In short, not much would happen to me if I could prevent hypothermia. In time my absence would precipitate a search, and I would quickly be spotted by air or by search and rescue folks who knew the area. How embarrassing that would be, so close to the road. But embarrassment ceases to matter to those in jeopardy, like the moment in deep water when you finally swallow your pride and enough water to yell "Help!" if you still can.

As the day waned, dusky shadows made injury more likely, and I knew my chances of getting out without a bivouac were waning as well. My uneasiness grew out of anticipating cold, hassle, and failure. It wasn't fear of the place or its creatures, though the Big Lava Bed would make a marvelous set for a cinematic version of the deep, dark woods where sinister things lie in wait. Dark woods have never seemed sinister to me, but my own shortcomings can be truly frightening.

When you read about lost children or hunters or hikers in the papers, you wonder what they're going through, at what point they panic, and then what happens. Everyone knows that the disoriented are likely to walk in circles and get more dislocated with every step. Now I knew something of that feeling. The pines looked identical, the rocks were repeats. There was the squirrel midden again, or was it a different one? The squirrels made fun with their piping hoots, the ravens honked discouragement. Panic? No, but a nauseated wave when I realized how a short ramble had become a desperate scramble by the easiest, silliest increments. Though sweaty in my wool, I was cold, and it looked like a bad time coming.

Then, just as I was thinking about pulling together a rough shelter and gathering a few berries and chanterelles before dark, I stepped between a clump of pines and a lump of lava onto the rough track I'd come in on. I had indeed gone in at least one circle, probably circumscribing the oval on my map. In the end I had arrived very near where I thought I was aiming for. I hadn't so much misplaced myself as taken leave of my confidence. The Big Lava Bed will do that to you. I stepped lightly onto the flat surface of the track, feeling the way you do coming off a long, awful drive, hitting the pavement, and throttling down.

Coming out south of my entry point, I found a dozen or more sinkholes. Unlikely to be from meltwater or rainwater at this season, the little lagoons must have artesian sources. Whether the disappeared Lost and Lava creeks tie in to the underground system and reemerge at the south end as Lava and Moss creeks, only the lava bed knows. And perhaps the plants, which know how to find the water wherever it runs. The Big Lava Bed is an ericaceous haven — a heathland full of kinnikinnick, manzanita, their hybrids, two salals, wintergreens, pipsissewa, huckleberries, and others. The odd shrub *Garrya*, heathlike but in a family by itself, is a specialty of the lava landscape. Its flowers hang in silky tassels. Now old tassels dangled among next year's firm buds and tough, shiny green leaves. I ate a "little apple," the fruit of the manzanita. It was sweet and tasty, with little meat and lots of big, hard seeds, but with water in its tissues. A raven alighted in a snag, howled to let Seeahtlks know I was about and stealing his little apples.

In the dusk I could see that the ponds had drawn some attention. There was an old handmade picnic table, an elaborate fire pit of lava rocks, but no litter. Heaven forbid, I thought, that this should ever become an interpretive site. So far it seems unlikely. According to the forest planners, the Big Lava Bed receives only an estimated two hundred RVDs — recreation visitor days — per year. Or perhaps that's how many come out after venturing in.

- - -

Without a doubt this was one of the wildest, most forbidding landscapes I'd ever known. The only place that came close was the Valley of Ten Thousand Smokes in Katmai National Monument, Alaska. Marching across the polychrome pumice gulleys of that eruptive plain toward the caldera, I felt as far from anything as I have ever been. But I was never lost there.

Now, in a land of gaping black holes and razor scarps of lava, I had known the meaning of lost, if only briefly. It means being aloof from your whereabouts, unable to predict, let alone count on, what comes next. It means facing each footstep with a forlorn question, getting no answers from your logic or your heart. To lose yourself is to be cut off from communication with the ground underfoot, the sky overhead. It is almost the worst thing that can happen to a species whose sense of place is often forgotten and never enough. Lost is a peril, a trial, a torture; it is the only kind of certainty that you never wanted. And in the Big Lava Bed, where any false step can mean splintered bone, lost could mean dead.

No other animal has ever been lost. Disoriented, maybe. Temporarily confused as to location. But unless tossed in a rat's maze or transported far from home like a bad bear, every creature knows exactly where it is at every waking moment. Each "inferior" animal brain carries its own global positioning device and Geographic Information System as standard operating equipment. At least this is what I believe about the essential nature of wild organisms: by definition they are situated.

Only people get lost. Captain Jack did not lose his bearings in the lava beds of the Modoc country. Humans and other primates for whom the location of the furniture of the land means comfort, security, nourishment, happiness, and even survival never lose their way on their home ground. They may establish songlines or blaze trees to help, but they know. Only we modern ones do not know our way around. Landlorn, without a compass or a clue, we're stuck in the ruts to the who knows where.

Bigfoot doesn't get lost, not here or anywhere. Maybe it would show us the route, help us spot the path back to the land. If we don't find our way home soon, we will find ourselves instead out in the sun with Captain Jack, backs against the hot rock wall, hunted out by the howitzers of change. I learned two things here. Whether my compass works or not, I'll never go in there again without it. And if Bigfoot ever has to make a stand, it ought to be here, in the Big Lava Bed.

18

Mermaids, Monsters, and Metaphors

His parting from life
was no cause for grief
to any of the men who examined the trail
of the conquered one
saw how, despairing he had rushed away
ruined in the fight
to the lake of monsters fleeing, doomed
in bloody footprints.

— *Beowulf*

S O WHAT THE HELL IS IT?"
Sheriff Angleford shifted a stubby paw from his hip to his chin, then retrieved the drained Styrofoam cup from the truck's bumper and pretended to drink the dregs. "Damned if I know."

Hank Peterson prodded the duff beside the truck with his boot. "You know what they're saying, Ed."

"I know . . . they're starting to talk about goldurned Bigfoot again. I thought we got rid of it that last time around, when we pulled that prankster out of the woods and ran him out of town."

"Yeah, but this time there's that dead goat, all chewed up . . ."

"So? Cougar, bear. Ain't no goddamn monster."

"But there's more tracks like these over there, Ed. And the doc thinks he saw one, comin' home from the widow Bates's Saturday. Said it was bigger 'n Kandoll's ox stood endwise."

"That wasn't any medical call," said the sheriff. "And who knows how much schnapps doc and the Bates woman had between 'em?"

"Folks are worried, Ed. They're talkin' posse."

"Yeah, like that 'posse' they got up when Slade squeezed out of the county coop? That 'posse' ended up in the Triangle Tavern, as I recall." Angleford and Peterson kicked a little more dirt around. They had met at the end of the Cedar Creek road, where a hunter had reported a line of giant footprints.

The deputy's cruiser threw up a fog of pumice dust. Deputy Potrillo leapt out. "Hey, Hank, Sheriff, we got it! You need to get over to Jake Kandoll's place, and quick."

"Got what? What're you yammering about, Potrillo?"

"That ape-monster! Kandoll and some boys've got it pinned down in a canyon behind his place. He's pissed about that goat."

"If he's got anything in that brush-hole, he's got a bear. Or more likely a porcupine!"

"I saw it move, Sheriff. It's big . . . standing up and . . . and yowling and like that. And does it ever stink. Man, it stinks!"

"I told you," said Peterson. "I've believed in it for a long time, most folks around here do, really. Now you're gonna find out what I'm talking about."

Sheriff Angleford, a Montana cop before coming to Washington the year before, had lucked into the sheriff's job when two local men split the election. When he learned about the county ordinance against killing Bigfoot, he just laughed. "Hairy apes!" he said. "Next they'll put little green men on the endangered species list." Now he found himself swept along with a band of locals brandishing rifles at a brushy gully yelling about something he didn't even believe in. As the light faded, and howls continued to emanate from the ravine, some of the men wanted to start a fire to smoke the howler out.

"That's the only way," said Kandoll, the owner of the land, hoarse from the general excitement. "We sure as hell ain't going in there after it. It's all poison oak anyway."

Angleford, for the first time since he'd taken office, found himself supervising crowd control. Crowds didn't often gather in Skapoose County, but this one was growing fast.

"Hold on," he shouted, rolling his bulk in front of the mob. "You can't start a fire. You know the restriction's on. You're liable to burn the whole damn mountain down."

"How else we gonna get 'im out?" the truculent Kandoll demanded.

"Besides," said the sheriff, "I thought you people had some law around here protecting these so-called Bigfeet. Pretty big fine, isn't it?"

A spare man in a checked jacket and shiny tie spoke up, a county commissioner. "Ten thousand dollars. Yeah, statute's still on the books," he said.

"That's nothing," Kandoll grunted. "It's my land, I can shoot what I want. Besides, them durn scientists'd pay me a lot more than that to get a look at this here deal." Several of his neighbors laughed their agreement.

"Hell, I'd pay that much just to get a look at this thing," one of them said.

A woman from the Department of Fish and Wildlife arrived in a green pickup within minutes of the red Blazer driven by Peter Byrne of the Bigfoot Research Project. She saw the guns and sized it up. "Who's got a license to hunt at this season?" she asked. "What are you planning on shooting?"

No one answered. The young woman faced a row of stony faces. She was about to use her hand-held radio, when Byrne, stretching his soft British accent to be heard, said, "Listen up, you men."

"How'd the guy from *Wild Kingdom* get here?" asked a logger, and the others laughed. But they listened.

"If you really have a Bigfoot in there," he went on, "we're interested. But it won't do anyone any good to kill it. We've been trying to find one to make contact. This might be our best chance yet." Once he'd said it, some of the people jeered, but others concurred, including Kandoll's wife.

"Why should you shoot it anyway, Jake?" she said. "It just wants to be left alone. One goat doesn't matter that much."

"It'll be the ox next," her husband barked. "You're just being a softy . . . or else them old Indi'n stories are gettin' to you again. I told you to stop listenin' to them."

"But, Jake, there might be something to the stories . . ."

"This here ain't no goddamn *spirit*, Elma. It's a durned *ape*, and it *ate my goat*."

As dark came on, the sheriff and the wildlife agent and the commissioner and the Bigfoot researcher argued over jurisdiction and tactics of peacefully capturing or contacting the creature, while the roars continued from the brush. Suddenly the tone changed. The cry became a sharp whistle. All heads turned toward the head of the box canyon. Another whistle answered from the rim. There, profiled against the dusk skyline of the clear-cut above the ranch, stood a massive black figure.

A hush like an empty grave fell over the unruly aggregation of the curious and the fearful. Everyone saw the figure. Whistles flew like swallows back and forth between the beast in the brushy grotto and the one on the top. The rim-walker gestured, roared, and whistled again.

Byrne was the first to speak. "That's it," he said quietly. "That's what we've been seeking, all right. It's bigger than I thought." He was awed, amazed, moved. Then, the shocked spell broken, a clamor arose. A torch was lit. Men shouted, "Get it!" A rifle shot cracked open the night.

- - -

Hokey? Of course. But it would be like that. We've all seen a hundred movies like it. An unknown or mythical life form arrives stage left — space alien, subterranean, mermaid, whatever — and the reaction of the people on the scene is . . . well, reactionary. The sympathies of the movie audience lie firmly with the interloper, who tragically perishes at the hands of the army, science, or villagers with pitchforks or shot-guns. We feel communal moral indignation and pity for a harmless creature misunderstood and feared. And the conclusion, every time, is that it did not have to happen. The lucky ones, such as E.T. or the mermaid in *Splash!* escape with the help of the protagonist; but only after hair-raising episodes of wrong-headed persecution.

I know what I'm talking about here. When I was a preteen, my friends and I became completely bewitched by Bela Lugosi, Boris Karloff, and Lon Chaney, Jr. We began a monster club with ranks: I, as Frankenstein, was president, then came Dracula, the Wolf Man, and Caris the Mummy. I borrowed my father's boots for monster clogs, and my friends' mothers made batwing cookies and cherry Kool-Aid vampire punch for our meetings. Our delusions of grandeur ran toward making our own movie with my grandfather's wind-up Key-stone, a primitive sixteen-millimeter motion picture camera. We story-boarded the plot, and of course the monster (played by me) would meet a glorious demise out by the old canal. We never graduated to the slasher genre, two holes in the neck being about as much abstracted gore as we wanted. But for all the fun, some innocence was lost. Those old movies told us all we needed to know about the mean-spirited actions of grown-ups toward whatever they failed to understand.

After generations of movies with the same basic script, we should not be surprised if our baser motivations prevailed and we extended pitchforks instead of open arms to any outrageous beast that had the misfortune to walk off the set and into our midst. I suppose the theme survives because it never ceases to jerk tears and sell tickets; but does anyone doubt that we would react this way, given the opportunity? Or that we would feel anything but remorse about it afterward? The issue has been one for scriptwriters and dreamers so far, since few outlandish species have dared to show up. But if Bigfoot walked out of the woods tomorrow, how would we behave?

— — —

Several years ago Sally Hughes, my wife at the time, lepidopterist John Hinchliff, and I found a species of butterfly that was new for the Washington list at the foot of the Big Lava Bed. We had been seeking the golden hairstreak in the state for a decade, reasoning that where its host plant grew, the insect flew. Its larvae feed strictly on the foliage of golden chinquapin, a western type of wild chestnut. The shrubby tree and the butterfly are widespread in California and not uncommon in Oregon all the way north to the Columbia River. I had a feeling that if we could find the few golden chinquapins rumored to occur across the river on the Washington side, we would find the butterfly as well.

The Army Corps of Engineers' *Environmental Atlas of Washington State,* the same document that helped legitimize the search for Sasquatch, showed the chinquapin in parts of Clark County. We scoured the region but found none. A few years later a paper by professor of botany Arthur Kruckeberg, one of my long-time mentors at the University of Washington, detailed the whereabouts and ecology of the chinquapin in two Washington locations. At last we were able to visit them, and within seconds we confirmed the state record of *Habrodais grunus* as well.

Kruckeberg had been concerned about the effects of logging on the chinquapins. They are considered weed trees by many foresters in California and Oregon, and the few scraggly ones in Skamania County were certainly not being given any special protection from spraying and log-slash. By finding the butterfly and subsequently having it listed as a "Priority One Special Animal" by the Washington Natural Heritage Program, we doubled the reason for the USFS to attend to the dispersed chinquapins. Together the butterfly and plant people lobbied the Gifford Pinchot and gained the interest of USFS biologists. All this resulted in a few lines in the Forest Plan about both organisms and a degree of attention to their well-being. I have since heard from colleagues that at least some chinquapins have been flagged with ribbons meaning "do not harm," and the hairstreaks are thriving. The long-term health of these species locally is still in question, but if they are lost it won't be from ignorance. Unlike certain other novel creatures reputed to occur in the area but never "proven" with a specimen, at least they have been recognized.

One evening during my exploration of the Big Lava Bed, following a day's walking, I visited the site of our discovery to see if I could find the golden hairstreaks again. They appear in the late summer and fall and are reported to fly at dawn and dusk as well as in full sunshine. But perhaps this was too late in the season or the day even for them. I did not find them or any eggs. There were fewer chinquapins, and they were very dusty from a long season of logging-truck traffic.

In that autumnal haze, with the scrubby growth black on the black, scabby-toe lava, the idea that golden-leaved trees and golden-winged butterflies occurred here together seemed outlandish. Yet we know these life forms exist, not by faith or belief, but by Cartesian means: Professor Kruckeberg's paper, based on herbarium sheets, and our discovery, backed up by a small series of specimens in the state museum. In other words, the evidence is concrete. It depends neither on hearsay nor on the leaky memory of some field observer but on actual specimens. And there's the rub when it comes to Bigfoot: there is no body.

Nonconsumptive wildlife enthusiasts and weekend naturalists often fail to appreciate the need for collecting specimens. If we can see the creature or the plant in the field, they ask, why is there any need to kill it? Often their point is well taken. Christmas bird counts and Fourth of July butterfly counts have shown that sight records can be just as meaningful as specimens in many instances. After all, we have come a long way from the days when every bird had to be shot to credit its occurrence. Picking wildflowers is considered antisocial.

In some circumstances, however, field biologists require what they call voucher specimens. The initial scientific description of a taxon (species or variety) is a formal procedure; the International Code of Zoological Nomenclature (ICZN) insists on designation of a type specimen, a kind of yardstick against which all future examples of the taxon can be gauged. Voucher specimens are also required for proof that a species has been found out of its known range and for some teaching and research purposes. More and more we find ways of representing organisms with photos, models, or field notes, yet for some needs only an example will suffice.

People who oppose collecting are often surprised to learn that the small numbers of specimens taken by scientists have a negligible impact on populations — certainly nowhere near that of hunting, fishing, roadkills, bug zappers, pesticides, or habitat development — and collecting can contribute immensely to conservation. As the raw material of biogeography (plant and animal distribution studies), collections enable us to characterize where living things occur and where they don't — and then to question why they don't live where one would expect. Applied biogeography has led to more direct habitat conservation measures than any other process has. Without museum and amateur collectors, we would lack the necessary data to assess conservation needs. If sight records progressively replace specimens for this function, all the better. But especially for invertebrates, we are so far from classifying and being able to recognize most of the species (that is, most of life on earth) that to end collecting tomorrow would darken the prospects for preserving biodiversity.

So when Grover Krantz calls for taking a specimen of Bigfoot, he is not being bloodthirsty. As a scientist he is keenly aware of the role of anthropological artifacts and biological specimens. He firmly believes that a single body will establish the existence of the species and lead to its instant protection and permanent conservation, and that these considerations justify its killing.

To what extent is he right? Krantz, in *Big Footprints*, explains the attitude of many scientists as "I'll see it when I believe it." In other words, their minds (and eyes) are closed to unlikely possibilities. This, he says, is exactly the view faced by the discoverers of *Pithecanthropus* and *Australopithecus*, now considered major players in the ancestry of humankind. *Northwest Anthropological Research Notes*, in response to prods from John Green and others, decided to "welcome . . . any reasonably scientific paper dealing with the sasquatch phenomenon." Subsequently in that journal, Krantz proposed the official naming of Bigfoot, using casts of footprints as the requisite type specimen. Concurring with the suggestions of John Green in 1968 and Yerkes Primate Center Director Geoffrey Bourne in 1975, he concluded that Bigfoot is congeneric with the giant fossil ape *Gigantopithecus blacki*. Krantz erected the name *G. canadensis* for Bigfoot, reserving the possibility of changing it to *Giganthropus canadensis* if *G. blacki* turns out to have been a knuckle-walker instead of erectly bipedal like Bigfoot.

There is precedent for the naming of cryptids. In 1975 Sir Peter Scott, the distinguished wildfowl artist and conservationist, with Robert Rines, applied the name *Nessiteras rhombopteryx* to the Loch Ness monster in the journal *Nature*. The "Ness-marvel diamond-fin" description was based on impressive underwater photographs obtained by Rines's Academy of Applied Science of Boston, the same outfit that supports Peter Byrne's Bigfoot Research Project. Although a famous old photo of Nessie has recently been disclosed as a hoax, the AAS sonargrams have not been discredited. Sir Peter's action was criticized as wishful and premature and also praised for its prescience. His purpose was to promote the saurian's conservation. In 1976 Byrne followed suit by informally proposing adoption of the Linnaean name *Homo nocturnus* for Bigfoot-like creatures. In the absence of a type specimen or formal scientific description, this name must remain invalid, what the ICZN terms a *nomen nudum*.

So if Bigfoot has already been classified, why do we need a specimen? Because the world has not been quick to embrace Krantz's (or Scott's) description; most of the scientific establishment maintains an attitude of outright disdain or utter indifference. After the fact, Krantz's paper might be recognized for its priority in zoological nomenclature; but in the meantime, in the monolithic eye of Science, Bigfoot remains in the realm of mermaids, minotaurs, and unicorns. And conservation too takes the subject of hairy monsters in vain. So until there's a specimen, there will be no name, no page in the textbooks and field guides, no slot in the Forest Plan alongside owls and martens and salmon and cedars and chinquapins and butterflies.

Byrne and others who don't want to see even one Bigfoot killed argue that the animal will be recognized and protected if it is reliably sighted, with good films and multiple witnesses as articles of proof or, at most, with blood samples taken from a tranquilized animal. Krantz replies that if the authorities won't accept the Patterson film and footprints with dermal ridges, they are not likely to accept anything but a body.

Assuming that there would be value to science and perhaps to the species if an example were collected, three questions arise: (1) how to catch one, (2) what to do with the specimen, and (3) what ethical issues must be dealt with, both before and after the fact. I'll consider these seemingly contradictory questions in that order, since in my opinion the last is the most important.

All the hunters have their own programs and schemes for catching a Sasquatch. Grover Krantz has effectively discounted the effectiveness of most of these in advance. Plans for trapping, tranquilizing, and heat-seeking the giants all have big flaws. What's left is the blunt hunt, with or without guns.

Robert W. Morgan mounted a colorful search on the slopes of Mount St. Helens well before its 1980 eruption. A local source remembered Morgan as five foot six, bald, with a goatee and piercing blue eyes. His American Yeti Expedition 1970 included an archaeologist, a cinematographer, and several young men and women, some with degrees in biology. They are supposed to have tracked the beast in forest and cave with jeeps, night-vision devices, psychics, and, at one point, a nude female volunteer as "bait," though this detail creeps into accounts of many hunts and is probably always apocryphal.

The expedition was cosponsored by a Florida agent, a film company, and the National Wildlife Federation. George Harrison, managing editor of *National Wildlife*, went along and later wrote about it for the magazine. Morgan's plan was to capture a Bigfoot and fly it to Washington, D.C., for study. "Upon completion of the research," wrote Harrison, "Morgan intends to have the creature flown back to the Pacific Northwest and released unharmed in its native wilderness haunts."

The expedition spent $50,000 and found several sets of tracks not uniformly accepted as genuine before dissolving in disarray and allegations of hoaxing. A local Native American described the outing as "more Hollywood than science," and said his family was "haunted" by Morgan's crew. "There are two ways of dealing with the hunters," he told me, "and they're both wrong. One, don't talk, and they won't leave you alone, thinking you know something; two, talk, and the tabloids get you."

A different but equally ineffectual approach centered on a paramilitary Bigfoot cadre based in Vancouver, Washington. As Ray Crowe told me, members of this group held ranks and called their leader "El Capitan." They went forth in big-wheeled trucks, armed with assault rifles, spotlights, and camouflage. God knows what all they shot, but it wasn't Bigfoot.

Such weirdnesses might not represent the mainstream (if "Bigfoot mainstream" is not an oxymoron), but there are certainly lots of guys with guns out in the woods looking for giants. They are all hopeful of the result predicted by a veteran Bigfoot hunter in Kentucky, where the local ridge-dwellers call the animals "wild woolly bullies." Quoted by Marian Place in *Bigfoot All Over the Country,* James Vincent said that the backwoods people "hear them stomping along the ridgetops, and hear them screeching. These folks think the same as I do. Bigfoot is a very curious animal. One day this curiosity is going to get one killed."

And that, essentially, is a conclusion devoutly to be wished for, according to Grover Krantz. "If I could come up with the money," he told *Washington* magazine writer Michael Schmelzer, "I would hire a team of expert trackers and hunters and send them off into the mountains with very specific instructions: Bring me a Sasquatch, dead or alive."

Suppose Grover, or anyone, got his Sasquatch — then what? As he rightly suggested in his visceral presentation at Harrison Hot Springs, anyone who succeeds in the hunt or finds a roadkill will have to face this challenge. "There would be several gallons of blood," he said, "one heck of a mess."

Krantz divided this "nasty little problem" into a number of questions. How would you handle the specimen? Who would you trust to help you? How would you transport a rotting, stinking mass of that magnitude? Where would you take it to authenticate the find and establish your interest in it? What would you get from it? How would you protect it from being taken or appropriated? What legal threats would you face? What would you do about general harassment from the media? Would there be danger from pro-lifers? How should you pursue your legal rights?

Each of these questions, he feels, presents a major obstacle. You could hardly move the corpse by yourself, so you'd have to decide what parts to take. Any assistance would mean competition. Do you try for a refrigerated truck, and if so, would it be usable again? Fame and fortune, which might be the chief rewards, are easy to understand, stemming from straight selfishness. There might also be product endorsements for the discoverer; newspaper, magazine, and book receipts; and sales of body parts — but the negative impact on your life might cancel the benefits. (Krantz spoke with a soft irony that many listeners missed altogether.)

You would need to protect your find from theft by competitors, government confiscation, bears, coyotes, ravens, vultures, other scavengers, and the timber companies (who might try to destroy any sign of it). Everyone would want a piece of the action, not to mention the body — the media, the museums, the government, the "best of the Jane Goodall clones," who, Krantz feels, would be eager to study the creature.

Krantz thinks the Skamania County ordinance would not apply, since it proscribes "wantonly killing" Bigfoot, and scientific collecting is not wanton. As for other authorities, he says, your action would be to all intents and purposes "like killing a unicorn" — they can't prosecute you for something whose existence they don't recognize. He thinks the timber companies might try to buy a scientific opinion that the animal was human, in which case the Endangered Species Act would not apply and its killer would be a murderer. "Some nuts will almost certainly come forward to charge the successful hunter with murder," Krantz said, and they might try to prosecute. And failing that, to persecute. He wouldn't put it past the animal rightists to levy a Salman Rushdie–style *fatwah* on the killer of Bigfoot, and he evinced some concern that the discoverer might be subject to the same sort of hysteria that abortion doctors have had to face from murderous pro-lifers.

I asked Grover what he thought about keeping the specimen in liquid, the way invertebrates are preserved. Wouldn't it be easier to store and transport in alcohol, like Lord Nelson shipped home from Trafalgar in rum? The tallest gorilla ever held in captivity (Baltimore Jack, six foot three) is preserved in formaldehyde at Arizona State University. Krantz didn't think much of my idea. His own plan would be to get the skin and the head and whatever else proved possible. He knows he would be criticized, no matter how he approached it, for damaging or leaving important materials; and he would ask his critics just how they would deal secretly with an unidentified half-ton primate. The important thing, he believes, would be to have a specimen.

After a Bigfoot evening at Portland Community College, put on by enthusiast Richard (Rip) Lyttle, several of us were chatting over Chinese food and beer. Peter Byrne was there, along with Rip, Ray Crowe, and Jim Hewkin. I said, "Right, gentlemen. One of us has a road-killed baby Bigfoot in our trunk. What do we do about it?" Around the table eyes flashed with a mixture of mirth and earnestness. I got the feeling that no one, friendly as they were, would trust anyone else there enough to let them in on the find. Byrne assumed an authoritative and cryptic air and simply said, "We have a plan." In fact, as I later learned, the Bigfoot Research Project does have a detailed (and secret) plan, not only for dealing with the carcass of an unfortunate victim but also for detecting a living beast to make a nonviolent "find."

- - -

Plans and rationales aside, when it comes to killing a Sasquatch, we are entering the darkest of all the several divides that I considered during my days with Bigfoot. In short, since we proscribe the killing of humans, what about hominids, or hominoids? We have proved ourselves capable of truly bestial acts against creatures with whom we share most of our DNA, namely the chimps and gorillas, and in many cases we call it legal. But we define them as belonging to the Pongidae, the great apes, along with orangutans and gibbons. This seems to give us the distance we need to kill without feeling great moral distress.

The familial division between humans (Hominidae) and great apes (Pongidae) is an artificial distinction. Orangs and gibbons split off earlier, most agree, and the family Pongidae makes some sense for them. But if we separate *Homo* from *Gorilla* and *Pan* (chimpanzees) at the familial level, we ought also to split lions from tigers, foxes from wolves, ducks from geese, giving each group its own family. I asked Krantz what he thought of the hominid/pongid division. He said the traditional split makes sense from the standpoint of morphology (form) and common sense, but the phylogenetic (evolutionary) reality was certainly that humans and other apes, except perhaps orangs, belong in a single family. This expanded sense of the Hominidae raises serious ethical issues.

Krantz is not oblivious to these. He thinks Sasquatch deserves the same consideration we give the great apes — implicitly, general protection but not immunity from killing when it is judged to be in the interest of the commonweal. He believes that Bigfoot is not human, based on the animal's apparent nonusage of tools, a major criterion of humanity among anthropologists (though muddier now, with Jane Goodall's discovery that chimps are tool users). He feels the creature probably is no more intelligent than the other great apes. And if he is mistaken, he told me, and Sasquatch belongs in the genus *Homo*, then the need to know it and protect it is that much greater.

Before I knew Krantz, I had assumed that this lanky, broody, and sarcastically witty man was so invested in proving Bigfoot's existence that he was desperate to vindicate his name and willing to take any means toward that end. Some have called him a Bigfoot butcher. That characterization, I found in talking with him, is far from the mark. He maintains that he is otherwise content in his career and can take Bigfoot or leave it. Of course, since he is human, proof would be very sweet for him indeed. But he does not seem obsessed.

"Sasquatch," Krantz has written, "is not the most important subject in the world . . . [It] may well be the most important of . . . unproven animals because it is probably our closest living relative. Still, it is not human, and there are millions of real people in this world who need help far more desperately than the sasquatch does."

In a short conclusion to *Big Footprints,* entitled "Keeping It in Perspective," Krantz suggests that a Bigfoot specimen will cause a dust storm among a few government officials and lumber barons, will ruffle both the creationists and evolutionists, and the "news media will have a hey-day and will badger every participant so much that they will wish (at least for the moment) that it had never happened." His own prestige will get a blip, not much more, and then "life will go on, almost as if nothing had happened."

I asked Krantz what misgivings he'd have about killing "our closest living relative." Far from cavalier, he paused and gave me a thoughtful response that I took as both ingenuous and expressive of the conundrums involved here: "If the time comes when I have the choice of shooting or not, it will be the most difficult decision I have ever been faced with. And," he went on, "however I decide to act, I will regret it for the rest of my life."

- - -

Not all of the Bigfoot hunters express such compunction. Danny Perez's bibliography, *Big Footnotes,* is dedicated to "the first woman or man to collect a Sasquatch." A September 18, 1994, Associated Press story lionized an Idaho man named Ralph Squires. "When he enters Sasquatch's mind," said the AP, "his senses heighten, he feels a harmony within, and he's in tune with everything around him." Everything, that is, except Bigfoot. "Squires intends to kill the first Bigfoot he encounters, saying that the mystery needs to be solved." Pictured smug and ready to go in camouflage, with night-vision goggles and an elephant gun, Squires said, "I hunt hard, I hunt the wind. . . . All of a sudden Bigfoot'll be there, and I'll be ready for the challenge of my life."

Even otherwise peaceful men find their principles stretched when they contemplate such a treasure as the first Bigfoot. In hindsight some wish they had fired when they had the chance. When Patterson and Gimlin encountered the famous subject of their film at Bluff Creek, they both were carrying high-powered rifles. They had agreed not to shoot unless absolutely necessary, a point on which Patterson was adamant. Gimlin, covering Patterson as the filmmaker ran after the beast, never came close to shooting; later he wished he had. And in a 1992 letter to me Peter Byrne wrote, "I still think of Patterson, dying, sitting in a chair in the sun in his back garden in Yakima, a skeleton of a man (Hodgkin's disease) saying to me . . . 'You know, we should have shot that thing; then people would have believed us.'" Only near death, unvindicated, did Roger Patterson reluctantly change his mind.

In the opposite shadow of this divide stands Byrne himself, the primary searcher of stature to forswear a violent approach. As Byrne wrote in *The Search for Bigfoot,* "It seems incredible in this day and age that there are people who would want to shoot something like a Bigfoot. . . . [This] is cruel and unjustified thinking, and I would not condone it, not even for so-called scientific reasons." As for "wanting to shoot one for monetary gain," Byrne says "this is mindless cretinism of the lowest form."

Most Bigfoot hunters, even if they prefer that the animal not be killed, would not outright condemn doing so. Many others support live capture, study, and release. Byrne's book, *The Search for Bigfoot,* included an off-putting list of problems with this approach. Even if the technology was properly guessed and the animal was not killed by an overdose or hurt by half-drugged wandering, Byrne contended, a major problem would remain: Would those in charge be able to resist the pressures to keep it or kill it? He quoted George Hass of Oakland, who asked, "What would happen, if while you have the creature in hand, either drugged or in a cage, healthy and well, some powerful organization like Disney Studios walks up and offers a check for half a million for the body? Are you then going to let the thing go?" Even so, Byrne has recently decided to consider tranquilizing a Bigfoot, should his Bigfoot Research Project succeed in finding one, in order to obtain blood samples for definite proof.

It is fair to say that the great majority of amateur Bigfoot enthusiasts and members of the interested public want the animal to remain untouched, even if it means never proving its existence. For this reason, Byrne is seen as an exotic "good guy" in the field, while many cast Krantz (with media help) in a black hat. But is it simply a matter of Byrne taking the moral high road and Krantz the pragmatic means-for-the-ends approach? I think it is much more complicated. The two men respect each other's heartfelt positions, even though they differ. Krantz may be right to believe that only a specimen in hand will guarantee acceptance by the protection authorities, and Byrne's position may be completely unrealistic. And none of the Bigfoot investigators has had the opportunity to discover what he would actually do in the event. Several hunters have reported having Bigfoot in their sights and feeling unable to pull the trigger because the target struck them as "more human than animal."

Our actions and attitudes about killing are a mass of contradictions, confusions, and hypocrisies. We all must kill to eat, to live, to breathe, to walk, and each of us draws the line somewhere. Certain yogis wear masks, it is said, so as not to inhale and kill microorganisms. Vegetarians will not kill animals for their own nutrition (for a variety of reasons) but are content to kill plants, which are living things. I used to collect butterflies for the thrill of it, then for the trophies, then for discovery, eventually for college tuition money, and finally for research purposes. I have known all these motives and acted on them, and I still feel their contradictory tugs. Yet I am no more confused than three friends who have expressed abhorrence at my taking the lives of butterflies: one a fly fisherman, one a moose hunter, the third a fur broker.

Since I have found it possible to justify the killing of moths and butterflies, I have tried hard to sympathize with Grover Krantz's position. I find I cannot come around to it. When I sought out the vultures' find in the Big Lava Bed, I would have been as excited as anyone to find a Bigfoot corpse that had died of an accident or disease. But when I peered through the lodgepoles, sighting along the handle of my net at a lava pinnacle about the size, shape, and color of a Sasquatch, I knew that even if Marsha had been a buffalo gun instead of a butterfly net I could never shoot. I draw my own personal line somewhere between butterflies and Bigfoot.

As I wrote in my piece for *Washington*, "Should we kill one Bigfoot, there will be a blood-rush for specimens: museums, zoos, roadside attractions, labs — all will want their own. And like the great auk, Sasquatch might not survive this flood of lethal attention." Both Byrne and Krantz have pointed out the naive flaw in this reasoning: even if one Bigfoot was found, the rest would not be any easier to find than they have been these hundred years and more. And Krantz is probably correct that one killed Bigfoot would lead to statutory protection for the rest.

So why do I continue to resist gigantocide? And that raises other questions: Why worry about the fate of an animal that is not at all certain to exist in flesh and blood? What ethical standards apply — what scruples should we display — toward premeditated killing, when the victim might be an ancestor, a cousin, or a pipe dream?

I am certain that some of the would-be giant killers see themselves as exactly that — some Jack, some David, some Saint George or Saint Michael or Muhammad Ali — out to dance like a butterfly and sting like a broadsword. Such Uzi-toting dragon-slayers would rejoice in the act of righteously blowing away Bigfoot, which they vaguely imagine as an archetype of evil like that embodied in giants, dragons, monsters, and the Other. They are the kind of men who would take satisfaction in gunning down the last wolf. That way lies the pogrom, the bounty, and all manner of final solutions.

But these gun-happy Jacks (and Krantz is not remotely among them) have got it backward. We have here, if we have anything, the greatest gift of evolution in our time, just as Mount St. Helens is an immense gift of geology, and in the same place. If Sasquatches exist, we should cherish them. By so doing, we might reinforce how to treat one another better. At this juncture in our brutal history — after Rwanda, after Bosnia, after Tiananmen Square — would we not be well advised to take the humane approach at every opportunity, toward the broadest possible concept of the Family of Man?

Or shall we begin this new relationship through the sights of a high-powered rifle, like any despicable sniper; or the jaws of a great steel trap, as we did for wolves and grizzlies throughout their former empires? If Krantz is right, and Bigfoot is *Gigantopithecus,* it is hominoid; if Byrne is right, it is hominid. If Myra Shackley is right, and Bigfoot equates with Neandertal, it is human. If the Kwakiutl and Klickitat are right, it is both human . . . and spirit. And if the doubters are right and Bigfoot is nothing but thin air, then it still exists within the lineage of our hearts. If we condone the killing of our evolutionary companions — our friends, our brothers and sisters, our ancestors, our dreams — how far can we be from the brink?

We know that Bigfoot is one big metaphor — a model for wildness, the unknown, tumid and hirsute desires with no names, the godforsaken exile. But metaphors can get up and walk. How sadly ironic it would be if something amazing had to be executed in order to prove that it wasn't a stand-in for something else. Or as Blackfeet singer-songwriter Jack Gladstone put it: "What is the proper way to express what can't be seen? For our senses grasp only a glimpse of the mystery between. Therefore I'm resigned to weave my way through the forest of word-lore, Dyin' for a Metaphor." Will that be Bigfoot — dyin' for a metaphor? As if in reply, in "The Man in the Mirror," John Sparrow wrote, "Wouldn't it be nice to think that there was something left that the human could encounter without bringing death."

Surely we can agree to leave the question of Bigfoot's existence open until unimpeachable photographic or first-person testimony proves it for all but the most cynical skeptics, or until a roadkill or subfossil shuts the case tight. Krantz, Perez, and others will reply that photos can always be faked and that there have been plenty of solid testaments already; if doubters won't believe Patterson, then what? It has also been pointed out that no fine nature photographer has ever photographed a Sasquatch, and no professional biologist has ever reported a sighting. This is no proof against, it's just a circumstance. But I suggest that when an Art Wolfe brings in a picture, or a George Schaller presents a sighting, acceptance will surely follow. And if it doesn't? Then sweet mystery will survive another day.

In Hans Christian Andersen's *Little Mermaid,* when the unfortunate hybrid first sees children, she asks her sisters if the children will be her friends. No, the sisters say; when they see your tail, they will be terrified and run away screaming. Eventually she gives up her tongue and her tail for love and legs — and loses it all. The mermaid in *Splash!* would have made out no better if the scientists had had their way. These are fairy tales. But who can doubt that, faced with the real thing, we would behave any better than we do toward our myths . . . or toward ourselves?

For ourselves, as much as for the beast, I want us to be able to think of Bigfoot as an animal or an idea worthy of our best behavior. Bigfoot, I presume, has no desire to be our friend, but we need friends wherever we can find them. How much better poised we might be to approach the times to come with equanimity toward all nature if we could agree to forswear the acts most clearly destined for remorse.

Let's rewrite the end of this movie. Grover Krantz is no murderer but a dedicated and visionary scientist with the best interests of his subject ultimately in mind. Even so, I hope he and the others who want a Bigfoot in hand will reconsider. Bigfoot belongs in the bush.

19

Carson on the Columbia

⚏⚏⚏

Once you have been to his land
you may enter and leave at will
though few return from that journey
unchanged.
— Margaret Atwood, "Oratorio for
Sasquatch, Man, and Two Androids"

WHEN I LEFT THE LAVALANDS, I paralleled the route of the
old Broughton Flume, which still carried fir cants from Wil-
lard down to the mill at Underwood. I saw the yellow trains of the
Union Pacific, the green trains of the Burlington Northern, and the
red truck train of I-84. There was Mount Hood's sleek eminence.
There was the big river itself. I had come all the way, Cowlitz to
Columbia. To celebrate, I crossed over to the Whitecap Brew Pub in
Hood River.

The Columbia Gorge marked the end of the trip, but I wanted to
make it last. Besides, I was hours early to check into my room at
Carson Hot Springs. So I crossed the Bridge of the Gods back to the
Washington side and struck north and west into country with the
names of the wild: Panther Creek, Bear Creek, Cougar Rock, Trout
Creek, Wind River, Trapper Creek Wilderness. I wanted to feel just a
little more of this swatch of the West where giants are said to walk.

At a curve in the narrow forest road, a flock of waxwings and other
birds erupted from a blue elderberry they'd been busy dismantling.
Stepping out among them I heard their seeps, cee-dees, and about
half of the bird calls of the past month afield. It was one of those great
autumn feeding flocks where species mingle in common pursuit of
food before migrating or wintering in the north. As my presence

became known, they all vanished into the mist and the drop-laden conifers.

As I nosed up the Wind River, the wind off the gorge was cool, moist, and fragrant. Beyond the Wind River Experimental Forest (how many ways can you skin a cat?) I crossed a gentle divide into the Trout River watershed, where a road crew was fixing a muddy slide just in time for me, and came up under the eaves of the tiny but vital Trapper Creek Wilderness. On the ridges far to the north, plantations gave way to the gnarly tops of old growth, which came and went with the blowing fog-wraiths, making me uncertain if they were really there or not.

The Cat-skinners (Ray Wallace's skilled guild) had cut roads close to all the edges of the wilderness area. Bare Mountain, on the western border, richly deserved its name. I knew that the Siouxon drainage, off to the northwest, flowed yet unlogged and unroaded and that its future was an ongoing battle between those who liked it that way and those who wanted the spaghetti of roads to spill over the entire plate of the Gifford Pinchot map.

Outside of the national forest such options no longer remain. I rolled as far down the mountain as Chelatchie Prairie, headquarters of the Mount St. Helens National Volcanic Monument. Tumtum Mountain, a perfect isolated cinder cone, had been licked clean of trees from the bottom up. The Weyerhaeuser St. Helens Tree Farm appeared to be logged off right down to Canyon Creek. Where Fly Creek came in, a dramatic spot of mossy rock walls and merging white waters, a half-dozen or so trees had been left on the scenic cliff point. This was a land of vine maples strung with tight red leaves and a tinsel of heavy, long lichens, and replacement conifers that were about Christmas tree-sized, where they had taken.

I was working hard to appreciate Jim Hewkin's idea that Bigfoot is an opportunistic beast, happy in the logged-off hills. But these hills had been pretty efficiently logged off, and it stretched my powers of imagination to envision how a giant might use them. I escaped back into the national forest, where some of the streams had buffers, and a few patches of old growth survived, but where fragmentation was well advanced. Puny Creek was, but it would have seemed a torrent a month before, when I had gone thirsty in search of a slake.

As the day waned, I wandered easterly up Panther Creek, where panthers surely hunt yet. The road circled around onto the humped shoulders of Bear Creek. A land of lions and bears. Dropping through oaks into bigleaf maples slung with long locks of *Usnea,* I realized that I was really on the cusp between the dry side and the damp side of the Cascades, yet another divide. Travel much farther west and you're in the temperate rain forest; to the east you're in the sage desert. I was reminded of John Green's quip about the majority of Bigfoot sightings occurring on the wet side. Isn't it interesting, he asks, how people's need to invent monsters dries up where less than sixteen inches of rain falls?

Through rags of mist and ragged forest I saw a silver sliver in the distance and a black lump beside it that seemed to have tumbled down from the dark heights of the Divide to the north. The sliver was the Columbia; the lump, Beacon Rock. Golden god-beams fell across the distant river, and a patch of pale peach sky shone beneath a silver ceiling — a more fitting arrival. But the glory was brief. The day, never a bright one, was duller still for the melancholy of any ending. As I descended toward Carson, the dishrag sky mopped up the last of the light in the west, and the drear became complete. I thought I heard a donkey, but it was a last futile elk call of a bow-hunter about to give up and go home.

Ass or archer, that bleak bray seemed absurdly out of place in the gathering dark, but no more so than the apparition I encountered a few miles beyond. Driving directly into the cloud-glow of the fullish moon, I beheld scores of pale faces looming and crowding all around me. It was a big herd of sheep, or mountain maggots, as John Muir called them. They reminded me of hiking the Pennine Way to the Dark Peak near the English-Scots border, where I was seldom out of eye- or earshot of sheep. Masked by the wan moon, these faces were even dumber than those of the Derbyshire breed. Their fleece, certainly not golden, was full of burrs, tangles, and shit. Now there's easy food for Bigfoot, I thought, if it likes mutton. As I pulled through the bleating flock, a ruffed grouse pummeled the roadway before me. The night has no shortage of visions. If we don't see them, it is only our own blindness.

- - -

One person who has no lack of visions is Datus Perry, the resident Bigfoot guru of Carson. A skinny Santa in olive drab and flannel, Perry hangs out in the canyons above the Columbia, where he spots Sasquatch almost at will. In 1937, he claims, he saw one in full view at two hundred feet on the Observation Peak Trail. In 1963 a Bigfoot followed him down from the saddle south of Gifford Peak, and he saw it well from twenty feet. Since then he has seen them from Panther Creek to the Quesnel River in British Columbia, in every aspect from sunning to soliciting his favors.

Anywhere else Datus Perry might be considered merely an eccentric or worse. Around Carson he is certainly seen that way, yet he is also revered as something of a Bigfoot expert. Situated at the confluence of the Wind River and the Columbia, Carson lies in the very heart of Bigfoot country. The town team is the Carson Bigfoots. One of several annual Bigfoot revels around the Northwest takes place in Carson's Bigfoot Trailer Park. And the locals have blessed both the proceedings and the beast that inspires them.

Back in 1969, "at the peak of Big Foot sightings in the county" as they later put it, the *Skamania County Pioneer* of nearby Stevenson published its first "Big Foot Edition." A second came out on April 1, 1992. "Our hope," wrote editor Stacy Smith, "was to compile a comprehensive edition that would include past sightings for a historical perspective and more recent sightings for a timelier edge."

The original 1969 Bigfoot paper was stimulated by a spate of sightings at Beacon Rock, Bear Creek, and near the Big Lava Bed. The front page included drawings by artist Linda Ford, who worked with Washougal sportsman Don Cox to recreate the creature he saw cross the fogbound road at Beacon Rock. The encounter, the paper said, had the stone-sober Cox all shook up. Inside was a photo of Sheriff Bill Closner and Deputy Jack Wright making a cast of a twenty-two-inch track in the snow, with members of the Bigfoot Research Association (a group of former lawmen) kneeling over the sulfur cast. "I guess I'll have to stop laughing," said the sheriff.

The attitude of the Big Foot Edition was nonviolent. As editor Roy Craft wrote, "To be honest, I think there is such a creature, and I think that more than one was forced down out of the high mountain lava cave area by the most severe winter in the history of the Cascades." He went on, "Let us hope that when the day for irrefutable evidence by way of perfect photographs comes, the ape-creature will be left alone to the wilderness home he has chosen." A reader commented, "The monster (and what right have we to call it that?) . . . is self-supporting, owes no debts to anyone and asks for naught but its God-given right to pursue its own life with malice toward none."

A portrait of Datus Perry, white-maned and pointing with a stick, graced the front page of the 1992 Big Foot Edition. Within was a 1969 photograph of Robert Morgan and a young female assistant, her long hair swept back in the style of the times, displaying casts of tracks purportedly found on his American Yeti Expedition. A map indicated the Ape Cave area, Babyshoe Pass at the eastern end of the Dark Divide, and the southern part of the Big Lava Bed as "the most probable places to find Big Foot." The paper included drawings of Bigfoot by Stevenson Elementary School students and a table of "Big Foot Facts."

The centerfold featured photos of and comments by eight local business people and elected officials who were asked, "Do you believe in Big Foot?" Sheriff Ray Blaisdell and Prosecuting Attorney Bob Leick both gave replies suitable to their positions. "I don't believe in it, but I do believe people have been seeing something," said the sheriff. "I'm willingly suspending my disbelief," replied his colleague. "I don't know whether it exists or doesn't exist."

Only Arlene Johnson, executive director of the Chamber of Commerce, took a hard line: "I have a hard time believing in anything I can't see or have not seen proof of." Jim Joseph, a sporting goods shopkeeper, told the *Pioneer*, "I think there's more to it than we even begin to understand." Bill Yee, the manager of the public utility district, gave a hearty "Yes, I believe Big Foot exists," then qualified it, "just as sure as the Lock [*sic*] Ness monster exists. I have never seen Big Foot myself, but I have never seen the Lock Ness monster either."

Perhaps the most surprising responses came from the three elected county commissioners. All three looked on the phenomenon positively. "I'm not a disbeliever," said Ed McLarney, "but I'm not a total believer yet either. People have to be seeing something." Commissioner Ed Callahan went a little further, saying, "I do believe there's something out there we can't explain." And Kaye Masco left no question: "From the information that I have gathered and the reading I've done, I absolutely believe Big Foot exists and has a watchful eye over all of the people in Skamania County." That is a remarkable degree of open-mindedness about a topic that causes discreet people elsewhere to smirk or swallow their thoughts.

But it was not just the local attitude that drew me to conclude my ramble in Carson, nor the fact that a line drawn from my starting point through the middle of the Dark Divide leads to Carson Hot Springs, with its promise of a cheap bed and a fantastic tub and massage. It was the Skamania County Bigfoot law of 1969: Ordinance No. 69-01 Prohibiting Wanton Slaying of Ape-Creature and Imposing Penalties. The ordinance reads:

BE IT HEREBY ORDAINED BY THE BOARD OF COUNTY COMMISSIONERS OF SKAMANIA COUNTY: WHEREAS, there is evidence to indicate the possible existence in Skamania County of a nocturnal primate mammal variously described as an ape-like creature or a sub-species of Homo Sapian [*sic*]; and WHEREAS, both legend and purported recent sightings and spoor support this possibility, and WHEREAS, this creature is generally and commonly known as a "Sasquatch," "Yeti," "Bigfoot," or "Giant Hairy Ape," and WHEREAS, publicity attendant upon such real or imagined sightings has resulted in an influx of scientific investigators as well as casual hunters, many armed with lethal weapons, and WHEREAS, the absence of specific laws covering the taking of specimens encourages laxity in the use of firearms and other deadly devices and poses a clear and present threat to the safety and well-being of persons living or traveling within the boundaries of Skamania County as well as to the creatures themselves, THEREFORE BE IT RESOLVED that any premeditated, willful and wanton slaying of any such creature shall be deemed a felony punishable by a fine not to exceed Ten Thousand Dollars ($10,000.00) and/or imprisonment in the county jail for a period not to exceed Five (5) years. BE IT FURTHER RESOLVED that the situation existing constitutes an emergency and as such this ordinance is effective immediately.

The ordinance was signed by Commission Chair Conrad Lundy, Jr., and Prosecuting Attorney Robert K. Leick. The fact that it was adopted on April 1 did not escape notice. However, the commissioners insisted they were completely serious. "Although this ordinance was adopted on April 1, this is not an April Fool's Day joke," Commissioner Lundy told the *Pioneer* at the time. "There is reason to believe such an animal exists."

Likewise, as long-time commissioner Ed Callahan told the paper, he and his comrades were very serious when they amended the ordinance in 1984. At that time Prosecutor Leick realized that "the county had exceeded its jurisdictional authority by making the crime a felony," according to the supplement.

The new version declared that a person found "guilty with malice" would be guilty of a gross misdemeanor. If the killing were premeditated but without malice, it would be a misdemeanor. The penalties were reduced to a maximum of one year in jail and/or a $1,000 fine. Perhaps mindful of the wacky faction of Bigfooters, the revised law prohibited any defense based on "insane delusions, diminished capacity, or . . . a diseased mind." If the county coroner determines "any victim/creature to have been humanoid," the crime would be considered homicide.

Leick credited the idea for the original ordinance to the late Roy Craft, then editor and publisher of the *Skamania County Pioneer.* "You never knew whether Roy was being mischievous or whether he really felt it was something that needed to be done," Leick told the newspaper. But whether the originator had giants, a joke, or a civic promotion in mind, Skamania officials treated it seriously. The amended law also declared the animal "an endangered species" and created a "Sasquatch Refuge" coterminous with the million-acre county. Presumably the intent was not to protect habitat from logging. Nevertheless, Prosecutor Bob Leick summed up the business this way: "I think Sasquatches are at least as important as the spotted owl."

In spite of their elected officials' openness, most people who encounter hairy apes still keep their sightings quiet, according to the newspaper, for fear of being thought crazy. Such a concern has never bothered Datus Perry. He doesn't give a hang. You can take his stuff at face value or you can stuff yourself; it's all the same to him. "I don't just believe in Bigfoot," he says, "I *know* it's out there . . . so I'm beyond the need for belief."

If this oddly echoes Grover Krantz's words about belief versus knowledge, the resemblance doesn't end there. Both men have white beards clipped close under their chins, though Datus lets his throat-mane and hair go long and silky. Both are tall, slender, lank. Both wear spectacles and gesture emphatically. Beyond that, two Bigfoot hunters could scarcely differ more than Krantz and Perry. Krantz comes across as vaguely astonished at everyone else, tolerant under protest, suffering no fool gladly, sarcastic, and world-weary. Perry is a gnome, ever surprised at himself, both naive and sly, grateful. The first is a university professor, the second a mountain man. They share a fascination but few opinions. Their languages do not have many words in common beyond "Bigfoot."

In an interview by Carrie Robertson for the *Gorge Current* of Hood

River, Oregon, Perry estimated the number of Bigfeet in North America at a mere fifty. He said that they migrate great distances and hang about civilization as well as in the deep woods. There have been many hoaxes, he believes, but insists that his own sightings are real. "You see," he told Robertson, "I tell it like it is. I have a photographic memory." That recall gives him a picture of a rather iconoclastic model; in his statues and drawings, Perry's Bigfoot is eight to eleven feet tall, narrowly built but with broad shoulders and a tiny, almost neckless, and strikingly pointed head. The point, he believes, is a sharp ridge with a punkish tuft of hair, which can wear off, running its length.

Another one of Perry's apostate views concerns the beast's putative putridness. "The common thread among all the [reports] to give them credibility was the strong, strong sulfur smell," Sheriff Ray Blaisdell said to the *Pioneer*. Yet Perry believes that Bigfoot is odorless and that the reported strong smell might come from the skins of deer and other animals it wears as shawls or necklaces. The Bigfeet bury their dead, eat them, or flush them down glacial rivers, he says. "They live in mountain alder and in willow, where there's good cover overhead, and where the sun doesn't come in too much. They keep hiding better, going farther away." They may resort to cannibalism since we are taking all the fish. "You wouldn't eat your own kind — but you might eat somebody else's. Sasquatch is not above [eating other Sasquatch]." They also eat fruit, rodents, big mountain angleworms, and dogs.

Unlike many enthusiasts, Perry actually lives in the forest, and going into the wilderness has been his chief pleasure. "Anthropologists need to come out in the bush with me and get a full account of my findings," he told me; "that way they can see how the real thing fits their bones and teeth." So far Grover Krantz has not obliged him.

When I came off the Dark Divide, Datus was not to be found. I later learned he'd been up in the hills working on his main project, enlarging, by hand, a cave that he believes will connect with a big lava tube. I finally met him at Carson's Bigfoot Daze the next autumn. Around the first night's campfire, the confab running to wild tales, Datus told a few of his own, like that of his friend who was raped by a "big, snaggle-toothed, breath-reeking female." The friend had a mineral springs that tasted like beer, made friends with another Bigfoot he named Nancy and taught her a few words. Other stories concerned a diesel tank whose valves were mysteriously opened, a Bigfoot who stopped a Caterpillar tractor, and a bulldozer left running, high-centered on a stump. "He'd love to stop the logging," said Datus. I thought of dozer-driver Ray Wallace, who reported Bigfoot doing just that by intimidating his road crew; and of how Ray, like Datus, democratically tells stories that raise interest as well as those that merely raise eyebrows.

The next morning, when Datus took the podium again, he said, "I've been screamed, chattered, whistled, yodeled, and knocked at by Sasquatch. Seems like they hang around to protect you from other animals. One man alone with a couple of poodles has the best chance. You can whistle three times and they might answer . . . Say, 'Bigfoot, come on in.' Hold your hand up with a limp wrist, that means non-aggression. Hold up a flower or a bough as an offering; that's the best defense, better than a forty-five Magnum." Datus was getting warmed up. "Worst thing you can do is carry a gun. Or have a rough dog on a chain. I guarantee one thing — first time you meet one the skin on your back will wrinkle up and your hair will stand up. You'll be so darned scared you won't know what to do. Just walk away like nothing was wrong."

He had a big tablet of drawings, notes, and findings, and he flipped the pages as he went. "One time I was scared by something on the trail — hey, I got the right of way! — it was evidently a Bigfoot, I never saw it. It screamed, I answered. This went on until I felt like Tarzan of the woods.

"I have fallen into a lot of experiences with Bigfoot. I think maybe it was meant to be that way, so I could tell you about it." He told about sightings up above Government Springs, by Trapper Creek, and elsewhere. "I sat and chewed licorice fern and waited, looking at a rock ledge with tore-up moss. I found a track and was trying to figure out how to get a cast, and while I was pondering, ol' Sasquatch appeared."

Someone asked if Bigfoot ever said anything. "I've heard them talk five times," he replied, "but it sure ain't my language; more like Asiatics or something." Does Perry carry a gun? "Never! Just a machete." He told of having a heart attack and of regaining his strength by building a switchback trail up the nearby mountain, where he knew he could find his friends from time to time. Then, just as a new tale seemed imminent, he said, "I don't know what to say . . . I think I'll turn this microphone over to Rory . . . no, Ray, that's his name." And Datus Perry sat down.

After the screenings of videos (*Harry and the Hendersons* for the kids, Patterson and an episode of *Unsolved Mysteries* for the adults); after reports of rows of trees mowed down by Bigfoot on Cinnamon Mountain near Ape Cave; and after a hunter's tale of an apple-picking Bigfoot, backlit in the moonlight, near Seaside, Oregon, that "smelled like an outhouse" and of one in the Coast Range that looked "like a big black biker," Datus weighed in again. By then what he said didn't seem so bizarre, but one got the impression that he was always *ready* to see Bigfoot — not an unusual trait among the faithful. For example, he took as "signs" an apple in an orchard with a single tooth impression (a starling?) and a cherry tree completely stripped that had been full a week before (a bunch of starlings?). He spoke of a far-off dark pattern that he admitted "could be shadows" and of stones that he took for knives and scrapers, reminding me of Ray Wallace's concretions that he took to be missiles for killing deer.

"I've been hoping I could make a breakthrough and talk at them," he said. "Maybe build a fire and whittle on something to put them at their ease, and they'd say something . . . But what the heck, I might get friendly with them and then I'd have to tell people about it. They'd think I was *really* crazy then."

- - -

When I visited Datus another autumn he was living in a trailer at the Bigfoot Park with his former wife, Lillian Dillingham. They had recently sold their ranch of many years across the road. Perry was born in 1912. "I was conceived in Home Valley," he said, by a fussy school-teacher and a trapper, and brought up in Washougal by his grandparents. When he came to Carson to explore the caves in the sixties, he met Lillian. Later he was a machinist in the Vancouver shipyards and an engine man on troop ships and diesel barges on the Columbia. "We got froze off the river in 'forty-eight," he said. He got pneumonia then and later; the month before I visited him, he almost died from it. Exposed to asbestos and fiberglass in the shipyards and gases from burning wool when he worked for Pendleton Woolen Mills, he has very little breath left.

I found Datus recumbent on the bed in his trailer, his drawing pad on his narrow knees. Though thin and pale and sucking oxygen, he was as feisty as I remembered. His beard was short, his hair still long and silky. He showed me his drawing, a cone-headed female with a monkeylike face and round breasts (he has never found them either "pendulous" or "perky," as others have reported). The caption said, "I don't need a chin or beard. My eyes reflect red at night. Imagine me in total black or brown. 1200 #. 10′ to forehead, 10′8″ to top." On a fresh sheet he sketched a leg and a hand, showing fingers that stopped eight inches above the knees rather than hanging below, apelike. Next to it he drew a hairy, clawed bear paw.

"Deal is," he said, "their hair's short and breaks off. If you see a picture showing long fur around the hands like a bear, you got a bearskin." He said Patterson's Bigfoot, for example, was bearskins. "And he had a tall son-in-law," he added.

He gave me this drawing, and I asked him to sign it. "If I do you'll prob'ly just go," he wheezed, then laughed and signed it.

I wasn't nearly ready to go as long as he was talking. I told Datus he seemed to know a lot of natural history. He said, "I keep my eyes open." Then he reeled off some of it. "These creatures? Fastest thing but a cheetah. Outrun pretty near anything in the forest. Deer? No problem. Are they throwers? Oh, shit, are they ever — and accurate! Hones a true course at a deer or a horse. I've never seen any sign of a sharp tooth . . . but then I've never had one mad at me. No lips, either. Face is black velvet. Roman nose" — like his, I noted. "Mouth might be like a black slit, but how do you see a black slit in black velvet? Like to eat pine beetle grubs, dig 'em out of rotten wood with their nails. Also grasshoppers, which are a different outfit from flying ants."

After hearing him describe behavior and features that might belong to any woodland creature, it was a mild shock when Datus told me about the arenas where big male Bigfeet fight. One of these he had found up behind Augsburger Mountain as a young man. Tracking a buck deer with a rifle, he came to a solid wall of thorn apple (hawthorn) which the animals had planted foursquare to make an impenetrable enclosure. He went up on a knob, which he later figured as the bleachers, to look down inside, and saw a Bigfoot sleeping. "The females sit up there to watch the big ol' guys fight," Datus said. "Rocks, clubs, ever' damn thing — survival of the fittest. That's why you see such big ones." From an Indian he heard about another square arena on the south side of Mount Adams. An Indian woman saw four Bigfeet at once headed that way, and a Portland Bigfoot hunter is supposed to have seen four going, one at a time, toward there from the north.

I didn't want to make Datus talk too much, and I thought Lillian might be protective. But she and Thea were having a good time talking and playing with two small dogs at the other end of the hot little trailer. Datus told me a long, detailed story about when he was working in California on a surveying team and "ran a Bigfoot right out of bed" in a huckleberry thicket, where it had a neat den. He didn't see the animal, but his boss did and ran like hell. The boss was scared to death but wouldn't admit to seeing anything. When Datus pressed him, he said, "Bullshit! Can't a guy run if he wants to?" But with a transit? Datus asked. "If you want to keep your job," said the boss, "you'll say nothing about this." Datus laughed over the incident. "Then I found a surveyor's pipe pulled right out of the ground." Many years later Datus found a similar Sasquatch bed in a swamp north of Carson, up near Pete's Gulch.

He says lots of people have his boss's attitude. The forest and game people agree there's something out there but won't admit it's Bigfoot. They get out into the field too late in the day and leave too early, so they never see it. Two of his friends, a forester and a chemist, had experiences of their own but later denied them, refusing to talk about it further. The forester then cruised the hill where Datus's trail was for the Forest Service: "Shit, they logged the hell out of it." His sister's husband was "quite a nature man. But he was scared shitless when he saw his first Bigfoot."

It was in 1932 or '33 when Datus saw his first, though he had seen a good track when he was twelve, on a clam-digging trip to Pacific Beach. Gathering blueberries for his hotcakes, he saw that the berries had been picked over, and then he found the track in moss on soft dirt. He has known what Bigfoot was ever since. His trapper dad, a contemporary of John Dark, had seen a print too, but didn't know what to make of it.

Datus, who once weighed 212 pounds, had gone down to 110 with the pneumonia and was now back up to 117. He raised a bony left hand and said, "It won't take on no meat." He wanted to get back up to his cave but could barely get around. "I'll have to get some young guys to help me," he said. And he probably will.

Datus was tired, and I felt we should go. Then he told me with some urgency that some of the Indians feel, and he shares their belief, that there may be several types of Bigfoot — some with the head bristles, some without, some maybe with longer hair — and that they may interbreed. "But that's as far as it goes," he said, "like a horse and a donkey. They'd make a mule." The types haven't arisen through evolution, he figured, because they can't mix. This was a fresh view of hybridization biology, which others employ to demonstrate evolution, not disprove it; but it didn't bear pursuing.

As I left, I gave Datus greetings from Ray Crowe and Peter Byrne. "Poor guy," Datus said about Byrne. "He works so hard." He thinks all of Byrne's gadgets and gizmos will just scare the Bigfeet away.

The night of the Bigfoot Daze at Carson, Peter Byrne and I had shared a cabin at the Hot Springs. As his daughter, Rara, and sheltie, Robin, slept soundly in camp beds, Peter and I chuckled over some of the things we had heard.

"Datus might very well *see* and *believe*," Peter said thoughtfully. "But at the same time and place, others might not."

Later I heard Peter's words echoed in Wayne Suttles's view that "while Sasquatch-like creatures may inhabit the real world of the Indians, this may not be relevant to the question of whether they inhabit the real world of Western science." And Chief Lelooska spoke of things you could see only when watching "with Indian eyes." Many would conclude that Datus also sees the world with eyes different from ours. So why do we tend to venerate the one as spiritual and write off the other as deluded?

- - -

Separate realities aside, what has Datus Perry seen in those wild hills behind his home? For that matter, what has Ray Wallace seen? And what, if anything, did Paul Freeman and Ivan Marx see? Freeman is the former Forest Service employee who made a name for himself with Bigfoot tracks, Indian artifacts, and films of encounters, which are widely regarded as hoaxes. At a meeting of the Western Bigfoot Society in a narrow hall beneath Ray Crowe's North Portland book-shop, we watched Freeman's video sequence as featured in a television program on Bigfoot. In it Freeman said he was too scared by a close encounter after the fuzzy filming to continue, and was getting out of the field. Most present felt that would be a good thing. His bad rep stems from his admission on *Good Morning America* that he had faked tracks before finding real ones; from an expert man-tracker's assertion that his tracks went nowhere; and from the unconvincing nature of his films, among other inconsistencies. Freeman is said to be a skilled artisan who has worked in orthopedic shoe labs. Yet

Grover Krantz considers one of Freeman's tracks, with dermal ridges and sweat pores, to be one of his linchpin exhibits. Has Paul Freeman been misjudged?

Ivan Marx, a former bear and coyote hunter, was involved in Tom Slick's Pacific Northwest Bigfoot Expedition in northern California in 1960. In 1969, having taken the search north, Marx claimed to have found a series of tracks and films of a partially disabled Bigfoot in northeastern Washington. Almost all of the other serious investigators went to see for themselves. The story is complicated, and its radically varied tellings by John Green, René Dahinden, Peter Byrne, and Grover Krantz reveal the relativity of experience and the roots of dissension and acrimony. The various camps, at first cooperative, became embattled and embittered. In the end Byrne had bought a blank film, Dahinden was convinced of an absolute hoax, Green was bemused and disgusted, Krantz had another key track, Patterson had nothing to show for his high hopes of a follow-up to Bluff Creek, and Marx was off to points unknown.

I went to Bossburg, far up the Columbia from Carson, and asked around about Marx and the Bossburg Giant. It was difficult to imagine this bucolic old village as the center of the Sasquatch world, as it briefly had been in the winter of 1969–1970. The local garage man who had rented a place to Marx told me that everyone considered him completely bogus. "I've seen those slabs of wood he made the tracks with," the man told me. But again, Krantz has a track from Bossburg of a foot-wounded animal, and he considers it completely genuine, impossible to fake by anyone less knowledgeable than himself, and a critical piece of evidence. Both Marx and Freeman made casts of hand prints that Krantz considers good candidates for reality, as well as footprints.

Krantz's acceptance of tracks from two men considered fakers by the others has led to charges that he is gullible. Byrne, a master tracker, feels that Krantz has been fooled. Two papers in the *Skeptical Inquirer*, published by the Committee for the Scientific Investigation of Claims of the Paranormal, analyzed and dismissed Freeman's evidence. Though *Newsweek* called the prints "startling new evidence for Bigfoot," writer Michael Dennett found them wanting. Joel Hardin, a U.S. Border Patrol tracker extraordinaire who has never lost the trail of a fugitive, examined the site for the Forest Service soon after Freeman's report and found no trail continuing beyond the distinct impressions. Dennett proposed how the dermal ridges in Freeman's tracks could have been faked, and the second paper attacked the sweat pores as bubbles.

Yet in *Big Footprints* Krantz analyzed both sets of tracks from a morphologically sophisticated viewpoint, rebutted the doubts, and produced arguments that are quite convincing. Clearly, persons of goodwill disagree in the matter, if any Bigfoot hunters can truly be said to have goodwill toward the others.

- - -

When I think of Marx and Freeman, Wallace and Perry, I see two men considered charlatans by many of their Bigfoot peers and two broadly thought of as hyperbolical at best. Each has his champions, and each has his convictions, or so we presume. It makes me wonder: Can it happen that people have experiences that are quite authentic (at least to them) and that arouse their interest and then, in the absence of further excitement, attention, or reward for their efforts and hopes, cross the divide into the manufacture of their own kicks, either in the damp sand of a creek bed or in the soft gray putty of their brains?

When I mentioned this thought to Peter Byrne, he doubted it applied to Marx and Freeman; but he felt it might be true of others. He mentioned a man who had a quite credible sighting, which many others investigated to their satisfaction. But he went on having sightings over the next dozen years or so, "all the way to the last one when a BF walked up behind him and put its hand on his shoulder. Oh, yes, indeed!"

Is this another dark divide that Bigfoot illuminates in the glare of its red headlights, the too-human border between truth and desire? Maybe Marx was always in it for the money; perhaps Wallace has been a jester from the start. But then again, perhaps the casts are real, and only some way into the chase did the line of tracks trail off into ignominy. When men begin with gold and try to salt the mine with base metal instead of the other way around, when they concoct clumsy prints, silly films, and even sillier statements and expect to be taken seriously, they must have changed within themselves.

Many Indian groups speak of Bigfoot-like spirits, such as River Otter, as having the ability to bewitch. In one Tlingit lineage men were driven into the forest by whites in the early days of contact. There they were bewitched by Otter and mated with her, and the unfortunate offspring were the Kooschtaka, or Bigfeet.

I think Bigfoot bewitches men. They fall in love with the idea of

Sasquatch when they first see something or find a print on a muddy bank. They love the attention it brings them, and they see the glittering prospects of catching what everyone else wants to catch. They think they have an inside track in the chase. Or they find a friend in Bigfoot, who becomes the object of their passion. When their devotion is unrequited, with no more tracks or sightings and nothing to film, they grow desperate. Ignored by men and monsters, they contrive to renew the thrill by making their own evidence, and once they do that, they are lost, for they will never be believed again. Or else imagination takes over from observation, with the same result. Hoax and hallucination: the twin bewitchments of Bigfoot.

Or perhaps, as Marjorie Halpin wrote in *Manlike Monsters on Trial,* "As long as Sasquatch is a personal rather than a collectively sanctioned experience it will remain hallucinatory as officially defined by Western culture." I guess Datus Perry doesn't much care. He just sees what he sees.

- - -

I lay in the deep porcelain tub on the men's side of the bath house at Carson Hot Springs. When I climbed out of the steamy spring water, an attendant named Larry mummified me in hot towels and reclined me on a cot. After that a masseuse named Corrie macerated my muscles. This process put me in mind of the reverse of a plaster-of-Paris casting. I came in hard and set, softened in the bath, melted to a gel in the body wrap, and completely liquified under Corrie's gifted hands in the massage. If I hadn't had to move at last, I would have dribbled down the drain, run on into the Wind River, and merged at last with the Columbia.

When I had solidified enough to move, I strolled a leafy lane behind the old hotel to a path leading to a suspension bridge over the Wind River. The relaxation remained, but I lost the light and returned. Downy hazel leaves brushed my hands; maple and mud made a scent, strong and fragrant like that of witch hazel or horehound or some herbal preparation dimly recalled.

After dinner I read in a worn, would-be-leather rocker in the shabby-comfy lobby of the old false-front St. Martin's Hotel. The last of the old Russian bathers, who live across the river in the Oregon Cascades, had retired to their cabins. After the desk clerk donned her nylon tavern jacket and left me with "Good night now . . . have a good one," I was alone in the hotel.

I didn't read for long. I knew I would sleep the second I hit the bed, so I stayed down a little longer and ran over the past month in my mind. What did it prove, this crossing of the Dark Divide, besides re-radicalizing me on forest issues, as if I needed that? I did not find Bigfoot, but then I wasn't looking. I had a chance to use my plaster of Paris and came away with a nice cast of a somewhat footish impression on a rock. I found big tracks in a muddy pond and heard strange whistles at Yellowjacket Pass, a likely collaboration between black bears and gray jays. Among the ancient trees of Quartz Creek I was briefly overwhelmed by a truly foul stench that could have been anybody's body.

If, occupied by my own too-human concerns, I never quite slipped into the skin of Grendel, I did feel a powerful empathy for his harassment by jets, trucks, cycles, saws, and the people who wield them. Perhaps unfairly, I transferred my own irritation with them, to a beast whose back yard is invaded daily. After eating a lot of berries and mushrooms and things I hadn't eaten before, I convinced myself that the land could support another large omnivore, if only we would support the land in its annual battle to grow more than we take away.

Now, at the foot of a one-million-acre Sasquatch refuge, where to kill one with malice was a gross misdemeanor, I was no closer to knowing whether there was anything out there. That, of course, was never my objective. I'd been stewed in a Bigfoot brew as hot and steaming as my afternoon mineral-springs bath, but nowhere near as clear as those mountain waters. My mind was massaged with a million attitudes and the opinions of those who share their green and rocky space with a famous myth.

I had a copy of a drawing Datus Perry had made of a Bigfoot: "A very accurate sketch of one that followed me to my shelter." Unrolling it, I read his annotations scribbled near her feet:

Mowglee *Sasquatch* hand her a flower I walked up to 25′ from her
— she never moved till after I left.
　7 ft. tall Oct. 20, '85 sundown at my camp
　Back again in '86 Datus Perry no harm

Lovingly drawn, she stands erect and at attention, her hands at her sides. She wears a buckskin tied around her shoulders like a tennis sweater; her tiny ears barely show above her sloping shoulders; and her petite, peaceful face is topped by a sharp crown like a dunce's cap.

Datus told me that they stand still like this, hoping to be mistaken for a snag. Others have suggested that a snag is exactly what Datus saw. I rolled her up.

So who knows? Maybe she is up there, just as Datus saw her. Maybe the remarkably apelike stone heads found not far from here in the Columbia Gorge represent real animals known to the ancient makers. And maybe the Skamania County ordinance pertains to actual flesh-and-blood creatures that can be shot to death. Perhaps the final notation on Datus Perry's drawing could be taken as the last word:

"no harm"

There are worse ways for people to spend their time.

- - -

Of course, there never will be a last word on Bigfoot.

As I turned in that night, the words of two old rock 'n' roll songs ran around in my head as a medley, a super-group duet by the Grateful Dead and the Moody Blues. "What a long, strange trip it's been," crooned the Dead, and the Moody Blues replied, "We decide which is right, and which is an illusion."

A strange trip it had surely been, and I considered it essentially finished. All that remained was to go home, think it over, and write it up. The Dark Divide, crossed once and crossed again, had expanded to embody a whole mountain range of divides, perhaps paramount among them that muddy slide between right and illusion.

Little did I know as I drifted off to sleep that the strangest part of the trip was still to come, that one more night, one more passage, and one last event would crack my imagination wide open in the matter of Bigfoot.

20

Something in the Night

Now in the night
the dark walker came
gliding in shadow.
— *Beowulf*

WHEN I AWOKE at Carson the next morning, October 4, I knew it was time to leave the hills. I was more than ready for home and Thea and Bokis, my cat. I had a dentist appointment, a month's mail and phone messages, a manuscript to finish. In other words, life. And I had to drive to Olympia for a meeting of the Natural Heritage Advisory Council the very next morning.

I slept in, idled over breakfast and a bath, then walked up the river again to the suspension bridge. I would have remained willingly, suspending my obligations, suspending my disbelief, seduced by the breathy utterances of the Wind River into staying behind just a little longer. Then, having succeeded in using up much of the short gray day, I could dawdle no longer.

But on the edge of Carson the Wind River Trading Post, a junk shop with secondhand books and a Bigfoot statue, lay in wait. I had to check it out. Adjusting my eyes to the dim light within, I spotted a copy of Victor Calahane's *Mammals of the World* and dived in, to learn about pikas that live in slab piles or logjams in streams. I wondered how long it would be until we could pick up a mammalogy text and read about the natural history of *Gigantopithecus canadensis* alongside *Lutra canadensis*, *Castor canadensis*, and *Cervus canadensis*.

I came out an hour later with three books: an old Thornton Burgess Bedtime Stories volume, *Mother West Wind's Children* (a wartime reprint edition by Grossett & Dunlap); a little leather-bound book of Lamb's *Essays of Elia* ("half genuine English calf, super-extra hand-finished, gold top, untrimmed edges, sewn with silk," $1.75 in 1893 from Henry Altemus, Philadelphia, now $8.50); and a 1932 anthology, *Washington Poets*, mostly rhyming, its brown cloth spine split from loving overuse. By now it was late enough for dinner so I took my treasures into a Mexican restaurant down the road, which surprised me with excellent tamales.

I began to read Bigfoot into everything. Burgess dedicated his book "To all who love the green meadows and the smiling pool, the laughing brook and the merry little breezes." Well, who is that if not Sasquatch? When Charles Lamb wrote in "Witches and Other Night Fears": "Gorgons, and Hydras, and Chimeras dire . . . may reproduce themselves in the brain of superstition, — but they were there before. They are transcripts, types, — the archetypes are in us, and eternal," surely he was foreshadowing Bigfoot. And when Muriel Thurston, the former owner of *Washington Poets*, in her own poem "Fugitive" wrote, "Everywhere I go I find / What I thought to leave behind," she had me in mind.

I just couldn't face the freeway yet. I realized I could get to Olympia just as well by crossing the Dark Divide on dirt roads as by following the Columbia to I-5, if I didn't mind losing a night's sleep. After having the forest roads largely to myself for so long, this seemed infinitely preferable to sharing a rainy freeway with semis and motor homes. I wanted to buffer my emergence from the mountains until the last possible moment. So, leaving Carson at last, I turned left instead of right and headed north.

By nine P.M. I had shot up along the western fringes of the Big Lava Bed and Indian Heaven. Near one of the trailheads I stopped to cut some noble fir boughs for a silkscreen Thea had in mind. Then over the top of heaven and down a narrow green slot between close alders on the gentle grade of little Forest Road 3211. It followed Rush Creek, here a minor torrent of white spray, but I remembered it as a dry bed of black pebbles on the Indian Heaven plateau. The road felt and looked like an old logging railroad bed, and in the rain I realized that it could easily be washed out or made unpassable by a deadfall; I might have to retrace the long wet drive. But it took me to the major forest thoroughfare, No. 90, which carried me west along the Lewis River to No. 25, the post-eruption Mount St. Helens "expressway," at Eagle's Cliff. Images from my journey flooded my mind as I peered through the rain-washed glass, my traveling chamber fragrant with the terps of the fir boughs.

The rain diminished as I rolled northward along the eastern verge of the Mount St. Helens National Volcanic Monument. At ten I crossed Elk Pass where Boundary Trail No. 1 intersects the road. I pulled into the trail parking lot to get out and stretch. This was becoming a long night. To wake up, I walked a way in the black rain and fog. Realizing where I was, I crossed the Dark Divide for the last time, hailing it with a Pyramid Pale Ale. Later it would become important to note that this was the only beer I drank that night.

Striding back toward the car, I heard an eerie whistle; in the fog it chilled my spine just a degree or two. I stopped, it stopped; I resumed, and it resumed. Then I realized the sound was the whistle of the wind in the neck of my ale bottle. I recalled the sound of air escaping my car seat up at Bluff Creek and how that had momentarily caught my attention, and again I laughed at myself and shook my head. "Ha," I snorted. "Dummy."

But back at the trailhead, as I make notes in the comfortable glow of the overhead lamp, I hear another sound, definitely from outside. "Wheeeouh," it shrills, descending the north hillside ahead of me. Sharp, loud, it is no bird I know, no owl I've heard. What bird *would* it be in the cold fog and rain and dark? And it is real — a real, sharp *whistle* — repeated at intervals. It pauses, and I drive back onto the road.

Coasting down the road past a creek, I stop and hear the whistle again. The sound is quite close to my left on the hillside — loud, piercing, and not always shrill. It has a hoarse or grating or metallic undertone, not so different from what I heard by the shore of Cultus Lake late at night.

The rain has become a mere drizzle. The night is entirely black, the full moon masked by sopping clouds. All is silent; then the whistles begin again. They are fairly rhythmic, as bird calls are, and sometimes have a nasal, reedy (birdy) quality. But the sounds vary and move about the hillside. I whistle back, "Wheeeough." The whistler answers, now shriller, more urgent. It seems almost enraged, or at least irritated, as the Cultus caller did. I am tingling. I have often talked with owls, sometimes, indeed, even by blowing across a bottle, but this is different.

The whistles seem to come from no more than a hundred feet away. The maker moves back toward the creek, a little behind me, over my left shoulder. Then it fails to respond to my whistle. I've turned off the engine to hear better and not intimidate whatever it is. My lights are doused as well, except the brake lights. I listen through my open window, carefully, quietly . . . I am about to pull over, get out, and shine my flashlight up into the brush of the hillside. Then, with the suddenness of a gunshot, something strikes the roof of the car like a slap.

Involuntarily I yell, punch the clutch, key, and throttle at the same instant, and, if an old Honda can be said to burn rubber on a wet mountain road, it does. I don't stop until my heart slows down, a quarter mile later. Shaken, I get out. There is nothing on top of the car, no dent or mark, and I feel foolish for having panicked. But it was not my decision. Like the autonomous nervous system, like smooth muscles, the action occurred on its own. I didn't pee my pants, but I got the hell out.

I went back to the site where the car was slapped. There was nothing to be seen on the road, and no more calls to be heard. I kicked myself again for not remaining to have a look. *Something* had been up there at the Dark Divide. Something that whistled loud and clear, something that struck my roof. I checked again to confirm that there were no trees overhanging the car or anywhere near, only the low alders on the hillside. Nor had there been any wind. Whatever struck the car had been propelled.

There was nothing for it but to continue north. I would have loved to look the area over in daylight, but I had to be in Olympia by nine in the morning. As my blood pressure and heart rate dropped back to their normal lows, I reluctantly left the scene.

The road followed Iron Creek past Ferrous Point to the Cispus and thence down to the Cowlitz at Randle. I stopped for coffee at a tavern, where rude spotted-owl T-shirts were a big item. I kept my mouth shut. On the seemingly endless downramp of State Route 12 from the foot of Mount Rainier to the interstate, I had hours to run the tape of the whistles through my mind. I'd heard way too many people say "It had to be Bigfoot" about this or that event to do the same myself. I hadn't a clue. After midnight the full harvest moon picked out the rain-dampened flower fields of Mossyrock, and a barn owl crossed the highway in my headlights.

- - -

Two or three days later, Peter Byrne came to Swede Park, our home in the Willapa Hills. "Shame on you," he chided good-naturedly when I told him about my hasty departure from the whistle-spot.

"I know, I know," I said, laughing. "Even if it were you-know-what, I fully agree with you that it doesn't represent a threat. In fact, *nothing* up there does. So why did I turn tail?"

"Things that go bump in the night," Peter suggested, tipping his glass toward mine. "I've had that feeling when tracking the pugmarks of a large black leopard in the Indian dusk." That seemed to me an altogether better reason for getting spooked. There are panthers on the Dark Divide, but they don't whistle, they scream; and though it's unnerving, you know they are unlikely to attack. Leopards are another matter. Anyway, Peter hadn't cut out; he'd merely felt like it. Maybe that's the difference between tiger guides and butterfly hunters.

We had been considering the basic humanity of Bigfoot, something Peter is more and more convinced of. And if it pops from our head, like the children of Zeus? All the more human. Whether or not we ever get a chance to run gene-sequencing tests on a bit of tissue to determine our genetic propinquity, we are plumbing what it means to be human. One thing it means, Peter and I agreed, is to skedaddle smartly when the affrighted imagination overcomes curiosity and common sense.

But I couldn't leave the puzzle alone. Five days after I'd left the hills, Thea and I headed up the Lewis River bound for Elk Pass on a bright, colorful autumn afternoon. We arrived at the Boundary Trail as the day began to cool.

The place of the sounds was a low, wooded slope beside the two-lane paved highway. There were, I again confirmed, no trees overhead to drop cones or debris onto the car top. Between the pass and the site I had fled, a small rough track diverges westerly into an old quarry or borrow pit. Above its rim bracken and fir were outlined against a rapidly moving cloud in a cold blue October sky. The odd dump truck and RV passed on the road, then it was quiet until a fighter blasted overhead at a few hundred feet. Lots of rain had fallen since that night. Everlastings nodded with the burden of it, the pumice looked like grainy March snow against the earth.

While I poked around the borrow pit, Thea explored a patch of nearby old-growth noble fir and found a *Hemphillea* (an uncommon, vestigially shelled species of slug), the first we'd ever come across. Being a gut-level Cartesian like me, and not having been present the night of the cries, she lacked my sense of the significance of this place — the westernmost edge of the landscape on which I'd focused my being for many days. So she was surprised when I hollered with some urgency to come see.

Crossing the Dark Divide at midnight, I heard an eerie whistling and stopped to listen, but when something struck the roof of my car, I sped away. Returning later, I found a long line of huge tracks crossing the pumice slope near where I had stopped. Though eroded by rain, they were deeply impressed in the steep slope.

Each of the prints from the Dark Divide was sixteen inches long and six and a half inches wide. No hunter, elk, or bear made these tracks, and no hoaxer could have known I would be there.

I had climbed a slope to a small shoulder that ran from the road up to a higher ridge and formed one side of the quarry. Immediately I saw a line of large impressions ascending the slope on the other side. Careful not to disturb the marks, I worked my way down the loose bank to a spot where I could see them clearly. My mouth dropped. These were tracks — big tracks.

The spoor came from a rocky-floored stand of firs uphill from the highway. The first fairly distinct impression lay in mossy sand at the edge of the woods. From there the tracks came a little way down a pumice slope to a rotting stump above alder scrub, where they were indistinct and scuffled. This was precisely the area from which the whistles seemed to have come. Next the tracks moved across the slope (as had the whistler when I whistled back) before striking uphill. The prints crossed a line of eroded elk tracks, then merged into a well-trodden game trail that headed up the shoulder to the rocky ridge above.

Some ten tracks were individually discriminable, three of them marginally clear. They were impressed about an inch into steep, loose, granular pumice that had sustained rain for days, and they lacked the structure to take a mold even if I'd had my plaster with me. The battery on the flash attachment was dead, and it was too dark to photograph the mossy, shady print without it. But the others, in the open, exposed fairly well. I measured the best track by cutting marks of its dimensions on a dry alder twig, then compared it against the second-best. They were identical: $15\frac{7}{8}$ inches long, $6\frac{3}{8}$ inches across the instep, and $3\frac{3}{8}$ inches across the heel. By comparison, my size-ten EEE feet measure $10\frac{1}{2}$ by $4\frac{1}{2}$ by 3 inches.

No print showed distinct toes, except a fairly distinct big toe on the inside, a primate trait according to master-tracker Jim Halfpenny; other mammals, such as bears and weasels, that exhibit a "big toe" have it on the outside. A heel was still visible in two tracks. I had the definite impression of bare, humanlike feet. If these prints had been left by a hunter, his huge boots were more footlike and smooth-soled than most, certainly not waffle-stompers. There were no shoe marks of any kind in any of the prints. The stride varied because of the slope, but the longest step (two steps equal a stride) was about four feet, going uphill at about forty-five degrees.

Thea was less impressed by my tracks than I was by her slug. Spotting the elk trail, she reckoned the big tracks were just elk prints eroded together. But it was chilly, and she didn't linger. Up the slope, where this line of tracks crossed a line of equally eroded elk tracks, I could clearly see the difference between the two. Even if they were hoof prints that had run together into larger impressions, it seemed unlikely that two such composites would have the same dimensions. I photographed my own hooves in their big Frankenstein boots next to the two best impressions, and they looked petite by comparison.

Okay, so something or someone had walked across the slope not long before or after the time I'd heard the whistles. Supposing these tracks had been made by the whistler, what about the thump on my car?

Beside the spot where I had parked when I traded whistles, I found a ten-inch-long twisted-off twig of cherry. I asked Thea to fling it at me as I replayed the scene. She tossed the stick at the car several times, and it made the appropriate sound and impact.

Does this prove anything? Of course not. I remember a short story having to do with a teller of tall tales who, when pressed, would produce a physical object reputed to come from the scene described. A matchbox from a certain tavern, for example, was supposed to provide proof positive that the story had occurred as told. This is just the sort of logic often employed by reporters of paranormal or extra-normal phenomena, and I am not about to fall prey to its seduction. A stick is a stick. The fact that it appears twisted rather than broken, and Sasquatch is often said to twist branches rather than snapping them, and that it makes a satisfying "thump!" about like the one that sent me skittering, demonstrates nothing.

But there was the other stick, the alder twig on which I carved notches showing the precise distance from the rim of the heel to the tip of the toe, identical on the two best tracks. This alder switch is a little more difficult for me to dismiss than a cherry twig that looks twisted off and that thumps nicely.

- - -

In the failing light we dashed off to see the violent scene of St. Helens's Windy Ridge up close for the first time, caught the pewter sunset glow over the ashen eruptive landscape, then left for home. I had a roll of film, a couple of sticks, some notes and drawings in my yellow "Rite in the Rain" field notebook, and a hell of a lot of questions. Thea brought the slug home for identification. We would keep it alive in a terrarium for a long time. At least it could be said that one strange creature roams the Dark Divide at Elk Pass, sliding along the ancient forest floor on its one big slimy foot.

I did not announce my "find." I considered it scarcely dramatic enough for anyone else's attention. The last thing in the world I wanted as I began writing this book was notoriety. I had dodged attention ever since receiving a well-publicized grant for the purpose of looking into the Bigfoot myths. For one thing, I am not enamored of the sort of quick-brush, sensational publicity usually given the topic by newspapers and television. For another, as Peter Byrne pointed out to me, if my movements were known I could easily become the target of hoaxing, either to throw me off whatever track I might be on or to entertain the hoaxer.

When I went into the hills, almost no one knew where or when. I have no reason to think that anyone followed me at any time or attempted to delude me with false findings. As for the whistles and tracks, no one could have known that I would change my mind at the last minute and travel over the Divide and stop at Elk Pass that dark and rainy midnight; I hadn't known it myself. It defies belief that what I saw and heard could have been the objects of a hoax aimed at me.

And what about a hoax perpetrated by me? What can I say, other than to parrot Dave Barry: "I am not making this up." Thea, already doubtful of the tracks, pointed out how hokey it would seem that I heard the whistles on my last night out — "a convenient climax," I believe she called it. Then to go back and find tracks in the same spot? It's too much. But I can't help the way it happened.

I did show the photographs to Peter Byrne and, much later, to Grover Krantz. Peter showed polite interest but felt he could say little without having seen the tracks himself. Indeed, I wish I could have returned to the site with him at the time. Grover was more positive. After examining the slides, he said, "I'd say you've got a darned good case." He said he had seen people become believers over much less. "If this was all I had," he went on, "I'd be very interested. I wouldn't posit an animal on it. But when you have a thousand of these . . ."

Well, I had ten. What kind of case did I want? None, really. I never set out to find Bigfoot or evidence of same. I have no interest in joining the ranks of the seekers, the true believers, the obsessives with something to prove. As a biologist, I would be as interested as anyone in the field if a new primate turned up. As a naturalist and a prowler of the deepwood, I would not be as surprised as some. As a conservationist, I would be highly intrigued to see how the discovery played out. But as a writer I have no wish to use my pale "evidence" to convince anyone of anything. Least of all myself.

I took some pains to explain my accidental findings by known phenomena. Could the whistles I heard have been made by some species of owl whose repertory I didn't fully know? I narrowed down the possibilities to saw-whet, spotted, and barred owls, of which saw-whet seemed the least likely. This past spring Thea and I went afield with Bob Pearson, a dedicated northern spotted owl researcher who works on his own time. We joined him at a café in Randle, where the breakfast clubbers swapped round damnations of the creatures we were seeking and of those whom they see as caring more for owls than people.

"They'll do just what they want," said an obese man in overalls. "See, they've got the numbers. And they've got the laws — all they've gotta do is find a species." His breakfast partner, a trim older man with a clear-cut flat-top, told of seeing two Forest Service Suburbans full of college students surveying wildlife up on Elk Pass; this he saw as a bad sign. I wished that their bitterness and my enthusiasm — and vice versa — did not have to flow from the same source. There was no point talking it over.

From there we drove to several spots in the hills that I will not name. As we drove, Bob told us about the first time he'd heard a spotted owl call. He'd been plotting known locations in a computer mapping system for the Forest Service for some time. "I knew the owls in the abstract through pixels and paper, as dots within estimated circles of home range, and as numbers." Then he went out on his first survey with an experienced caller. "We called, asking, 'Is anybody out there?' And when the first owl called back — it might have been saying 'Go to hell,' for all we knew — it came as a revelation: we had talked to an owl."

At the first stop Bob struck down the slope into the old growth, and we followed. Varied thrushes, golden-crowned kinglets, and western tanagers called through the dense vegetation. Bunchberry and anemones bloomed at our feet. Vanilla leaf and sword fern glittered in the sun filtering through the crowns of immense Douglas-firs.

We descended five hundred feet over a quarter mile before Bob paused and called. Unlike many owl-census workers, he calls with his own voice instead of using tape recordings. Soon an owl barked back and Bob replied. Before long it swooped down to a branch ten feet from our faces. I was surprised to learn that the birds could be called up during the day. Pearson placed one of several white mice he had with him on a branch, and the female owl swooped down, grabbed it, and swooped up again. Watching and following, we were able to locate her pair of young, fledged but still near the nest. We tried the same with three pairs of owls and found two. At one nest site both parents and both young were perched within yards of us at the same time.

I looked into the black black eyes set in the taupe face, with heavy black brows, a pale "H" of fluff around the chartreuse yellow bill, and a rich brown widow's peak flecked with opal. Such a bird! "About as big as a football," said Bob, and a political football it certainly has been. I doubt that anyone, face to face with this stunning creature, could say the violent things that are said on the T-shirts and in the cafés at Randle. But I wouldn't want to risk it. The young, almost as big as the adults, were fluff-balls. Thea said they looked to be made out of hummingbird nests.

I heard a logging hooter in the near distance. Bob said it was a timber sale allowed under an agreement to get some logs flowing while the timber plan was being worked out, and that sometimes the owls respond to the whistle. But there is nothing for them there. If the timber plan fails to protect these woods in the long run, these owls will of course be gone, along with these trees and the mollusks and the rest of the old-growth specialists. The people in Randle would be more cheerful — until these woods too were gone.

When Bob whistled and the owls whistled back, I listened carefully. The whistles and barks were much softer than what I had heard, and tended to be ascending rather then descending. But when the mother whistled to one of her young (it had to respond in kind before she would deliver the mouse), her querulous call carried something of the tension and the tenor of the Elk Pass sounds. Bob said the mother has a much louder and sharper alarm call, but he did not want to elicit it because of a worrisome redtail hawk in the area. He said that call is often given at night in the autumn when an interloper gives cause for alarm. But either sex can give the agitated whistle at any time of day or night and at any time of year.

I had heard reports of spotted owls flying at people and other objects, and I asked our guide about this. He said a habituated owl (the sort that biologists condition to pop for a mouse at the appearance of any senator or reporter), which these owls were not, once struck his mouse tube. One Forest Service district biologist who laughed off the reports was swooped on, and when he fled, he fell and broke his ankle. Another companion was knocked flat, Bob said. And as he was telling me this, the male owl flew directly at my head from behind, swerving at the last moment.

Back in the truck, Pearson said that barred owls also whistle and swoop and are more aggressive. The barred owl is a generalist that has spread from the East and is competing with its relative, the much pickier spotted owl. Barred owls will dive while giving the loud, raspy, descending last part of their "Who cooks for you, who cooks for y'allll?" call. Bob has been swooped on by a barred owl, and it freaked him so that he split, leaving his coffee cup on top of his car — even though he knew who the swooper was and knew it wasn't likely to hurt him.

That confession made me feel better about my behavior at Elk Pass. It also reminded me of my grandfather's story of being swooped on by a "hoot owl" nearly a hundred years ago in Kentucky. I always assumed it was a great horned, but maybe it was a barred. Far from merely striking him, the owl hooked its talons into his shoulders and held on as GrandPop ran, yelping. I had seen the scars left by that experience. So maybe Bob was wise to drive off, and maybe it was just as well that I stayed in my car and put the pedal to the metal when the roof was rapped.

Earlier I suggested that the discovery of Bigfoot would make the spotted owl's impact on forest planning look mild. Wouldn't it be rich if it turned out that the spotted owl accounts for many of the sounds that Indians and whites have long reported as giants' whistles? I think of Tah-tah-Klé-ah, the Owl Woman Monster, and realize that the connection is not new.

At any rate, after going out with Bob Pearson to call and hear and see the small, beautiful birds at the center of the logging tempest, I am willing to admit that my encounter might well have been with *Strix* instead of *Homo nocturnus* or any other bipedal ape. That those sharp, piercing whistles were born of a feathered throat instead of a furred one. That had I flashed my light on the hillside where the whistles arose, the eyes they found would have been round and black instead of almond-shaped with a red-reflective tapetum. That the thud on the roof of my car was a body blow from a self-propelled missile instead of a twisted twig of wild cherry hurled by a thickly muscled arm. All this seems highly possible, if not probable.

But what about the tracks? No owl made *them*. With due respect to my favorite field companion, no elk made them either. And if it was a megapodal hunter after a grouse or a deer, he must have been wearing Birkenstocks or moccasins, because those looked like no boot prints I'd ever seen.

Fred Bradshaw, a former Gray's Harbor policeman who claims two dramatic Bigfoot sightings, recently found a line of tracks on pumice in Oregon with similar proportions to those I saw. To him the prints he saw meant that Sasquatch had likely been there. What did the Elk Pass depressions say to me once I'd had time to think about them? Many writers before me have concluded that either Bigfoot walks or there has long been a secret track-faking conspiracy so sophisticated and complex as to make most other conspiracies look as simple as pie. "My" tracks weren't the best, but they had impressed the expert, Grover Krantz. Just how impressed was I?

I had gone into this investigation hoping to keep an open mind on the subject of Bigfoot. To me, having a truly open mind is a rare state, easier to define by its opposites. One thing it does not mean is *belief;* faith is the opposite of an open mind. Another condition that has nothing to do with open-mindedness is gullibility or credulousness, which are just forms of faith-hunger. Coming from the other direction, I can further define the term by stating that it also opposes the hard head and the set jaw. It refracts impressions rather than reflecting them. An open mind is a window, not a mirror. Now we're getting closer.

On the dark and stormy divide between what you want and what you get, there strides a slippery essence. I call it power, and a kind of freedom: the power to change your mind, the freedom to grow. I think this essence is the source of the strength the Kwakiutl Hamatsa sought when he went into the woods to contact the wild ones. John Napier called it "entering the Goblin Universe," and we can still do it.

Twice more I returned to Elk Pass. The first time the stale snow of spring on the Boundary Trail held big melted tracks that honestly could have been anything to a receptive mind. The pumice slope was rain-harrowed and elk-gouged. The second time was by moonlight in summer. I took off my clothes and walked nude for half a mile or so, the white pumice path a soft and softly lit beckoning through the high, hairy firs. When I returned, my clothes were where I'd left them. I whistled and nothing whistled back; there was one loud, weird noise off toward Pinto Rock, and that was it. The tracks in the pumice were my own.

"What a good poem inevitably hears, sees, and speaks," wrote poet Jane Hirschfield, "is that point where perceived and perceiver join, where inner and outer worlds meet." Then my walk in the nude was a poem, and a good one. I didn't hear Bigfoot or see it; I *was* Bigfoot. The pumice and the moonlight met in me, and through me Bigfoot gave voice.

An open mind neither rejects nor limits itself to the scientific method but considers it among the other tools for palping the universe. It doubts everything and accepts everyone. It is completely skeptical and wholly receptive, seldom wishy-washy but often unsettled. The open mind is not afraid to be made up, then, like a bed, to be thrashed, stripped, and made fresh all over again. Convictions? The open mind has them. But like everything else, convictions are liable to amendment.

The possessor of this mythic mind has the ability to slither hither and thither, to poke and prod and dodge. This is the only way to take the world, and it is an ideal almost never realized.

The proud owner of a closed mind would never have interpreted my clues as revealing anything like a Bigfoot, especially if each clue were taken separately on its own merits. But the inmate of the sort of vacuum-packed oatmeal tub of a mind that often passes for open when actually flaccid can spot a Bigfoot anywhere: in elk tracks, in snow tracks, in my tracks; in a pale and naked hulk moving gingerly through a moonlight mile, barefoot.

What I want is a state of brain aloof from arrogant dismissiveness, free from superstition, and rich in question. That seems to me the only way of approaching Bigfoot that would be acceptable to the subject — and the only way to be a naturalist. When I showed Grover Krantz my plaster cast from Indian Heaven, he said he doubted it had anything to do with a foot. "But the important thing is," he said, "you *saw* it."

According to Bergen Evans, author of *The Natural History of Nonsense,* anyone "who for one moment abandons or suspends the questioning spirit has for that moment betrayed humanity." To see is to be open, to take it all in without being taken in, to be aware of the sweet possibilities of the world. What more could you want? How much more fun than being the willing slave of instant opinion, pro or con, closing the door from either direction. "Freedom of speech and freedom of action are meaningless without freedom to think," wrote Evans. This is the kind of mind I wanted to bring to Bigfoot: free, and open.

Weird whistles, a bump in the night, and a set of tracks at Elk Pass brought me these gifts of happenstance: a lever to keep my biologist's brain propped open on a topic that begs for closure; a rare glimpse of my own myth; and the knowledge of what it is to be among the charmed or cursed ones who have encountered something in the night.

Epilogue: Monsters in the Mist

Are we or are we not simians? It is no use for any man to think anything else out until he has decided first of all where he stands on that question. It is not only in love affairs: let us lay all that aside for the moment. It is in ethics, economics, art, education, philosophy, what-not. If we are fallen angels, we should go this road: if we are super-apes, that.

— Clarence Day, *This Simian World*

GORILLA, GIRILLA, GORILLA! Gorilla, girilla — see the beautiful girl turn into a gorilla, right before your eyes! Gorilla, gorilla, gorilla!" The barker repeated his weird incantation as he drifted through the crowd, winding down the midway and back again to the tent with a garish poster of a part-woman, part-ape in front. "Girilla, gorilla, girilla!"

I was visiting my former wife JoAnne in southern Florida, where she was a ranger-naturalist in the Everglades. I was living in New Haven, Connecticut, at the time. I'd been sick for weeks, but the March sun and the birds and butterflies of Shark Alley soon put me back on my feet. We'd gone with friends of JoAnne's to see a carnival that was limbering up before heading north with the spring. We considered paying the buck to see the gorilla girl but laughed it off. I've always regretted that decision. Though repelled by its premise, I was also fascinated. I wanted to see how they would make a human become an ape before my very eyes.

Recently, on National Public Radio, I heard it again: "Gorilla, gorilla, gorilla." Steeped in Bigfoot and all things anthropoid, I listened up automatically. The commentator was telling about seeing the same carnival act I had passed up some twenty years before. He described the amazing metamorphosis in the dim light, as the young woman faded out and the hairy ape emerged. Later, walking between the tents, he stumbled on a small woman and a strapping lad sharing a break. The sideshow huckster shooed him away, but the illusion was gone. The girl was not the gorilla.

- - -

What makes a silly freak show perennially compelling and profitable is certainly not the visual effects, no doubt clever but bush league in this day of Crichton and Spielberg. Nor is it the sexual subtext, no more subtle here than it was in *King Kong* (for what is the subsuming of a nubile woman by a hairy ape meant to convey, like the famous scene on the side of the Empire State Building, if not a kind of ravishment?). No, it is the merging of our kind with another kind too close for comfort that draws in the gawkers year after year.

This too is the fascination of Bigfoot — the not-quite-us of it. As I found again and again in my visits with Bigfooters, no question enthralled and confused them as much as the animal's possible humanity. Those who advocate killing one define Bigfoot as nonhuman and not very intelligent, while those who venerate it almost as a green god tend to feel that Bigfoot blends the best of humanity with more desirable wild traits. In Skamania County it is the coroner's call whether any apelike animals that do get shot shall be deemed human. Until that melancholy scene occurs, maybe a look at our previous struggles in finding the obscure line of demarcation can help us envision what we and Bigfoot may be vis-à-vis each other.

Ever since Darwin, the darkest divide has been the one between ourselves and our ancestors, or our surviving siblings. However we hang the known fossil and living species on the anthropoid bush, no one can avoid seeing the connections but those who persist in exclusive creation myths. To Darwin the exact point of departure mattered much less than the process. "In a series of forms graduating insensibly from some ape-like creature to man as he now exists," he wrote in *The Descent of Man,* "it would be impossible to fix on any definite point when the term 'man' ought to be used. But this is a matter of very little importance." And so it should be. But not everyone agrees.

Darwin's descendants have since provided the fossil evidence and Mendel's the genetic, to end any residual doubt about our origins. The remaining questions concern order of species differentiation, rate of evolution, breakpoints, and the faces of the absent personnel.

The outline is clear. But familiarity with the story has not made us uniformly comfortable with our company in the fossil record.

We stern Europeans have always indulged vicious attitudes toward primates other than ourselves, including other humans. It was not unusual for races considered strange (by the dominant culture) to be exhibited, enslaved, exterminated, even collected. Ota Benga was an African pygmy taken from the Congo by missionary Samuel Phillips Verner and displayed next to Geronimo at the St. Louis World's Fair. In 1906 he became a caged exhibit at the Bronx Zoo. The British Museum of Natural History acquired the skins of Australian aboriginals, and a steatopygous female from the African Kalahari became a Smithsonian specimen. Linnaeus optimistically named us *Homo sapiens* — "wise man" — and Darwin argued for our common species identity, but witless acts of supremacist barbarism continued.

While Europeans routinely considered black people to be a different species, native peoples have often failed to differentiate between themselves and other primates. Some pygmies, one biologist with African experience told me, do not consider themselves fundamentally different from chimpanzees. Another told me of Borneans who considered orangutans to be people who chose not to speak so as not to have to deal with the Dutch tax collectors. And the !Kung San of the Kalahari call baboons "the people who sit on their heels."

Western attitudes toward monkeys and apes have seldom been so collegial, but there have been exceptions. British journalist Richard Boston wrote in a 1977 *Guardian* column about Lord Monboddo, an eighteenth-century learned eccentric "who believed that orang-utans belong to the human race. This is a very likeable idea. The only orang-utans I have seen were in Chester Zoo. They were delightful, gentle, graceful creatures and far more human than most of the people who regularly make the front-page headlines." Boston went on to describe a well-known incident that took place when a French ship went aground off Hartlepool, England, during the Napoleonic War. The only survivor was the ship's mascot, a monkey. "Its stature, grimaces, and jabbering caused it to be taken for a French spy and hanged."

We have needed no such excuses to torture and execute vast numbers of primates in the name of medical research. Even if we accept that animal rightists sometimes become terrorists and that much human good has come from research, most thinking people abhor the excesses of the laboratory. The public disgust with gratuitous research using primates (and other animals) can be gauged by skimming any issue of the *AV Magazine,* a venerable and respected antivivisection journal far removed from the firebombs of some animal rightists.

"We now have sufficient information about the capacities of chimpanzees, gorillas and orangutans to make it clear that the moral boundary between us and them is indefensible," *AV* quotes Peter Singer. The Australian professor of bioethics, supported by people as diverse as primatologist Jane Goodall and author Douglas Adams, has launched The Great Ape Project to eliminate the use of these animals in research and entertainment.

But respect for even the higher primates is far from uniform. As I began writing this chapter I was listening to *A Prairie Home Companion* on American Public Radio, a variety program in which I ordinarily take great pleasure. One of the ersatz "sponsors" that week was "Oranga-Help," promising freedom from housework to those who would "hire a primate," which would cook, clean, and even pick off your fleas. Ironic? Perhaps. Harmless enough? Maybe. But the joke's premise — that hiring minority human "help" has become non-PC so why not move one rung down — struck me wrong.

I remember one of my sister Susan's first 45-rpm records: "Abba dabba dabba dabba dabba dabba dab, said the chimpee to the monk; babba dabba dabba dabba dabba dabba dab, said the monkey to the chimp." Debbie Reynolds and Carlton Carpenter performed the duet in the 1951 MGM recording "Abba Dabba Honeymoon." I loved the tune, luckily, since Susan played it incessantly. At least the songwriter differentiated between monkeys and chimps, something that pop culture has rarely done, and the message was a sweet one: "Then the big baboon one night in June/he married them and very soon /they went upon their Abba Dabba honeymoon." Simians have seldom fared so well in human entertainment.

The misestimation of our near genetic neighbors in the cinema has never abated since *King Kong* set the high-water mark for countless scary gorilla movies. Degrading stage acts with live chimps and orangutans dressed in human clothes began in vaudeville and continue today. From the indignities of the organ grinder to *Bedtime for Bonzo,* primates have never had a chance to be themselves in our eyes.

As columnist Boston wrote of primates, "Perhaps it is precisely their proximity to the human that has made people so beastly to them." Not that they have always stood by and taken their mistreatment. As a teenager I felt a righteous pleasure watching the monkeys at Colorado's Cheyenne Mountain Zoo as they gaily flung their droppings through the bars or masturbated before shocked dads and moms and curious kids. But their opportunities to bite back have been few. When we tell someone "Don't make a monkey out of yourself" or "Cut the monkey business," we express our true attitudes; and we can be sure that in all of our dealings with them, apes have had less fun than a barrel of monkeys.

Nothing reveals our genus confusion as sharply as gorillas. Reports of gorillas, brought by Carthaginian seamen, reached Europe some 2,500 years ago. But the lowland gorilla *(Gorilla gorilla gorilla)* was not actually seen by Western scientists until 1847, and the mountain gorilla *(G. g. beringei)* not until 1902. When an American explorer, Paul du Chaillu, went to Africa in 1861 and brought back hides and bones, he colored his find with lurid and false accounts of the animal's vicious behavior. "The Great Gorilla Controversy," as the *Daily Telegraph* called it, erupted in Britain concerning the true nature of the beast. Recently sensitized by Darwin, Europeans wanted to know whether they were indeed related to the gorilla and whether it was the monster du Chaillu had described.

Zoologist Richard Owen and others doubted du Chaillu's veracity, but another century would pass before George Schaller's gorilla field studies first illuminated the animal scientifically. Not until Dian Fossey's remarkable and courageous study of the mountain gorillas in Rwanda was their truly gentle, complex nature understood. Her tragic murder in 1985, four years after publication of *Gorillas in the Mist,* underscored just which primate is capable of monstrous behavior. Of course, she already knew this; gorillas with whom she had bonded were decapitated by poachers who sold their heads and hands for souvenirs. Fossey was sometimes accused of caring more for gorillas than for people. Had she lived to see Rwanda ripped by tribal butchery in 1994, Fossey would have found her species loyalty even more severely tried and her concern for the beloved gorillas magnified.

When media magnate Ted Turner announced a large prize for a novel that would point to a positive way out of our environmental dilemmas, the winner, in 1992, was *Ishmael* by Daniel Quinn. The title figure is a gorilla who has acquired deep knowledge and the ability to communicate with human beings telepathically. Ishmael becomes a teacher in search of a student, who turns out to be the narrator. The gist of his lesson is contained in this quotation:

The people of your culture cling with fanatical tenacity to the specialness of man. They want desperately to perceive a vast gulf between man and the rest of creation. This myth of human superiority justifies their doing whatever they please with the world . . . But in the end this mythology is not deeply satisfying. The Takers are a profoundly lonely people. The world for them is enemy territory, and they live in it everywhere like an army of occupation, alienated and isolated by their extraordinary specialness.

By chance, when I was buying Quinn's book at Powell's Books in Portland, I first spotted Roger Price's *J.G., the Upright Ape.* This 1960 novel also employs the device of a gorilla as the protagonist. J.G. is a member of a fictional high-elevation subspecies called the silver gorillas. His search for his abducted mate, Lotus, in America becomes a vehicle for sharp, witty satire of contemporary culture. "For the first time in his life, J.G. was unhappy. It required great concentration on his part, because it isn't easy to be unhappy when you have such a tiny brain."

Neither author can challenge Schaller's and Fossey's gorilla scholarship, but their fictions point to a conclusion that the researchers might recognize: gorillas — gentle, cooperative, environmentally benign — are in some ways better than humans. Similarly I concluded that by certain measures Sasquatch seems to be the superior animal.

As with Bigfoot, our attitudes toward gorillas are ambivalent. People don gorilla suits in parody of scariness, then behave sentimentally toward the real thing. When Ivan, an orphaned gorilla who spent twenty-seven years on exhibit in a Tacoma shopping mall, was finally transferred to a colony of his species at Zoo Atlanta, scores of well-wishers saw him off, and many tears were shed. It's the same with Sasquatches: they're a little frightening, but we'd hate to see them go.

Another similarity between gorillas and Bigfoot is their absence from the fossil record. As John Napier liked to say when he was director of primatology at the Smithsonian Institution, "The story of the gorilla is the very essence of myth except for one thing . . . it happens to be true." Chimpanzees also lack fossil confirmation, and they too skated between myth and reality until their physical presence became commonplace. Even their Latin name, *Pan troglodytes,* suggests a mythic dimension. Yet chimps are very much among us, and if our attitudes toward gorillas betray the shapelessness of our apehood, a look at chimps should really rub our noses in our primate connections. Dian Fossey often called gorillas the greatest of the great apes, and so they may be, but chimps are closer to our own kind. *Homo* diverged from *Gorilla* around twelve million years ago and from *Pan* only about eight.

Evolutionary biologist Jared Diamond goes so far as to call *Homo* "the third chimpanzee" in a book of that name, subtitled *The Evolution and Future of the Human Animal.* Diamond outlines the genetic-clock (DNA rate of change) experiments that show we share 98.4 percent of our DNA with chimps and 97.7 percent with gorillas. He claims that we should share not only our family (Hominidae) with chimps and gorillas but our genus *(Homo)* as well. As in the carnival act, Diamond would have the apes blend with us. Some might find that difficult to swallow; but "whenever taxonomists from Outer Space visit Earth to inventory its inhabitants," he writes, "they will unhesitatingly adopt the new classification."

For those who lack Diamond's certainty or Darwin's equanimity in the matter, who need a sharp distinction between *Homo* and the rest, cross-breeding experiments might settle the issue. In his unforgettable evolution classes, Yale biology professor Charles Remington used to suggest that interspecies hybridization would demonstrate how the pongid/hominid split is really a silly act of anthropocentrism. "And I will happily volunteer to be the male donor," he would quip. He was speaking hypothetically and ironically; deeply involved in bioethics classes on campus, Remington was far from cavalier about primate experimentation. But his lectures left me wondering whether such experiments had ever been undertaken.

In 1992 I had the opportunity to meet psychologist James Harlan Elder, the father of a good friend, writer Jane Elder Wulff, shortly before his death at nearly ninety. Elder had been a student of R. M. Yerkes and had supervised all reproductive research at Yale's Primate Research Laboratory (later named for Yerkes) at Orange Park, Florida, in the 1930s. Later he served as chairman and professor of psychology at Washington State University for twenty years. His former student Alan Hartman wrote that "his work . . . was pivotal in establishing the value of experimental method in the study of infrahuman primate sexual behavior." By respecting them as individuals, Yerkes and Elder showed clearly that chimps are no mere pawns of instinct; rather, their mating is "a complex biopsychological phenomenon," as is our own.

Jim and his wife, Leona, became very close to the chimpanzees at

Orange Park. Jane Elder Wulff spoke of "a quality in JHE that caused him to respond to sustained intimacy with chimps by becoming more tuned in, expanding his connection with them, becoming their champion — instead of sealing over, seeing them always in the same limited way, as many animal researchers do with their subjects." That description also applies nicely to Jane Goodall, who might concur with Elder's declaration that "if there are no chimps in heaven, I don't want to go there."

I asked Elder if he was aware of any hybridization studies conducted at the Yerkes lab or elsewhere. (When I put the same question to Grover Krantz, Elder's erstwhile colleague at WSU, he said he had heard many rumors and a few jokes but knew of no confirmed instances of actual hybrids.) Elder, still sharp-minded in his terminal illness, responded, "Something like that might have happened, but I didn't know too much about it."

Yet I felt Jim knew more than he let on about interspecies mating and that he almost wanted to talk about it. On a later visit he brought up the topic and began to tell one of his wonderfully detailed stories about chimp behavior and human response. But his speech rambled and faded, and he either lost the train of thought or decided against pursuing it. Perhaps if we had known each other earlier in his life, he would have felt safe in sharing his knowledge with me. But before I could visit again, Jim Elder was gone. I've often wished I'd met him earlier, and not just because of this point. He was a delight, and I would have liked to discuss Bigfoot with him. But with both Yerkes and Elder gone, we have lost the chance to hear a hidden tale that could cast a glimmer on one of our darkest divides.

— — —

Clarifying our relationship to other primates is important scientifically, but it also influences our interpretation of the Bigfoot myths. As anthropogenist Noel Boaz states in *Quarry: Closing In on the Missing Link*, "When [the missing link] is found and the circle is closed, there will no longer be a reason to set humanity apart from nature."

Such a time might be getting closer, with the recent find of seventeen "new" fossil humans in Africa. Presently dated at 4.4 million years, this age makes them a half-million years older than Lucy, the previous "oldest human known." These forms are said to have some chimplike qualities, not surprisingly, since their date puts them more than halfway back to the time when chimps and humans diverged. Language studies with bonobos, or pygmy chimpanzees, also point toward common ground. "The boundary between humans and apes has finally been breached," wrote Sue Savage-Rumbaugh and Roger Lewin in *Kanzi: The Ape at the Brink of the Human Mind.* Kanzi, the most linguistically advanced bonobo to date, can communicate readily and complexly with humans using colored symbols and sign language, and is beginning to make attempts at speech.

But we have a very long way to go until society as a whole embraces its origins. In written testimony to the 1925 Scopes trial in Tennessee, President Woodrow Wilson said, "It surprises me that at this late date such questions should be raised." How surprised he would be to learn how many people, presidents among them, still agree with Attorney General Stewart, who told the court: "I don't believe that I came from the same cell with the monkey and the ass." Or with William Jennings Bryan, who testified that the theory of evolution had dragged Darwin "down and down and down to helpless and hopeless agnosticism." Bryan complained that to Darwin "it was all animal, animal, animal." Of course Bryan was right.

"We must stop pretending we are something we are not," wrote Carl Sagan and Ann Druyan in *Shadows of Forgotten Ancestors.* "Somewhere between romantic, uncritical anthropomorphizing of the animals and an anxious, obdurate refusal to recognize our kinship with them . . . there is a broad middle ground on which we humans can take our stand." We can seize that ground by seeking a bond that will serve our own survival as well as that of our animal associates. Such a way of thinking is neither pantheism nor animism, for we should worship animals no more than we do men. But as Sagan and Druyan also write, "Those who deny or decry our 'animal' natures underestimate what those natures are. Isn't there much to be proud of . . . in the lives of monkeys and apes?"

In *Visions of Caliban: On Chimpanzees and People,* Dale Peterson and Jane Goodall masterfully outline our centuries of inhumanity toward our nearest living relatives — what Diamond would call *Homo troglodytes,* returning Pan's name to its rightful owner. Peterson identifies chimps with Caliban, the monstrous central character in Shakespeare's *Tempest.* He writes that "Shakespeare imagined with astonishing brilliance and foresight how people might behave toward a being they considered to be neither quite beast nor quite human." Goodall says that "in fighting for the chimpanzees' survival [humans] are also fighting for their own," and her coauthor adds, "Only when we free Caliban will we free ourselves."

These ideas are illuminating, but they refer to an animal whose existence everyone accepts. Great apes can be seen by anyone near a zoo or a TV, and no one has any excuse to act monstrously toward creatures that we all know are not monsters.

It was different for Shakespeare. The first accounts of African anthropoid apes arrived in London in 1607 with the seafarer Andrew Battell, and *The Tempest* (a mariner's tale) was written in 1610–11. For all Shakespeare knew, these subhumans warranted the ignominious descriptions of poor Caliban: "a freckled whelp hag-born . . . got by the devil himself . . . a thing most brutish . . . most scurvy monster." Peterson's guess that rumors of chimps inspired the character is a good one. But Shakespeare was seldom one-dimensional in his derivations. What if he had in mind not only apes but all the monsters that dwell within our earthbound brains: what if Caliban is equally Bigfoot?

In 1867, working with pelts and bones brought back by du Chaillu, London artist Joseph Wolf rendered a remarkably accurate portrayal of a gorilla. Like Shakespeare, the artist brewed bits of evidence with his own fecund impulse to concoct his vision of manlike monstrosity. In the same way, on the basis of tracks and firsthand descriptions, various artists have undertaken to depict Sasquatch. The walls of my study display many such images, ranging from the rather gorilla-like rendition on an illustrated touring map of northern California's Bigfoot country by Robert Filbey to a postcard of Jim McLarin's bulky, neckless redwood statue in Willow Creek, from Datus Perry's stoic and coneheaded version to a whimsical hippie-ape on a produce carton labeled "SAS squash." We all have an image of Bigfoot, whether we believe in it or not. And that's how it was with the apes before they finally appeared in zoos. Until we can actually see the face of the beast, we imagine one for it.

Why must we have our Calibans? Not a range of hills, not a hollow, not a shore, not a village of any age at all lacks an ogre, serpent, troll, or some such shade. It is interesting to me that trolls and headless horsemen often are connected with bridges: in the case of the latter, a covered bridge, as in Washington Irving's "Legend of Sleepy Hollow." A neighbor of mine, a fourth-generation farmer, told me about our local monster. A ninety-year-old covered bridge crosses the river between Larson's place and mine. When he was growing up, Brian Larson told me, you never crossed the covered bridge on foot at night without looking out for Old Greenface. I have not garnered many details, but it is clear that Old Greenface is a fright and has been a part of this small community for many years. I can only assume that he survived the recent refurbishment of the bridge; I've never seen him, though I go down to the bridge every Halloween midnight.

We come to our monsters young. Bill Watterson's popular comic strip "Calvin and Hobbes" is richly populated by gruesome under-the-bed fiends whose reality Calvin's parents will never accept. In Bruce Coville's darkly compelling story "There's Nothing under the Bed," a boy whose parents didn't believe him is finally abducted into the monster-hole beneath his bed, where he is groomed to be a bringer of unwholesome visions to others. And writer Ray Bradbury tells of his irritation that his mother couldn't see the monsters on the penultimate step as he went upstairs to bed.

In an essay entitled "Why We Need Our Monsters" in *National Wildlife,* John G. Mitchell wrote that "there is something about the human condition that seems to demand monsters." He believes that monster figures arise in cultures that no longer have to deal with real ones: "Who needs monsters when there are lions and elephants and rhinos and crocodiles and mountain gorillas . . . Where there are grizzly bears, who needs Bigfoot?" Mitchell may be right in thinking that we replace vanished terrors with made-up ones, but in fact even places with extant big beasts produce mythic monsters. Sasquatch stories abound in Alaska, where grizzlies thrive. Mitchell's theory isn't enough.

Others have theorized that giants, in particular, are the memories of creatures that once cast shadows beside our own. Russell Ciochon, John Olsen, and Jamie James, the authors of *Other Origins: The Search for the Giant Ape in Human Prehistory,* write that our awareness of giants might be a mote in our collective conscious from a time when *Gigantopithecus blacki* and *Homo erectus* both inhabited the same areas. Since our precursors once walked with giants, they suggest, perhaps all the giants since, including Bigfoot, have been atavistic memories of Giganto. *G. blacki* is not the only candidate. In *Gulliver's Travels,* Jonathan Swift's Brobdingnagian philosopher says, "There must have been giants in former times." And so there were. There was Giganto. There was *Arctodon simus,* a giant bear that inhabited much of North

America until about 12,000 years ago. Oregon naturalist Jim Anderson reminded me that there were enormous Pleistocene ground sloths in North America, which are his candidate for the giants of our ancient dreams.

And there was — or is — the Amazonian jungle sloth that is said to have stood six feet tall and weighed six hundred pounds or more. Conventional wisdom says it became extinct some 8,500 years ago. Yet some biologists are taking seriously reports that the sloth lives on in the remote rain forest, which may account for Mapinguari, the Amazonian cognate of Bigfoot. It is characterized as having the body of a bear, the face of a monkey, a "disabling" stench and a "terrifying" roar "like endless thunder" — monster enough for anyone. Rubber tappers have described the creature for many years, and now some scientists think they have found evidence for it, including huge round tracks with backward claws, hair, and twenty-two pounds of poop.

There were indeed giants in former times. But perhaps group memory, hereditary tale, and myth all avoid the main issue. For as Mapinguari shows, there is another possibility: that there really *are* monsters among us.

Wayne Suttles, in his paper "Sasquatch: The Testimony of Tradition," says, "Any hypothesis that we human beings have an innate propensity to create mythical wild men or apemen might be plausible if there are *no* wild men or apemen in the real world. But if there *are*, then this hypothesis becomes unnecessary; beliefs in wild men everywhere might then be the result of direct observation plus that old anthropological explanation — diffusion."

By whatever route — diffusion from real but scattered events, atavistic experience of extinct beasts that we outlasted but once knew, or the spontaneous generation of gremlins and creeps wherever folklore grows, the monsters continue to arrive on our doorsteps, usually at night. We make them as much like ourselves as we dare, but we seem to require a certain distance — a green face, no head . . . huge feet.

After apes became common knowledge, they remained monstrous only through hyperbole, such as fake jungle tales and King Kong. Since Fossey, the gorilla has lost its last shreds of monstrosity. In the film version of *Gorillas in the Mist,* with Sigourney Weaver playing Fossey and the gorillas playing themselves, Hollywood finally atoned for *King Kong.* The ape as monster was dead. Now Bigfoot has taken over the role. If and when its myth too becomes truth, we will have to look even further for a monster made after our own image. And as both faces of Rwanda have shown, there is only one place left to go. We are the last monster.

- - -

When George Schaller left the high haunts of the mountain gorillas, he said that "all I could do was wish them luck and a free life of roaming about the mountains." That is exactly what many would wish for Bigfoot. And again, in *The Last Panda*, concerning the long-standing question of the relationship between red and giant pandas, Schaller wrote, "Just as I hope that there is a yeti but that it will never be found, so I would like the panda to retain this minor mystery."

Schaller is not alone in wishing for the hairy giants' continued anonymity. Many believers have told me they will be seriously disappointed if Bigfoot actually turns up. In a contracting world, they feel, what is left when mystery flees? Yeti proponent Edward Cronin, for one, wrote, in the *Atlantic*, "I would be deeply saddened to have it discovered. Every time man asserts his mastery over nature, he gains something in knowledge, but loses something in spirit."

Or as Peter Steinhart put it in *Audubon*, "The search for hidden animals is a skirmish in our continuing war against the death of wonder." He worries that "if we ever find one of these creatures, a star will blink out in the heavens. Another mystery will die." I understand the feeling, but I do not agree. As any entomologist knows, of mystery there is a plenitude. For me, wonder can never die, but habitat can. In itself, knowledge of the natural world can never be a sadness; it's the outcome that counts, and we do not protect land for will-o'-the-wisps.

- - -

I am continually asked by those who hear I am writing about Bigfoot, "So, tell me — do you believe?"

I have never answered yes or no, and I don't intend to now. Not because I am afraid to take a stand, but because it has never been my desire to finally decide. Bigfoot as beast, or Bigfoot as Rod Serling saw it, "an apparition walking in the landscape of our minds"? That's up to others. I am content to have walked where Bigfoot walks for a season or two.

Sasquatch walks, all right. Whether as a hank of hair and a hunk of bone or a boon companion in our hearts is something we may never know. And it might not matter. When E. O. Wilson met Kanzi, he was unnerved by how much the encounter with a bonobo felt like meeting a two-year-old child. "I had to ask myself," he wrote in *Biophilia*, "was this really an animal?"

It is time for us to see, as Darwin saw, that the point of separation between man and not-man has no fixed place and "is a matter of very little importance." It is time for us to say, as Thoreau said, "We are conscious of an animal in us."

Maybe now, more than ever, the dark divide between the monsters in our minds and the monsters in our midst is the shadowland we walk together, hand in hand with Bigfoot.

MAP

-

APPENDIX

-

REFERENCES

-

ACKNOWLEDGMENTS

-

INDEX

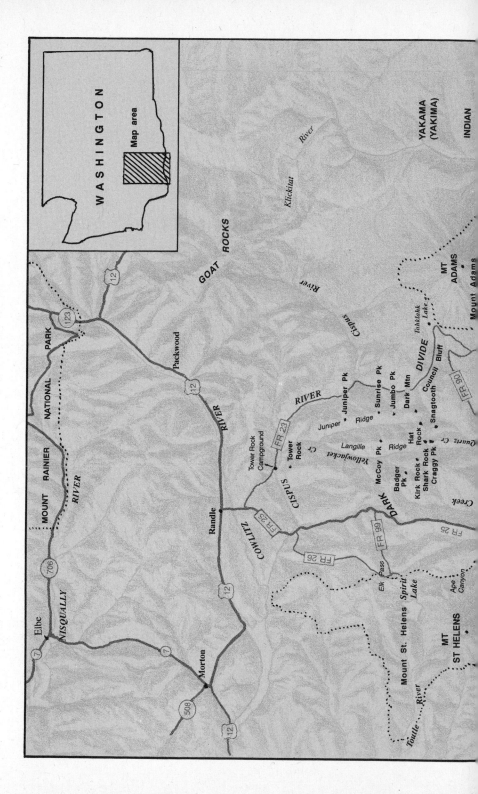

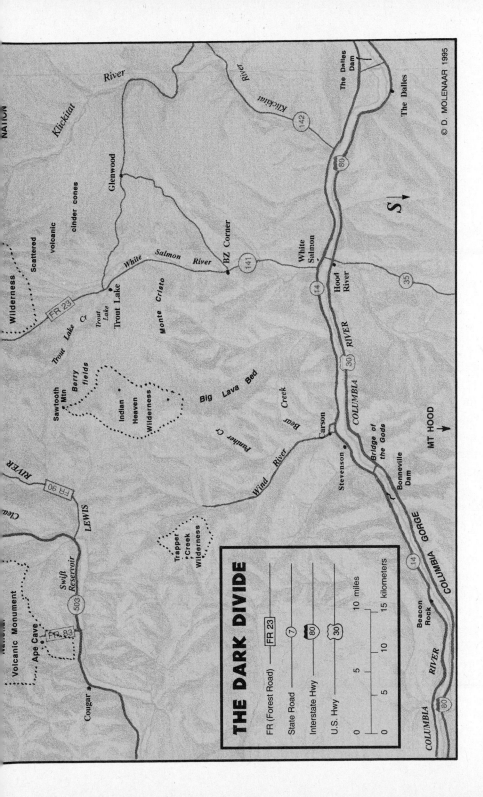

THE DARK DIVIDE

FR (Forest Road)	FR 23
State Road	7
Interstate Hwy	80
U.S. Hwy	30

© D. MOLENAAR 1995

Appendix:

A Protocol for Encounter

That we do not know you
is your perfection
and our hope. The darkness
keeps us near you.
— Wendell Berry,
"To the Unseeable Animal"

I favor broad, if provisional, acceptance of Grover Krantz's description of *Gigantopithecus canadensis* based on the tracks he has examined, followed by the preventive listing of this species under the Endangered Species Act. Then the penalties for killing a bigfoot would have to be harsh enough to prevent a killer from recouping the fine through media rights and sideshow or museum sales. If not manslaughter, the crime should at least be an imprisonable felony.

I do not propose using the species designation to dramatically disrupt the forest planning process without better ecological information. Rather, serious research efforts should be launched by federal, tribal, state, provincial, and private groups and coordinated by the National Biological Service and its Canadian and Indian Nation counterparts to determine the likely range of the species and its ecological requirements. Then, if logging must adapt to a new protection priority in the woods, let the chips fall. Such a change won't be easy, but the results of overharvesting for all these years aren't easy either. Bigfoot could drive the change toward better use of logged-off private and federal lands at a time when the electronic revolution is supposedly reducing the need for pulp. Thus Bigfoot's listing, if temporarily a nuisance because it causes us to look much more closely at how the forest works and what it needs to keep on working, could help create an eventually stable logging industry. And if the animal is never found, little harm will have been done by these measures.

And what if it is found? I have long favored the adoption of a protocol for first contact with Bigfoot or with any other outlandish life form. Such a plan could be adapted for extraterrestrial aliens, dinosaurs in the Congo, or plesiosaurs in Loch Ness and Lake Champlain, as well as for the five or so unproven manlike primates. Each of these categories, and others of seeming unlikelihood, have their serious-minded champions — people with both oars in the water.

Roy P. Mackal, a former University of Chicago biologist who went to West Africa to track a putative dinosaur, told *Audubon* writer Peter Steinhart, "We are far from the bottom of the barrel. We may penetrate all the areas on Earth and establish that there are no more large species. But we are a long way from that now." Rory Nugent followed Mackal to the shores of Lake Télé and came back to write *Drums along the Congo: On the Trail of Mokele-Mbembe, the Last Living Dinosaur.* Nugent never saw the animal, but a local witch doctor, thumping his chest, told him "Mokole-Mbembe is in here, and out there in the forest. He is a great spirit, so he is everywhere." While this certainly doesn't prove the physical existence of the dinosaur, it hardly proves otherwise. As George Zug, Smithsonian herpetologist, told Steinhart, "There *are* unknown things."

One of the most eminent biologists ever to give his serious attention to cryptids was G. Evelyn Hutchinson, the Yale ecologist whose theory of the *n*-dimensional hyperspace in the 1920s spawned the popular concept of the ecological niche. As his 1959 *Herald Tribune* review of Bernard Heuvelmans's *On the Track of Unknown Animals* stated, "Many long and slimy beasts from forests, swamps and the depths of rivers must be essentially night mares, whose true home is the unexplained terrain of the unconscious mind. Yet some of these beasts may be lurking in forests or mountain valleys waiting to disturb our complacency."

But the actuality of the phenomena need not be at issue. Statistically there is a good chance of eventually finding more creatures like the coelacanth, the mountain gorilla, the Komodo dragon, and they might be far weirder than any of the above. Should we not have a plan in place for the event? If we don't, we might as well ask Hollywood to script the news release in advance, for we know the ending.

So how to avoid that ending? We might start with the International Society for Cryptozoology (ISC), which was founded in 1982 as a forum and clearing-house for questions and information concerning unknown animals. Perhaps ISC could coordinate a working group of concerned scientists and others to write such a master plan. The World Conservation Union (IUCN) should be involved, along with the wildlife and conservation authorities of each affected governmental district. In the case of Bigfoot, IUCN's Primate Specialist Group, the International Primate Protection League, learned societies of primatologists and anthropologists, the Bigfoot Research Project, the Western Bigfoot Society, and similar organizations and institutions should be invited to contribute.

It would be neither possible nor desirable to exclude the local, state, and tribal police, the sheriff's departments, and perhaps the FBI from the plan. None of these should be in command, however. The Bigfoot "situation manager" should be appointed by a council of the Smithsonian Institution, the American Museum of Natural History, the National Biological Service, and Nature Canada. He or she should have full authority to direct the response, after the fashion of a fire boss on a forest fire, within the context of an agreed-upon procedure, which would include neither killing nor dangerously confining the subject.

In order to give credit for prior involvement and to ensure maximum cooperation for verification and follow-up, a first-call list should be drafted of major Bigfoot researchers who have agreed to participate without remuneration and without arms. Thus, if they agree and are willing to cooperate with one another, Peter Byrne, John Green, Grover Krantz, René Dahinden, Bob Titmus, Bernard Heuvelmans, and perhaps certain others should be notified simultaneously and invited to convene.

All signatory agencies and individuals would agree to abide by a set of behavioral prescriptions. When a scenario occurred such as the one that begins Chapter 18, the sheriff would telephone a coordinator who would activate the communications grid. The principals would travel to the site as soon as possible. In the meantime the sheriff's main job would be to maintain public calm and to protect the animal or corpse. The military should sign the protocol but remain uninvolved unless riot conditions required the National Guard to maintain safety.

For the scene to unfold as peacefully as possible, agreements would have to be made in advance at the highest levels of security and intelligence. This would be especially important for contact with aliens (as so many films have shown), but to some extent it would also hold for Bigfoot. Therefore the protocol should be signed by the secretary of the Smithsonian Institution and a cabinet-level representative of the president and the Canadian prime minister.

But what *should* happen and what will are two different things. I don't think such a protocol has much of a chance of being created until it is too late to prevent a tragedy, because most of the relevant officials agree with the scientist who told *Washington* magazine: "It's as pointless a pursuit scientifically as the man in the moon." Only the commissioners of Washington's Skamania and Whatcom counties, to my knowledge, have had the foresight (some say good humor) to pass protective ordinances for Bigfoot in advance of definite proof.

And even if a plan was in place, everyone having put his or her neck out to sign it at risk of derision, would it be followed? Or would human nature, driven by fear and base motives, lead to a dead or wounded creature after all? Even if the plan worked splendidly, I can't say what should or would happen next. Without an iron-clad promise to release any captive creature within a specified time, the temptation to keep the animal (and the danger of confiscation by authorities above the treaty) might frustrate the intention of peaceful encounter.

Nevertheless, I feel we should try to devise a civilized and intelligent procedure to protect our unwilling quarry. For in the end, how much better for all concerned if we could hear the words of Ralph Waldo Emerson above the soundtracks of the monster movies we all grew up with:

> Hast thou named all the birds without a gun;
> Loved the wood-rose and left it on its stalk;
> Unarmed faced danger with a heart of trust;
> And loved so well a high behavior in man or maid,
> That thou from speech refrained,
> Nobility more nobly to repay? —
> O be my friend and teach me to be thine.

References

I have made no attempt to systematically survey or summarize the large Bigfoot literature, though I have drawn from it freely and widely. The following titles are some that I found particularly engaging, worthwhile, helpful, or otherwise meritorious. They will lead you to many sources of further information.

BOOKS

Byrne, Peter. *The Search for Bigfoot: Monster, Myth, or Man?* New York: Pocket Books, 1976.

Coleman, Loren. *Tom Slick and the Search for Yeti.* London: Faber and Faber, 1989.

Cronin, Edward W., Jr. *The Arun: A Natural History of the World's Deepest Valley.* Boston: Houghton Mifflin, 1979.

Gardner, John. *Grendel.* New York: Alfred A. Knopf, 1971.

Gordon, David George. *Field Guide to the Sasquatch.* Seattle: Sasquatch Books, 1992.

Green, John. *Bigfoot: On the Track of the Sasquatch.* New York: Ballantine Books, 1973.

Halpin, Marjorie, and Michael M. Ames, eds. *Manlike Monsters on Trial: Early Records and Modern Evidence.* (Proceedings of the conference "Sasquatch and Similar Phenomena," University of British Columbia Museum of Anthropology, 1978). Vancouver: University of British Columbia Press, 1980.

Heuvelmans, Bernard. *On the Track of Unknown Animals.* New York: Hill and Wang, 1959.

REFERENCES

Hunter, Don, with René Dahinden. *Sasquatch/Bigfoot: The Search for North America's Incredible Creature.* Buffalo, N.Y.: Firefly Books, 1993.

Krantz, Grover S. *Big Footprints: A Scientific Inquiry into the Reality of Sasquatch.* Boulder, Colo.: Johnson Books, 1992.

Mackal, Roy P. *The Monsters of Loch Ness.* Athens, Ohio: Swallow Press, 1980.

Napier, John. *Bigfoot: The Yeti and Sasquatch in Myth and Reality.* New York: E. P. Dutton, 1973.

Patterson, Roger. *Do Abominable Snowmen of America Really Exist?* Yakima, Wash.: Franklin Press, 1966.

Perez, Danny. *Big Footnotes: A Comprehensive Bibliography concerning Bigfoot, the Abominable Snowmen and Related Beings.* Norwalk, Calif.: D. Perez Publishing, 1988.

Sanderson, Ivan T. *Abominable Snowmen: Legend Come to Life.* New York: Jove/HBJ, 1977.

Shackley, Myra. *Still Living? Yeti, Sasquatch and the Neanderthal Enigma.* New York: Thames and Hudson, 1986.

FOR YOUNG READERS

Baumann, Elwood D. *Bigfoot: America's Abominable Snowman.* New York: Franklin Watts, 1975.

Douglas, William O. *Exploring the Himalaya.* Eau Claire, Wis.: E. M. Hale, 1958.

Place, Martin T. *Bigfoot All Over the Country.* New York: Dodd, Mead, 1978.

Soule, Gardner. *Trail of the Abominable Snowman.* New York: G. P. Putnam's Sons, 1966.

PERIODICALS

There are a number of regional Bigfoot newsletters. Inquire at your local library or watch the newspaper for features on local "experts."

The Track Record: News Bulletin of the Western Bigfoot Society. Portland, Ore.
Cryptozoology: The Interdisciplinary Journal of the International Society of Cryptozoology. Tucson, Ariz.

NOTE: Serious reports of possible encounters should be shared with the Bigfoot Research Project: 1-800-BIGFOOT.

Acknowledgments

This book grew directly out of a Fellowship to Assist Research and Artistic Creation from the John Simon Guggenheim Memorial Foundation. I wish to thank the foundation and its officers profoundly, as well as my referees: Willard R. Espy, Sue Hubbell, David Rains Wallace, and Ann H. Zwinger. My writers' group — Jenelle Varila, Lorne Wirkkala, Pat Thomas, John Indermark, Diane Matthews, and Susan Holway — gave treasured responses to many drafts. The Bigfoot Research Project and its staff — Peter Byrne, Tod Deery, and Deborah Wolman — extended enormous courtesies, as did Grover Krantz. Dee Molenaar kindly made the map, and the Wilderness Society's Pacifiic Northwest Regional Office provided the Dark Divide diagram. I am humbly and deeply grateful to Alan Hall and the Haisla Nation for sharing Billy Hall's story, to the Hoopa and Klickitat people, and to all First Americans who generously gave of their rich tradition and experience.

About a billion people and institutions assisted me, of whom the following are a few. Those whom I have forgotten to name or whose material I did not use directly can be sure that their contributions are deeply embedded in the text. Thank you to JoAnne Heron, Fayette Krause, Laura Smith, Ed and Cathy Maxwell, Ann Musché and Alan Richards, Jim Fielder, Susan Saul, Bob Pearson, Carl Forsgaard, Keith McCoy, Stuart and Mildred Chapin, Mary Schlick, Marlene Simla, Fostine Lone Tree, Sally Dole, Patti Fawn, Don Smith (Lelooska), Martha Dementieff, Gerald Amos, Ken Margolis, Arthur Dye, Spencer Beebe, David Campiche, Bill Holm, Tony Angell, Jeanne Gammell, Robert Dirig, David Wagner, Harriet Reinhard, Barbara Deutsch, John and Florence Hinchliff, Sally Hughes, David Shaw, Howard W. Pyle, Jim and Leona Elder, Jane Elder Wulff, Bill Crary, Harry Cody,

ACKNOWLEDGMENTS

Josh Haney, Alan Cossitt, Kevin Landacre, Howard Bulick, Joel Freeman and Debby Schaefer, Martin and Luzette Witter, Glenn, Dotty, Ian, Libby, and Hilary Dorsch, Jack Gladstone, John Sparrow, Steve and Kristi Nebel, Richard Cook, Dean and Caroline Wood, David Branch, Monty West, Edgar Wymans, Paul Dorpat, Arthur Kruckeberg, Peter Matthiessen, Pattiann Rogers, Chris Merrill, Ron Carlson, Jane Hirschfield, Scott Sanders, David Quammen, Peter Steinhart, Gary Nabhan, Dick Nelson, David Guterson, Kim Stafford, Edwin Wirkala, Mathew Tekulsky, Gary Cummisk, Brian Doyle, René Dahinden, John Green, Ray and Theata Crowe, Ray Wallace, Danny Perez, Cliff Crook, Steve Harvey, Sally Newberry, Bonnie West, Fred Bradshaw, Jim Hewkin, Larry Lund, Richard Lyttle, Al Hodgson, Mary Roberts, Jimmy Jackson, Stephen Suagee, William Saxe Wihr, Henry Franzoni, Captain Gutz-Balls, Mojo Nixon, Karölis Bagdonas, Datus Perry, Lillian Dillingham, Bill Lawrence, Mary Stough, Jim Anderson, George Earley, David Gordon, David Burlison, Orin Bridges, Bob Walls, Richard Wiggin, Ken Clark, André Stepankowsky, Cat Warren, James Halfpenny, Kent and Irene Martin, Carolyn and Don Maddux, Susan Balikov, Jerry Powell, Pam Pratt, Susan and Ted Kafer, Jean Anderson and Ugo Pezzi, Jan and Ray Chu, Ron Wahl, Ron Cisar, Sheri Sykes, Dede Killeen, Su Rolle, Paul Sullivan, David Somdalen, Emily Hiestand, Chris Simons, Nonie and Grant Sharpe, Pauline Larson, Brian Larson, Hilary Richrod, Eleanor Robinson, Jay Windish, Chuck Williams, Mel Hansen, David Stone, Bob LiaBraaten, Libby Mills and Rusty Kuntze, Marc Hudson and Helen Munde, and Rainy Knight.

Special debts are due the archivists and librarians of the Timberland Regional Library System, Longview Public Library, Astoria Public Library, Washington State Library, and the Weyerhaeuser Company Archives; the Cispus Environmental Learning Center, the Skamania County *Pioneer*, Skamania County Prosecutor's Office, the Yakama Nation, the dedicated professionals of the Gifford Pinchot National Forest, and the good people of all the towns around the Dark Divide; Powell's Books, Carson Hot Springs, and the White Cap Brew Pub.

My warmest thanks flow to my agent, Jenny McDonald, and the people at Houghton Mifflin who made the book (and made it better), including Peg Anderson, Michaela Sullivan, Susanna Ralli, Melodie Wertelet, Mab Gray, and, especially, my long-time and much admired editor, Harry Foster.

As always, Thea Linnaea Pyle and Bilak Bokis deserve the best of my love and appreciation.

Index

Note: the index does not include entries for names and terms that appear frequently throughout the text, such as Bigfoot, Dark Divide, and U. S. Forest Service. The names of most people mentioned are included, but the names of most species, landforms, and minor places are not. Specific sites may be found on the map.

SKY TIME IN GRAY'S RIVER
Living for Keeps in a Forgotten Place

"Robert Pyle is one of America's exceptional naturalists and one
of its finest natural history writers."
— Sue Hubbell, author of *A Book of Bees* and *A Country Year*

With his contagious enthusiasm for the natural world, Pyle compiles his
seasonal observations of the remote, roughly 2.3-acre expanse in southwestern Washington where he has lived for more than twenty-five years.

Houghton Mifflin hardcover / ISBN-13: 978-0-395-82821-2 / ISBN-10: 0-395-82821-x

CHASING MONARCHS
Migrating with the Butterflies of Passage

"A pleasure: informative, funny, wonderfully absorbing in its
curiosity and erudition about the natural world."
— *San Francisco Chronicle*

Pyle accompanied migrating monarch butterflies from British Columbia
south to the Mexican border and back up the California coast. While de-
scribing the mesmerizing behaviors of his winged companions, he also
creates a brilliant travelogue of the terrain, plant life, and the compelling
cast of characters—both human and animal—he encounters during his
two-month journey.

Mariner paperback / ISBN-13: 978-0-618-12743-6 / ISBN-10: 0-618-12743-7

WHERE BIGFOOT WALKS
Crossing the Dark Divide

"Pyle rejoices in the beauty of the world, and communicates his
enthusiasm and expert knowledge with a rare modesty."
— *New Scientist*

Awarded a Guggenheim fellowship to explore the legends of Bigfoot, Pyle
set out on a fascinating trek through Washington's southern Cascade
Mountains. This enchanting chronicle of his findings examines a wild,
rich territory where folklore and natural history converge.

Mariner paperback / ISBN-13: 978-0-395-85701-4 / ISBN-10: 0-395-85701-5

VISIT OUR WEB SITES: www.houghtonmifflinbooks.com and www.marinerbooks.com.